Twenty Thousand Mornings

~

AMERICAN INDIAN LITERATURE AND CRITICAL STUDIES SERIES

John Joseph Mathews, 1938, in a photograph submitted with his
Guggenheim Fellowship application (Courtesy of the Western History
Collections, University of Oklahoma Libraries)

Twenty Thousand Mornings

AN AUTOBIOGRAPHY

~

John Joseph Mathews

EDITED AND WITH AN INTRODUCTION BY
Susan Kalter

FOREWORD BY
Charles H. Red Corn

UNIVERSITY OF OKLAHOMA PRESS : NORMAN

This book is published with the generous assistance of the Wallace C. Thompson Endowment Fund, University of Oklahoma Foundation.

Twenty Thousand Mornings: An Autobiography is Volume 57 in the American Indian Literature and Critical Studies Series.

Library of Congress Cataloging-in-Publication Data

Mathews, John Joseph, 1895–1979.
Twenty thousand mornings: an autobiography / by John Joseph Mathews ; edited and with an introduction by Susan Kalter; foreword by Charles H. Red Corn.
    p. cm.
Includes bibliographical references and index.
ISBN 978-0-8061-4253-1 (hardcover : alk. paper)
    1. Mathews, John Joseph, 1895–1979.
    2. American literature—Indian authors—Biography.
    3. Osage Indians.
    I. Kalter, Susan, 1969–
    II. Title.
PS3525.A8477Z46 2012
813'.52—dc23
[B]
                                                    2011032480

The paper in this book meets the guidelines for permanence and durability of the Committee on Production Guidelines for Book Longevity of the Council on Library Resources, Inc. ∞

1 2 3 4 5 6 7 8 9 10

To Carter Revard, who made this good thing happen

To the *Pa-Ci-U-Gthi'n*, the Top-of-the-Tree-Sitters, who became the Big Hills people

and

To the *Ni-U-Ko'n-Ska*, all the past, present, and future Children of the Middle Waters

Contents

~

Illustrations

~

Foreword

~

CHARLES H. RED CORN

Twenty Thousand Mornings recounts an exciting span of history as seen through the eyes of a naturalist, patriot, sportsman, and citizen of the world all wrapped in a single person, a brilliant descendant of an Osage woman and a mountain man.

John Joseph Mathews is best known for telling the story of the Osage people beginning more centuries into the past than we know, when we were becoming a tribe, and continuing through an intense century and a half of cultural and scientific change. Yet there was more to his personal story than he had time to tell.

Susan Kalter does an exceptional job of bringing to focus the story of John Joseph Mathews the man and the writer through his personal diaries and unpublished papers.

Whether the reader is a follower of John Joseph or a student of American Indian culture or an admirer of beautiful prose, there is much to appreciate in this memoir. (In Osage country, mention of "John Joseph" is understood to be John Joseph Mathews, so please forgive my relaxed references.)

Not long after publication of *The Osages: Children of the Middle Waters,* I ran into John Joseph on Kihekah Avenue in Pawhuska, Oklahoma. I told him there were many young Osages reading his book and that it was having a positive influence on their lives. With that distinctive posture of his, holding his pipe, he said, "So, I am proselytizing," followed with a laugh that let me know he was pleased to know his writing was appreciated by Osages.

John Joseph planned a three-volume memoir and drafted Volume 1, *Twenty Thousand Mornings,* which begins with a view of his early years. He titles this first section "Boy, Horse, and Dog." Who among us could write of our childhood and make it so interesting? But then, how many of us have spent summer days and nights on the prairie, alone with only our horse and dog, while we lay watching the Red Tail Hawk circling above, brought to tears because we could not soar like that Osage life symbol?

Then came John Joseph's early college years playing football at the University of Oklahoma and his subsequent service in World War I when he, like 159 other Osages ineligible for the draft, enlisted and served. He became one of the earliest fighter pilots.

Following the war, John Joseph spent time in Europe before returning home. He referred to his postwar period as John-Without-Purpose. This may have referred to the period of adjustment that many soldiers experience after a war. Later he returned to college and received a degree in geology. While waiting for graduation, he was approached about applying for a Rhodes scholarship. After some soul searching, he proposed that he not apply for the scholarship but instead pay his own expenses, thus freeing up funding for someone not able to pay. He was then accepted at Merton College, Oxford, England.

Delaying travel to Oxford University for one term, he went hunting in the Rocky Mountains. Then he went on to Oxford and earned a degree in natural sciences. After more travel, "John-Without-Purpose" returned to the Osage Hills and in time began writing.

Although this gifted man of letters ran out of time before he could write the complete three-volume autobiography, his daily journal writings allow Kalter to piece together the pages of his life in search of that total picture. Those pages are of interest not because he is John Joseph Mathews but because his life's work reflects aspects of the human experience not found elsewhere.

The original Mathews home, site of John Joseph's early experience, is in Pawhuska, on a hill next to the Osage Agent's Residence and the government Indian Offices, today the offices of the Osage Nation. The prairie where the boy and his horse and dog roamed was the Osage Reservation, a closed reservation that required permission to enter.

John Joseph's writings provide links with an ancient past through his retelling of Francis La Flesche's recorded teachings of Osage clans and traditions, through government records, and through his face-to-face conversations with Osage elders whose knowledge of oral history dated back centuries.

In piecing together those histories, one might begin with a description John Joseph wrote in the introduction to *The Osages: Children of the Middle Waters,* where he wrote of his childhood. In that hour just before dawn when the silence was heaviest, he would awaken to the sounds of Osage prayer chants. Prayers he could never describe, not even to himself, filled his little boy's soul with fear and exotic yearning. When the prayers ended, he lay in an exultant fear-trance, hoping fervently there would be more of the prayer, and yet afraid there might be. These pre-dawn prayers, which seemed to outlast the prayer-chants, were Osages greeting Grandfather Sun.

His late-night fascination with the Osage *I'n lon schka* Drum as a little boy lasted a lifetime. He wrote that those experiences were the seeds of that which would disturb him all his life.

Those childhood experiences later grew into a search that took him to college, to a World War, and to Mexico, Africa, and Europe. Then back to the Osage Hills and the Black Jacks, where during the ensuing fifty years John Joseph wrote five books and numerous short stories and articles.

Other parts of John Joseph's body of work are *Wah'Kon-Tah,* and *Talking to the Moon.* Both are extensive accounts of Osage life. *Sundown* is a work of fiction dealing with struggles of a young mixed-blood Indian.

When piecing together his work, one might, possibly, consider John Joseph's five published books to be Volumes 2 and 3 of the memoirs he conceptualized but never wrote.

The Buffalo Clan blood flowing in John Joseph's veins came from his great-grandmother, *A Ci'n Ga,* of the Big Hill Osages. His other heritage was French and Welsh. While Buffalo Clan traits were not apparent in the tone of his complexion nor in the color of his hair, Osage was abundantly present in his heart, mind, and soul.

John Joseph awoke each of those twenty thousand mornings with an awareness of nature. He was aware of seasons and the earth itself and of those who peopled the earth, both human and sacred animal. He spent his life appreciating and striving to understand all that was Osage, then shared what he had learned with his readers.

I am fortunate to have known him.

Preface

~

John Joseph Mathews (1894–1979) got his start as an author when the University of Oklahoma Press published his book *Wah'Kon-Tah: The Osage and the White Man's Road* in 1932. At the time, he was one of a mere handful of Native Americans writing for Native and non-Native audiences. These Native authors told the modern stories of their people to a wider audience; they acted as literary ambassadors to the United States from the First Nations. They wrote at a critical time, when the forced relocations of Native Americans onto reservations and the political destructiveness of the Indian Relocation Act were beginning to effect the misconception that Native Americans were extinct or truly vanished, a perception that still plagues Native communities today. Their publications impressed upon the other citizens of the United States the continuing survival of these people.

Mathews was one of the founders and shapers of the Native American novel in the twentieth century. Of Osage, French, and Welsh descent, he drew in part upon his own experiences to craft his well-known modernist novel *Sundown* (1934), one of the earliest treatments of the dilemmas of mixed heritage. The University of Oklahoma Press also published Mathews's *Life and Death of an Oilman: The Career of E. W. Marland* (1951) and *The Osages: Children of the Middle Waters* (1961), and it reissued his *Talking to the Moon: Wildlife Adventures on the Plains and Prairies of Osage Country* (1945), a well-known and beautifully written book about human beings trying to live in harmony with the natural flow of life.

Mathews left an extensive archive of unpublished works in the Western History Collections at the University of Oklahoma. Among these is this "lost" autobiography, *Twenty Thousand Mornings*, a work of great importance to anyone interested in Mathews and his work, in Native American culture, or in early-twentieth-century American history. It provides a deeper understanding of Mathews's childhood growing up within the Osage Nation and, in doing so, allows readers for the first time to recognize significant differences between the author Mathews and his character Challenge Windzer from *Sundown*, who has often been assumed to be an autobiographical persona rather than a fictional character.

In tracing the first quarter-century of Mathews's life, from 1894 through 1921, this book also records some of the most remarkable historical events of the early twentieth century. Mathews became a pilot and flight instructor during World War I, when aviation was making its rocky debut as a facet of war. With him, we experience humankind's first emotions at joining birds in flight, and the fears of rookie pilots of finding themselves inside a "spinning incinerator" plunging to earth. We fly solo with Mathews, aloft and free over the beautiful mesquite plains of the American Southwest.

Aside from giving voice to these wartime memories, Mathews makes impeccably precise observations of the first automobiles to appear in Osage County, the dawning of the cinematic age (of which he became an enthusiastic participant as an early amateur motion picture photographer), the transition from reservation life to statehood on his thirteenth birthday, and the setting of the sun on the Old West during his travels into the Rockies in his young adulthood. His writing infuses these historical milestones with a meaning that carries them far beyond the descriptions in a textbook. Whether he is talking about the struggles of an illiterate man to express the beauty of a sunset in the Tetons, or the grumblings of a groggy chauffeur on the half-built campus of the University of Oklahoma who is driving Mathews out of Norman in the middle of the night to be present at his dying father's bedside, he allows us to inhabit his intimate responses to his experiences.

I came to know Mathews's work around 1998 when Ross Frank, a member of my dissertation committee at the University of California–San Diego, called my attention to *Wah'Kon-Tah*. The book impressed me and taught me so much that I wrote an article about its significance soon after I arrived at Illinois State University in the summer of 2000. Meanwhile, the Osage poet and medievalist scholar Carter Revard began a correspondence with me regarding our mutual interest in the little-known indigenous writing systems of North America. I occasionally asked Carter questions about his perspectives on Mathews. In 2006, he mentioned the existence of a Mathews archive containing an unpublished autobiography. The University of Oklahoma had received Mathews's papers in 2005 after John Hunt, his stepson, deposited them in the archive that Mathews himself had established in April 1963. Assuming that others were working to bring the work to press, I did not pursue the project until 2008, when I learned otherwise. Encouraged by Carter, I stopped in Norman on my way back from the first Native American Student Advocacy Institute in Tsaile, Arizona, that summer and discovered not only the manuscripts of the autobiography but also a huge body of unpublished writings and recordings that floored me then and floor me still.

I immediately requested photocopies of the manuscripts in five folders labeled "autobiography," and in the following summer, on a second trip to the archive, I discovered the missing pieces of the work. Through that intervening year, I had compared the manuscripts to one another, made notes on each, and converted each into electronic files. Perusing Mathews's extensive diaries in June 2009 allowed me to date each draft, determine which were likely sent out to publishers and which he was editing just before his death. Unfortunately, Mathews's plans for a second volume never materialized, and his final edits, though extensive, were nowhere near completion. However, the work that did emerge—at the end of a life writing from the Blackjacks (Osage County, Oklahoma)—is rich and complete.

I would like to thank Kristina Southwell and all the dedicated faculty, staff, and students of the Western History Collections at the University of Oklahoma, Norman, Oklahoma, who have assisted me with the John Joseph Mathews Collection, the University of Oklahoma Press Collection, and other collections. Work on this book was funded by the College of Arts and Sciences and the Department of

English at Illinois State University, and I am quite grateful to both. Thanks also to Kathryn Red Corn and Lou Brock of the Osage Tribal Museum for their generous help in locating and providing photographs of the Mathews family. Finally, I owe my deep gratitude to Carter Revard for his scholarly and moral support throughout the project.

Introduction

~

[T]he old men talked more eagerly and with more patience
to me than they had ever done before. . . . I suddenly
realized that they were worried; they were worried about the
disruption of father-to-son history. They were worried about
the end of their own gentile and tribal importance, and that
the sheet water of oblivion might wash their moccasin prints
from the earth.

—John Joseph Mathews, introduction to *The Osages*

In his tour de force *The Osages: Children of the Middle Waters*, John
Joseph Mathews brought forward the fear of two continents. The
writer—who was never to be known, understood, or appreciated
well enough in his own lifetime—expressed the fear of the indigenous peoples of the Americas that no trace of their great histories
would remain. His words pertained specifically to the Ni-U-K'on-
Ska, known to the English-speaking world as the Osage tribe, from
the mispronounced name of the Wah-sha-she, one of their patrilineal
clans. Yet they expressed the sensibility of millions of human beings.
The historical memory of the Fourth World was being left to die, as
though unimportant, insignificant to humanity's understanding of
itself and human beings' understanding of one another. "Their only
chance now of immortality," Mathews wrote, "was to live in the word
symbols" of a foreign people, a foreign tongue.[1]

Mathews would not have rated his own hopes for immortality as having the same importance as those collective hopes of the
Osages. Yet one must ask whether the completion of his forty-year
journey into the history of the Little Ones prompted his yearning to
talk eagerly about his own life.[2] Certainly an autobiography was not

the first project he conceived after the publication of *The Osages*, an enormous work, which he read and reread to the end of his life. Early in 1963, a little more than a year after its publication, he was toying with an idea for a novel.[3] At the time, he had already launched the concept for a book of nine short stories intended for boys ages nine through twelve, and later that year he completed it. Yet, in early 1962, he was reading *The Middle Span*, the second volume of George Santayana's three-part autobiography, *Persons and Places*. He read it again in May 1965, the month before he started composing *Twenty Thousand Mornings*.[4]

To our regret, he completed only the first volume. Over the next fourteen years, until his death in the summer of 1979, he struggled with patience in a way he never witnessed among the Little Old Men of the Osages.[5] For Mathews did not have the responsibility for preserving centuries of collective history to sustain him when met with discouragement. Yet his life story forms an important chapter in literary and intellectual history, just as his chapters in *The Osages* commemorate the substantial place of the tribe in world history. He often garners attention simply as one of the early shapers of the Native American novel. Frequently, we focus our attention on only two of his published works: *Sundown* and *Talking to the Moon*. These abbreviated references merely reflect the paucity of information we have heretofore had about his activities and contributions, the dearth of words with which we conceptualize the thick history of this continent. Mathews was not just an inaugurator of new forms in age-old Native discourse nor merely a forerunner for a Native American "renaissance" often obtusely imagined as more significant than all the centuries and decades preceding it. He was as important as a strong strand binding together numerous ropes of world thought and action as he was in any single capacity or field.

A gathering of rivers

Mathews was born and raised in Pawhuska, Osage Nation, twenty-two years after the Osages moved from Kansas to this reservation—their "last"—in northeastern Indian Territory, "roughly . . . a million and a half acres" along the eastern shore of the Arkansas River with Kansas as the northern border. Throughout their century and a quarter of trade with the French and Spanish empires through 1803, the Osages had built a powerful hegemony that stretched across most of the current states of Missouri, Arkansas, Oklahoma, and Kansas.[6] Now they moved onto land previously theirs that had been taken to serve the United States' Removal projects. Some sources place them along the Ohio River prior to their seventeenth-century presence west of the Mississippi. Others associate them with Cahokia, the urban center of the seventh through fifteenth centuries near present-day St. Louis. As a historian himself, Mathews left open multiple possibilities.

Mathews and his family were firmly embedded within the tribe, even though they were also in another sense nearly thrice-removed descendants of it. Their lives document the complexities of Osage nationality, dual Native-European ethnicity, and their own commitments to the Big Hills people from whom he, his father, and his siblings descended. As Mathews tells it, his great-grandfather William Shirley Williams "lived with the Osages and married an Osage girl," "A-Ci'n-Ga, [a] Big Hill girl of the Buffalo gens." Both their daughters married "John Mathews from Kentucky": Sarah Williams, John Joseph Mathews's paternal grandmother, married him after her sister, Mary, died, leaving John a widower. Though it appears that both his father's parents had died long before Mathews's birth, Sarah, through her son (Mathews's father) and daughter (Mathews's aunt Sue) evidently handed down to Mathews his understanding and knowledge of Osage traditions, although no direct male tie to the patrilineal clan heritage had ever existed.[7] His Anglo-Welsh-Osage father, William Shirley Mathews, married a second-generation French-American woman, Eugenia (Jennie) Girard. French traders had intermarried with Osage women for over a century prior to the Louisiana Purchase, so Osage culture had inherited a French inflection. His father's marriage to Jennie Girard thus sealed in Mathews a historical memory of the French heritage of Osage identity, though again no direct tie to the older French traders' marriages with Osage women had ever existed.

John Joseph Mathews was born at a time of significant change that he observed intensively as he grew older. Three years after his birth, oil was discovered on Osage land. Mathews's life was shaped largely by the privileges, destructions, opportunities, and tragedies associated with its pursuit and with the global rise of Big Oil. Because of the unusual fact of their purchase of the land compared with other tribes for whom the United States held the land in trust, the Osages were able to retain rights to the subsoil minerals, and soon became one of the richest per capita groups in the world . . . for a time. Their wealth brought upon them parasitic outsiders, murderers, and ecological danger along with political clout and a degree of continuing independence. The Mathews family's oil headrights, their income from leased allotment lands, and William Shirley Mathews's mercantile and banking businesses apparently afforded Mathews his college educations at the University of Oklahoma and Oxford University.[8] These opportunities led him to become the first known Osage novelist and historian in written English, predecessor of poet Carter Revard, literary critic Robert Warrior and others.

Fittingly, he became famous for his intricate understanding of the crises of mixed blood identity through his 1934 novel *Sundown*. In the Osage Tribal Museum that he helped establish a few years later while serving as a tribal councilman, he takes a humble place beside soldiers, sports figures, statespersons, and the hundreds of other allottees honored in their permanent exhibits. Although Mathews's prominent place among American Indian authors is well established, too little has been known of the details of his life to allow readers the intimate knowledge and understanding of him that his work deserves. His autobiography opens for us a view of the parallels and dissimilarities between him and his contemporaries and near contemporaries, both Native and non-Native, as pertains to their creation of authorial personae and their paths toward authorship. For example, unlike fellow life-writer Zitkala-Ša, eighteen years his senior, Mathews never experienced the dislocation of removal to boarding school that so many Indians of his generation were forced to undergo, though some of his relatives did. While both authors challenged the religious presumptions of the dominant society, they did so from different backgrounds: Mathews had been raised within French Catholicism, whereas Zitkala-Ša strove to retain her traditionalist roots. Unlike Creek, Chickasaw, and Scotch-Irish humorist Alexander Posey, Mathews wrote primarily for national (U.S.) and international audiences, even while focusing on the local and regional, educating those audiences about Osage perspectives arising from Osage intellectual, social, and tribal history. Yet like both Posey and Zitkala-Ša, he actively participated in political lobbying on behalf of the Osage Nation and the wider Indian community. Among non-Natives, Mathews might best be compared to his friends and models, such as J. Frank Dobie, Jack London, Ernest Thompson Seton, and W. S. Campbell—many of whom are unfamiliar to the majority of present-day readers. He also bears similarities to Ernest Hemingway, William Faulkner, Antoine de Saint-Exupéry, and other contemporaneous and now canonical writers, and he has been compared to Henry Thoreau.

The autobiography touches upon such an enormous wealth of topics that any attempt to characterize its main attractions for readers and scholars would close rather than open vistas. One can only provide a foundation upon which others will build with more in-depth studies and observations. Certainly, it will attract a wide variety of readers, from students of American Indian literature and historians of the progressive era to those interested in early aviation, World War I on the home front, Native American military service, hunting narratives, and chronicles of the eastern Plains and the West. Mathews is first and foremost a philosopher of his own life. Beyond that his interests range from Osage prayer, comparative religion, Catholicism, and the universality of fetishism in societies denying its power to the interplay of gender and sexuality in the shadow of the Victorian era. He writes about the "cultural heteroglossia" or the meeting of many cultures in one place that so profoundly shaped his childhood, and of one's love for one's parents and their elusiveness to their own children. He is a keen judge of the psychology of children, adolescents, and young adults; a critic of educational methods; and a champion of technological achievements in aviation, the military, and transportation. His interest in language—capturing precisely how people speak—is as strong as his fascination with the bonds that humans and animals form with one another. His investigation of "earth laws," the biological parameters of human existence, deserves recognition as distinct in its grounding from the biological determinism of writers who shaped his consciousness. Finally, ever and always, Mathews had his finger on how the confluence of empires in the middle region of North America played out among ordinary people, on detecting minute shifts amid epic historical change and on relations *among* Indian tribes in this center as well as within them.

Although *Twenty Thousand Mornings* is conceived and executed as a conventional autobiography insofar as it presents a "comprehensive and continuous narrative in chronological order," it will challenge, defy, and perhaps redefine studies of American Indian autobiography as a genre. Mathews consistently exercised a degree of agency often seen as unusual in this genre, dominated and surrounded as it has been by collaborative projects of life telling made to conform to the expectations of print narration, as-told-to narratives dubiously mediated through non-Indian interlocutors with motives powerfully divergent from their subjects', and oral and pictographic forms such as coup tales, vision stories, and sketchbooks. Inevitably, the work will be compared to the earliest known autobiographies of Native Americans such as Samson Occum, William Apess, and Catharine Brown; to nineteenth- and twentieth-century narratives by Black Hawk, Charles Alexander Eastman, Francis LaFlesche, Zitkala-Ša, and John Milton Oskison; and to later works including *Family Matters, Tribal Affairs*; *A Salishan Autobiography*; *On Native Ground*; *A Chief and Her People*; *Rez Road Follies*; *Bead on an Anthill*; and *Interior Landscapes*.[9] Mathews himself might invite comparison to the autobiographers he chose as models for crafting his own, among whom none of the above explicitly appear. How he tells his own life in this volume also invites comparison to his role in collaborating with others to tell theirs.

It is not my aim here to attempt a full-fleshed analysis of Mathews, his published and unpublished writings, or his place among writers. Rather, I concentrate on the conditions under which the autobiography was produced and how this work challenges our previous conceptions of Mathews. Despite this work's merits, particularly its meticulous witnessing of history, Mathews met with frustrations and interruptions that stymied its publication and torpedoed his plans to complete it. His dedication to Osage causes, because time-consuming, compounded these difficulties. Yet the work enhances our appreciation of Mathews's fictional and nonfictional characters by revealing his differences from them, challenges various readers' obsession with authenticating his "Indianness," and exposes how the marketing of Mathews as an American Indian shaped his career in positive and negative ways. It gives us greater insight into Mathews as an author and as an adept navigator of a shifting modernity than does any previous publication except for his five published works.

Because the truncated nature of the unfinished volumes inevitably raises questions about Mathews's life after 1920, I devote a large amount of time to his diaries and other papers in the archival collection where the autobiography is housed. As a de facto continuation of this autobiography, his diary may be considered one of his thirty-plus yet-to-be-published works. I pull only a small fraction of diary entries into service here, but they help us to see how Mathews actively shaped national scholarship about Osages and Indians. They also introduce us to the prolific nature of his lifelong writing career, exposing a much wider corpus of works than has been previously imagined. Readers are left at the end of *Twenty Thousand Mornings* wondering what happened next. I sketch the answer in brief here, spinning out a thin filament between "Liber Primus" and *Talking to the Moon*, Liber Tertius.

"A mint-flavored whisper on a jet airfield"

Mathews wrote *Boy, Horse, and Dog,* this first volume of his autobiography *Twenty Thousand Mornings*, between June 1, 1965, and March 11, 1967. His taped diary for 1965—the only version available—is perversely inaudible for the first of June, but he clearly planned at that time to write three or four volumes. These intentions suggest he was following Santayana's model. Mathews saw *Talking to the Moon* as one of the volumes, either the last or second-to-last. The first would extend from 1900 until 1920, or from his early childhood through his World War I service and the completion of his degree at the University of Oklahoma. The second, for which he was still toying with inadequate titles, would presumably have covered the period from his arrival at Oxford University in 1921 (after the wonderfully dilatory gentleman's hunting trip to the Rockies narrated here) through the late 1920s or early 1930s, at which time *Talking to the Moon* would have picked up the story.[10]

Discouragement appears to have stopped him short before he did any substantial work on the second volume. He perceived the world as uninterested in his story, and the East Coast publishing establishment as unable to convert it into merchandise and unwilling to publish anything that could not be converted into a salable commodity. "It's just not commercial press merchandise. Looking over the lists of the last five years, one can find practically no titles that have to do with native and hinterland America; the writers who are published seem to be writing only for money, and are careless of everything else one associates with literature with a capital 'L.' The successful commercial press authors seem to vie with each other in the presentation to the reading public of fornication, Lesbianism, homosectuality [*sic*], masochism . . . . The public at the moment would not be interested in the American earth, to which they must flee later from electronics and over-population and 'Flower Children.'"[11] Having been raised in a more reserved era, Mathews felt acutely that the United States and its publishing houses had moved into an "age of vindictiveness, vulgarity, common man stridency and sex both aberrant and normal."[12] Throughout his life, Mathews moved with and often anticipated the times, but he never fully shed the values with which he had been raised. Many aspects of the 1960s abraded his sense of propriety.

The discouragement was actually quite slight. Mathews sent the manuscript to only three publishers, none of whom had lists that conformed to such a project. Two commercial publishers in New York were attempting to form the cutting edges of postmodernism, science fiction, thriller, and detective novels. However, Mathews took too much to heart the new discourtesies of the industry in the mid-1960s and the impersonal nature of entirely meaningless rejections. He astutely recognized that the editors were now more concentrated on making money than forging good relationships with authors of standing or potential. Still, the experience of receiving the manuscript back, barely examined and probably never actually read, from Seymour Lawrence, with whom he felt he had a personable connection, provoked in Mathews wide emotional vacillations about the project over the next fourteen years.[13] Even before submission—to companies that no longer even sent postcards acknowledging receipt of manuscripts—he wrote in one mood that "the whole business of writing seems dull and ineffective. If one were really a dedicated writer, this sudden impression of dullness would make one very unhappy; perhaps in some cases almost suicidal. . . . As for me the Philistine, non-writer, I should have liked to saddle a horse and lope across the prairie into the goddamned wind of Just-Doing-That-Moon."[14] In other moods, he would recognize and wallow in his own narcissism (as he and his wife observed it), his love for the sound of his own words in the manuscript. Later, he would wonder how well written the retrospective really was. By October 1967, he acknowledged, "I can't judge it. . . . In this stage of our culture, this sort of book would be—one was about to say, like shouting in the wilderness—perhaps like a mint-flavored whisper on a jet airfield."[15]

As readers of this posthumous work, however, we cannot fully attribute the fact that the first volume was never published and the second volume apparently never written to Mathews's sensitivities to rejections lacking in both substance and diligent review. In fact, throughout his writing career, he had experienced such highs and lows. He often spent many more years in the composition of his manuscripts than first pledged. *Life and Death of an Oilman*, for example, conceived by April 1943, had originally been due to his publisher on January 1, 1946. He did not even start composing it until November 1946, nor did he send the initial chapters out for review until March 1948. During this time, like most writers, he experienced periods when he was simply not inspired to continue with it.[16] So it is not surprising that we find Mathews between his seventieth year and his death distracted from writing his life story by any number of other projects that had always drawn him away from writing. Significantly, he experienced a major illness requiring surgery in 1975–76 for which he may have been experiencing symptoms as early as 1967. Yet he returned to editing the first volume in 1978. His attention to his grandchildren and long vacations to visit with them also claimed priority. As a writer, Mathews spent much of his time writing for family, friends, and himself rather than a larger public. He would spend hours illustrating letters and diary snippets for his children and grandchildren with the pen-and-ink work that was one of his major (but little-known) creative talents.[17]

Besides private affairs, the usual public obligations drew him off his ranch—The Blackjacks—and away from writing. The year he finished volume one of the autobiography, the Osage Tribal Museum reopened. The tribe had withdrawn funding during and after World War II, forcing it to close. So in the late 1960s, Mathews poured energy into trying to turn it into a national monument, to preserve and fund it as well as to bring attention to Osage contributions to American history. He also met with what he perceived as indifference toward this museum on the part of the staff and volunteers, a museum which he had been instrumental in founding in 1938 through negotiations with the Bureau of Indian Affairs. During the late 1960s, Mathews frequently checked the museum at night to see if those in charge had locked up. Finding once that they had not was enough to obsess him for a decade.[18] Perhaps the mood of the new post-relocation era of tribal sovereignty and civil rights clashed with the orientation of the older generation. Younger Natives may have perceived a tribal museum as a cop-out to Amer-European values, a making static of a living culture from which they had been forcibly detached. Their parents and grandparents had "thrown away" those traditions they perceived as jeopardizing their children's future on the "white man's road," making deep appreciation of them difficult to attain. Whatever the situation, Mathews frequently despaired of his efforts to "rescue Osage culture," yet spent his own time and gave money from his own pocket to keep the museum alive.[19] He also continued to consult with Chief Fred Lookout's son and others regarding legislative bills affecting the Osages, helped researchers with his tape recordings of Osage ceremonies and his knowledge of them, participated as a shareholder in the Osage Realty Company, and cooperated more and more reluctantly in an acquaintance's proposal for the filming of *Wah'Kon-Tah*.[20]

Regardless of whether *Twenty Thousand Mornings* would have been published in Mathews's lifetime had he had more persistence, more time, or a better sense of appropriate publication venues, the value of the narrative to his readers is unquestionable. Not only does the autobiography throw into much greater relief the distinction between the persona Jo-Without-Purpose and the older Jo's character Challenge Windzer, but it upends a number of misguided attempts to corner Mathews with regard to his Indianness or whiteness. Robert Warrior put it nicely when he wrote that "both American Indian and Native Americanist discourses continue to be preoccupied with parochial questions of identity and authenticity." It is my hope that with the publication of a host of heretofore unpublished works by Mathews, stereotyping categories within these discourses (as well as within those regarding American and world literature) will cease to reign over, to reduce, to constrain, to contain American Indian literature and thought; and that the focus of scholarship will increasingly be to engage in the myriad critical issues crucial to an Indian and global future. My hope is, further, that readers will be as interested in the John Joseph Mathews who read Western autobiographies as models for his own and wanted to live like a gentleman as in the Mathews who wrote of the Little Old Men and told the story of the spider to his granddaughter visiting from France one pleasant June.[21]

For despite Warrior's sense in 1995 that Mathews "did not rely on the popularity of Indians in writing his books," the archival record strongly suggests otherwise, not with respect to Mathews's own mindset but with his publishers' marketing of him and his works. For example, in February 1933, the University of Oklahoma Press received a letter indicating that Mathews was being described as a full-blooded Osage to the public by someone (apparently not the Press editors through 1967, who were lifelong friends of Mathews's). Book-of-the-Month Club displays of *Wah'Kon-Tah* featured kachina dolls, Southwestern pottery, and blankets that appear to be Navajo.[22] Henry Seidel Canby's review of the book for the Book-of-the-Month

Club newsletter sells it based on its rather tenuous connection to President Herbert Hoover. Canby characterizes Mathews as a young man who has been "sufficiently stabilized in the ways of the white man to resist degeneration" because of Agent Miles's introduction of compulsory education among the Osages. This reading ironically strips the book of its critiques of Miles's coercive imposition of Western education onto the Osages while ignoring Mathews's missionary great-grandfather, Confederate-allied grandfather, and a father who appears to have been educated in the Western style quite independently of Miles or other agents. University of Oklahoma Press releases also emphasize Mathews's Osage heritage rather than his half-French background or his father's Anglo-Welsh parentage.[23] Mathews's autobiography might have been rejected had any of his editors seriously read it, because the Jo Mathews within it does not conform to the Osage man presented to the public in the early 1930s. Even by 1961, four of his five published texts pertained centrally to Osage topics, despite a much larger body of work that could not be consolidated under such a singular identity. Mathews's larger frustrations with publication, then, likely derived (whether or not he focused on the fact) from institutional disinterest in those works that could not be "sold" through reference to his Indianness, regardless of their quality.

The present moment in history is different for this book's appearance in print. Mathews suggested to himself repeatedly that only "illusional nostalgia" would sell the volume. Moreover, its reception could not possibly, he believed, depend upon reader identification by the masses, who buy books and live detached from the earth in cities.[24] Given how few people who were born in the nineteenth century remained alive even at the time Mathews was writing, true nostalgia—the actual remembering of a bygone time that one experienced firsthand—is now virtually impossible. Nor will *Boy, Horse, and Dog* seem more important to people in the cities simply because the green movement is motivating them to reattach to the earth or at least treat it better. However, despite his self-avowed narcissism, it seems that Mathews's underlying reasons for writing his life were not fully self-absorbed, nor centrally concerned with immortality. Rather, they conformed to what I also see as this writer's enduring attraction: that Mathews was a magnificent witness to a remarkable historical period that is becoming increasingly distant and inaccessible. "Well," he said on January 1, 1970, "I've reached the 7th decade of the 20th Century. I must get onto the second volume of my autobiography, *Twenty Thousand Mornings*; tell the world about my life spanning the greatest achievements of mankind, in which the world, shouting, postulating, screaming, organizing, busy saving the unfit, who will eventually destroy us, can not possibly be interested."[25] Although I very much doubt that Mathews's list of those who will eventually destroy us conforms neatly to my own, his minute observation not only of the greatest achievements of the twentieth century but of day-to-day life, character, introspective self, and region are invaluable.

Thirty Thousand Mornings

Of course, any autobiography is more than a historical record. It is a story made unique by the specific perspective that a writer brings to his or her experiences and by the ruminations they elicit. This work is no exception. The beautiful and touching portraits Mathews devotes to his father and mother, for example, give us enormous insight not only into them but into him and his development as a man and a writer. Hilarious reminiscences, which sometimes turn painful, about his relationship with his older sister Josephine give us glimpses into patterns in his early relationships with women. They also show him beginning to reflect upon the elements of her behavior that were shaped by forces beyond her control: the apparent attention to the sole surviving male child of the family, the shaping of her views of civilized behavior by a boarding school that may have been chosen by the family rather than forced upon them, the assignment of parental responsibilities to her as the oldest sibling, which she had some cause to resent. It is important for us to note that Mathews showed these parts of his manuscript to his three younger sisters—Marie, Lillian, and Florence—a year prior to submitting it to publishers, asking them to check his memories of their childhood. There is no indication that in 1967 he was reticent about revealing these private incidents to public eyes. In the absence of editorial feedback regarding the draft he submitted to publishers, however, Mathews intended to cut out several of these superb passages. He was personalizing the inattention of the presses to his manuscript and trying to mind-read what within the draft might have discouraged its immediate embrace by them, though he had to have known on some level that they had never read it.[26]

If, then, the autobiography is of interest for the delicate ways in which it tells human stories of great filial love and bewildering sibling rivalry, it is also intriguing because of the kind of writer who wrote it. Known for his incredible skill at creative nonfiction, Mathews cannot be read without piquing in his reader a curious quest for the border between fact and fictionalization. Of course, it is a widely understood concept in studies of autobiography that they are shaped by a kind of fictionalization that masquerades as memory unmediated. What draws one's attention with Mathews is less the creative attempt to disguise faulty memory as unquestionable truth, as the lengths to which he went to verify his own recollection of events. In addition to passing the first volume by all three of his living sisters, he researched through outside sources details regarding the Mitscher family, Guynemer, and the precise wording of the leaflets dropped on Beaumont, Texas, not to mention the genre of autobiography itself. Yet the primary source of his story was likely not recollective memory, or "emotion recollected in tranquility" at the age of seventy, but his own diary entries through 1921 recorded very close to the events he describes.[27]

He was right in predicting that some "future researcher" would be "compelled to stumble over" his unpublished manuscript, even if it was not published in his own lifetime. He ended up writing this manuscript for the mere "pleasure of writing" it.[28] Yet if it is the case that the primary source of his story were his diary entries (and he mentions referring to them several times in his narrative), this researcher would very much like to know: Where are those diaries? Are they still extant? How might being able to compare them to the autobiography aid our comprehension of Mathews's writing process?

Perhaps a segue is in order.

After reading *Twenty Thousand Mornings*, one might easily be disappointed that it never goes beyond young adulthood. However, Mathews's written life story does not end with the last sentences of this volume. Nearly every day of his life from April 21, 1921, to November 1978, he entered his activities, thoughts, and feelings in his diary. The great bulk of that diary is housed—thanks to his own forethought and the diligence of his beloved stepson John Hunt—at the Western History Collections of the University of Oklahoma Libraries. It is an extraordinary record. A record to be envied by any researcher of nearly any other writer or historical figure. A record nearly complete and comprehensive. Yet in its expansiveness there are maddening silences and gaps. Among those gaps are *all* the yearly diaries prior to 1920 to which he refers within his autobiography. In 1940 he wrote a letter to Elizabeth Hunt, who would become his second wife, saying, "I have found myself going back over the nineteen years the present Diary has been going—from April 21st 1921. The one before that, the war one was lost, and for several years I refrained from keeping one at all. Suddenly, I felt the need, and I began again."[29] So one must conclude that the lost war diary was not the entire record of his childhood and young adulthood, yet there is no archival trace—yet—of the diary from 1905 or so onward.

Mathews was a fascinated observer of life with an eye for details. Several of the diaries are not only typed but carefully illustrated by Mathews. They show his immersion in creative reflection upon the events of the human and nonhuman world and his own impressions and expressions of joyously being alive. They also show us that the diaries themselves were works of elaboration. Script versions of the diary do not precisely match their typed transcriptions or audiotaped renditions. His own statements within them about his work with them reveal that he filled them out over the days and perhaps months or years following the initial record of events. When he showed them for the first time to Elizabeth as a way to share with her his activities in Mexico during his Guggenheim Fellowship, he clearly was beginning to conceptualize them as potentially interesting to a wider audience. "You seem to enjoy the carbons so much, you have me wondering if I am not really writing something that might be readable to others as well. I might even submit [it] when I get back if you think it worth while. . . . Your letters then, have made me Diary-conscious. . . . You, by the way are the only person who has ever read any of my Diary." Even before this, he had been transcribing the previous nineteen years of it into uniform volumes.[30]

So although the diary that we do have left helps to reconstruct and straighten out the record heretofore left fragmented by statements that Mathews and others made about his life, it nevertheless leaves important questions unanswered. First, did Mathews destroy (intentionally or unintentionally) the diaries that shaped the material within volume one of *Twenty Thousand Mornings*? Or did someone else? If not, and if they survived the prairie fires that destroyed some of his early papers, it is to be hoped that they will eventually be added to his archive at the University of Oklahoma. Second, to what extent were the diaries lent to the same fictionalization processes that characterized nearly all of Mathews's published work? When one picks up the diary of 1921, for example, the sheer beauty of the writing sets the mind to wondering which snippets of Oxford conversation were reworked or polished by Mathews for the record, even prior to and during their first drafting. It even crosses one's mind that they could have been made up out of whole cloth, so consistent are they with the well-known spirit of Oxford life in the 1920s. Yet the diaries of the same decade and certainly those of the 1960s and 1970s bespeak a remarkable lack of premeditation on Mathews's part. Frequently, he punches his cherished tape recorder on and off over the course of a day, inspired by the voice of a field sparrow or a nighthawk, or taking a break from a morning of writing. His early pledge to the diary of absolute sincerity and the repetitive minutiae of quotidian life also speak to a reliable firsthand record. So do his published fact-faithful historical narratives. Even Mathews was fascinated. Reading his 1921 diary forty-five years later in preparation for drafting the second volume of *Twenty Thousand Mornings*, he wrote, "I had no idea that I had kept it so meticulously and had written so well."[31]

The care with which Mathews kept his diaries and their sheer length make it difficult here to give a sketch of the man that would do justice to him or to them. Once more widely available, the diaries will be seen as a critical component of his artistic profile and teach us much about the creative process. It is also difficult to re-create at second hand the emotion they stir as one learns about the major turning points of his personal life. However, like the autobiography itself, they so completely transform our image of Mathews that an overview is imperative of the major ways in which they extend the story of his thirty thousand mornings on earth. Aside from the information they will give to researchers of Osage politics, history, and legislative intervention in the twentieth century, they enable a most significant discovery.

At a time when most imagine that American Indians were rendered nearly impotent to shape the discourses about them, Mathews was actively and meaningfully shaping the body of scholarship that would emerge about the Osages and affect their lives. From 1933 through 1967, he worked as a manuscript reviewer and consultant for the University of Oklahoma Press. In that capacity, he could not control the decisions of an entire industry. Yet his influence appears to have helped quash the publication anywhere of at least one unworthy book, driven others to publishing houses with less reach and reputation, and promoted works of significant merit. As important as this work was, equally important is the fact that Mathews was not the only American Indian writer shaping academic discourses about American Indians in this way.[32]

Mathews's first reviews were in October 1933. He rejected a manuscript by Corabelle Fellowes titled *Blue Star*. This title, which was actually an as-told-to life history authored by Kunigunde Duncan, did not come out until 1938 and ended up being published by a then local Idaho press, Caxton Printers (which also published the yet unknown Ayn Rand's *Anthem* that year). He also wrote a positive review for *Oklahoma Place Names* by Charles N. Gould. In 1936, he was sent a manuscript by Basil Hayes titled *Blackjacks on the Horizon*. This one, too, he rejected. The Press wrote Hayes: "The reviewer can readily understand that a book of this genre may be pleasing to patriotic Oklahomans, yet understanding and appreciating the objective of the University Press, he is not ready to suggest that the publication of this book comes within the province of such a press."

It appears that this author went on to issue only one, self-published book, not the one Mathews reviewed.[33]

Also rejected by the Press during the late 1930s was a more interesting manuscript titled *The Osage Mission: A Factor in the Making of Kansas*. Written by Sister Mary Paul Fitzgerald and issued the following year as *Beacon on the Plains* by the much less well known printer for St. Mary's College in Leavenworth, Kansas, it was a manuscript that Mathews not only appreciated reading but later used as a source in *The Osages*. He emphasized in his review that it was "worthy of publication" and that he "enjoyed reading" it, but his critiques are worth repeating and may have influenced Savoie Lottinville, the Press editor, against it.

> First: The term "half-breed" should not appear in a scholarly book. It is indefinite in the first place and very offensive and barbaric in the second. I object to this crude smugness on the part of the writer. Then I see no reason why the term "squaw" should be used when "Indian woman" is perfectly expressive. These terms should not be used in University of Oklahoma Press books, stressing the "civilization" of Indians, and appearing in a Series which has as one of its purposes the bringing about of a better understanding between two races of people.
>
> Second: I was constantly shocked by the studied avoidance of facts in the documents used in this manuscript, which did not contribute directly to the glory of the missionarys [*sic*]. One feels that their glory would not have been dimmed by fairer analysis of the materials, which would have made the manuscript more convincing.
>
> . . . Certainly there is little to be gained by the reader about the raison d'etre of the Mission—the Osage Indian; his religion, philosophy, his life. And the Mission as a factor in the making of Kansas remains little more than a sub-title.

In his correspondence with Sister Mary Paul, Lottinville stressed that the two anonymous reviewers were "well established scholars in their respective fields." Sister Mary Paul responded to Lottinville "in the interest of historical truth" to find out more about the material not creditable to the missionaries to which Mathews had referred. So

Mathews's work clearly influenced the shape of the future publication and her thinking. She also used *Wah'Kon-Tah* as one of her sources.[34]

His contributions that same year to the publication of the Albert J. Salvan translation of Victor Tixier's *Voyage aux Prairies Osages*, edited by John Francis McDermott, also lend insight into Mathews's style as a reviewer. He wrote to Lottinville that he had read the manuscript with "deep interest and much care" and highly favored the book's publication. He then made several sensible corrections of the translations, the most significant indicating that Mont des Tombeaux meant not "burial mounds" but Hill of the Tombs. These he referred to as "a few discordant notes which fell 'plunk' on my Osage sensitiveness." Calling Tixier's Osage Glossary "putrid," he recommended that the Press either correct it or leave it out entirely. In this same letter, Mathews, who by then was at the end of his patience with Osage, state, and national politics, confided in his friend Lottinville that he was "abandoning hope of civilizing the State of Oklahoma and the Osage County—I shall attempt to revert to the life of gentleman." It is an interesting comment for a man who frequently penned in quotes when he used the word "civilization."[35] It clearly indicates his greater interest at the time in reviewing manuscripts than in solving problems of public policy.

Mathews's diary entries for the 1940s indicate that he reviewed Angie Debo's *And Still the Waters Run*. On July 7, 1946, he wrote that it was "a book for which I had been a reader, and which carries a quotation from me on the wrapper." Debo and he became acquainted as well: he occasionally mentions meeting with her. During this decade, he also rejected a manuscript by Tillie Karns-Newman, likely the book that was published nine years later by an out-of-the-way Boston publishing house under the title *The Black Dog Trail* (1957). He said of this one that it had not been worth his time. As Mathews received no pay, but only one Press title per review as compensation for that time, this must have seemed particularly egregious during a year of terrible financial worry.[36] Likewise rejected was a manuscript on James Bigheart of the Osages by Orpha B. Russell, this in 1954. In 1961, Mathews gave a favorable review to a manuscript by Royal B. Hassrick, probably *The Sioux: Life and Customs of a Warrior Society*.

The next year, he also favored *The Otoes and the Missourias* by Berlin B. Chapman, though the Press did not end up publishing this title. Mathews found it "meticulous, and extremely detailed" but "difficult going . . . a package of documents between two . . . covers." Though he mentions reading a manuscript on d'Iberville in his journal for June 1962, it is unclear whether he favored or discouraged its publication, or which title it may have been.[37]

Mathews also consulted with the University of Oklahoma Press in 1967 on a book it was publishing (*On the Western Tour with Washington Irving: The Journal and Letters of Count de Pourtales*). Asked to help identify Osage sacred symbols in three pictures, Mathews consulted five members of the tribe: Paul Pitts, Ed Redeagle, Wakon Iron, Henry Lookout, and Charles Whitehorn. They had little luck. Mathews determined that because these men were boys when Peyotism was adopted and their fathers didn't want to hand the traditions of the old religion down orally, believing it might be harmful or cause death, the knowledge had been lost among his acquaintances.[38]

Mathews's most intriguing encounter as a reviewer came in 1954 when the Press sent him A. P. Nasatir's manuscript *Life on the Spanish Mississippi, 1792–1796*.[39] It appears that Lottinville initially showed the manuscript to Mathews not to review, but because it concerned his "undertaking on the Osage." Five months after inviting him to Norman to "have a look through" it, Lottinville asked him if he was finished with it yet. Three and a half months after that, he wrote "A.P. Nasatir says that you have not been out to see him yet. I'd asked him to send the material here on 'Imperial Osage' to see whether we might have another fling at it. Do let me know what you think." Of course, the latter manuscript was not published by the Press until 1983. *The Osages* became one of its sources.[40]

The admiration of Lottinville and his predecessor, Joseph Brandt, for their good friend derived partly from Mathews's superb talent in writing, partly from his connections, partly from his unique ethnic background, and partly from his enthusiastic advocacy for the Press. In February 1936, during one of his frequent visits to Washington, D.C., on Osage business, Mathews lobbied senators and congressmen by distributing free copies of *Deserts on the March* by Paul Sears, a man he greatly admired. Impressed by Sears's argument on desertification and the causes of the then most abysmal Dust Bowl, Mathews influenced public policy debates and conservation efforts while simultaneously promoting his loyal publisher. Two months later, Mathews wrote to Brandt that he had spoken with the sitting Commissioner of Indian Affairs John Collier about a book that the Press would be interested in seeing Collier write (perhaps one of Mathews's suggesting). "He said that such a book ought to be written—that Ickes [Harold Ickes, secretary of the Interior] was also interested in it, but he wasn't sure that he would have the time. He would enjoy writing such a book however." Later that year, the Press used its connection with Mathews to try to acquire Frederic Voelker's biography of Old Bill Williams (Mathews's great-grandfather), apparently after seeing signs of Voelker's disaffection with a University of North Carolina Press volume, the A. H. Favour biography of the man.[41]

If the Western History Collections archive reveals Mathews's unknown identity as a scholarly reviewer, it also allows a fuller picture of his writing career. Mathews has been known primarily as the author of five books. Though the works were substantial and appeared about once a decade (1932, 1934, 1945, 1951, 1961), Mathews was immersed in the process of writing continually, much more than this publication record shows. He daily crafted entries for the diary, which (especially considering the amount of polishing he did to the writing) he may have considered one of his central works. Some of these entries are substantial and thoughtful. Some are quite beautiful, and many of them are intellectually interesting because they expand our understanding of Mathews's thinking and values. But sometimes they do so in ways we might rather not know, as many of his views are at odds both with the current Native American intellectual establishment and with the wishful fantasies that have grown up around him.

For example, in 1924 Mathews avowed himself to be "very anti-Jew." He hated male homosexuality and viewed it as degenerate. (One would have to work quite a bit of overtime to convert his hatred into a homophobia that might be a reaction formation against tendencies within himself, a present-day ideological practice that in effect minimizes the real virulence of widespread early- and middle-twentieth-century sentiment against those who practice sex with persons of the same sex.)[42] Although we might wish to associate Mathews with civil rights, his reactions toward blacks in general and the leaders of the civil rights movement were ambivalent at best. He appeared in 1963–64 to be disgusted at the "Christians still burning Negro churches" and at the assassination of Medgar Evers. Yet in the 1920s, he was telling "nigger stories" to his pals at Oxford, in 1967 he called Martin Luther King, Jr., sanctimonious, and he thought black Africans to be "Paleolithic" and "a perfect tool for the Fascists and the Communists." The chances for racial equality in the United States, which he probably did advocate, were, he felt, "very small . . . if [blacks] continue through riots and screaming" to demand it.[43] On their anniversary in August 1970, he somehow was able to convince himself that the dropping of the first atomic bombs had been a "most effective bluff," similar to the bluff of a male animal that does not want to fight, ignoring the inconvenient fact that not a single bluff among nonhuman beings kills more than two hundred thousand (or even one) of the bluffer's own species.[44]

If the diary is itself one of his unpublished manuscripts, it also shows Mathews conceiving, completing, or publishing several manuscripts that most of his current readers do not know he undertook. Around the time when *Wah'Kon-Tah* was being publicized, Mathews wrote Brandt that he was working on a handbook of the birds of the Osage and another on the geology of the Osage. Sara Jane Richter discusses the articles that he published in *Sooner Magazine* between 1929 and 1933, yet these ten articles have never been excavated from the magazine's archives to round out our knowledge of Mathews's corpus.[45] Though apparently his least studied form, poetry was among Mathews's endeavors during the 1930s and 1940s, and he sent one poem to "Dibbs" (Elizabeth Hunt). So although our information is sketchy about his career through the 1930s, in part because of the absence of diaries, it is clear that Mathews was writing regularly. *Wah'Kon-Tah* and *Sundown* are only the best known of his works prior to 1940.[46]

As Mathews hints in his acknowledgments in *The Osages*, the 1940s and early 1950s were unkind to him financially. His diary entries starting in 1943 betray a much greater sense of distress than that brief but sincere line of gratitude to Frank Phillips, Allen G. Olliphant, and W. G. Skelly. He had taken on not only the college tuition payments for his two children from his first marriage and at least one of his two stepchildren, but in at least two instances their private secondary school tuition as well.[47] The impact on his writing was both depressive and proliferative. On the one hand, he became dependent at one point on his family and on Paul and Gladys Buck, the lessees of his allotment, for transportation. This put the brakes on the travel that he needed to perform to complete research for the E. W. Marland manuscript. On the other hand, the situation prompted him to start writing short pieces for money, a plan that unfortunately coincided with the recessions of 1945 and 1948–49. Still, between March 1939 and December 1949 he wrote *Talking to the Moon*; the political philosophy *Without the Sword*; something he referred to as the Peyote manuscript; fourteen short stories; a 120,000-word novel titled *Within Your Dream*; *Life and Death of an Oilman*; and articles for at least three newspapers and magazines.[48] The timing suggests that the desire to earn money, and not just an interest in editing, may have been their impetus. He toyed with an idea for a book to be called *The One Who Weeps*, as well as one for a biography of former U.S. senator Thomas Gore of Oklahoma, and had an idea for a novel about his mother's childhood and family in Missouri that he seriously considered writing in the mid-1950s.[49] In addition, he encouraged the apparently short-lived aspirations of Elizabeth and her daughter Ann in fiction.

In the absence of diaries or letters from 1941 and 1942, it is hard to know the precise dates of composition or ultimate venues of all of the completed projects. In September 1940, he wrote from the Blackjacks to the secretary at the Guggenheim Foundation that he had returned from Mexico early after contracting jungle fever and that he was laying the manuscript for his fellowship aside because two old men upon whom he depended for information on Peyote Church ritual had been ill recently.[50] So he may have completed the "Peyote manuscript" prior to working on *Talking to the Moon*. However, given the number of stories about peyote in the latter, it is unclear that this manuscript was ever completed in a discrete form rather than being folded into *Talking to the Moon* or *The Osages*. The fate of *Without the Sword* is a good touchstone.

Mathews completed that manuscript, originally titled *Earth's Children*, within eight months of first mentioning it in his diary in February 1943. The actual writing (at least 41,500 words) took only from mid-August through mid-October. At the time, Mathews felt rushed to finish the project. He was afraid his idea would get scooped, and he knew that publishers were facing wartime paper shortages. Also, he wanted to get on with his search for a government position to help with the war effort and to stabilize his income so that he could marry Elizabeth. When the book went under informal review at the University of Oklahoma Press, he responded defensively to the good-faith critiques by Lottinville and the anonymous reviewer, Cortez A. M. Ewing. Disheartened, he asked Paul Sears for advice about the manuscript. Before receiving any, Joe Brandt, who had moved to the University of Chicago Press, encouraged him in a plan Mathews had conceived to integrate the ideas into *Talking to the Moon*.

Lottinville was taken by surprise when the University of Chicago Press announced the publication of *Talking* in December 1944, and he wrote Mathews a curt letter that evidences his hard feelings. Mathews replied that his economic need had been a major consideration in his decision; Brandt had promised monetary advances for the revision integrating the two manuscripts and for the Marland biography. He acknowledged that the timing of his negotiations with both presses was delicate but assured Lottinville that the negotiations were also ethical. When Lottinville was approached in 1948 by William Couch, the new editor of the University of Chicago Press, who wanted someone to take over the press's contract for the Marland biography, Lottinville initially declined. He told Couch that Mathews was "a superlative writer" when "under discipline" and that "an editor working closely with Mathews can do both himself and the author a lot of good." But his hurt feelings also surfaced: "That's what

I thought I was doing on the book [the University of Chicago Press] ultimately published," he wrote.[51]

After seeing *Talking to the Moon* through publication, Mathews immediately started writing short stories. He composed and submitted at least two in August 1946. Though he thought in 1961 and 1970 that he had not read his own 1934 *Sundown* since its publication, he did reread it in 1946 "for style" for the short stories. He also found it better than expected when he returned to it while writing short stories in 1948.[52] He then wrote twelve more and hoped for a regular monthly income from them, a hope that was soon dashed. The whereabouts of four of the stories remain a mystery, so it is possible that these four alone were published (perhaps anonymously). It appears that *Within Your Dream* was another rapidly composed piece. Though the diary entries are missing for the stretch, Mathews says at the end of 1949 that he had written it between August 11 and December 2. Perhaps for that reason—Mathews was generally uncomfortable with hurried drafts—he put it in "cold storage" rather than sending it out right away.[53] The novel emerged again in March 1952, at which time he "lifted" a short story from it and planned to submit that story to a magazine not yet launched called *The Wild Catter*. In August 1953, he found the second part of the novel "wild" and "full of chaff" but containing "valuable grain." He finally decided on an ending in January 1955. The whereabouts of the manuscript, which he sent off to a publisher, and of the short story are unknown.[54]

Though their quality hides the fact, his foray into short stories was mainly to finance his work on the biography of Marland. He conceived and began researching that 1951 work—originally titled *The Wolf of Reality*—in 1943. In September 1944, the University of Chicago Press offered him a $2,500 advance plus a Newbury Scholarship to facilitate completion of the work.[55] Whether he was able to accept the latter is unclear. Certainly Mathews met his share of frustrations with the book. He ended up breaking ties with the press because he chose to be a gentleman, refraining from the demand that he delve into Marland's unorthodox love life. He thought that the writing of it would involve him in a prurient sensationalism that he despised. It would also have betrayed his friends and two of the sources of his information: Lydie Marland, E. W.'s second wife; and her brother George Marland. It is also unlikely that Mathews felt in a position to judge Marland, given his own lengthy separation and then divorce from his first wife during an era in which whispers, rumors, and moral condemnation overrode all common sense.[56] Lottinville also once again suppressed Mathews's hopes to illustrate one of his own books. Though Mathews created an array of important pen-and-ink sketches that highlight the Indian and Mexican contexts of E. W. Marland's activities much more than do those chosen by the editor, Lottinville judged them erroneously and unkindly "a notebook of very poorly done sketches." He told the illustrator he used for the book, Craig Sheppard—whose career he was trying to promote—"you alone can do the artistic job that is required."[57]

During and following completion of *Life and Death of an Oilman*, Mathews experienced a period of severe dejection over writing. In April 1948, he mentioned in his diary that he was unable to pay his taxes or insurance. By September he was wondering how he would make it financially, given the timing of the publication of the Marland book and his doubts that there would be public interest in his short stories. "Terrific food prices, Ann's college, interest keep me broke so that I have nothing for myself." The interest was on various loans: at least one from "the Equitable," another from his great friend and lessee Paul Buck, possibly others. "The situation is the worst I have ever experienced and I seem not to be able to do anything about it." He despaired that he had nothing but his "natural income" (probably the lease on the ranch, and perhaps both his annuities as an Osage from the 1870s Kansas land sale and his oil headrights) upon which to depend. The following December he wrote, "I saw my short stories as liberators. . . .This failure dimmed my confidence quite a bit." He felt that he was a "prisoner on the ridge dependent upon the Bucks and the family." It comes as little surprise then that the diaries for 1950 and 1951 are absent from his collection. By May 26, 1952, the situation sank him to an ironically insightful low: "Bothered all day. Wondering why in the hell I set out to write. I feel today, that writing is stupid. If you write for money you must write for the great mass of Christians, who love sex, murder and God." However, by September of that year, the financial situation must have begun to ease, as he and Elizabeth traveled through Montana, British Columbia, Washington, Oregon, Idaho, and Colorado. But the impact on his self-esteem and will remained. In April 1953, he read through old diaries to get an idea of the thread of the Osage story through the 1930s. "Nothing can be more starkly convincing of my failure than the details of my life during the period between 1934 and the autumn of 1939," he wrote. "What a waste of time and talent; what a fool I have been." He then quoted Cassius's lines to Brutus about where fault lies.[58]

Remarkably then, Mathews's lengthiest and most important work emerged from this decade of intermittent despondency and self-accusation. Equivalent in size to three *Talking*s or *Marland*s, and much more complex, *The Osages* might truly be counted as his life's work. *The Osages* corresponds better to the work described in his application for the Guggenheim than *Talking to the Moon*, though the latter was published closer to the time of his fellowship. His planned book will be

> based on the conflicting expressions of two races in religion,
> philosophy and creative arts. The two races being the
> American Indian and the invading European. The expressions
> of the former growing out of, and in harmony with the
> natural environment. The balance thrown out by the invading
> European, resulting in destruction. Then readjustment of the
> Indian to the changed conditions, and readjustment of the
> European to the natural environment. The book dealing with
> the resultant drama in one region. . . . Observations within
> the field of my project began twenty years ago [1918]. . . . I
> was in the bewildering position of being a part of both and
> understanding both.

As early as March 1936, Mathews and Brandt were in negotiations with Simon and Schuster about financing the research to develop the idea. In September 1938, around the time of the Guggenheim application, Brandt wrote to Mathews to discourage him from feeling obligated to Simon and Schuster simply because he discussed the idea with that press first: "Anything you write will not want for a publisher. You are, after all, one of the best stylists in America, and, as Canby put it, you have something important to say. . . . You have a name which deserves the medium of not a good, but one of the best publishing houses." Asking Mathews to pardon his complete frankness, he confesses, "If I did not have a keen personal interest in you and your writing future, I would scarcely write as I have."[59]

In favor of *The Osages*, two other books planned during 1953 and 1955 fell by the wayside: *Gasconade*, the novelized saga of his mother's family to be modeled on *War and Peace* and in his mind demonstrating how truth was stranger than fiction; and a biography of oil magnate William Grove Skelly. Lottinville frankly and wisely discouraged the latter idea: "I think you ought to think very seriously whether the book should be done as a third person account, or whether Skelly ought to tell it in the first person. This obviously would leave you in the role of 'as told to John Joseph Mathews,' but it would save a hell of a lot of research, if you understand what I mean." After receiving this advice, Mathews appears never to have considered the idea again. Given the timing of his revisions of *Within Your Dream*, he possibly used Skelly as the model for his hero or one of the characters. In August 1953, he was trying to get in everything he knew about acquisitive men.[60]

Although he was studying the short story again during that same year, he did not launch any further projects in that genre until a decade later. In September 1963, when he was almost finished with a story book for boys, he spoke of having completed another book that same month. Which manuscript he is referring to is a mystery. In January, he had decided to steal one of his own titles for a new novel. A story in the magazine *Encounter* "exposed unconsciously the predicament of men and nations . . . when they have lost their power," he wrote. "The idea is about a novel to bring all this out. I shall steal my own title from an unpublished MS *Without The Sword*." In addition to these two book-length manuscripts, Mathews was writing "Osage Vignettes" in the early 1960s for the *Pawhuska Journal Capital*, as well as a short treatise against the fascism he witnessed emerging around Barry Goldwater's candidacy for president. Later that decade, he sent an article to *Oklahoma Today* and may have written for the *American Sportsman* magazine. But his main project during the late 1960s and the 1970s was *Boy, Horse, and Dog*. Missing are his diaries for March 1973 through March 1978 and for 1979, but it is unlikely that he started another project, given his surgery during that time. His other main creative activity during this fifteen years was pen-and-ink artistry, often for his letters to grandchildren and children or for his diary.[61] His love for and his involvement with his grand-children cannot be mistaken.

By far the most gripping story to emerge from the Mathews archive is the one of his ties to his wives, children, and grandchildren. The autobiography brings us through his early experiences with sexuality, but it cannot tell the deeper story of his loves and disasters. Perhaps it is a great story of enduring faith; perhaps it is a mundane story of acrimony and alimony. Surely it is one that should not be eaves-dropped lightly.

When World War I ended, Mathews was still a young man. He was only twenty-six when he left for Oxford in April 1921. By his own report, he had never truly finished college. Veterans returning to the University of Oklahoma had been rushed through, according to his account. A story he tells about his visit to France that sum-mer displays how little hardening or trauma his World War I ser-vice stateside had effected. He had gone to Paris with two brand-new acquaintances. One, whom he called S.G., was very anxious to visit Chateau-Thierry. He wanted to see the spot in Belleau Woods where he had been covered—that is, buried—by a shell during the attack by the Marines in 1918. S.G. pointed out to Mathews the machine-gun nests of the Germans and found the spot where his buddy had fallen. They visited his grave in the American cemetery there. Merely three years after the battle, the trenches were still visible. Mathews wrote: "Nature is quicker than man in many cases in hiding her scars. . . . I saw the helmet and bits of the olive-grey tunic of a Boche soldier, and close by the skeleton of the owner. He was lying just as he fell, in a small depression. Already he was scarcely discernible in the growth of herbage grew up through his ribs and scattered bones. A tall straight weed had grown up through the pelvis, and had bloomed. I saw the flower first, and then was attracted by the half-hidden gleaming, pelvis." Mathews's experience had been nothing like S.G.'s. He had seen the war from the air, and then only in his eager imagination.[62]

In 1972, Mathews gave the impression that an incident of joy-shooting by Kabyle tribesmen in North Africa sent him straight back to Osage County out of homesickness and a renewed interest in his own people's culture. The actual sequence of his early travels as recorded in these early diaries tells quite a different story. When they pick up in mid-June 1921, Mathews is at Merton doing very little work and about to get in trouble with the Oxford Dons about it. "Even in the very midst of spring, I have begun to deprecate my lotus-land existence. I haven't thought of a text book or a lecture for weeks, nor have I written letters. My whole being is full of spring, and I am unhappy because I can't express it—yet there is Sanity, standing guard armed with the halberd of Sense of Duty,—what a stiff, narrow, bigoted, Puritanical phrase—'sense of duty.'" Mathews had been courting an "Isis Girl" to whom he gives only the initials B.G. This entry was written days after he confessed frankly to her that he did not love her and loved his freedom too much to ever marry.[63] So when he pronounced himself full of spring, he was clearly recognizing his biological urges as a human animal that were bound to make him unhappy in a society gone back to "normal." The crazy war days and their releases were a thing of the past. Mathews had to learn to live somehow with the Puritanical guard at his neck.

He and B.G. could not have known one another more than a month or two, given the timing of Mathews's arrival at Oxford. By going away for the summer, he escaped her likely confusion of intense and highly ornamented attraction with love (which he feared because he felt it becoming a "form of lunacy"). In late June, he and a friend whom he calls W.J.H. (probably one of the Hobbs family whom he mentions in a later diary) took his motorbike—still a technological innovation at that time—and sidecar on an excursion to Scotland. He felt "wildly happy and delightfully free" as he left B.G. These friends had completely opposite tastes just like Tom Mitscher and young Jo—Mathews loving nature and solitude, W.J.H. loving crowds and cities. They toured through Hornsea-by-the-Sea, Newcastle-upon-Tyne, Edinburgh, Blair Atholl, Inverness, Wick, Thurso, Dingwall, Fort William, Glasgow, the English Lake District, Liverpool, and Stratford-upon-Avon before returning to Oxford. There he prepared to leave for the Continent, a trip he apparently intended to be solo. "W.J.H. left this afternoon for France, on his way to Vienna. I am glad he has gone. I am extremely glad to be alone again. He is not a bad travelling companion, but I am of a solitary nature. Every one does not like the things I like." However, he soon encountered C.E.L. and S.G., newly arrived from the States. They were soon buying a "Royal Enfield bike with side-car" to join him on a tour of "eastern France, Germany and Austria." They also investigated securing a visa for Russia but were discouraged in all ways by the American ambassador's secretary, Mr. Winslow. They did obtain a visa for the newly formed "Zcheko-Slovakia."[64]

The three friends spent time together in France and Belgium through late August. The next entries in the disorganized, archived diary are for September 23–27, 1921. Mathews is back at Oxford. He leaves for Shrewsbury in Shropshire to join several friends there, one new. "I was immediately attracted to Dolly's lush body; drawn by a fundamental urge." When the diary picks up again, it is January 6, 1922, and Mathews is in Biskra and Sidi Okba a hundred miles or so from the border with Tunisia in Algeria. Mathews, C.E.L., and another acquaintance named C.W. stayed in Biskra until at least January 10. Unless Mathews returned to Algeria at some later date, it is likely that the joy-shooting event by the Kabyle that Mathews recollected in 1972 took place seven years or more before he finally returned home.[65]

Mathews must have traveled again after Hilary term at Oxford. In April 1922, we see him returning from New Quay. There are sections cut out of the pages of this diary, one just after the mention of a woman named Hazel. However, it appears that Mathews is now dating several women, a Rose, possibly a Mavis. He mentions someone named Beryl who seems likely to be B.G. By this time, he has buckled down to work and at term end travels with a friend named John Moseley to Obergammerau to see the Passion Play. "The crucifixion was the most realistic thing I have ever seen."[66] Mathews and Moseley then tour Germany by train, stopping briefly in Prague, where President Wilson seems to be everywhere. After a week's visit in Berlin where he had also been the previous year, Mathews appears to finish the tour alone. By September 1922 he has gone to Paris and then Vichy, where he stays at least a month and is on the verge of leaving for Spain. While in Vichy, he worries that he is not reading enough history in preparation for the next term. He is also trying to acquire French, finding it difficult despite his childhood familiarity. "I rather like being alone," he says. "I am my own boss in that case and do as I please. I have always been rather solitary in my habits." His entries in this piece of the collection do not pick up again until almost a year later, June 26–27, 1923, when he is at Merton. He is taking exams and engaged in light flirtation with a girl named Cissy, whom he calls "Miss Industrial Revolution" and finds difficult to talk with. He appears, however, to be single.[67]

Throughout all these years, there appears no mention of the woman who was to become his wife on April 20, 1924. Her debut on January 1, 1924, suggests that Mathews had known her less than six months before proposing to her and less than a year before the wedding. Perhaps the lacuna that appears after December 31, 1924, is a mercy. We do not again hear Mathews's solitary voice until autumn 1939. Correspondence prior to the early 1930s is also absent. What we find in the Mathews of 1924 is enough to tell. Writing from Caux, Switzerland, on January 1, he describes joining Ginger (Virginia Winslow Hopper) and her sister Phyllis at a "fancy dress ball" on New Year's Eve where his "sole disguise" as a bohemian was "a flaxen wig." They toast the couple's future happiness, but the next morning he feels that he doesn't "want a future at all—all I asked was to die in peace." The next day, he is dreaming of living alone in a small cabin in the Rockies. The following day, he writes that he is "still enjoined to Ginger and I am delaying the day when I must write home and tell mother and the girls." He is indifferent to the wedding preparations. "I dislike the idea of giving up my history studies at Oxford after winter term." Rather than following his early inclinations at Oxford to study history instead of natural sciences, he was on the verge of sacrificing a chance that he would never get again, a chance to earn a graduate degree.[68]

Two weeks later, we feel that we have just stepped off a high and unforgiving cliff: "I am anxious to get back to Oxford. I have a strange feeling that I wish to 'find' myself again—this should not be the case with one who has engaged himself to be married—I have made the mistake of my life." On his way back to Oxford on January 23, he chastises himself: "I felt rather free once more, and rather enjoyed it—shame John you are supposed to be in love and lovers are not supposed to be happy away from their sweethearts." The self-policing continued in early March when he told himself he "mustn't flirt" with Irene Burnsides because Ginger loved him. And though he ran into "Cissy" Norton on a detour back to Switzerland and she had "been engaged and dis-engaged . . . since [he] saw her last," and he felt she "could inspire love in" him, he accused himself of being "damned queer" and commented that he did not understand himself. It never occurred to him to return to his self-aware convictions of three years before and break his engagement. His sense of honor, his feeling that he was probably in love despite his other wayward emotions, and perhaps the pressure of being single at age twenty-nine overcame his better judgment.[69]

After the marriage, one detects only undercurrents of the problems that would drive him and Ginger apart. It is far from certain that they emerged from Mathews's suppressed ambivalence alone. After their honeymoon through Italy and Switzerland in May, June, July, and August, they briefly set up living quarters in Geneva. One must conjecture from their mind-set that they would have stayed had Ginger not become pregnant within a few months of the wedding. By late September, they knew. By early November, they were on their way back to the States. They settled in Montclair, New Jersey, near mother and father "H." All the way back across the ocean, Ginger was sick and scared, believing that she would die in childbirth. As early as September, Mathews wrote: "Poor little prospective mother how will she be able to undergo the actual birth of her baby—I sincerely wish I could do it for her, or at least have the pains for her." On New Year's Eve, he waxed philosophical, recalling Algiers in 1921, the Elks dance at Pawhuska in 1922, Switzerland in 1923, and believing in his heart that he would soon meet his son. Virginia Winslow Mathews would be born on March 9, 1925, to be joined by the anticipated son only later. In his 1972 interview, Mathews suggests that what took them to California later was the prospect of a job with Standard Oil Company that might eventually have involved relocation to South America.[70] What is certain is that he considered the events of the ensuing years his tragedy. In 1964, he was transcribing the diaries of 1927–29. Regarding 1929, he spoke into his tape recorder about how unpleasant the transcription was, because it had to do with his leaving home and "the definite separation from my babies."[71]

Although told from Mathews's perspective alone, the story he tells makes it easy to grieve with all the parties and to imagine how it must have felt for each. What ultimately splintered the family is unclear. We know that Mathews returned to the Osage in the year of the stock market crash and during the last few years of massively declining income from his oil headrights. Possibly he simply got fed up with Ginger's perceived histrionics and decamped. Yet it is also conceivable that Mathews wanted his wife to return with him to Oklahoma and that she refused. Indian census rolls for the period suggest that the children were with him in Pawhuska in 1930, so Ginger may have been there as well. We also do not know whether she knew he was part Osage when she married him. He was likely seen by some in New Jersey or California or even Pawhuska as a man who had abandoned his family. Yet a 1939 letter to the Guggenheim Foundation indicates that he had voluntarily been sending Ginger an "allowance" for the past decade. The money, though, would not have lessened the emotional burden on any woman suddenly finding herself a single mother in an era when such was unheard of outside of widowhood. (By 1939, she and her sister were still living with the children in a rented house in Maplewood, New Jersey.) Nor would it have filled the gap—however delicately explained—created in Virginia's and his son John's lives by an absent though still living father. In March 1945, Mathews marked with frustration in his diary that he wrote to his children every month but that they did not write back. When he met them in Washington in late February 1939, seemingly for the first time in ten years, the powerful realization of all he had missed overwhelmed him.[72]

Talking to the Moon leaves the impression that Mathews's life at the Blackjacks between 1929 and 1945 was solitary. But by October 1932, he had met and begun to court Elizabeth Hunt. Their love story must be left for another day, except to say that the courtship with "Dibbers" lasted nearly thirteen years, and the marriage that commenced on April 4, 1945, lasted another thirty-four. It was to marry her that Mathews began in March 1935 to seek either a divorce or custody or both. He wrote Dibbs in January of that year from Arizona: "I am no more a solitary person." By September 1938, Mathews was still not free. On his Guggenheim application he stated that he is "Married, but separated from wife during last ten years." He avoided returning from Mexico to Pawhuska in December 1939, writing to Dibbs, "I must hear from Paul Humphrey [his attorney] about the jeopardy of my coming to the U.S. during certain times; called into divorce court sort of business—the very thing that I want to avoid for both of us." In January 1943, in the midst of his financial troubles, Mathews wrote in his diary that Virginia (Ginger) had accused him of being in arrears with his payments. In the following month, he referred to her as his "former wife." So he may have been divorced by this date but postponed marriage to Elizabeth for two more years because they were expecting him to be called into government service in the administration of conquered lands overseas.[73]

In December 1943, Mathews received a citation to appear in district court and complained in frustration about his sense that Virginia did not value the children's college education. "Virginia is demanding for her own use the money which I have been spending on the children's education." His daughter was at Goucher College, and his son at St. George's School at the time. He does not appear to have taken on Ann Hunt's tuition yet. Mathews felt certain that the court would recognize his contributions to child support and to their education, as well as his strained financial status. Yet by January 1946, nine months after his second marriage, he still owed court-ordered payments to Virginia from autumn 1945. In September, he talks of that last payment of "that which I do not owe her" and is anxious to get it settled but does not have the money. The situation and perspectives were obviously complicated, especially given the international dimension of their marriage. Clearly, though, Mathews strongly supported all four of his children's aspirations, sacrificing his own career to put three of the four through college. He also supported his first wife financially for more than twenty years.[74]

Luckily this man who is best remembered for preserving histories that might have been lost had a short memory when it came to the struggles he faced in his own life. On his seventy-fifth birthday, November 16, 1969, he mused: "I have lived three quarters of a century; almost a perfect life. I have done as exactly as I chose to do. It is difficult to believe that my gay and insouciant existance [sic] is terminating." It would be nearly a decade before there would be any need for eulogies. When they came, they were praiseworthy. Ed Red Eagle, the Assistant Chief of the Osages, mourned that "the man who knew more about our heart and what we thought is gone." Lest anyone doubt his "Indianness," it shall be remembered that his will of May 1976 had to be approved by the Department of Interior, because he owned 1.20000 Osage headright interest and was "Osage Allottee N. 1501," having received his competency certificate in the same year the Osages became citizens of the United States.[75] Asked seven years before his death if he was concerned that there was not very much written about him, he replied "Well . . . no, no, no, because, uh, um . . . well, probably I'm a little bit afraid of . . . misconceptions . . . misunderstandings. . . . You know, it's very difficult for someone . . . out of a man's heart . . . to understand . . . why I live as I live . . . and why I love that which I love. So that they can't . . . not being able to understand, they've got to have some . . . they've got to be empathic at least."[76] It is indeed devoutly to be wished.

Note on the Text

~

The text is based on the version in Box 4 Folder 32 and Box 4 Folder 33 of the John Joseph Mathews Collection at the Western History Collections of the University of Oklahoma in Norman, Oklahoma. The drafts in these folders are apparently the draft sent out for publication in 1967, with additions and corrections from the other versions. Pages 14, 73, 77, and 219–26 MS are from Box 4 Folder 33 only; pages 101, 102, 160 insert (two pages), 201 insert (two pages), 204–205, 208–209, and 227–29 MS are from Box 4 Folder 32 only.

The version in Box 4 Folder 32 appears to be a carbon copy of the version in Box 4 Folder 33 from page 1 MS through page 112 MS. From page 113 MS through page 212 MS, the version in Box 4 Folder 33 appears to be the duplicate (carbon), whereas Box 4 Folder 32 appears to be the original. From page 213 MS through 226 MS, the version in Box 4 Folder 33 appears to be the original. From page 227 MS through 229 MS, the version in Box 4 Folder 32 appears to be the original.

Mathews edited and corrected the apparent originals, possibly in 1972 or later. In some cases, I have not retained the edits or have listed them as alternatives in the notes. Mathews wrote in his diary that he felt the original manuscript "overwritten," but many of his changes (as well as in the structurally edited and unfinished 1972/1978 version in Box 4 Folder 31) intellectualize or use abstract language that was plainer and more straightforward in the original. These changes have been omitted unless the passage itself is more intellectual or abstract. I indicate in the endnotes the variations that I judged to be significant.

I had several reasons for working from the posited 1967 version of the manuscript rather than the version edited in August and November 1972, September and October 1977, and April, July, and October

1978. My principal reason is that those edits appear to be incomplete (and there is uncharacteristically no final, polished draft typed by Mathews or his wife); what Mathews intended is often unclear. For example, several handwritten additions, though largely illegible, contain key words. Mathews adds text, then second-guesses himself: his final decision is not indicated. He repeated some additions in ways that seem accidentally redundant rather than artistic, and the final placement is left undetermined. Others are noted for inclusion but were never written up. Moreover, the draft from which he worked was filed in four different locations within the archive. The bulk of it is found in Box 4 Folder 31. An unedited duplicate of the draft in this location was discovered in Box 5 in a binder in May 2011. It was not indicated on the finding source. However, a key section that he may or may not have intended for publication was found in a separate binder in box 4 that had not been labeled by the staff of the Western History Collections before June 8, 2009 and that was also not indicated on the finding source. Additional pages from this version were also discovered in Box 3 Folder 13, which the finding aid (mis)labels as parts of his 1978 diary. On some of these pages, which at first appear to be excisions, Mathews indicates that he is saving the excised episode for a space later in the manuscript. For example, Mathews wrote: "Reincorporate this incident as the bran box" in the margin of 14 MS of Box 3 Folder 13. Finally, there is every indication that Mathews intended in 1967 to publish the version found in Box 4 Folder 32 and Box 4 Folder 33 and all its episodes had he found a willing publisher. His diary indicates that he undertook the 1972/1977/1978 edits without feedback from an acquisitions editor or other professional advisor (and apparently without the feedback of familial or other advisors, perhaps with the exception of his wife). The revisions seemed to have been under the imagined duress of rejection for cause, even though the manuscript content was never peer-reviewed or even editorially reviewed beyond determining whether its genre fit with the list of the target publisher. Mathews mentions in his 1978 diary that after his surgery in 1975 or 1976, he struggled with his memory for a long time. Though this appears to refer to short-term memory, it may explain his self-questioning notes in this late draft to reconsider certain episodes. In one case, he apparently cannot recall whether the incident happened to him or someone else, though subsequent paragraphs make clear that it happened to him. Apparently, his note to "reconsider" meant "rewrite" in some instances, rather than "excise."

Although choosing to create an edition that does not incorporate all Mathews's later intentions risks omitting important additions and corrections or including excisions no longer intended for publication, choosing to use highly marked-up drafts would force any editor to determine the final shape of his manuscript and potentially to put words in his mouth. I have used edits from Box 4 Folder 31 sparingly, mainly for clarification or expansion of Mathews's philosophies; they are generally indicated in the notes.

Version 4.31 *has* been used as one guide to excisions that were required by current costs of production, marked in the notes as "excision," and amounting to approximately 15,900 of 108,560 words. I hope to make these excisions available elsewhere. They may be found in the Western History Collections' Mathews archive.

In general, editorial corrections have been of the same nature as those that the manuscript would have undergone during copyediting on its way to production under Mathews's supervision. Mathews reports in his diary that his wife, Elizabeth, prepared the final drafts of the manuscript, so it is not clear whether the source of any errors is him, her, or simply the technology or the times.

Twenty Thousand Mornings

Volume I: Boy, Horse, and Dog

⌒

Being the only boy in the family, I was given a room of my own; even as quite a small boy I had my own room.[1]

There were south windows from which I could look down into the valley, and onto the village which was the Osage Indian Agency. There were several native sandstone buildings, built by the United States Government: a blacksmith shop, a livery stable, as well as the traders' stores, one surrounded by palisades, and there were several private residences.[2]

Sounds floated up from the valley into my windows; the creaking of the freighter's wagons, neighing of horses, the freighters' braying laughter, the coyote chorus from the hills across the creek, and from the tree near the window, the eerie cry of the screech owl. However, these were sounds which I associated later, after the raising of the curtain of memory, with this period of my extreme youth. These sounds were still floating up from the valley after the curtain of memory was raised, and my impressions could then crystallize into memory.[3]

"Memories" of that time behind the curtain are not memories at all, but incidents recalled to the very young later by their parents or their older sisters and brothers, and they are never able to distinguish actual memory from those things which have been told them.

But there was an impression from early childhood before the curtain was lifted, that did crystallize. The soul-stirring sound that floated up into my window from the hills across the valley, that predawn many years ago, was incised in my plastic memory through profound emotionalism, and when the following period of the raised curtain and crystallization of impression came, the scar was already there: a precocious memory.

3

The sound I heard that pre-dawn, was long, drawn out and broken by weeping. I could hear the sobbing. After I had heard my first lobo wolf, I had something with which to compare the chant, and after I heard my first bull wapiti challenging in the moonlight, I had something else to which I could compare it, despite their diversity. My prayer-chant had something of both the lobo's howl and the wapiti's challenge.[4]

But the lobo's howl and the wapiti's challenge had endings, and this prayer-song, this soul-stirring petition was always left unfinished by a sob of frustration.

The prayer-chant that disturbed my little boy's soul to the depths was Neolithic man talking to God.

These Neolithic men, the Osages, were profoundly urged to communicate with their god each pre-dawn, embodying him in the morning star.[5] They arose from their bear skin beds, wrapped their robes about them, and strode out into the darkness, and raising their faces to the morning star, they chanted and wept in frustration.

I have never forgotten that pre-dawn, and that memory from behind the curtain has ever been in the back of my consciousness, and wherever I have traveled the memory of that early morning has succeeded in disturbing me, always making me conscious of mysteries of existence that cannot be pigeon-holed or card-indexed through reason, scientific analysis, logic or philosophic rationalization.

The memory of the chant-petition comes forward if I only stop to look at [a] Gothic cathedral or as I listen to the Muezzin calling from his desert tower.[6]

At such moments a vague idea presents itself, suggesting that man has not yet developed sufficiently, or advanced far enough in his progression to be able to understand an Omnipotent Being, or even begin to interpret the Force behind life, since the sobbing frustration inherent in that prayer-chant so long ago, might indicate a universal frustration even in civilized man.[7]

My disturbance as a child was not in the least religious, wherein I might have been perfectly contented with the acceptance of Christian forms and of a credo. However, not being able to read or write I followed them pro forma, but now I can understand that I was closer to the chanter to the morning star who sobbed in frustration than I was to the crystallized formalities of the Mass, and the atmosphere of assurance in the recitation of the Apostles' Creed.[8]

There wasn't much left for the imagination to be nourished on in this pro forma acceptance, except for the anthropomorphizing of God, but this of course was a memory from the period after the curtain was lifted. When I knelt to say my prayers at the bed side or with my sisters at mother's or grandmother's knee, I had to visualize God; I couldn't possibly pray to an abstraction.

As I held my hands together just so with thumbs properly crossed, and with eyes shut, I could see God sitting on a cumulous cloud (I have always thought them the most beautiful of all cloud formations) holding his sceptre (man could never get above his king and emperor orientation). He wore a species of toga and his white beard reached to his cord belt, and he looked down upon the good little Mathews boy with approval.

But I never, it seems to me, felt shriven. I arose from my knees with the image vanished, but even though I had kept the image constantly before me as I prayed, I always felt that there was some remissness on my part; that the white bearded patriarchal man on the cumulous expected much more from me than the Hail Mary rote. It in some strange manner seemed to me to be too smug; I certainly could have felt that it was, even though I couldn't reason that it wasn't.

After coming from mass, or after our prayers, mother assumed a shriven manner. Perhaps it would be better to write that she felt assurance. There was something intangible in the pattern of her mouth lines implying spiritual cleanliness and charity and acceptability. And, in the manner in which my night-gowned sisters rose from their knees, touched lips to cheeks all round, and ran brightly off to bed, there was something much more than relief from a nightly duty. They too were "in."

And there was a strange feeling that they and their prayers were acceptable to my visualized anthropomorphic God on the cumulous cloud, while mine were received (not accepted) out of indulgence and with ultimate hope.

I suppose my disturbance—not unhappiness certainly; there would be wonderful night voices coming into my bedroom windows—was created perhaps, and certainly nourished by my eagerness to understand, rather than to accept and be contented.[9]

I think I must have got my image of God from some picture cards, the kind called holy cards. There is a memory slide of a hot afternoon and two sandalwood perfumed ladies arriving in a livery carriage, hot and breathless and dusty, wearing large hats with the nuptial plumes of the snowy egret on them.

The lovely plumes associated with the incident make it a very clear memory.

They later came out of their room refreshed and dramatically told of their adventure in being driven from somewhere to somewhere by one of cousin Will's drivers from the livery stable, who "would you believe it, Jennie, he had had a dram or two."[10]

They talked down to Jennie, my mother, as most of my father's relatives did, or seemed to do, because she was a Catholic. I don't believe that cousin Fonte and Bea Price knew firsthand about the disastrous plunge the Catholic faith had suffered by being burdened with Irish immigrants in the atmosphere of the East, where they were chiefly domestics and unskilled laborers, and discriminated against. It is not likely that Fonte and Bea Price knew about this unless the facts had seeped down to Missouri, but they seemed to know instinctively that Catholics had been sneered at as Papist by the Puritans and the early Protestant colonists in general, and believed them to be not quite acceptable socially.

When they had finished their dramatic tale, Fonte motioned to me to come to her. She searched in her reticule, and brought out some holy cards. I am quite sure that they as Protestants did not believe in holy cards, but Fonte being consciously thoughtful as a gracious lady should ever be, she had had a card blessed for each one of her cousin Will's unfortunate little Catholics.[11]

My younger sisters got very blond, simpering angels, and a white bearded patriarch on a cloud, while mine was of the crucifixion. There was the Christ on the cross, the Roman soldiers, the amphora of vinegar, and at one side the group of soldiers dicing for the robe.

Allotment photograph of John Joseph Mathews (Allottee #1501) with his sisters Marie (Allottee #1502, left), Florence (Allottee #1504, center front), and Lillian (Allottee #1503) (Courtesy of the Osage Tribal Museum, Pawhuska, Oklahoma)

The soldier with the spear was just about to stab Jesus. He evinced a bestial grimace, and his knotted muscles and lamp globe calves were hairy and obscene.

The next day when the "Price Girls" were leaving, Fonte said, "Did you show your sister Josephine your nice holy card; she's never seen it?"

I could assume a stupid expression at times, I have been told, and I suppose I assumed it now.

"Go get it, honey; that's a good boy, and show it to big sister."

I remained silent, and must have appeared guilty, and my stupid expression must have been provoking. The female jumped to conclusions.

"Well, well," she said, "what a pretty how-de-do; cousin Fonte gives him a holy card one day, and the next day he's lost it. Well, there's one thing certain; there won't be any more gifts for bad little boys—only for good little girls."

As she said this she fondled one of Marie's braids.

Marie was the favorite of my father's family. However, if my father had been present Fonte would not have criticized the princeling, but since only mother and my sisters were present she rather enjoyed censuring me. Mother was not only a Catholic but a Frenchwoman as well. Cousin Will had certainly married "beneath" him. Jennie might have been alright, but what about Frenchmen in general, when it came to morals?

I hadn't lost the holy card; what was left of it was in the old cast-off trunk in my room where I kept my treasures. The card was safely put away in the trunk with many other treasures, among them being the shed tail feather of a buff cochin rooster, a quail's wing, and a wren's egg I had found in the grass, a few hackle and saddle feathers from a brown leghorn cock, and which I called "silks," and a peacock feather I had found in the barnlot and had brought back from Aunt Sue's ranch.

The card had been mutilated, but I didn't so consider it. The Christ was still on the cross, the dicers casting for the robe, the mourners at the foot of the cross; all, except the mean old soldier who was about to spear Jesus. I had cut him from the card and had buried him out in the yard under a lilac bush.

I apparently had little sense of the dramatic which my sisters enjoyed. Most any child brought up in the Catholic faith would have gone to the card periodically in order to enjoy compassion, tragedy, even poignant bittersweet tears. The mean old soldier would have been a prerequisite for the full enjoyment of drama.

I suggest that memory slides projected onto the screen of memory, are just that: isolated memory transparencies, and I can't fit them in as links in the chain of chronology. So, I am not sure which came first: the above memory slide or the following one.[12]

Our long, rambling barn was a wonderful place in which to play. There were the two shiny vehicles for swank, the C-spring single buggy and the surrey; and there were the lumber wagon and the "Indian wagon." The latter was a light wagon which was the type supplied to the Osage Indians by the government, and they had a bad reputation among the Osage Chieftains to whom they were issued, for trying to outrun the team downhill, the simple mechanism of a brake being quite beyond the racial experience of Neolithic men.

It was fun to sit in the driver's seat in one of the vehicles in the barn and travel almost anywhere fancy urged, even tapping the rumps of imaginary horses with a real whip taken from the whip socket.

Then there was the hayloft, redolent of the wonderful odor of hay. The bales could be moved about with the aid of my older sister, so that they formed rooms of an imaginary house, or formed a stage from which we recited, or they could be made to form tunnels through which we crawled as animals.

One day my sister Josephine and I had huffed and grunted trying to drag the bales over the glass-slick floor, to form a theatre stage and at least the walls of the theatre, so that Marie and I could perform a scene from Bethlehem, which Josephine's class from the parochial school had performed the Christmas before.

Marie and I were to be angels under Josephine's direction, but the walls tumbled almost as soon as we got them into place, and one stepped into the cracks between the bales of the stage.

Finally, defeated, we sat on the bales to rest.

Josephine was born didactic and histrionic, and her fictions repeated only a few times became facts to her in which she believed sincerely.

She was as convincing as a medicine show pitchman.

I don't have any idea how old I was, but I should guess I was five and Marie three. Josephine was seven years older than I was, whatever my age, and she was suffused with catechism.

Defeated by the bales and uncomfortable in the loft's heat, an idea flashed and Josephine became almost effervescent.

"You kids," she said, "could be REAL angels; do you know that?"

I can't recall what I thought of the suggestion, but surely I must have been unconvinced, with my then, or later feeling, that I was an "outsider." Also I had never seen a boy angel on the holy cards, and this, as I remember, seemed quite as it should have been: definitely *comme il faut*.

Josephine now warmed by her idea became enthusiastic, and carried on with her pitchman's cajolery: "You kids COULD be angels. You know why? You haven't reached the age of reason; seven's the age of reason, and after that you hafta go to confession and be absolved of your sins. And you know what? You can never be sure you won't hafta spend a lot of time in purgatory."

We knew about purgatory; mother had us pray for the poor souls in purgatory, periodically. There was always the thought that one might have relatives there; the "lukewarm" Catholics who had been remiss in attending mass, and had neglected their "duties."

Purgatory was a boon though, since Protestants couldn't even have a chance of being purged by fire in purgatory. I used to visualize them sliding all the way down to hell on a chute-like contraption; like the one that we used to run water from the hydrant to the horse's watering tubs.

We knew of course that our two brothers George Martin and William Shirley, Jr., and our sister Frances—George, Billy and "Frankit"—had died much before they had attained the age of reason, and were therefore angels—(friends at court—sort of thing,) and didn't need our prayers. We might have prayed to or through them;

my sisters probably did, but I don't remember having done so. I was a direct actionist, and when I prayed, I shut my eyes and shut out all other thought so as not to blur the image of my anthropomorphic God; so that the visualization would be bright and clear. The efficacy of my prayer seemed to depend directly on the crystalline brightness of that image.

I can't remember how long it took Josephine to convince us that we shouldn't lose this wonderful chance to become angels.

The three-year-old Marie must have accepted the idea with mild, but free enthusiasm. Josephine had been born didactic and histrionic, but Marie had been born tranquil, and even before she could reason, seemed to be influenced by wisdom and logic and justice, while I suspect I might have been born happy and a bit confused.

Marie's baby logic, unreasoned and hopeful, and my academic inquisitiveness aided Josephine's plan. What we accepted was an intriguing method of transformation, which the imaginative, medicine-show pitchman Josephine presented to us. The pitchman had sold the elixir; the purchasers had not yet thought about the nature of the contents of the pretty bottle.

"Alright," she said, "come on down."

We climbed down the ladder from the loft, and she led us to a large bran box which was at the head of a long passageway that ran the length of the mangers.

In order to defeat the mice and rats and weevils Q. had fitted it with a heavy lid and lined the under edges with felt, thus making it airtight when closed.[13]

We lifted Marie into the box and I climbed in with Josephine's aid, then when we were seated on the soft, flowing, sweet-smelling bran, she closed the lid.

I don't know how long we sat in this dark, cave-like silence, but since the box was perhaps two-thirds full of bran, I suspect it was not long. The oxygen was being used up fast.

Soon Marie began to whimper, and when Marie whimpered there was usually an important cause.

I began pounding on the lid; I couldn't move it, and began to shout that we wanted to get out. I remember the dialogue with Josephine through the lid. She was sitting on it, and the more the pitchman cajoled, the more frightened I became and the louder I shouted and the harder I pounded.

Marie began to cry; we were smothering.

Finally the lid was raised, and there looking down upon us was Gabriel in a school girl's frock. Her face expressed not only righteous indignation, but a sneer that had been absent from Gabriel, the true messenger's, face.

I am sure this is a true slide memory since Josephine wouldn't have told our mother, or anyone, ever, about the incident. I am sure I didn't tell anyone, so that the story could have been told back to me later. The incident took place before the memory curtain was lifted for Marie, and I feel sure she couldn't have remembered, but having heard the story of the bran box much later when I referred to it facetiously to annoy Josephine, it may seem like a memory to her.

$\sim$

I remember the hot summer evenings when my mother and father sat on the front porch with palm leaf fans, where they quite often talked desultorily with my grandmother Girard. The sounds from the valley flowed up over our hill from the few stone buildings and the trader's stores and washed over us.

The freighters would have driven their wagons in from "The States," which were for us children represented by Elgin, Cedarvale, Arkansas City and Chautauqua Springs in Kansas just over the border with The Osage Nation in Oklahoma Territory.

In front of the Pawhuska House, where they gathered, there would be horseplay during these hot summer nights, and their great raucous laughter, and sometimes their oaths would come up to us as we sat talking; that is, mother and grandmother talked. Our father and we children usually sat silently, listening to the insect chorus from the grass roots.

There was one man, I didn't know whether he was a trader's clerk or a freighter, whose voice came up to us in a sort of falsetto, changing to baritone. It was a shout as if expressing pain or dramatic fear, and usually came after a protracted silence, almost at a time when you might have supposed that the freighters had dispersed.

One night when there was a lull in the conversation on our front porch, which had, as usual, been carried on chiefly by mother and grandmother, this dramatized falsetto shout came to us after a dead silence down in the valley, and was followed by the greatest braying laughter I had as yet heard: a definite cacophony of laughter and shouting.

This was a night when my grandmother who lived with my uncle Nick and his family was paying us one of her periodic visits.

When the ridiculous cry broke the silence this particular night, I asked my father what could be wrong with the man. He said: "nothin'; he's goosey, that's all."

My mother said, "Will, little pitchers have big ears," and glanced at the little girls sitting about or lying drowsily on pallets brought out for them.

"What's wrong with that?" my father asked, "that's what they call it and that's what he is."

Grandmother said, "Naturally," and contempt was implied in her inflection, and there was also an implication that there were no goosey Frenchmen. There was a further implication that Anglo-Americans might be expected to be goosey.

"But what is goosey?" I asked.

"Never mind, son," my father said, "I'll tell you some time when we're alone."

"Well, I should think so," said my mother, and immediately started a new conversation in French with my grandmother.

~

About a mile east of our house and a little north, in the broadest part of the valley, was the village of that physical division of the Osages called Thorny-Valley People, and in June they danced a traditional social dance called the In-lon-schka. They danced each afternoon and each night for four days, and on the fourth day they "smoked" gifts to certain visitors from other tribes.[14] These gifts were horses, blankets, silver dollars or piles of potatoes, beans, etc.

They usually invited only their kinsmen, the Poncas, the Otoes, and often there were lithe, sinewy Sioux with their Plains eyes with their crow's-feet. These came all the way from their reservation in South Dakota.

The dance usually began on Thursday afternoon and after a feast they returned to dance that night. Sometimes the rhythm of the drums and the rhythmical tinkling of the hawk bells tied just below the dancer's knees, were ruptured suddenly by the raucous laughter of the freighters closer by, just under the point of the hill. The singing that came from one of the churches in the valley between our ridge and the Thorny-Valley Village, did not completely rupture the rhythm of the In-lon-schka, but the choir of the church and the singing of the drum men produced a sound that was ridiculously antiphonic and certainly a cacophony.

When the air was right, you could hear the high-pitched coyote-like ululations of the lead-off or head singer, and the beginning of the TUM-tum—TUM-tum—TUM-tum of the great kettle drum, along with the earnest paean, "Will There Be Any Stars in My Crown" flowing out the windows of the little church and up our hill.

The tintinnabular rhythm of the dancer's little garter bells was the same as the metallic rhythm of the grassroots chorus of the insects in the yard just in front of us.

Sometimes on hot September evenings when we had an early dinner and came early to the front porch to escape the heat of the house, and if there was no braying laughter from the valley, we might hear the wild turkeys fly up to roost along Mud Creek. This is the feeder stream that flows into Bird Creek opposite the floodplain that formed the valley of the agency.

If grandmother was with us, she and mother would talk on and on during such evenings, and our father would sit silently with his own thoughts, and sometimes my baby sister Lillian would go to sleep induced by the soporific rhythm of the insect chorus from the grassroots, and the hum of conversation.

Grandmother might be saying something like this: "Several people have seen him in the shadows back of the house, and that happened to be the time when—" Mother would put up her hand and look significantly at us children, sprawled here and there on the porch, and grandmother, noticing, would remember that little pitchers had big ears, and continue, "Tu sais bien, Jennie, que—," and thus carry on in French about the certain woman who was having a secret affair with a handsome mixed-blood younger than herself, when her husband was in "The States" on business.

Their French gradually became a thin smoke screen to me; I had begun, it seems, to understand it at an early age, chiefly because I had a profound love of words and sense of rhythm, and their accompanying gestures were as fascinating as Osage gestures.

I learned one night that this certain woman was not only deceiving her husband while he was away in "The States," but "J'ai bien entendu, que—" she had a "woods colt" when she was a girl in Kansas. Here, I seem to remember that this empirical Frenchwoman pretended Puritan shock. This is of course a sort of retrospective interpretation; I couldn't possibly have had the impression at the time.

I should probably have been just as confused about the "woods colt," if they had been talking in English. This image of a woman leading a woods colt around puzzled me for some time. I was afraid to ask about it due to the secretiveness of the thing. Whatever was a "woods colt" in the first place?

Quite likely since the matter of the "woods colt" had to do with exotic Kansas, I could easily assume that it might possibly be beyond my understanding. A woman leading a "woods colt," whatever that might be, COULD happen in Kansas.

~

The little Kansas border towns and Kansas itself were as romantic then as the Taj Mahal became to our imaginations later.

I don't remember if at this time I had visited Babylon-Cedarvale or Samarkand–Arkansas City, Singapore-Elgin, Baghdad-Sedan, or Tivoli–Chautauqua Springs. Possibly I didn't visit them until I was ten or twelve years of age.

I may have been quite a bit younger when I first visited Arkansas City, since I do have a memory of it which could only be associated with extreme youth.

We had to drive to Arkansas City to have my mother's teeth "fixed," and this consumed two days, staying with my aunt Sue and uncle Jim Simpson at their ranch on Beaver Creek.

We put the horses in the livery stable and we stayed at the Fifth Avenue Hotel, no less. There were no bathrooms attached to the rooms, and we had to go down a long hallway to the very end. In the little room, the reservoir was covered—encrusted, is a better term—with carved oak, and on the end of the chain as a grip was a carved pine cone, the flushing chain was really a pair of chains like the pre-electric bell cords. The reservoir was high up near the ceiling for the benefit of supplementary gravity one might suppose.

As a gesture to the prudish attempts to forget earthy associations, there were no directions to this obscure little room, and no brazen lettering on the door.

I was always being disturbed there, and one day when the door was opened by three young ladies, I became frightened and ran all the way back to our rooms with my pants down. The young ladies giggled; perhaps with their fans over their mouths.

This incident was the index to this particular memory slide, I feel sure. This incident and the vivid image of the drunken man yawing down Summit Street, swearing at an imaginary persecutor. I watched him from the window of the dentist's office, while mother was in the chair.

Everything exotic and beautiful came from Kansas, especially I believe from either Cedarvale or Elgin; villages which had arterial connections with the outer world, represented by railways, and out of the outer world came the exotic and the beautiful things, and we associated the little border town of Kansas with them.

But only the strange and romantic things came from these towns; our clothing, our utilitarian shoes and kitchen ware, and axes and harness, and staples, and stoves, came from the Osage Mercantile Company where we could get merchandise at cost.[15]

The Company handled everything from wagons to chocolates that melted and ran in the summer. The odors were a remarkable mélange of greased harness, cinnamon, onions, apples (these latter in the autumn) and cigar smoke.

You could buy ladies' hats with ostrich or heron plumes, Indian blankets, shrouding wrap-arounds for the Indian women, whimsically printed silken materials for the making of Indian men's shirts, from the bolt. You could also buy from the bolt, chintz, and percale and calico, measured from the bolt by the saleswomen who were guided by brass tacks along the edge of the counter. Single tacks representing inches, double tacks, feet and three tacks yards.

Of course my sister's beautiful piano didn't come from the Osage Mercantile Company but from the great outer world by way of Kansas and especially Cedarvale, and inspired obscenities among the sweating freighters that were fascinating.

The freighters bringing the piano from Cedarvale had four horses hooked to the wagon in order to make our steep, dusty hill. One of the lead horses soon had enough of it and balked in the middle of the climb.

I saw all this squatted under a tree on the brow of the hill, watching and listening intently. I came away with a wonderful epithet.

Several days later, after the family had stood and admired the piano, mother asked me to run the chickens out of the yard. They ran free in the barn lot, and their house was a part of the group of buildings which included the smokehouse, the icehouse, and that part of the barn where the surrey and the C-spring buggy were kept.

Mother went in for Light Brahmas and buff cochins, ridiculous atrocities of man's whimsies: biologically ornamental if not esthetically ornamental. Of course in their feather-legged and short-winged clumsiness they, mother's chickens, couldn't possibly have cleared the fence between the garden and the horse lot, but my father kept chiefly for egg production, blue Andalusians and brown leghorns, and they were quick witted, alert and strong-winged, and the primary feathers of one wing had to be clipped to keep them on their side of the fence.

Despite this handicap, a few of them managed periodically to get into the garden and they were delighted to dust-bathe under the rose bushes. This was sacred ground.

When I came back into the house breathless and red-faced, mother asked, "Did you run them all out?" Before I could answer she began berating my father, Q., blue Andalusians and brown leghorns, intimating that there were holes in the fence and both Will and Q. knew there were, and that men didn't care about flowers.

Both she and grandmother personalized that French logic which hints that there are just not a sufficient number of Frenchmen in the world to ensure tidiness.

All the time she was talking, she was busy with this and that going about with her characteristic swiftness from cupboard to stove, then into the dining room and back, then suddenly froze with a stove lid lifter in her hand, when I took advantage of a brief stoppage in the flow of her words to finish my report about the invading chickens, to say, "Mama, there was one son-of-a-bitch that wouldn't go out."

She stood for a moment looking at me, then lifted the stove lid and placed a kettle on the hole. "Pookie," she said, "I don't believe I'd say that ugly word anymore; nice people don't use vulgar language like that. Where did you hear that, is what I'd like to know."

I told her about the balky horse and the freighters, and "Mama," I said, "they said—"

"Never mind, never mind; I don't want to hear. You mustn't use that word anymore, or any of those other words the freighter used. Better not let your father hear you using bad words."

The epithet if that is what it really is, if a phrase can be called an epithet, had no true application at all to that silly chicken of my childhood, any more than it had to the freighter's balky horse, or to a United States Senator, a Congressman, a politician, or politicians in general to whom it may be applied. It has no application to Presidents, secretly applied of course, and most certainly not in the case where a President of the United States called a United States Senator an over-educated S.O.B.

It has in reality lost its meaning, like the English "by-the-lady" which eventually became "bloody." The word bloody became a descriptive adjective, and son-of-a-bitch became an epithet, with self-esteem-satisfying, hackle-smoothing, vicious steel trap finality to it which soothes resentment, and jealousy and damaged pride in the user.

18

The other obscenities shouted by the sweating freighters failed to appeal to me, but love of words being inherent, I felt the pride-satisfying snap and sneer in the last word "bitCH," which had given me a sense of a greater superiority than was really mine, even though the rattle-brained chicken had actually defeated me.

The epithet is certainly a great boon to those who are linguistically impoverished, lack poise, and have little of cultured satire and wit at their command.

However, now, in 1966, I have a fellow feeling for the intellectually frustrated; all I am able to do about far away, immaterial TV and radio pitchmen, is to hurl the freighter's hackle-smoothing, comforting epithet at them. If that fails I can push the button, and become vindictively self-sacrificing.[16]

~

[1901–1903]

Even during the most intense periods of my life, corresponding with my college years, when my academic inquisitiveness had few distractions, other than romantic ones, I never really tried seriously to solve the mystery of man's relationship with the Force, whose very existence seems to have made of man an incredible paradox and a disdainer of his placental attachment to earth. Beyond the fact that I knew the Force to be quite beyond my comprehension, (and this is one of the reasons I felt empathy with the Neolithic, pre-dawn chanter of my childhood, and never lost it all my life) was the illogical tendency of men through the ages with their many concepts of the Force, to create laws and rules and ceremonials which they asked the Force to honor, then in their incredible egotism, contented themselves with the illusion that it had.

My humility (a profoundly sincere one) in the presence of Nature and the Force, has not effected my academic interest, which has nothing whatever to do with religiosity.

I have, in my animal feeling for my natural environment, naturally experienced frustrations in trying to understand, very much like the

Osage chanter to the morning star and to grandfather, the sun, but I have never felt frustration so profound that I wept. I have experienced only euphoria.

The Neolithic chanter to the morning star was afraid.[17]

My formal education failed to disturb my feeling in the least, chiefly I believe, because education was a matter of "induction" and not, as was assumed, "eduction."[18] Education was a duty and a formality; the pre-dawn prayer-chanter had stirred my soul.

My formal introduction to the almost incredible achievements of man through the centuries, began in a little private school building perched rather arrogantly, for its size, on an outcropping of the same sandstone that formed the backbone of our ridge finger, and only perhaps two hundred yards from my father's house. We were so close that my sisters and I could be gulping a last spoonful of oatmeal, when the bell rang and still make it, breathing rapidly, to find our places in line, waiting to march into the building at the command of Mrs. Tucker, the teacher.

Mrs. Laura E. Tucker had a Hussar's sense of order and deportment, and there was never any doubt in her mind as to what was Right. She was as enduring and as cherished as McGuffy's reader, which, incidentally, I don't remember ever having seen.

She came to the reservation of the Osages with her two handsome sons, and they became my father's partners in the Osage Mercantile Company.

She was one of the most important people in my life.

From the first grade to perhaps the sixth, Mrs. Tucker, with her rightness and her rugged certainties, laid a wonderful foundation upon which later I was to build my formal education and culture. She seems to have noted from the beginning the fascination words held for me; these symbols upon which civilizations had been built. I can't remember what form her encouragement assumed, now, after all these years, but it must have been subtle. I think I must have been as one imbued, as some children might be inspired by beautiful music. I can distinctly remember going about whispering to myself such words as "extravaganza" and "Santa Maria."

There are other memory slides of my parents and just-after-the-rising of the memory curtain, there were memory crystallizations, but I recall a Tucker's slide at this point, ignoring chronology, since my first day at Tucker's, was definitely crystalline, uncluttered by suggestions from my parents or my older sister.

I engaged in my first fist fight.

Mrs. Tucker's was comprehensive; she taught grades from the first to a stage which equated with the sophomore year of High School. On this September morning, I was like a maiden-voyaging boat unaccountably dropped by her pilot, and was shy and confused and dwarfed by the eighth- and ninth-grade boys.

I set out into this strange and wide world following my older sister, Josephine. She insisted that I walk behind her, but I didn't know why; I should have felt much more comfortable holding her hand.

I suspect that our mother with her Gallic loquacity and repetitions, had warned Josephine that she must take special care of the only little male in the family; watch him for wriggles of discomfort, and see immediately that he got down the crooked, precipitous path that led to the door marked "BOYS."

The outhouses were at the end of two trails, which began at the schoolhouse and ended, one at the girl's and one at the boy's outhouse, at each leg of a V. The little houses were like the knobs at the ends of crooked, exploring insect antennae: the schoolhouse representing the head of the insect.

But my sister was annoyed with me; my very existence seemed to annoy her, and she abandoned me among the big boys. I was afraid and shy and speechless, when one of the big boys approached me and said, "Hi kid, whur's your curls?" I couldn't answer, but I was relieved to remember that my coil spring curls had fallen to the floor of Bill's Barbershop, the week before.[19]

The big boy looked at me as if now, since my curls were gone, he could appraise me against male standards. "Can yu fight?" he asked, feeling of my arm. Then he gripped my arm and pulled me toward the grouped big boys and led me into a circle they had formed. "Here's my entry," he said.

Gentner Drummond had been pushed into the circle, and there was a ring scratched out in the dust. Gentner came forward blinking.

Even at six years of age he wore glasses, and with a Scotsman's caution had taken them off and laid them carefully by a stump.

Gentner's father was a trader, and later established the Hominy Trading Company, at the trading center of the Upland Forest physical division of the Osage Indians, called Hominy Post.

We faced each other and I may have been a blur to his naked eyes.

I stood and he stood, then someone pushed us toward each other, and we collided but moved backward away from each other immediately, and stood looking at each other again.

Then someone put a chip on Gent's shoulder, and told me to knock it off. By this time I was losing my shyness and was becoming stubborn, and when I made no move to touch the chip, it was placed on my shoulder and Gent was commanded to knock it off.

He blinked like a diurnal owl and looked about him as if he were searching for a hole in the circle, through which he might escape. Just then two of the big boys pushed us together, and soon our tender, six-year-old fists were pounding each other.

We each had our partisans and they were shouting to us words of encouragement, but were so engrossed that they failed to see the wrathful Mrs. Tucker until she had actually reached the edge of the circle.

The younger boys ran like quail, and the older boys gave way, and pretended interest elsewhere, but she sent Basil Hickerson and Orel Hunt home, saying I believe, that they could not return until they had brought notes from their parents, assuring their future good behaviour. Then, they could apologize. Mrs. Tucker never demanded an apology, but gave one permission to apologize, saying, "Now, you may apologize."

My sister Josephine and Gentner's older sister Blanche came up with a group of girls and must have sensed some reflected importance, as they pretended concern over us and looked for wounds, but found none, then with female self-righteousness and assumed authority made us shake hands. Then arm linked in arm they walked off. They were good friends.

It would have been much more dramatic if there had been blood.[20]

~

My mother as I have noted, was a Frenchwoman, who came with her mother and brothers, and a half-sister to the Osage Nation from the French settlements of Missouri: the environs of Jefferson City and St. Louis.[21]

My grandmother Girard was in the government employ as a play-it-by-ear nurse, who had great experience in New Orleans during the yellow fever plague.[22] Her energy and her Chauvinism compelled her to go to the aid of distressed Frenchmen.

She had come to the United States at the age of sixteen, and when she died in her eighties, the United States had never quite enjoyed her approval.

The European diseases such as smallpox, diabetes, syphilis and cholera had perhaps destroyed 50 percent of the Osage tribe during the nineteenth century, and infant mortality had risen to an alarming percentage of the births.[23] Every infant or adult Jeanne Girard, my grandmother, could aid the government doctor in saving fired her vanity. She seemed to assume an attitude of vindictiveness, as if she might be spiting the Anglo-Americans.[24]

My mother was much like her in energy and in spirit, but grandmother had been formally trained in the best schools of Normandy, before coming to America, and mother had had to depend on the backwoods log schoolhouses of the Missouri French settlements, where there was a daily massacre of the English language.

She never quite mastered English. She would become so entangled in English syntax, that she often had to bring her French to the rescue, then allow it to flow beautifully without realizing that she had switched languages, the smooth flow of her mother tongue making her insensible to the puzzled faces of her listeners.

As a young woman she looked like Mademoiselle Liberté on the French five-franc piece. A quite remarkable woman of dynamic energy, and with deep interest in birds and animals and trees and flowers and Things in general, although she might not be able to spell the names of any of them. She had a very deep maternal tenderness, a sacrificing love, and a complete unquestioning faith in the Catholic Church's concept of God.

I have an incidental memory of her Titian figure framed in my bedroom doorway, making the sign of the cross at the bed where I lay, believing me to be asleep, saying some blessing sotto voce.

This is not only a memory from childhood, but she did this every night I happened to be spending at home. She asked this favor of heaven, until her last illness confined her to the downstairs rooms: until, as a matter of fact, her eighty-ninth year.[25]

My father's people fascinated me, especially his three nephews and his niece, my cousins. They laughed with their eyes, and were quiet and unexcitable, and gave an impression of honesty and fairness that was not in the least aware of laws or regional customs and mores, Christian or otherwise. There was something inherent in their sense of honor: something that belonged to the family and was handed down from generation to generation like the Hapsburg Jaw. The memory of my father's strict ethics comes to make me uncomfortable, at times.

My father's and his brother Edward's unostentatious and unconscious fairness was so much a part of them that no vicissitude of their barbaric 'teen-age environment could influence it.

They had been compelled to flee from their home in southeastern Kansas after their father, John Mathews, had been killed by the Free Staters in 1861. His trading posts were burned, his property confiscated.[26] His sons, aged ten and twelve years of age, set out for Texas, under the protection of a Confederate-sympathizing family, the Audrains. They could take nothing from their home before it was burned except the clothes they wore. Two of the Mathews slaves fled with them: one "Ole Aunt Millie," the nurse, and the stable man, "Uncle Ned."

In Texas, Southern sympathizers aided them but they were soon on their own, and they became cowboys in their 'teens.

When the Osages were moved to their last reservation in 1872–73, they came there to make their home among them, since they were, by virtue of their inheritance, members of the tribe, and could improve parcels of the community acreage, and establish a ranch.

They rode horseback over the creek and river-veined areas of the approximately one and a half million acres of the reservation, camping, hunting, examining the heights of the drifts of the high water on the Caney and the Arkansas Rivers. Only in the river and creek bottoms could they find the alluvium necessary for growing of corn and grain.

They found the drifts too high on the Caney and the Arkansas, indicating that their crops might be subject to flooding periodically.

After weeks in the saddle, and after examining the lenticular alluvial creek and river valleys of the reservation, they found a floodplain on Beaver Creek wide enough to accommodate the periodic spates, and the volume of water here would be much less than on the rivers.

Here my father and his brother established a ranch, and had their headquarters in a dugout on the banks of the creek.

After my father had been permanently crippled by a horse, Uncle Ed became a Deputy U.S. Marshal, and my father became interested in a trading company and a bank.

~

I shall always associate my father and the memory of him with horses. I have seen him sit for many minutes just looking at a horse: not calculating the worth, or its usefulness as the half of a matched surrey team. Since being crippled he could never hope to ride again, so he would sit on, or rather braced against his cane as one uses a shooting stick, watching and dreaming and I found later that he spent hours planning some felicitous future for me with horses in it; wherein he could experience chivalric happiness again, even though vicariously.[27]

He kept a shiny black pair of Morgans: mares whose coats shone with metallic highlights. This was the carriage team, and he had not planned to breed them until the time had arrived when he must think of training a new pair: their colts. But there would yet be time for the breeding to a Morgan stallion. It would only take three years for their colts to replace them as a carriage team.

One Saturday morning in May, he said: "Son, I want you to come with me out into the country—you're old enough."

I helped him harness the mares; such things as hooking the traces, and then we drove off in the C-spring buggy. As we creaked and jolted along, the mares' hooves thudded in the sand of the trail, and immediately later the sand flowed through the spokes of the wheels.

Finally he spoke. He said, "The mares are both in heat at the same time, and that's what we're doin'—we're takin' them to a stud. That doesn't happen often: a buggy team in heat at the same time. That way, the colts will be about the same age."

There was a long silence; only the sound of the tyres rasping on the sharp, resonant limestone, as the team climbed a prairie hill, then he said, as if he were stating a conclusion, that had been reached after months of careful consideration: "Reason I wanted you to come along, and didn't have Q. take 'em out, is because one of these colts is gonna be yours; thought you might like to be in on the beginnin'."

A mystery of adult life was being revealed to me, and with the revelation, the promise that I would have a colt of my very own.

As I have suggested, I have a remarkable memory in recalling certain incidents in my life that have moved me deeply; these, and those incidents of my childhood associated with the feathers and birds on ladies' hats. From this moment it seemed I would remember vividly as well, every incident associated with horses.

I remember the prairie hill we were climbing as my father made his laconic announcement: the very shape of the clouds of the moment, and a dickcissel singing on a wind-swayed weed.

We came to a little white house just on the edge of a blackjack ridge, and it seemed to be intimidated by the great red barn.

Behind the barn was a corral, and in it circling with arched neck and flowing mane and streaming tail was a great stallion, his flanks dark with worry-sweat. He sent a challenge over the prairie that was feral and primordial and thrilling. The prairie breezes had brought him the message the mares bore.

The man from the barn started to help my father unharness the team, but he stopped suddenly and looked toward the house, covertly, then re-hooked the traces and said: "Judge, rekon maybe you'd better drive 'round back of the barn, kindy."[28]

When the team had been driven back of the barn they were closer to the corral, and the air brought their message to the stallion full strength. He reared and struck at the logs of the corral with his front feet. He whinnied and fluttered his nostrils, and began to coax and cajole through rumbling grunts, as we unharnessed.

The man looked at my father and then at me as he walked toward the gate to the corral and my father pointed to the buggy and we went quickly to it. The man opened the gate and swung it wide, then pinned himself between the gate and the corral's logs, as the great beast came out in a run, then stopped to nose one mare and then the other, then with great nose flutterings he made a complete circle of Molly, with his tail high and his flaxen mane like a pennant. His cajolery, a rumbling in his throat, he circled again then mounted; his ecstatic whinnying in diminuendo, finally ceasing during the orgasm.

After both mares had been served this magnificent blood-red beast with the flaxen mane became tranquil, and began nipping at the grass, and the man had no trouble in leading him back into the corral.

By the next spring, the bellies of both mares became as great barrels, and they were given a long vacation from the harness.

I came each morning to watch them as Q. let them out of the barn to roll and sun bathe. And one day just as my father had predicted, I could see Maud's foetus kick as she stood dreaming in the soporific spring sun. Then two days later, ever watchful, I saw Molly's foal kick, and it kicked so vigorously that Molly laid back her ears in her annoyance and pain.

Q. had been watching. He said: "Your pa said you could have airy one you wanted. Figured you might pick one 'fore they's dropped; er maybe you'd better see 'em first."

"Yes," I said, "I believe I want Molly's."

He spat tobacco juice. "That's hit ever time," he said. "You take one that kicks regular and hard like that 'n o'her'n, 'en you ain't gonna make no mistake; never seen hit to fail."

I had made up my mind but really, I didn't know I had. Molly had been the stallion's first choice, and Molly was restive while Maud was tranquil and cautious. Only Molly became excited when there were races at the George Carter race tracks in Clear Creek valley southwest of our house. The tracks were several miles from our ridge, but

Molly used to sense the excitement. She would trot along the west span of the lot fence with mane and tail streaming, then stand with her head over the top plank and gaze wildly for minutes at the far-away dust and excitement, as if she were being disturbed by racial memories passed down to her from her quarter horse Morgan ancestors.

My father often called her a fool, and we children referred to her as "silly Molly," but I liked her spirit, though reluctantly, since this was not being common sensible. Not to have "common sense" in our empirical world caused one to feel out of things.

It wasn't exactly a secret between my father and me, this imminent foaling of the mares, but we didn't talk about it to anyone except Q.

However, one day at breakfast, I allowed my eagerness and uncertainty to overbalance my caution, and said, "Papa, you think one of 'em might come today? You could write an excuse and I'll take it to Mrs. Tucker this morning."

Mother looked up: "Will, are you going to let that boy see those mares foal?"

My father said: "It's all planned, mother; won't hurt 'im a bit—do 'im good, and teach 'im about life. Make a stemwinder hossman out of 'im. Let 'im know about life; it's life." He turned to me, "Son, I'm not goin' 'round the bush; I'm gonna tell Mrs. Tucker the truth; she'll understand and what's more approve. Let's see, today's Thursday, so you can stay home and watch—only miss two days, and one of the mares'll have hers this weekend, unless it storms, and then she'll have it anytime: maybe at night. Anyway you can stay out in the lot and watch; you'll have four whole days. Q. says you're takin' Molly's. Now don't get too close; stay away cause you might make her nervous."

I couldn't finish my breakfast that April morning.

My mother began to deplore my haste in eating. At breakfast, I wasn't made to ask permission to leave the table, so I would leave a half bowl of cereal or a half-eaten egg, grab my cap and rush to the lot.

My younger sister Lillian was very sensitive to Mother's feelings, so on the second morning of my watch, she came out to the lot to scold like a true and universal female, grabbing at authority and a power not delegated. Mother called her back to the house with a strange Victorian shock that didn't harmonize well with her beautiful voice and the charming after-ring of her Gallic-tinted words.

As I have written, my father's house was built on the backbone of a sandstone ridge finger, and naturally the soil was shallow, and mother had to have alluvium hauled up from the creek bottom, and manure from the livery stable. These stables were another of my father's enterprises. They were just under the ridge.

The Osage Nation was a wonderful hunting preserve. The Amer-Europeans were not allowed to hunt here without invitation and/or permission.

But my father's stables catered to hunters from "The States," and the letterhead was crowded with deer, wild turkeys, quail and prairie chicken, overbalancing the other, the right-hand half of the paper, bearing the name of the stables and the pictured, high-stepping horses pulling a buckboard.

Our barn on the ridge formed one side of the horse lot, with its back to the agency barn across the alley. The lot, not having the care given the yard, was barren and sandstone outcrops were visible all over it.

There was one in particular in the middle of the lot, which each year became more conspicuous through erosion. It was like the hip bone of a long dead and deflated mammoth, and the erosion ripples in the soil, the shrunken skin.

It was here, lying partly on this sandstone outcropping, that Molly decided to give birth to her colt. This decision was quite in harmony with Molly's dramatic whimsies; she was ever doing the unexpected.

I saw her lie down with a protracted groan: that part of her body from which my colt would make his exit, actually resting on the outcrop. This worried me and I thought something ought to be done about it.

I wandered unhappily about looking for Q., but failed to find him, because I didn't search long and diligently, being afraid to miss the birth.

Thus, I sat and worried from a distance.

Soon, she stood up and seemed puzzled. She looked toward me, as if she would say, "I think I've been poisoned." She turned completely around and lay down again exactly in the same position, with her rear end on the outcrop, killing my hopes that she might settle with the exit end on the soft soil.

Soon, she got up again, this time more slowly; and she seemed to wobble a little. She took a step toward the pan of bran I had had set out for her. Of course there was no need for this pan of bran, whatsoever, but I was filled with worry that I might be remiss in some detail, upon which the successful birth of my colt might hang, that I cared little for whatever opinions my father or Q. might have about such silly precautions.

Molly, of course, was not the least interested in food at this critical moment. She walked up to the pan and blew through her nostrils and the bran went flying, then she took a mouthful, chewed a little, then allowed the flakes to flow out with her slobberings.

The poor thing was mechanically, in her distress, associating the bran with deep pleasure and relief from another pain: hunger.

Then when she lay down again, there was no part of her body on the outcrop.

Suddenly, it seemed, there was a whitish, slimy, poisonous appearing, reddish, quivering mass behind her, and at that moment Q. appeared carrying a piece of rope, but when he saw there would be no need for it, he did something about the mass, and motioned to me to stay where I was.

After a few minutes Molly groaned and stood up, and then he motioned me to come near.

Q. kept talking about something; as I remember it, he seemed to be talking about "what a man orter do" about something or other. I heard little of what he was saying, since my thoughts filled my consciousness completely, and I was profoundly happy. I shall remember this moment always; this moment when my happiness was all-absorbing, and my consciousness was closed against outside ideas.

I do remember the large cumulous clouds racing over the lot, and over the barn, making dark shadows over us: cloud shadow and sunlight each having its turn.

The colt's hair had begun to dry, and here at my feet was a beautiful sorrel with flaxen mane and tail, like the prancing, primordial beast who had sired her.

This beautiful colt had come into the world with head up and was immediately attempting to focus on it, as if she would know the earthy problems confronting her without wasting time.

Suddenly I was aware of Q.'s voice, like a sound in the dead of night that wakes one from a dream.

"Looks like you got yourself a damned filly, 'stead o'uh horse," he observed.

"Oh, that's alright," I said, "I want her anyway."

Fillies were not highly prized in the ranch country, except as brood mares.

I repeated, "I want her anyway." Louder this time as if the gods were listening, and they might think that I could have the least doubts about my beautiful colt, that had just miraculously come into my world.

I was afraid of a hubris and tried to conceal my buzzy happiness.

When Q. got things cleaned up he started off, then said back over his shoulder, "Now yu ken show 'er to your Ma and 'em."

I had no intention of blowing the trumpet—ever. I would announce the miracle later at dinner, not at the beginning when my father was serving the plates, and not at the end, but somewhere in the middle.

I was not ready for the oh's and ah's, or the later exclamations when the family went to the lot to see her. When I made my announcement, it would be too late in the day and the "oh's" and "ah's" and "what a funny tail" and "is it a boy or a girl" would be postponed until the next day.

As I stood looking at my miracle, planning the announcement of her birth, she struggled to her feet, wavered in her struggle with gravity and lost. She went down in sprawling disorder like a shot sandhill crane.

The next time she attempted to stand, she made it, stood for a minute perhaps, seeming to be afraid to move one of her long legs for better balance: fearing it might be the wrong one. She stood against gravity, with an expression on her face exactly like one trying desperately to remember which prop to move in order to conquer gravity.

31

She finally succeeded, and began to search forward and aft for Molly's teats but failed to locate them. She moved away and had to spraddle to keep from falling, but she shook her head playfully at the world. It must have been good to be free of the womb's black restrictions, and to show her gratitude, she began to frolic jerkily about her mother, who characteristically overdid the mother business as she did everything else. She gave throaty warnings with exaggerated maternal solicitude.

After a time the colt not only stood with assurance, but walked toward me to investigate. I backed away and she followed, and I held out my hand to her and she touched it with her nose and got her first man-scent. Two animals, two sentient things became attached to each other with that understanding that no adult can ever know.

This was perhaps the instinctive understanding one notices among small children meeting each other for the first time, that older children and grown-ups can never experience. It was also the way of a boy with a horse or a boy with a dog.

As I backed up, the colt followed uncertainly, reaching out her muzzle to lick my outstretched hand. I stopped and when she came up to me, I, flooded with emotion, hugged her neck.

All the time Molly was disturbed and followed us, making deep, coaxing throat sounds.

~

That June my sister Josephine came back from boarding school, with her beautiful head full of wisdom: a wisdom that somehow had just appeared and had not heretofore existed for the guidance of previous Girard-Mathews generations.

She was filled with propriety and poetry and Latin and liturgy, and she knew how one ought to eat soup properly. She came around behind my chair at dinner, and holding my right hand just so, showed me how genteel people ate soup. You dipped your spoon into the soup just over the edge closest to the diner, then slid it through to the other edge of the bowl or to the middle, then bringing it gracefully to the mouth. Horrors, "nice" people didn't reach out to the opposite edge of the bowl, submerge the spoon, then bring it toward you, like—like, a clod.

There was something in the manner in which she stressed the word "clod," that made any future attempts to teach me how to eat soup futile. I became obstinate.

I hated with all my impatient heart, the little rhyme she chanted as she moved my hand: "The spoon is a little ship—see? I send my little ship out to sea, and it brings its cargo back to me." The "cargo" were croutons, of course.

I jerked my wrist from her grasp, and splashed soup on the table-cloth, and mother frowned at her from across the table.

As she went around the table to her own place, she stopped at her chair, and with arms outspread and eyes turned to heaven, she looked straight through the ceiling of the dining room to the under-standing mysteries for help, even though she might not expect much indulgence from that quarter where there was a grimy little boy as the subject.

For years I could never understand how a boy with a rainbow imagination could have given his horse the name Bally. She was blaze-faced certainly, and the name "Baldy" was undoubtedly the source, but this prosaic name was no better than its derivative.

My stupidity shocked me later when I recalled the image of my beautiful horse and my boyhood.

The fact that the learned Josephine might have suggested Pegasus as a fitting name, could have had something to do with my prosaic choice. During one dinner when I had been called from the horse lot, she observed with her affected boarding-school-for-young-ladies daintiness (a convent far away in "The States") holding her fork just so, "and he even smells like a horse; ugh."

It was after this, I seem to remember, that she made the suggestion that I should call my colt Pegasus. If she had just allowed the matter to rest after the suggestion, and had not catechized me about Pega-sus, knowing quite well that I had never heard of the winged horse of mythology, my spirited, beautiful horse might have had a name

Josephine Mathews, John Joseph Mathews's older sister (Courtesy of the Osage Tribal Museum, Pawhuska, Oklahoma)

in harmony with her beauty and swiftness and grace. She would no doubt have been called "Peg," which would of course have been much, much better than Bally.

I spent most of the Saturdays that spring with my colt, and practically every comfortable afternoon after 4 o'clock, when I returned from school. Soon, she was following me around the lot, much to the annoyance of Molly.

At first when her stilt-like legs grew tired after play and long standing she would lie flat and go to sleep in the sun. She didn't lower herself, when she wanted to lie. She couldn't quite understand which legs she was supposed to bend so she allowed all four to collapse like a segmented tripod, and she went down in a heap. I would sit down by her and lift her head onto my lap, and pat her as she slept.

Eventually after a week or more, when she grew tired, she would nudge me and I would sit, and then she would collapse her tripod legs, often missing my lap with her head, and I had to move under it.

Josephine's horse Eagle had to be brought in from the Ridge ranch that summer, where he had been on pasture during her absence. He became a menace. He would lay back his ears and, baring his yellow teeth, make runs at my colt. He seemed to be bent on getting his own back from a world that had cut short his range horse freedom. He had belonged to an Osage of the Big Hills division of the tribe, and as the Osages say, his "pride was taken" too late, and he was thick-necked and ill-tempered and vindictive.

He had been given to Josephine by a man of the Buffalo gens, which was the gens of my father's grandmother.

When it was noticed that Molly had difficulty protecting her colt from his menacing rushes, he had to be confined to his stall in the barn most of the time. This meant that Josephine had to exercise him daily, and since there was no one to ride with her, this became prosaic and a chore.

She would come out to the lot dressed in a divided skirt—an exaggerated culottes—, shiny boots, a black, flat straw hat and gauntlets. She slapped her divided skirt with a fancy, braided quirt.

Eagle, the Indian pony, never lost his deep interest in the flappings of the divided skirt as she approached him, but he seemed always subdued under her "equitation from 'The States'" hand.

She sometimes helped me up behind her, and with [my] arms tight about her waist, she would put Eagle into a lope. She asked me to go along only when she was to bring the milk cows from pasture. There was a board gate to be opened.

Before there was a village herdboy, there was purpose; the three milk cows had to be brought in at the end of her ride, and this rather drab ending to her late afternoon rides, sometimes put her in a temper.

"What I'd like to know," she asked one day as we were "cutting" our cows from the other cows of the agency, "is, who ever gave such stupid names to our cows,—sounds cloddy like you."

I hadn't given the names, but they sounded alright to me: quite the proper names. There was Redneck, and she had a red neck, and certainly Muley was properly named since she had no horns. Of course Lily, the third cow, made one think.

Being an Indian pony, Eagle knew what he was supposed to do about herding cattle, and he must have appreciated the simple mechanics of bringing three listless milk cows home from the pasture to the barn lot: a distance of perhaps a mile. He had only to walk behind them, and the cows knew the routine as well as he did, and neither wanted nor expected any deviation from this routine: this daily comfortable monotony, with the same comfortable end, day after day. The cows could look forward to relief for their full bags, and Eagle could look forward to being relieved of his saddle and bridle, and he could roll and be free from the discomfort of his itchy and sweaty back.

On a particular day, Eagle and the cows and I were contented; I was happy and was very careful about my behaviour. I slid down from behind the saddle to open the gate for the cows, and climbed laboriously back up behind the saddle as quickly as I could and as efficiently as possible.

My sister's moods were mysteriously sourceless, but on this afternoon the heat was depressing and the flies were a nuisance, and I noted that she gave me no aid in climbing back to my seat behind the saddle, after I had closed the pasture gate. I was unusually silent and efficient this particular afternoon.

The cows were walking indolently in a line along the trail, and behind them was Eagle with head down, half asleep.

Sometimes when we were strung out along the trail coming home, one of the cows on seeing a particularly luscious tussock of bluestem, or a patch of exotic Bermuda, would stop to tear at it. The line would stop momentarily, then move on. If a cow had to step out of the line to tear at a bit of grass, we would stop and wait for her to come back to the line.

However, the cows at such times were conscious of misbehaviour, and would often jerk at the grass while still moving.

But during this hot, fly swarming afternoon my sister was in a mood; I sensed it.

Muley triggered the incident by stepping out of the line quickly and guiltily to snatch at a tussock. Josephine raised her quirt, kicked Eagle in the belly with her spurless heels, and started for Muley. Eagle woke up and became excited and began to buck, but only tentatively, to express his disgust. However with his head down almost between his front legs, his convulsive jumps caused the latigo to snap off at the cinch buckle, and off we went, saddle and all, and fell among the sandstone rocks and running oaks.

My sister regained consciousness first, and when I awakened, she was sitting, disheveled and bloody, rubbing her arm. She looked at me accusingly and accusingly asked, "Are you hurt?"

"My head aches," I admitted.

"Mine does too," she said, frowning at me.

We rose and walked about; we were still intact except for scratches that bled rather dramatically, but went unnoticed because of her headache.

When we arrived at the lot gate Eagle was standing there, with the reins under his feet waiting for someone to let him in.

We approached the house through the yard, and as we neared the house, Josephine looked down at me with contempt: "I'm gonna tell Papa you flanked him," she said.

"I didn't."

"You did."

"I didn't."

"You flanked him alrighty."

"I did not."

Mother examined our wounds carefully and applied arnica salve, and when she had convinced herself that we were not seriously hurt, she began to scold my sister, reminding her of her responsibility for her little brother. The rocky brook dashings of her English solecisms, were soon lost in the swift current of her French.

Our father laughed.

~

[1903]

I wasn't one of the bright pupils at Tucker's. As a matter of fact I have always had the feeling that I was ranked rather low in effort and interest. Years later when I was far away from my native hills and prairie, a feature writer came to interview Mrs. Tucker, who by then was quite old, and lived alone with bright enthusiasm.

My informant indicated that the feature writer needed for the dramatic effect his article must attain, some revelation of my assumed precocity or genius as a small boy. He wanted dreamy-eyed reminiscences, but the honest old lady said simply, "He was shy." She needed no reflected glory as a one-time guide or Mentor to a blown-up concept.

During the three years I was waiting impatiently for my horse Bally to be rideable, the years preceding my glorious chivalric ones, Tucker's absorbed my thoughts, and they were of primary importance during the period before I discovered the great world from my saddle.

I remember distinctly the happy period each morning when Mrs. Tucker read aloud to the room, from Jack London's *The Call Of The Wild*, for one half hour after we had sung the Lord's Prayer.

This half hour was disturbing to a lover of the wild; some mornings

I didn't get back from the Yukon country for several hours, and there were times when I didn't even hear a question from Mrs. Tucker. She referred to this, as "wool gathering."

Jack London's *The Call Of The Wild*, is a graphic, colored slide memory, as is the yellow-shafted flicker that made a hole in the overhang of the school house roof. He made the hole in October, but he came to hammer and shout in April as well, and this was a distraction, especially when the window was open on a warm day. It was romance to me.

Of course he was the monitor's responsibility. The monitor—a new one each week—was appointed to go down one aisle and up another, carrying a small pail of water. As he/she came to each desk, the pupil dipped his/her sponge and squeezed it out.

One warm, bright April day, the flicker was ecstatic; he pounded at the overhang with such energy, shouting, "wicky-up; wicky-up; wicky-up," that the recitations could not be heard.

Mrs. Tucker frowned and walked to the window, trying to look out and up; her pointer, which we referred to as her "ruler," must have been made of walnut or mahogany—or so it seemed to those who had felt it across their knuckles—was the sword of Britannia.

The monitor on this day the flicker disturbed recitations, was a girl whose ribbon on the back of her head was like an unlikely, exotic butterfly of tremendous size; her stockings were pulled up, and every button of her high-button shoes was in order. Since obviously she couldn't be expected to handle the flicker situation, Mrs. Tucker sent two of the older boys to throw rocks at the bird, with the last moment's warning: "just to scare it; don't throw to hit or hurt it."

The boys were back and scarcely seated when the flicker began his hammering and shouting again. Mrs. Tucker was always searching for that which she called "object lessons," and it suddenly occurred to her that if she had to be defeated by a trespassing lower form of life, it would seem less like a defeat if she could use him.

She had the impeccable little monitor close the window, then she looked over the room, and her bet-you-don't-know-the-answer expression came to her face, as she said: "You see the lower animals have reasons for what they do, the same as men have. Now there is a reason for what that yellowhammer's doing—a good reason; now, who can tell us what it is?"

Looking back over the years, I remember having the feeling that she was about to launch into a long explanation concerning the human traits manifested by "our brothers of the fields and woods," and since she was our teacher she might *really* know something about the earthy reasons for the excited shouting and hammering of the flicker, and if she hadn't called him a "yellowhammer," I am sure I wouldn't have raised a jerky, hesitant hand, during her dramatic stop at the end of her question.

I had a grimy little field guide to birds; I seem to remember it was by Chester A. Reed, and I know now after all these years that Mrs. Tucker was about to repeat some moral from the Medieval or the seventeenth-century Bestiaries: some mincing theological interpretation.[29]

My later reasoned contempt for anthropopathy may have had its origin that April day at Tucker's, and I had no idea of being didactic, but I seemed to wish to obviate such treacle and save myself annoyance, chiefly, but also to aid the "brothers of the fields and woods" in maintaining self-respect.[30]

Of course all this was then instinctive and not reasoned.

Before I realized it, my hand was in the air, and when Mrs. Tucker looked down the aisle at me, nodded and said, "Yes?" I should have like[d] to hide under my desk.

I rose weak-kneed, and mechanically picked up my Reader, thrust my forefinger among the leaves, turned the book around and pressed the backbone to my shoulder, and stood at uhlan attention.[31] This was perfectly mechanical; the forefinger thrust among the leaves was for the purpose of "keeping the place" in the reader and the heels together, and the book against the shoulder, was possibly due to some Prussian influence in the parochial and private schools of the period.

Mrs. Tucker smiled indulgently, and said; "You may put the reader down, Jo; you're not reciting, yu know."

This suggestion shattered my composure completely. I could hear titters.

I put the book down and knew that every thought concerning flickers had fled as I stood. Dear old Britannia was charming in situations of this sort. She spoke softly and with inspiring empathy: "Take your time, Jo; we'll wait.

A moment later, she said, "Now, do you want to go on; we should all like to know what you have to tell us about yellowhammers."

There was that "yellowhammer" business again, and suddenly my thoughts and my courage came back together.

My scorn for anthropopathy certainly must have been born this day long ago, since I remember now talking with conviction, to obviate moralizing from an ancient Bestiary, which I instinctively felt that Mrs. Tucker was eager to present as one of her inexhaustible object lessons.

I first assured the room that the bird was a flicker and not a "yellowhammer" and that he had made that hole in the overhang for his store of winter nuts and acorns. He did this in the autumn but in the spring since the hole was his, he would make his nest in it.

"The hole was big enough last autumn for his store of nuts, and big enough for a nesting hole, then why does he make so much racket now in the spring; hammering until we can't hear ourselves think—what about that, Jo; that's what we want to know. Is he just trying to aggravate us?"

I was suffused by courage now: "He's just doing that," I said, then I told the room about the tall galvanized tin stovepipe sticking up out of Mr. Gibson's kitchen roof, and how each spring the flicker would come to cling to the joints where he could get a foothold and hammer and shout "wicky-up; wicky-up." He didn't want to make a hole in the tall pipe, and he knew he couldn't, and he wasn't trying to make the hole in the overhang larger either.

Mrs. Tucker's empathy was evident; I can remember her expression graphically after all these years, when she observed: "But the point is, Jo, why does he hammer on Mr. Gibson's stovepipe and our building if he isn't trying to make a hole?"

"Well, it's because he can't sing, mam," I said, with glowing assurance. There were ripples of laughter over the room, and even Mrs. Tucker smiled despite her attempts to control her mild amusement.

She must have wished that I was being facetious, so that she might have no fear of embarrassing me.

I wasn't the least embarrassed; truth was my aegis. I said: "May I sit down?"

I did speak a truth that day at Tucker's, even though an unconscious one, and as I look back I am not quite sure that Chester A. Reed, of my guide book knew why the flicker hammered and shouted ecstatically in the spring. I didn't know until much later that the demonstration was really nuptial, and he was more than figuratively "beating the bounds" of his range, just as the mockingbird, the orchard oriole, the robin did with their singing.

~

The Osage Reservation was in the category of a "Closed Reservation" until 1907. This meant that the approximately one million and a half acres of land in the Reservation belonged to the Osage Indians, and that they held the land and the minerals in community. They were referred to as being a Nation within a Nation. Technically then, I had not been born "of" the United States but "within" their boundaries.[32]

One entered and remained by permission, if one were not a member of the tribe. Traders, nurses, schoolteachers, domestic servants, and some of the agency employees were permitted to live on the Reservation specifically because of their service to the Osages.

Just across the road from my father's house was the beginning of the southern boundary of acreage set aside—about '87—especially for the agent's residence and the campus on which were built the Osage Indian School buildings: the girl's dormitory, the boy's dormitory, the chapel, stable and engine house. The latter would now be called the power house.

All were of native Elgin sandstone.

In the valley, as I have mentioned previously, were the administration buildings, the doctor's house, the council house and the blacksmith's house: also built of the native Elgin sandstone.

Next to the agent's house was my father's house, then the Gibson house south of ours owned by the son of the agent who came with the Osages to their last reservation. Then there was the Skinner house, with one of the great rounded sandstone water reservoirs, standing above it gloweringly. On the point of the ridge finger was the Palmer house.

Both Allen Gibson and John Skinner were licensed traders to the Osages, but John Palmer was a lawyer-politician, orator and a breeder of racehorses. He needed no permit to live on the Reservation since he was not only married to a member of the tribe, but was himself a Sioux who had been adopted by the Osages.

He appealed to me much more than the taciturn Friend, Allen Gibson, and the monotoned John Skinner, the trader. Even the neighbor on the north, the superintendent or agent of the Osages, Oscar A. Mitscher, with his bright attitude of allocated authority from Washington, D.C., was not quite so interesting as John Palmer.

John Palmer spoke with gravity and declaimed with dignity when he spoke at the cemetery on Memorial Day, not with upraised arms and pounding fist that made the frail, red, white and blue bunting-covered rostrum quiver. His satire when he made a political speech, was according to my father, "like a wound you don't know you have until the next morning."

I am sure, I was fascinated by his manner of speaking, when his turn came on the Memorial Day programs, and even when he quoted Shakespeare, Byron, Poe or Kipling, without the usual histrionics of the other speakers, but I am also sure that I was associating him with his thoroughbreds and the large barn high on a prairie hill south of the agency, and this association alone would have given birth to the memory slide which I have had through the years.

There was a flock of pit game chickens foraging there among the stalls. Later, when I could ride to "Palmer's Barn," I sat long hours listening to the talk of the trainer and stable men. There were the odors: a mélange of scorched hooves from shoeing, and hay and oats and horse droppings, and the prairie winds singing around the eaves and over the roof.

I picked up some words of Belgian French from trainer Jack Noel.

And that was not all; John Palmer had built a summer house on the very point of the ridge, and from it you could look straight down onto the area in front of the Council House.

In winter, with my sister Marie and the two younger Palmer girls, [I] would coast down the ridge from their house into the valley on our bobsleds.

One hard winter when the snow lay long, the Palmer handyman, Casey, made a sleigh out of a C-spring buggy, and drove over the agency with a dozen or more bobsleds attached to the rear. There was not room for more than five sleds to attach directly to the rear axle, and the other sleds had to be attached to the ones in front, forming a flowing, rasping apron of stocking-caps and mittens.

If Casey turned a corner too sharply, the tail-end sleds were snapped off the apron to roll over and over in the snow: the sledders shouting, usually with glee.

When Casey had a bottle at his side, he became smug and prideful with his illusions of dexterity, and once the whole apron of stocking caps and mittens snapped loose from the buggy sleigh, when one of the horses stepped on the acute turn, and fell; and I came home with a bloodied face and a scratched knee.

The bobsledders' nemesis rasping behind the sleigh were the frozen horse droppings.

The barn on the high prairie visible for miles; the dignified but stinging oratory; the summer house; the precipitous coasting with Teeto and Clemmie Palmer; Jack Noel and Casey, made of John Palmer a memory slide of rare sharpness and color.

I can associate only the great sandstone water tower that dominated the house of John Skinner, with its occupants; I can't remember one member of the family.

The great tower was one of several built by the government as reservoirs in the water system, into which steam engines pumped water from wells in the valley. Inside there was a drip from the tank high above, that had a ringing sound and reverberated as one might expect the implacable footsteps of Fate to do.

There was cold, twilight mystery inside, and sometimes a screech owl sat and peered down at you, making a detailed examination of you, as if he might know your intentions. He sometimes trilled sadly; like a lost soul, which the Osages knew all screech owls to be.[33]

I used to remain there for minutes, the screech owl staring down at me and the water drip tinkling rhythmically. There was a Fairy story here for the writing.

Mary Ella Gibson and I played through the picket fence that divided our family's properties; I should have written the picket fence that divided our gardens. There was no space for lawns.

My neighbors on the north were, as I have noted, the Mitschers. Tom and I were about the same age and were good friends, and the road between our houses and the serrated iron fence around the agent's residence and the picket fence around ours were never barriers. We never used the gates but climbed both fences when we had the urge to visit

Tom was as tough and as courageous as his older brother Marc, and had the same sense of fairness. He was certainly no bully but he had an inherent urge to compete, and when there were no games to be played, and we grew tired of climbing trees or playing "follow the leader," Tom was compelled to wrestle or fight.

So we fought each other because Tom had to fight, and I had to fight with him because I had a terrible temper. We were evenly matched, and usually succeeded in bringing blood to each other's noses, but in the end we washed our faces and got on with boy's business, until the urge came upon Tom again; perhaps a month later, and again he would goad by calling me "curley," an epithet which I hated. He would look at me with his face raised the least bit, holding it to one side. He would then smile his tight, diabolical smile, and call me "curley" again. He could sneer more effectively than anyone I have ever known. His sneering smile was the same as that on the face of the devil on the picture postcards.

When Marc, Tom's older brother, happened to see us fighting, he intervened and divided our fight into rounds, and warned us about below-the-belt punches. When he was present he would stop the fight when he thought it had endured long enough, and make us shake hands.

There was really no need for these Marquis of Queensbury formalities, since Tom and I were as close friends with bloody noses as we were when robbing birds' nests, or playing in the haylofts of either the government or our barn.

Marc belonged to the group known as the "big boys" at Tucker's; boys in the eighth and ninth grades. They occupied the row of seat-desks along the north wall of the building, alternating with the "big girls."

South, across the width of the room from the eighth and ninth graders' desks, were the rows of descending status. The last row of diminutive seat-desks, the row along the south wall, was occupied by the first and second graders.

I don't know at what point Mrs. Tucker started teaching her pupils geography but I remember that the big boys and girls had the large atlas, red-backed, and perhaps 15 by 11 inches, which everyone referred to as "jographies."

We small boys of that time were fascinated by the great variety of things the big boys could do behind their "jographies." They whittled, shot paper wads at the girls across the aisle with a rubber band. The girls always pretended they were annoyed or indignant.

The big boys had a deep urge to cut their initials in their desk tops. This urge to immortality was deep and clean, and wholesome. It was simply an urge to say, "I passed this way."[34]

~

We had study hours at Tucker's when there were no recitations, but there were diligence and silence, and Mrs. Tucker sat at her desk, reading or writing arithmetical problems; perhaps even an algebraical one on the blackboard back of her desk.

During one particular study hour, we in the back of the room on the first-grade side could hear a scratchy sound; it was like the persistent, secretive gnawing of a mouse, making a hole in a cupboard. The big boys and girls were studying "jography," and as usual the boys had theirs upright in front of them, and half opened like screens.

Those in the back of the room knew that the mousy, gnawing sound came from Marc Mitscher's desk; as a matter of fact we in the rear seats could see him carving something, glancing up to peek at Mrs. Tucker with his icy-blue eyes.

We of the back rows had known about Marc's absorption for some time; at least I had, since my seat was the last one in the first-grade row and his the last one in the eighth–ninth-grade row, so that I had only to turn my head ever so slightly to watch him covertly.

Those of us just across the room from Marc were only pretending to study. The atmosphere was tense, and we were waiting for drama, not just diversion; such was the seriousness of the laws of the Victorians.

Mrs. Tucker was really too far away to hear the gnawing sound, in the back of the room, and very likely Marc, might have finished carving his name that day—and he was carving his full name and not just his initials—long ago, and that desk might be in the Smithsonian Institution this moment, or in some other national archive, and it is quite possible that Marc Mitscher might not have put General Doolittle and his sixteen B-24 bomber pilots in position to bomb Tokyo in World War II, and there would have been no heroic commander of Task Force 58, if the little girl in front of me had not suddenly raised her hand in grim desperation. She had been wriggling for perhaps ten minutes before she suddenly shot her hand into the air to get Mrs. Tucker's attention.[35]

Mrs. Tucker, absorbed by her work at her desk far up front might not have seen the urgent hand, if several of us barbarians near her, had not started snapping our fingers in mimic urgency.

Mrs. Tucker raised her head, nodded to little Rien, who with deep concentration and agonizing control fled out the front door. There was no rear door to the little building, since the downhill end of the foundation must have been eight feet high.

Then came into play Britannia's remarkable intuition. Marc Mitscher's killer-blue eyes were on her as if waiting, and she KNEW. She picked up her pointer ("sword"-"ruler") adjusted her shield, which was actually the pounding of her whale-boned midsection with her fist to relieve her flatulence (we were quite accustomed to seeing Mrs. Tucker pound her midsection periodically for relief, especially when she stood up suddenly—after lunch) and marched grimly down the aisle toward Marc's desk. Those in the front of the room turned their questioning heads as one, but for those of us in the rear of the room there was dramatic expectation.

When she reached Marc's desk, she held out her hand and said: "Marc Mitscher, give me that knife."

He held out his hand with the knife lying on the palm, and as her hand was about to close on it, he closed his fingers, and his hand became a fist, but remained extended.

I am not sure, but I believe she demanded a second time, "Marc Mitscher, give me that knife," but he responded only with his glacial eyes turned up to her face, and there was no hint of a grim smile, or any other emotion on his face.

The clash of indomitable wills: Right and Laura E. Tucker on one side, and tenacity and almost frightening, deeply respectful courage of a 'teen-age boy on the other. Respected Right and respectful Courage having a showdown, and neither lost nor won.

The silence was broken only by the cracking sound of the pointer on Marc's knuckles, wrists and his closed fingers. She brought his arm back over the sharp edge of the back of his seat-desk, and put pressure on it, and whacking it with all the strength she had. Her face became reddened, and her tongue made marble-like impressions, first on one side and then on the other; you could hear her breath, escaping through her nose.

Marc's face still showed no expression whatsoever. There must have been pain but there was no expression of it, either in his face or in his body.

Right was furious and emotionalized and aggressive, and Courage remained passionless and passive.

The atmosphere of the room was one of awe and drama and fear and a deep, primordial, silent admiration: unfathomable.

I know of only one result of the silent conflict between Right and Courage many years ago in the little white school house perched precariously on the sandstone outcrop; Marc Mitscher was possibly expelled and was certainly appointed to the United States Naval Academy by the then Congressman Bird S. McGuire.

After being "bilged out" once, he returned to the Academy and graduated, eventually becoming an international hero as the commander of Task Force 58, and to become later a full admiral before retirement. Less than 75 naval officers in the entire history of the United States had attained this high honor.

It was cold, reticent courage that made Marc Mitscher of Tucker's school a hero, and the pupils of Tucker's felt this that day, and this unreasoned fact made us primordially comfortable and partisans, and suffused us with tingly admiration, but at the same time made us uneasy, because Victorians believed that Right and Courage ought always to be on the same side.

~

[GAS LIGHTS AND A "HOEDOWN"]

Sometime after my younger sisters entered Tucker's, we had natural gas lights, and I can remember our father like an old European lamplighter, going from one room to the other, with a special taper, turning the keys at the bottom of the fixture and then lighting the mantles. He was very meticulous about this lamp lighting, because he was afraid of gas, and he always assured himself that the gas was turned on and lighted properly and turned off properly.

But before we had gas from the local gas fields, we had kerosene lamps. The fuel had at first been made from coal, and called "coal oil," and was for a long time, as a derivative of petroleum, the most popular and profitable product of petroleum.

The lamps had to be carried from room to room, and as they were carried thus, shadowy and fantastic figures danced on the walls, and the ceilings became flooded by yellow light.

After a late winter's dinner, the lamp was carried into the large room we called the "front room," and here our father had his swivel chair and he settled down to reading, while mother had her rocker and soon had her lap full of "sewing." The round table where we children studied our lessons didn't quite contain the pool of yellow light, and it overflowed the edges, and fell in ragged splashes on the carpet. Our mother had her pool of yellow light, and our father his, and my sisters and I around the table with the yellow flood in our eyes, absorbing the wisdom of the ages, as the wood fire in the heating stove made the pot-belly of it, red.

It was the time of the yellow pools of light that traveled from room to room that my father's nephew Owen came to live with us. He was the son of my father's brother Edward, who had died. I remember that both Aunt Sally and Uncle Ed were dead, and he had no home, and I believe I heard a story about his running away from school in Carlisle, Pennsylvania.[36]

My father had apparently sent Owen and his twin brother, Walter, to Carlisle, but Owen had run away back to the Reservation, so my father had given him a room and some chores to do concerning the horses. He was not a horseman, and seems to have been born without special interest in anything, while his twin played end on the famed Carlisle football team, and won fame in track.[37]

Owen was contented to do his chores around the stables and attend the country dances, and in general associate with the wild young mixed-bloods of the Reservation. In this atmosphere his unprepossessing physique, his readiness to agree with almost any statement, seemed strange and submissive.

He, however, had pretensions to manliness, and his urge to compensate for his small stature and incredible thinness, his ready repetition of aphorisms by some rugged extrovert, his dallying with mother's domestic helpers known in the parlance of that time as "har'd gurls," seemed almost a conscious expression of such pretensions.

One never used the term servant in our part of the world; this was not out of courtesy to the settler's daughters who came as domestics by special permission into the Reservation from Kansas, but because of a queer pride in the employer. Free men in a free country meant just that; that they were freeing themselves from centuries of European subservience; from racial memories concerning churls, house carls, peasant retainers, tradesmen, ladies' maids, fief holders, and they believed in the magic of terms; therefore if you called a nursemaid, a cook, or a girl of all work, a "har'd gurl," you served your own and her parents' pride, at least, if not hers.[38]

I can't quite fit this slide memory of Owen into the memory projections chronologically, but I feel sure it is from my first years at Tucker's.

Of course, I don't know how far he went with his dallying, but from later reasoning, I must suppose that he had no intentions of going very far; just far enough to nourish his male pride. Also, he had to maneuver under the eye of an empirical and logical Frenchwoman.

My mother came upon him once with one of the "har'd gurls" sitting on his bony knees. In his embarrassment he let her fall to the floor by separating his knees. Naturally, I knew nothing about this until I heard it discussed later out on the front porch in French, the smoke-screen language of the long summer evenings accompanied by the grassroots chorus.

One of the duties of the girl of all work was the gathering of the eggs; there were no milkmaids of literature and rhyme. Owen did the milking at that time and later that fly-pestered chore fell to me. One day the prairie Don Juan left some chocolates hidden on the surrey back seat under a laprobe, for the girl of the moment, whom he was trying to impress. However, Josephine got wind of this gesture, and found the chocolates, and with my father's connivance, divided them equally among her siblings. The details of the incident came out during the jolly family chaffing of Owen.

But the sharpest slide of this period was one of Owen getting ready for a country dance.[39] I think I remember this incident vividly because it is sharply associated with the shooting that happened later.

I sat in his room as he dressed. I sat on a hump-backed trunk as he adjusted his red sleeve holders just so, and snapped his new red suspenders after he had adjusted them for length. He blackened and polished his shoes (I can't imagine why he didn't have a pair of high-heeled cowboy boots) smeared some kind of grease in his very black hair, and combed it before the mirror until it gleamed like patent leather.

Then came the most thrilling phase of the preparations; he came over to the trunk and motioned me to get off, then raising the lid he took out a holstered 45 cal. revolver. He closed the trunk and I crawled back onto my seat, and watched with even more awe, which I know now he appreciated, even though the silent admiration and awe came only from a small boy.

He shoved the revolver down into the top of his trousers and then clipped the holster to the belt. He tied his tie meticulously, put on his coat, then spent some time turning to get a rear view with the hand mirror. He kept feeling of the gun through his coat and made sure that there was no impression of it visible.

When he was ready he walked out into the twilight to his horse hitched to the hitching rack at the front gate.

I followed him out and watched him as far as I could see him, down the dusty hill.

That night at the dance there happened what was locally known as a "knock down and drag out."

The prairie fiddlers were never, during this period of Victorian mores, accompanied by their wenches or "bitches" as were the fiddlers of Restoration England, but the epithet came over with the immigrants, so one said that some floor-pounding cowboy, or settler down from Elgin or Chautauqua, Kansas, doing a buck & wing as he waved his hat was as "drunk as a fiddler's bitch." These settlers and cowboys always became raucous and exhibitionistic, while the Osage mixed-bloods usually wavered with exaggerated dignity, but ever ready for gunplay.

The next day the news spread over the agency that young Lusting had been killed, and the dramatic story went that there had been not a single kerosene lamp left un-shattered when the fight was over. They said that young Lusting was endangering the lives of his host and the others through shooting at the ceiling and shouting menaces, being of course, as "drunk as a fiddler's bitch."

The people of the agency chaffed Owen, saying that when the smoke finally cleared and the lanterns were lighted, he came out from under a table. No matter how sensible he apparently was in his urgency when the guns were blazing, his pride was damaged.

The matter of the "fiddler's bitch" was finally understood by me, but for some time I had to concentrate on this business of a fiddler taking his dog into the room where people were dancing, and giving her whiskey, so that she became drunk. I can still remember my visualizations in my straining confusion, one being of a female dog lifting her feet high, stepping over imaginary obstacles, with glassy eyes focused on nothing, like the well-known agency drunkard.[40]

~

Victorians of the prairies and the blackjacks, driving their teams over the dusty trails, or riding horseback over the prairie were traditional visitors. One's relatives might appear suddenly, and after one had asked them to "stay for dinner," and had had their sweaty horses unharnessed and fed, might find that the visitor had planned to stay the night and perhaps several days. There were two hotels in the agency, one the Pawhuska House, and the other the Leland, but pride wouldn't allow a householder to suggest an hotel. He must put his visitors up (usually relatives, close or removed) no matter if he and his family might be inconvenienced by so doing.

However, when we went every Thanksgiving season to visit father's sister, my aunt Sue, we were more or less carrying out a tradition, and we looked forward to driving the thirty some miles to Beaver Creek.[41]

Aunt Sue was some twelve years older than my father and fourteen years older than her brother Ed, and therefore escaped the barbaric struggle between Slaveocrats and Free Staters, during which my grandfather lost his life and property. She had lived comfortably in Kentucky even during the Civil War days.

She had married a Kentuckian, James Simpson, and they had come to the Osage country with their heads full of dreams of Southern Plantation living with horses and apples and peacocks.

I have such a mélange of memories of "Aunt Sue's," that I am sure some of them must date before the curtain of memory rose to allow the recording of babyhood impressions: incidents talked about which were not my memories at all.

The trip to "Aunt Sue's" consumed a whole day, and we stopped at the Salt Creek ford to have lunch, water the team and allow them to rest. There was an outcropping of flattish rock here that made the fording of the creek possible.

Mother loved the busyness of preparing the lunch. Sometimes when the day was not windy or chilly, we built a fire for making coffee and heating milk, and sometimes we children were allowed to roast bits of meat which we stuck on the sharpened ends of hickory branchlets.

My father usually waited until we arrived at Beaver Creek before trying for the wild turkey, which would be served at the traditional dinner, but on the way, Jack and Gay, the bird dogs running along with the surrey, would point quail and/or prairie chickens, and there would be mallards flying in clouds over the prairies where the cattle were grain-fed.

When I became old enough I would help my father draw the mallards and the prairie chickens and stuff the cavities with grass, when we stopped for lunch at the Salt Creek ford. This was not necessary on cold days, but almost a necessity on warm days.

As I have noted, Aunt Sue and Uncle Jim had dreams of reproducing an "Ole Kentucky Home" on the wild banks of Beaver Creek. There were tall catalpas standing like a guard of honor on each side of the flagged walk that led to the white house from the gate in the white picket fence.

There was a large barn, an exercising lot for the thoroughbreds, and a crude race track for "breezing" them. Uncle Jim and his neighbor Sylvester Lawrence owned this track in partnership. There was a sort of catch-all building with a weathervane atop it, and a lovely metal thoroughbred facing in the direction from which the wind was blowing. The pigeons cooed and strutted along the ridgepole, seeming to be conscious of their iridescent feathers.

My uncle and aunt had no children, and the impression that we might have destroyed the tidiness of their ranch remains distinct. At least we were not allowed the freedom of the parlour which had the odor of immaculate staleness. The cast iron turtle by the fireplace fascinated me. You could put your foot on the head and the carapace would rise, and uncle Jim could spit into the cavity that was the insides of the turtle—if he ever dared.

There was a piano in the parlour, in front of which was a padded, velvet-covered stool with gilded tassels hanging from it all around. On one side of the room was a sort of cupboard with a ghastly vase, on which were alabaster men carrying long spears astride roachmaned horses. They rode bareback and wore sandals. In the vase was a handful of tail feathers from one of the ranch's peacocks.

If one intended to re-create "My Ole Kentucky Home," even on the savage Osage prairies, one had to have peacocks. I can remember how they screamed like witches from the ridgepole of the barn.

I don't remember the carpeting of the parlour, but I remember the table with the veined marble top in the center of the room. On it was a statuette of Apollo being foiled by Daphne, and a leather-bound book with uncut leaves. It seems strange that I can remember the uncut leaves so vividly, and not the title; perhaps I couldn't read when I was first interested in it. Very likely it was either *Vanity Fair* or *David Copperfield*.

Periodically, we the little nieces and the little nephew were allowed to enter the parlour, but only when accompanied by a grown-up. I believe Josephine was allowed to enter ad libitum, but it seems to me that she didn't always accompany us on our annual junket. Perhaps she stayed at boarding school over the Thanksgiving holidays or visited with a friend. In any case I can't seem to remember her at "Aunt Sue's," with one or two exceptions.

Aunt Sue was the image of her grandfather, William Shirley Williams, known in western history as "Ole Bill Williams." She and W.S. Williams both had long faces with a hint of Punch's chin and nose, but despite these prominent features she was comely enough, as I remember her.

She wore her hair in a "bun," and all her dresses were high-necked with incipient trains.

She preferred dogs and cats to children; she seemed to favor any animals above the human animal: the pre-adult human animal. She even adopted a chameleon I captured and brought to her.

She had the vanity of the virtuous, that conscious virtue which so silently and placidly made you conscious of the frailties to be found in others. She didn't really project frailties to others which she found in herself and refused to accept, since she couldn't possibly be aware of such frailties.

She sat with hands clasped on her lap, and with her feet crossed in perfect Victorian propriety and indulgence.

She was neither religious nor skeptical. She gave the impression that there was no need for outward manifestations. She sneered at people who pronounced the name of the agency village "Paw hŭh skŭh," instead of "Paw hūe skäh," and smirked when people said "crik" instead of "creek."

There was a wonderful orchard, and great vats of apple cider when we arrived for Thanksgiving. The vats were in a little house apart, and the odor was wonderful there. There were dippers hanging from hooks on the wall, and uncle Jim brought his guests into the little house, and dipped cider for them, after raising the cover to the vats ceremoniously.

The Samaritans lived back of the orchard, or at the end of it; I didn't get that far until I was older, and by that time the Samaritans had gone.[42] I have never known their business relations with "Aunt Sue's," but I imagine he was the orchardist and truck gardener, or he and his wife were there under some other arrangement with uncle Jim; perhaps they harvested apples and truck on shares.

He and his wife were mild, pleasant people. She always wore an apron and always folded her arms across her bosom as she talked. They both exuded Christian goodness and seemed always to be secretly exhilarated as if they hadn't the slightest doubts about getting to heaven: as if they had been assured by a clandestine whisper and a wink.

I liked them since they always treated me as an equal, stopping their work in the orchard to answer my questions, attributing importance to me and my little boy's questions, as if they were remembering what Jesus had said about little children.

Mr. Samaritan took me down into the cellar and showed me the great piles of potatoes, squashes, onions, the crates of eggs and dried corn, all the while smiling benignly, as if it were something he had always wanted to do.

The Samaritans' subservience was not of the marketplace, or to their employers, my uncle and aunt, but to God, and uncle Jim at times was a great boon to their Samaritanism; uncle Jim through his weakness, kept it strong and beautiful and ever aware of itself, by becoming trustfully drunk with owlish imperturbability on his way back from the Kansas towns of Maple City or Arkansas City on cold winter nights.

When the horses came home from such trips to "The States," drawing a driverless buggy or buckboard, to stand with that peculiar patience which well-trained teams had, at the lot gate, Samaritan would light a lantern and drive the team back to the last gate knowing that here he would find a rag-doll-like figure in the dust.

He would undress uncle Jim and put him to bed in the "spare room," since aunt Sue would ignore his presence for several days after such an episode.

After the team had been unharnessed and fed, and the merchandise and staples and the mail brought into the house, Samaritan would say good night to a silent house rather dutifully, as if he were bestowing a blessing upon a household that was not quite ready to receive it: a gesture to be recorded above.

I don't know how many years we traveled to "Aunt Sue's" for Thanksgiving, but I know that there were several junkets when I rode Bally, and Spot, my dog joyfully hunted quail and prairie chicken on the way there and back.

One time he scattered a flock of wild turkeys, and my father shot one, by sitting with his back against a tree and calling with a cedar box turkey call.

The team and Bally had been left out of sight, and the family warned about noise.

I think we had been still-hunting about half an hour, but when we approached the surrey, Maud and Molly, who had been unhooked, were dancing around the tree to which they had been tied. Spot was straining at his leash, slavering with worry; my baby sister Florence was weeping and Lillian had fallen into the creek.

Despite the fact that I rode back of, and to the side of the surrey, and loped ahead to open the gates, I could know from the slope of my father's shoulders, and from mother's aggressively forward thrust head and bosom, that she was giving him Gallic hell in machine-gun-fired English solecisms from her seat in the back.

I had only been allowed to sit with my father as he called up the scattered turkeys, but I had that day actually carried the young gobbler back to the disorganized family over my shoulder.

For me there was only the November sky; the whispering, brown prairie and euphoria. My sisters' unhappiness and mother's distress were of another world completely.

There are many memory slides from "Aunt Sue's": the neat orchard; the thoroughbreds; the peacocks; the cellar; the benign Samaritans; aunt Sue's English pug with his corkscrew tail, who hated children; the parlour with the fascinating iron turtle; and aunt Sue sitting at the piano with concave back, dewlap quivering, playing and singing "The Letter Edged in Black."[43]

Beaver Creek had often been our objective at times other than the Thanksgiving season and "Aunt Sue's." There had been the three homesteads along Beaver Creek, which my father and Uncle Ed had improved, so that when allotment should arrive, they would be permitted to file on them, as their first choices.

The ranch headquarters had been established on my father's land;— a dugout in the banks of the creek, and later a log cabin. Joining my father's land downstream was "Aunt Sue's," and south of these holdings was the land of Uncle Ed, but he and aunt Sallie were dead; the ranch was owned by their only daughter, my cousin Annie.

She was married to a Joseph F. Cooper and had three sons.

I don't remember my first visit to Cooper's, but all my memories are pleasant ones; of horses and fishing and swimming, the very earliest one having to do with riding behind my cousin Annie, with my arms tight around her waist as her cowhorse loped over the prairie. She was an excellent horsewoman, and wore the same kind of divided skirt which Josephine wore, a sort of glorified culottes.

She had the laughing eyes of her brothers, Allan, Walter and Owen, and the same inherent, imperturbable sense of honor and justice and courage. She was a lovely person, and she certainly has a memorial in my pleasant memories of her kindness and her readiness to pull me up behind her saddle and lope over the prairie to a little farmstead in the Kaw Reservation, where we stopped to talk with a young woman who wore a divided skirt and cowboy boots, and tapped her leg with a quirt as she talked.

The Coopers took me and their eldest son to the country dances in a wagon, and the memory of the fiddles and the "do-see-do" called raucously, and the excited horses whinnying to each other, is deep. So is the memory of becoming very tired and crawling into the wagon and going to sleep in the hay, and being awakened at the Cooper ranch.

The vivid memory of the whinnying of the horses during the all-day picnics at Kaw City, became for me later the very symbol for pleasant excitement.

Annie's brother Walter, lived south of the Coopers. He became my hero when he played end on the Carlisle football team, and had sent me the ball they had used when they came all the way across the Continent to beat Stanford. When visiting on Beaver Creek without my family, I sometimes divided my time between Annie and Walter's ranches.

One third of July we came back to Walter's ranch from Kaw City with a great variety of fireworks, and he aided his son Norman and me in celebrating the glorious "Fourth."

During the early hours of the 5th of July the house burned. We had obviously thrown some of the firecrackers from the porch.

As I stumbled down the stairs choking on smoke, I passed a closet on the landing, and as I passed I quickly encircled some clothing with my arms, and stumbled on down into the yard.

I had saved the "har'd gurl's" finery; her sole property, it later turned out, and this I seem to remember were the only things saved; this armful of clothing, except of course the clothes the family wore, or were able to grab as they ran out.

The poor girl wept uncontrollably with gratitude, and I was suffused with importance.

Eventually, the story of the burning grew dramatically, and the event grew and grew with each telling, until finally, people were saying that the "Mathews boy jumped outta the upstairs winda with that gurl's clothes, while the rest of 'em were gittin' out with what they had on their backs."

Loving words and exactitude, and being often annoyed by dramatic exaggerations, I have never been able to understand why I didn't make some protest. However, the fact that I actually came stupidly down the stairs rubbing my eyes, and subconsciously encircling the hanging clothes with my arms as I passed, grew dim in my memory, and finally, I wasn't quite sure that that was the way of it after all.

~

Mrs. Tucker believed that every pupil should participate in games. We played shinny and baseball in season, but the game in which everyone took part was a soccer-like game, in which we used neither our hands nor our heads; we called it association football.

We were divided into two teams, the captains of each side being elected by the school body, and then the captains alternately chose their players. The captains naturally were from the eighth and ninth graders—the "big boys"—and the last players they chose were the first graders; the very last to be chosen of course were the dainty little girl first graders.

These latter were a nuisance; always being run over, or weeping on the side lines, or with tear-stained faces going toward the school house to "tell Mrs. Tucker" on some one.

It was a harmless and sometimes exciting game. The ball as round as a basketball and was placed in the middle of the field, and kicked off, and the side to whom it was kicked had to kick it back and try to get it over the opponent's goal line.

Tom Mitscher and I were usually the first of the smaller boys to be chosen, and because of this we were seldom on the same side. After the big boys and girls had been named, the captains turned to us.

We thought well of ourselves, that we were the first of the smaller boys to be chosen. I, as I have written, was not in the least competitive, but as I have mentioned Tom was highly competitive and silent and tough, and I found myself not so much as a member of one half of Tucker's playing against the other half, but as a player who was concentrating on defeating a friend and neighbor.

But while I took part in all the school activities, and liked them, I was a loner. I spent hours by myself. Either in the barn or with the horses and the chickens in the lot; or watching squirrels and birds in the post-oaks and blackjacks back of our property and the agency reserve.

Tom was with me quite often, but he carried a slingshot in his hip pocket and flipped small, rounded stones and slugs from the black-smith shop at everything that moved. I carried one as well, but I shot only at bluejays, sparrows, squirrels and stray semi-wild cats.

We went together to pick up the small, irregular bits of metal that had been trimmed from the horseshoes as they were being shaped by the blacksmith, and had fallen to the native oak floor.

The blacksmith was fascinating. He was tall and swarthy, and there was at once the impression that the smoke from his fire and from the horse's hooves as he held the red hot shoes against them, had stained him so that he could be in color harmony with the interior of his shop.

He had the friendliness and the calm assurance of a happy man; a man who had no doubts about his skill.

He chewed tobacco but seemed never to spit, and somehow there was skill in the manner in which he held it in his cheek as he worked his bellows and smiled knowingly at some loafer, or the man who had brought the horses he was shoeing. His smile would indicate that the man was telling the truth, and that any fair-minded man couldn't possibly disbelieve him.

He would try the shoe on the hoof, then go back to his bellows, re-heat the shoe, then pound it on the anvil, still listening above the "ting-ting-ting-clank" of the hammer, to the visitor's story of self-appreciation or about troubles that had come to him through the machinations of some "stinker," but never saying a word; only wear-ing the smile of complete understanding, but really thinking of the beauty of his shaping shoe.

When he had finished with the shoeing, he watched with the pride of the artist, the horses pounding the oaken flooring of the shop with their new shoes; quivering at the flanks a little, rump-crowding, nervous and anxious to get out of the shop onto the comprehending soil.

Tom and I came away from the blacksmith's shop, weighted with slugs, and with renewed enthusiasm.

But when Tom was with me there were no panthers lying on large, grey horizontal limbs watching me, and no bears behind the great sandstone boulders in the woods back of the agency. If there was a mizzle, or a sudden shower, he wouldn't have understood that from a sheltered spot under an overhang, that I, when alone, could imagine myself a contented wolf.

When we played in the hayloft pulling the bales about, he wanted to build a fort, and I wanted to make dens with long, winding entrances: the dens of animals.

Both our barn and the agency barn were filled with wonderful odors: the acrid odor of the stalls, the comforting odor from the stanchions where the cows were milked, the warm, leathery odor from the saddles and the harness on hot days, and the poetic odor of the hay that had imprisoned the odors of the July meadows.

My memories are sharp of hours spent dreaming in our hayloft, alone and unmolested, perhaps being startled into reality by the dramatic boasting of an excitable brown leghorn hen, rushing forth from a crevice between bales; a neurotic who had "stolen her nest out."

One day when I had just finished a den at the end of a long tunnel which reached to the west end of the barn, I heard Tom coming up the ladder to the loft. He never went anywhere silently.

I was perhaps a panther that day and I could look out the cobwebby little window at the end of the barn onto my domain. I hated the interruption.

Tom called: "Hey, where are you? You're up here—I know it by golly."

I could hear him examining the bales. I had fortunately pulled a bale to cover the entrance to my tunnel; not as contemplative panther might do, but as a hibernating bear might have done.

He called out again: "Hey, come on out. You know what? Your filly's all tangled up in some bailin' wa'r—you better come help me get 'er out."

I could see my colt from my little window, lying in the sun with Molly standing over her, dozing.

He became restive, and I could hear his footsteps on the pine flooring of the loft. He whistled, then as he climbed down the ladder, he sang, "ta-rah-rah-rah—BOOM-dee-Ā—ta-rah-rah-rah-BOOM-dee-Ā," and then his song died in the distance.

By the time my horse Bally was three years old and ready for riding, Tom had Ingie, a smoky brown, and Button, an indecisive bay. I believe Ingie really belonged to Marc before he went to the Naval Academy. So Tom had a choice of mounts just as I had. There was Maud's colt, Brownie.

But when I became a cavalier, I became a greater loner than ever, and there was a wider gap between our interests than there had been as pedestrians.

Although we rode together, and raced down the road between our houses, and showed off before Mary Ella Gibson and Tom's cousin Rose Shear, Tom was never interested in objectiveless knight errantry.

I much preferred to ride off onto the prairie or up the creek valleys, filled with a tingly appreciation of being alive in a great, man-empty world, and failed to find much fun in riding out to the Village, and there attracting the attention of the vicious Indian dogs so that they would rush out with raised hackles and bared fangs to attack our horse's heels. Bally would dance among them with ears laid back, but Ingie would lash out with his hind feet and send a dog rolling in the dust, or send one or more back to their master's lodges limping and howling. Tom would be filled with delight, and ride on seeking more dogs to bait.

But we came in peace more often; to race our horses against those of the Osage boys, or swim with them, or play "rescue."

In the game of "rescue" a boy on horse raced at one standing, and as he came up to him would stretch out a hand to him, the one being rescued grabbing the offered hand and the saddle cantle to pull himself up behind the horseman.

There was a great difference in playing with the boys of the Thorny-

Valley Village, and the Anglo-Americans. When you played with the Osage boys, there was no stridency, no fist fighting (incidentally, Tom never taunted the Osage boys; as a matter of fact I think he was slightly afraid of them), no quarreling. When one lost a horse race, there was no accusation of unfairness, and no excuses. This was one of Tom's traits as well; he never made excuses for his defeats.

Also the games of the Osage boys were played in silence; like greyhounds at play.

The boys of the Thorny-Valley Village were inherently dignified and courteous and extremely cruel. They bluffed by scowling, despising you if the bluff succeeded, and this was a development away from the animal world, since bears and skunks and snakes and coyotes, carry on if their bluff succeeds, and make no attack. Perhaps this harassment of the weak, the cowardly and/or unfit had some biological reason for being in the tribal struggles of primitive men. Perhaps cowards and weaklings and the inept in general jeopardized the tribe in its struggle with the earth and other tribes, as such members do in flocks and herds and packs among the other animals. Perhaps the racial urge had not yet been destroyed by Europeanization, or perhaps it might be better to write, had not yet been displaced by a more refined European urge.

The Osage boys harassed misfits and the inept ones by teasing them, laughing at them, badgering them, making finger signs of contempt: forming with their fingers a vulva.

There was little physical contact; only a tentative shove, but that rarely.

When one had satisfied oneself with the reasoning that the Osages were only just emerging from the Neolithic stage, one was faced with the same urge in the Anglo-Americans whose racial urge was possibly born in primordial survival necessity but that should have vanished after four centuries.[44] One wonders about a kindred cruelty in English Public Schools, toward the extremely sensitive boys and those who can't play games, where the taunting of the inept ones is just as effective even though more sophisticated.

I remember quite distinctly an incident wherein I was a member of a gang that chased the little McClure boy home. I was just a member of the gang and went along, without ever knowing why we chased him home.

But soon I was riding away from Tom, my playmate, and the Osage boys of the Village; riding away from Tucker's, as soon as school was over for the day or for the vacations, and away from my younger sisters, who as little females, had begun to assume the responsibility of "telling papa," when I failed to feed the chickens, gather the eggs, fill the wood box in the kitchen, when Tom and I fought, and when I "said a bad word."

My sisters were holy and righteous and adoring, my baby sister Florence, a flattering tag-tail, but a knight had to go a-questing. I could be in the great spaces, as untouched by man as they had ever been, within ten minutes after leaving the agency.

But Nemesis took a hand here; she was jealous of my chivalric freedom. As if the formal feeding of me with the wisdom of the ages at Tucker's were not enough, my parents decided that I should take violin lessons. "Miss Agnes" had given Josephine "piana," and Marie had had piana lessons; Lillian had a beautiful voice and had also been given "piana," and Florence later took up the harp. So the princeling might as well learn to play the violin.

This meant that once a week, instead of riding out onto the spacious wind-singing prairies, I had to mount Bally, tuck my encased violin under my arm and ride the mile to Judge Clay's house, where Miss Florence Clay tried to teach me.

"Miss Florence," was willowy, wasp-waisted, tall, dark-eyed, and disturbingly gracious. She wore her black hair (frost-touched with grey strands) parted in the center, and twisted into a bun at the back.

The collar to her ruffled waist was high and tight, and was of net with stays and she wore a watch pinned to her waist (left side) supported by a golden Fleur de Lys.

Her hands were white and blue-veined, and her fingers as they moved over the violin's strings were like the legs of an albino tarantula making his way laboriously over the lawn grass.

One felt that blushes lay ready just under the surface of her face, but could never quite come to the surface to disturb the marble whiteness of her skin. The blush, one felt, no matter of what nature its source, could not possibly surface, and therefore could not manifest itself as a blush but remain only a disturbance.

And though she was Victorian Age proper, she was not the least bit cold and austere, and was always patient, constantly assuring me that I was doing "splendidly." I was always sorry that I had not washed my grimy hands when she guided them to bow and strings with her always very immaculate white ones.

After the lesson, she held the door open with one hand and held my cap in the other, and looking out to where Bally had been tied to the hitching rail, she never failed to have nice things to say about my "lovely pony." I was very proud of Bally, and liked to hear nice things about her, but I experienced a slight annoyance, when someone called her a "pony."

When the summer came, my weekly lopes to "Miss Florence's" became strictures on my freedom: almost tragic strictures. I was always reminded when it was time to go to my lesson, either by my mother or by one of my bossy sisters: either Lillian or Josephine, and when either one of them or both of them suggested that it was time for my lesson, I knew there was no escape from their vigilance. So, I saddled Bally, if she were not already saddled, tucked my violin under my arm and loped away up the dusty road running along the tall picket fence along the east boundary of the Osage Indian School campus, to Judge Clay's house on the point of hill overlooking the agency village.

Then one summer's day the prairies were calling to all three of us; Spot went with Bally and me wherever we went except to the Thorny-Valley Village. He had been slashed and lamed there once by a vicious pack of Indian dogs, and thereafter I made him stay at home when I went to play with the Osage boys. At the Clay home, he usually curled up under a wisteria and dozed as he waited for me to reappear.

When we got halfway to the Clay house on this day, a growth of coral berry (we called this delight of Cherokee basket makers, buck brush) gave me an idea, and I dismounted and hid my violin.

The agency was full of kerosene eyes, when the three of us arrived back at nightfall. The family were accustomed to my coming home late and there was nothing said. I had, of course picked up my violin. Appearances were quite normal.

I hid my violin and loped off to wander over the prairie, several times that summer, but "Miss Florence" seemed not to have noticed. Her patience and graciousness however awakened my conscience, and kept it aware for several days, but when the prairie called again, there was not the slightest protest from it.

One day, my father said, "Well, son, rekon, you'd better sell your violin."

I said nothing; I had no desire to go into the unpleasant business. I am sure that "Miss Florence" didn't report my faithlessness; she possibly refused the full amount of the fee, and then there were questions and troubled reluctance on her part to answer them.

~

[BOY, HORSE, AND DOG]

Since I have already introduced my dog, Spot, he is easily identifiable as the third member of the trio in this story of Boy, Horse, and Dog.

My father had a good prairie chicken dog in his German short-haired pointer, Gay, and a good quail dog in Spanish pointer Jack, but W. T. Leahy, a prominent mixed-blood member of the tribe, gave him a puppy, and we drove out to the Soldier Creek Ranch to pick him up.

He was emaciated, wobbly, and apologetic, and he came not to my father but to me and there again was empathy; this time between boy and dog, just as there had been between boy and colt.

When we arrived home with him, I gave him a bath and sprinkled flea powder on him, then took him out to the lot to meet Bally. I held him up to her so that she could smell him; they touched noses and he wagged his tail extravagantly. I put him down and Bally nosed him, and he fell over on his back with legs up, trying to show this great beast that he meant her no harm and was defenseless.

She sniffed at his soft belly, and Horse and Dog had met, and became friends for life.

Boy and dogs: A young Mathews with shotgun and hunting dogs (Courtesy of the Osage Tribal Museum, Pawhuska, Oklahoma)

He was called Spot by the people of the Soldier Creek Ranch, and when I asked my father, since he was a Llewellyn Setter, to give me a Welch name for him, he said, he'd think about it. Soon, Spot knew his name and it was too late for a fancy Welch one.

He was terra cotta and white, and grew up large, lanky and eager.

The first summer of my wanderings over the prairie and blackjack ridges, my father had suggested that during August, if we flushed quail or prairie chickens, that they would be the young ones still with their parents, but like all "young smart aleks," they wouldn't pay much attention to their parents' warnings, and would sit and stare like idiots. "Give your dog a noseful of 'em," he suggested, "but don't let him flush—keep him on stand if you have to hold him."

Spot and I worked hard at it that summer, the "smart-aleks" cooperating beautifully. Bally, with reins dragging would stand and watch us, slightly intrigued. One time I had Spot by the collar and we were already approaching some young prairie chickens, we had watched down. I was holding him by the collar and leading him, talking softly, and praising him, and was almost ready for the stand, when Bally came trotting to us, as if she might say, "What the hell you two up to without me?"

The young chickens had nerve failure and flushed, Bally snorted, and Spot broke and seemed intent on chasing them all the way into "The States."

But Spot became a good bird dog simply because when he finally understood what I wanted him to do, it was that which he wanted to do enthusiastically. By the time the summer was past, he was holding beautifully, and by the time cool weather arrived, he was retrieving.

The breaking of Bally to the saddle was simple; she even seemed to expect being saddled and ridden. From the time she was a few months old both Q. and my father, told me to put a little weight on her back every day, and then finally, I could lift my feet from the ground and hang over her back like a sack. If she started to run, I was to slide off before she might begin to buck.

My father warned: "Never allow a hoss to buck, son; never break a hoss's spirit. A hoss that has never been allowed to buck, always holds that final protest in reserve, and this gives him confidence; like a man who's got a little backlog in a safety deposit box. (My father, among other things was a village banker.) Nine times outta ten a hoss doesn't want to buck, but some of these damn-fool show-offs make 'em. Take your filly now; if you gradually make a saddle hoss of her, she'll always have the spirit of a thoroughbred. You take a hoss that's been allowed to buck, and then broken, he loses his spirit, and he's got nothing left but to be stubborn and sometimes mean."

Bally was never allowed to buck, and never had to. She had become halter broken as a colt, and I had saddled her perhaps three times a week and had led her around the lot, talking to her, petting her when she became nervous.

When the three years were passed, my father had Buck ride her for several days with a hackamore. Six months had passed before she had a limber bit in her mouth.

As I have mentioned, she was strikingly beautiful; she was sorrel with flowing flaxen mane and tail, and always held her short, box-nosed head high with ears forward, eternally expectant of excitement, whether we were in the agency or on the prairie. It was as if she might say, "How wonderful—I don't want to miss anything; horses don't live very long."

Of course there were other wonderful horses in history, I admit reluctantly, and if not as beautiful as Bally, certainly as faithful and admirable, and as loved, and fortunately more poetically named.

There was Bucephalus, who helped Alexander conquer the then known world. There was Morzillo who carried Cortez through the jungles and swamps and over mountains, finally becoming a god to the Iten-Itza Indians of Yucatan. There were the horses of Launcelot and Sir Galahad, whose names, I believe, I had never learned, along with King Arthur's palfrey, and there was poor old Rozinante who obediently and dispiritedly galloped into windmills to his masters' spurrings. And of course there was the horse who became a Roman priest and Consul, Caligula's Incitatus, who carried mad Caligula into Gaul on a smokescreen campaign.[45]

They all had purpose: Alexander must conquer the world on Bucephalus, and Cortez must conquer the jungles of Mexico and Honduras, and Sir Launcelot and Sir Galahad must fight for Right, and protect maidens and find the Holy Grail, and Don Quixote the most famous of crackpots must revive Chivalry.

Bally and Spot and I had no purpose, but we quested without purpose and were inspired only by *joie de vivre*.

For perhaps eight years, boy and horse and dog, quested over the Osage prairies and the blackjack hills, and we must have in that time covered thousands of the approximately million and a half acres of them. We quested in vast emptiness, where there were wind-songs, mauve shadows racing their mother clouds; climbing the prairie hills and sliding into canyons. We quested over the prairie swells that were like swells of the sea, where coyotes stood against the skyline and watched us, having no fear, and we were watched by long horned cattle with their harlequin color patterns, who would lose their nerve to disappear over the ridges.

In the autumn a white tail buck would stand and watch us with his great swollen neck of rut quite noticeable. He would stand and watch us, then turn and with mighty jumps disappear waving his tail flag as a signal to all white tails.

One day one stood in the game trail we were following, and as we drew near, stamped the earth in challenge. Our indifferent approach was an accepted challenge in his world, but he lost his courage, turned, waved his white flag and was lost among the black boles of the blackjacks.

Bally was ever aware of deer, cattle, rattlesnakes, rabbits, wheeling vultures, long before Spot or I were aware of them. There wasn't anything on the prairie she failed to notice, and in the case of a band of deer immobile in the creek bottoms, she seemed to be able to penetrate protective coloration as well.

Spot got most of his messages through his nose, and I had only to watch Bally's ears, the direction of her interested gaze, or watch Spot deciphering scent messages.

But I was keen-sighted as well, and one can see things from the saddle that one might miss afoot.

To see another horseman on the prairie became exciting and almost dramatic, and no matter whether he was a Stonebreaker cowboy or a bearded creek bottom settler, he would ride toward us, pull up, study Bally and examine the new Frazier saddle with keen interest. A line-rider was always ready to dismount and talk, even with a boy.

We would soon be squatting on our heels talking "man talk," and on such occasions, I always felt grown-up, and important, since the very fact that the cowboy had dismounted elevated me to his level of adult importance, and I was very careful to make the right comments about horses, cattle, grass and weather. The cowboy's horse being a working horse and being grain fed to supplement the grazing, would stand on three legs, resting the fourth, lower his head, and with lower lip drooping stupidly, go to sleep; these few minutes of rest were more valuable to him than grazing.

On the other hand, Bally was insatiable, since she had little time for grazing; only when I was lying on my back on a prairie hill, dreaming. And, when we had a rare meeting with a lone cowboy, she would graze with her reins dragging as we talked.

In the summer, we came to tranquil holes of water in the creeks, and I would pull the saddle off, then pull off my clothes and jump onto her back, and ride her into the water. Sometimes she would be compelled to swim, and at such times I would slide off her rump and catch her by the tail as she swam for the opposite bank.

After doing this several times, I allowed her to nibble the lush grass at the water's edge, while Spot and I played games, swimming about. He would become very excited and bark from the sheer joy of it.

He always grew tired of the game first, and he would pretend that there was something strange and interesting up the creek which needed his attention. He would climb out of the water, shake himself vigorously and search for scent messages. If he especially liked the place, he would immediately claim it. He would lift his leg against a sycamore, or against a willow, and perhaps finally against a hackberry, then contented, flop down with a happy groan.

Bally busy with the succulent grass of the water's edge, Spot dog-napping, I would stand in the cool water up to my middle watching a spotted sandpiper teetering up and down like a toy on a coil spring. I mused on the frogs; those that seemed to assume the role of scout. When we had first arrived at such holes of water the frogs would splash off their hunting stations, logs and jutting rocks, etc, then one would stick his nose above the water, watch me with great bulging eyes, then gradually climb out onto his log again, as if he would await a propitious moment for giving the all clear signal if there were such signals among the frogs; there must have been such signals, since they were used by many other species. Insects had color-flash signals, and voice signals and semaphore, and birds had color-flash and voice and that mystical unanimity of movement which I would later learn to name.

But the scout frog remained silent, and stared at me opaquely, and I stared back at him. We were like two animals of the perhaps Devonian world, only I, Homo sapiens would not have yet made my appearance.[46]

We must have puzzled the scout. He might have wondered what kind of animals we could be. Animals usually came to drink, then left, and there might be no need for the frog people to leave their logs, etc. But the three of us, each a different species, must have appeared insane to the scout frog.

When I moved to swim about or wade out to the bank the scout would plop back into the safety of the water.

All during the hot afternoons the cicadas sang in the trees. If we were in late July or in August, the "sophomore" great horned owls would call during the mid-afternoon; call listlessly as if they were bored, and it seemed that there was always a yellow-billed cuckoo calling from the tops of the wind-swayed elms, warning the world about something.

The Amer-European settlers said he called for rain, and they named him "rain crow."

As I grew older I stayed away longer, and was by the summer before I entered High School, well equipped for errantry. I had a new saddle from Frazier's of Pueblo, Colorado, and real military saddle pockets, and a scabbard for my 22 cal. rifle. Mother had given me a cast-off frying pan, which I tied to my long saddle strings, and had allowed me to take her binocular case for birds' eggs. The binocular case was perfect for this purpose, since it could be swung from my shoulder when I climbed trees. Being filled with cotton, the eggs would be quite safe even before they were blown, and in the original state.

I carried a side of bacon, which I got from the smoke house, or got one from the village butcher, Pete Spurling, who was an employee of the Osage Mercantile Company. While the bacon of course was quite fat and oozed grease on hot days, it was certainly edible, but I used it primarily for grease for cooking prairie chickens, squirrels or fish.

I stuffed the bacon into one of the saddle pockets, along with an extra pair of well-wrapped boot socks (they were sometimes smeared with grease, despite this precaution) and into the other went my extra shirt, and either *Kindred Of The Wild*, by Chas. G.D. Roberts or *Wild Animals I Have Known* by Ernest Thompson Seton, or sometimes both. I had, at that time, I remember, read each one of them twice.[47]

During the weekends and holidays I left the Agency at sun up and on school days after 4 p.m., but saddled Bally every day. Spot, as dogs often do, seemed to know the hour each day in the week, and became filled with expectation, impatiently watching me saddle Bally.

We stayed all day on the prairie during the weekend returning often after the lights had been lighted in the Agency.

During these days I lay on my back for hours on the prairie watching the red-tailed hawk, and the vultures sailing in wide [circles] trying to determine just what I was. Occasionally a golden eagle flew over the three of us, his head turned down to study us in detail.

I admired the red-tailed hawk above all the winged investigators, for reasons I have long ago forgotten. In his flight, there was something that [symbolized] freedom from Earth's restrictions. I admired him profoundly, and he inspired me to dream so poignantly that one day when I was quite young, [I started] to weep silently. I seemed, as young as I was to appreciate the urge of earth-bound man to give wings to angels, and I wondered why I had not accepted my sister Josephine's suggestion that I call my beautiful colt Pegasus.

But when not lying on my back on the whispering prairie dreaming of flying like the red-tailed hawk, I was learning much from birds and animals, which I could not identify by a name.

One day when climbing a tree to a mourning dove nest to get an egg for my collection (I took only one egg from each nest), the brooding dove flew off the nest, then free of the limbs and leaves, suddenly started to the ground, and lay on her side with a wing raised and fluttering.

I slid down the tree and approached her, but when I came near, she flapped away, and again stopped and lying on her side raised a wing and fluttered it.

She did this three or four times when I followed her, but when I came close she fluttered on. At some distance from the nest tree, she arose and flew off on sound wings.

Not until much later when I was an undergraduate at Oxford University in England did I learn this action was called "Distraction Display" to lure a possible enemy away from [the] nest of eggs or brood.

One spring morning we came too close to a nesting killdeer on the prairie and the brooding female left the nest in the tall grass, and after running a short distance, fell over on her side and lifted a wing moving it helplessly. Spot started for her and I called him back, and he came back to walk beside Bally, watching the fluttering bird with barely suppressed eagerness. I urged Bally to follow the killdeer as she alternately flew for a short distance, then fell fluttering as if wounded. Then after leading us off for perhaps a hundred yards span, she flew off across the prairie.

Another morning we came to a prairie ravine and Spot was interested in some scent along the exposed limestone bordering the ravine. Soon a female coyote appeared and she and Spot stared at each other. Spot made no move toward her, having no interest in coyotes. She turned as if to leave the scene, then started limping and looking back at Spot. When he didn't follow as she expected him to, she fell to the ground whimpering as if in severe pain.

When I guided Bally toward her, she struggled up, whimpering and limping, and after going away for about 20 yards, fell again and whimpered. As Bally approached she got [up] again and again limped and whimpered, even more piteously.

When about a hundred yards from her den, she arose and ran off looking back over shoulder.

On Saturday nights we slept on a blackjack ridge. Bally was free to graze, staying close without being tied to a tree. She was free from saddle and bridle, but never strayed off.

From my bedding roll, I heard the voices of birds; the owls and occasionally night mockingbirds.

However, the most compelling voice was that of the chuck-will's widow and since he flew in a wide circle about the spot where I slept, I thought that he was objecting to our presence, but some years later I learned that he was "Beating Bounds," warning other chuck-will's widows that he was marking the boundaries of the territory he was claiming.

He began his song, "chuck-will's-widow," from a tree to the north, then [would] fly to a tree to the west then to a tree to the south, to a tree to the east and finally back to the same tree in the north, singing constantly, as he flew the circle.

Again, it was much later when I was in England that I found out about "Beating Bounds" and the origin, which will come in a future vignette.

Every male bird marks the boundaries of his territory through warning others not to trespass as do animals and insects in their own way. Bears scratching pine tree bark as a bluff to other bears, and cougars and coyotes urinate at certain spots of the territory they have claimed, which has the form of a circle wide or narrow.[48]

At night I would unsaddle Bally, and turn her loose. She always stayed close to Spot and me, but I was warned by father and Q. The latter said: "You'd better take a halter and rope with yu, 'er hobble 'er, whenever she's come in heat, 'er by jucks, you'll wake up some mornin' afoot, a hunnert miles from nowhur."

However, the urges and emotions that came with coming in heat, never seemed to overwhelm her loyalty. She ran away from Spot and me only once, but that had to do with a tornado, and once through being in heat saved me from walking miles over the prairie, and averted a tragedy, which if it had occurred, might have changed my whole philosophy of life.

With the sleazy dramatics of men free but unaccustomed, after centuries of suppression by patricians, hierarchies and royalty in general, the writers in the journals of the border towns of Kansas and Missouri, had all train robbers, wanton murderers, and "bad men" in general taking refuge in the Osage Hills, and this in some strange way seemed to reflect importance on the area as well as on the mixed-bloods and the traders; restoring to them as free men importance which their ancestors had never experienced under the Patricians of England, Hierarchies and Emperors of Europe.

The journals dramatized both the train robbery and the escape to the Osage Hills, allowing factual details to take care of themselves. "It is believed that the bandit has escaped to the Osage Hills," they would inform their thrilled and mildly glorified readers.

Some of them did come to the Osage Hills. These men were not psychopaths, but quite normal and ignorant, superstitious, unimaginative, humanly cruel, and ferociously vindictive; they were neither psychopathic nor brutish, but just plain "man'ish."

One windy March day on the prairie I met one of these men. His horse's long winter hair was stiff in spots with dried sweat, and the cinch was loose, even though it had been pulled up to the last hole on the latigo. He had a 30-30 cal. Winchester of the 1894 model, and a Colt in his belt.

I couldn't identify him with banditry, even though he had a matted growth of beard and hair that curled over his neck like the tail feathers of a drake.

He studied Bally carefully, but there was nothing disturbing in this, since people were more interested in horses in this period than in their riders.

"Yore mare's a-horsin', h'aint she?"

"Yes, I think she is." She had whinnied when she saw the man's horse. She had whinnied several times, and this had attracted the man's attention. He had stopped and studied us, then had come toward us, and when he rode up to us there was no salutation. He had rested his weight on one stirrup, and with one hand on the horn and one on the cantle, had begun his close examination.

He sat back in the saddle, pulled his reins up a little, then said: "Whin I first seen yu, I figgered on a-tradin' horses with yu, but a horsin' mare is a plumb nuisance. Hit's like a-tellin' a goddam Deputy whur yore at." He rode off.

On this windy March day, I had no intention of staying out all night, so I rode home with my mind chiefly occupied with my anticipations; my thoughts in those days were a series of anticipations so warm and all-absorbing that they drowned fears and duties and obligations, alike.

It was late when we came off the ridge that was higher than the ridge finger on which we lived. Just past twilight, there were the red eyes of the kerosene lamps of the agency below us under the post-oaks. Off the high ridge and on the home ridge, Spot struck a wolf-trot and Bally changed to her crab-like sidewise dance, rattling the bits and slobbering. This was what Q. called "barn hungry."

In the barn, as I pulled Bally's saddle, the significance of my meeting with the man on the prairie came to me, and in my shock, I actually sweated, according to my little sweat- and blood-stained pocket diary. I petted Bally extravagantly and gave her an extra measure of bran, and stood for some time in the semi-darkness of the barn before going into the house. I knew I must be completely composed before facing my parents.

I didn't intend to tell them about the meeting, but I was afraid of my traitorous face. However, they failed to notice.

I have never told anyone about this meeting with the train robber; when he was shot later by a posse, still the potential tragedy of losing my horse very easily suppressed the reflected glory I would certainly have enjoyed, through the telling of the incident. And also my silence was self-protective as it should have been; had I told of my experience, my parents would have put an end to my knight errantry.

My fear, as I remember it was in retrospect; fear of the potential tragedy, not of future possibilities. I carried on with my wanderings blithely.[49]

I would throw my "soogin" (blankets) down wherever twilight overtook us that summer. My blankets were few, since I had to tie them back of the cantle, and soft earth was a boon, and found mostly in the yielding sand of the creek and river bottoms, where the sand adjusted to the body.

On quiet summer nights there would be the great horned owls, and an occasional barred owl, the mewing of raccoons, and rarely on nights of low barometric pressure the song of a lone coyote, or close by, the high-pitched staccato chorus of the "sophomore" coyotes disturbed by the camp fire.

Spot paid no attention to them.

There was also the grassroots chorus of insects, and sometimes the splash of a foraging carp or catfish along the water's edge. One night, I heard a lobo wolf, and it reminded me of the pre-dawn prayer-chant of the Osages, and thrilled me in the same manner.

During the nights Spot would bark at anything that moved, but I couldn't see or hear anything on awakening; only the nose-flutterings of Bally as she grazed.

It was that summer, according to my little black diary, that I was struck forcibly by man's pretensions.

The Osages made an elaborate ceremony of preparing their leaders and men with war honors for entrance into Spiritland. They dressed them in their finest clothing and valuable ornaments, painted their faces for recognition there, and carried them to a high hill, where their flexed bodies were placed facing west, then piled stones about them until they had built a cairn of sandstone, then they choked the man's best horse and allowed him to fall onto the skirts of the cairn, where he would be ready for his master's ride to Spiritland.

These cairns were sometimes robbed by ghoulish barbarians, searching for saleable artifacts, and my father warned me about even going near such cairns, but one day as we traveled along the flank of a sandstone ridge, Spot suddenly disappeared, and I could later hear him barking on top at the point of the ridge, and I as usual in such cases rode toward the barking which indicated "treed."

When we came in sight of him, I found him barking at an Osage cairn; trotting around it slavering and barking. I circled and approached downwind, and even so Bally snorted and tried to turn back, so I dismounted and walked the rest of the way to the cairn.

I could see through an interstice in the piled stones, that the gorgeously bedecked figure had slumped from his flexed rigidity, and collapsed forlornly when his spirit failed to make it to Spiritland, I wanted to believe.

Spot had stopped barking when I arrived, and was awaiting for me to understand the drama he had come upon. I knew there was something abnormal here, since we had seen several cairns during the year, and neither of us had been the least interested in them.

Even standing, peering from upwind, it was unpleasant there, but I began to make a larger opening; then I was startled, and froze like wild thing; and then my mammalian hackles remembered and tried to stand on the back of my neck accompanied by prickling.

The gorgeous, dejected figure actually moved, and I watched fascinated. Suddenly whipping out from the folds of a trade blanket, was the bare tail of an opossum.

I called to Spot, and Bally was so glad to leave the point of the ridge, that she swung into a lope as soon as I got my foot into the stirrup.[50]

Once when the three of us were traveling over the green, velvety prairie swells, Bally's flaxen mane wind-whipped and the high sound wind was hissing through her tail, we almost met with disaster.

It was June, the month which Osages called Buffalo-Bull-Pawing-Earth Moon because the buffalo bulls, feeling the rut upon them, became agitated, restive, and ill-tempered, roared across the prairie, stopping to paw the earth sending the dust high, and sending up clods of earth over their backs after a rain, like disturbed cowbirds.

They had been gone from the last Reservation long before the Osages arrived in 1872, but their wallows were still visible, and on this day, the mad south wind was raising dust from the wallows like smoke from a vent.

The weak songs of the dickcissels could scarcely be heard, and the meadowlarks squatted and ran low ahead of us, or ran to one side and squatted as we passed, loath to rise into the wind. We saw no prairie chickens since their young were small and almost earthbound by inadequate flight power, and were able only to flutter above the grass blades when they did rise, like flying fish. Their mothers would give the alarm twitter, then freeze and depend upon protective coloration for safety; her brood in cryptic freeze were indistinguishable from bits of stone or last season's seed pod shells. Spot paid no attention to them; either they had little scent during this season, or he wasn't interested in the chicks.

Beautiful cumulous clouds floated over us, their smoky-mauve shadows racing them to the north. Some of them were dark-centered with agitated edges and these soon became cumulonimbus, and eventually appeared to be inwardly disturbed, as well as agitated on the edges; it was as if they were about to boil.

We were in sunlight, then suddenly we were in shadow, then back in the sunlight again.

In this part of the Reservation were the headwaters of Pawnee Creek; the drainage veins and capillaries were as a map viewed from the limestone escarpment where we stood.[51]

To get out of the excited wind, I rode down under the escarpment, and started on down a feeder stream of the creek. Here in the stream bed the wind passed over us.

Just as Spot missed nothing, and knew through his nose the identity of everything that moved or remained immobile upwind, and knew through both nose and eyes the identity of things near, and Bally with her keen eyesight, and her protective alertness that domestic horses seem never to have lost, saw everything that moved and was interested in every strange conformation even in cryptic freezing, they now felt the barometric low.

Spot was not in the least worried, but kept close to us; he seemed to have lost momentarily his interest in things that normally interested him, while Bally on the other hand showed definite signs of restiveness, and scented the still air under the wind stream in the feeder vein, with her sweat. There were two kinds of horse sweat; the usual foamy kind that dripped from the belly on hot days when I had her in a lope across the prairie, and a nervous sweat that produced an odor that was definitely unpleasant.

This day she was nervous and sweated copiously, and moved her head up and down, slobbering her bits.

About halfway down the little stream, twilight murkiness came, and the wind ceased dramatically. The absolute silence and the murkiness disturbed me and filled me with animal fear only; there was no reasoning.

I turned Bally about to have a look at the western horizon and sky. That quadrant was blue-black, and overhead the clouds were boiling, with white fringes.

A little way up the side of the ravine, just under the escarpment, there was a shallow cave, and I rode to it. As a matter of fact there were several of these shallow caves, and some deeper than others, but I had no choice, and had to take the nearest one.

I had just dismounted when a hail stone hit the seat of the saddle, and Spot and I scrambled into the hollow under the limestone ledge. I knew Bally could take care of herself and she promptly did so. Just as the hail began to pound she trotted down into the second growth timber, with reins dragging to one side.

Just as she disappeared into the young, resilient growth in the bottom of the ravine, there was a terrific roar, like a train over a subterranean cave, and limbs torn from the trees passed our refuge; down in the stream bed an elm toppled.

The lightning zigzagged to earth and left a momentary greenish glow that seemed to come out of the prairie.

The twilight effect was only momentary, and soon a watery light displaced it, and with the watery light came air that was like the air one feels in front of an opened refrigerator. Then the sun came out and raindrops clinging to the leaves became diamonds and rubies, and feathery water ran down the little feeder stream.

Spot and I came out of our refuge, and he began to hunt for new scents, as if he thought that during the tantrum of nature extremely interesting and very strange things must have happened.

I slid in the mud of the hillside, as I started down into the ravine to look for Bally, with no worry whatever. She could have been carried away or have had a limb blown through her, or a tree could have crushed her, but my confidence in her instinct for protection was deep, and naïve.

There were no tracks of course; the rain had obliterated them completely.

As I walked downstream I saw grotesquely twisted trees. Some were up-rooted; these were chiefly the sycamores whose root systems had been partially exposed by stream erosion. The elms and the hackberrys were twisted and shattered; the shallow-rooted blackjacks pulling up their sandstone anchors as they fell.

I slipped on the mud of the bottoms and had to climb over fallen trees and limbs. It was late afternoon now and a wood thrush had begun to sing, just as I came in sight of a native sandstone house. As I approached it the trail hounds rushed out from under the porch and came at Spot, and he stopped and became stiff-legged with dignity and waited for them. Their white-tipped tails recurved over their back wagged ever so slightly.

Trail hounds were usually courteous to strangers, and always a bit apologetic, and like greyhounds, they seemed to care little about what happened to their master's property. They had only one joyous duty in life, and that was trail-singing under a starry sky, glorifying their masters. Other times they lay in jerky dreaming, or snapping at flies, or scratching fleas, and when hungry became doleful panhandlers.

They came rushing out to investigate Spot and not me. They circled him as he stood with stiff-legged dignity and raised hackles, his head high with bird-dog pride.

As soon as they had determined his sex, they became disinterested, except to lift their legs against different objects, to assure him that he need have no illusions about whose range he was trespassing.

A dugout door came up, and four bearded men came out, one with a deck of cards in his hand.

There were three young men and one old, grizzled one with a pot belly.

As I approached them, the old, grizzled one said: "Yore mare's in the barn, sonny. We lef' the bars down so's she could git in outta the storm. One'uh the boys yere'll unsaddle 'er and give 'er a good feed." He looked at Spot. "Is that there bird dog eny count?" he asked.

"Yes sir, he's awful good," I exaggerated.

After the younger men had left to go to the barn, to unsaddle and feed Bally and attend to their chores the storm had interrupted, he looked about him. The trees were intact here; apparently there had been no hail here and only straight wind; a tornado's path is narrow. There were still hail stones on the ground upstream.

"We's in the barn when she hit," he said. "That's whur we's at when hit first started, en yore mare comm'uh trottin' up to the corral, and we jist, by golly, had time to let the bars down fer 'er, and skedaddle fer the cellar. They musta bin some weather 'round clost."

I felt my importance. "There was a cyclone up Dry Prong," I said with a slight urge to dramatic coloration. I felt dramatic. This was certainly indicated by the entry in my diary for this day in blurred, penciled script.

The old man's interest enhanced both my sense of importance and of the dramatic. If I hadn't kept my diaries of that time, I should never have suspected these tendencies; they don't now seem to harmonize with the image I remember.

When the old man asked, "Wha'dit do?" I had my chance to be informative to experienced Age.

"Blew down trees," I said. But that didn't seem to satisfy the dramatic possibilities, and I added "raised hell." The situation seemed to call for the phrase with the steel trap bite of the three last letters, "tch," but still there was no way to fit it in. "Raised hell" seemed adequate, but the epithet of the sweating freighters of my earlier years would have implied more.

"Well," he said, "yu'd better stay all night. We'll git some grub together and fix yu a pallet—we ain't got airy woman."

During the meal, one of the younger men said, "What'yu doin' with that thur skillet tied to yore saddle string—must be a-stayin' out an a-campin'."

I was reluctant to admit my knight errantry, my version of knight errantry. It must have had something to do with the impracticality of it, I suppose. I should have liked to imply that I was doing something useful and practical, like riding line or looking for strayed horses.

My "yes" was weak.

The grizzled old man belched exaggeratedly, pushed himself away from the table and walked out onto the porch. I followed him with food for Spot, that one of the younger men had collected from the leftovers.

The sky was clear and there was an autumnal nip in the air; the post-tornadic air that came with the cold front. Just the right conditions for perfect trailing, and the old, grizzled man stood there, stood on the shabby porch and considered it, as he picked his teeth with his pocket knife. He looked at the stars appearing one by one as if by magic; studying them for some propitious message that would resolve his problems. He thoughtfully lowered his eyes from the stars, folded his knife, farted contemplatively, then after a moment turned to the door, and announced: "Hit'll be better fer cats tomorrow night; whur's yore deck, Heck?"[52]

As I lay on my pallet, just going off to sleep, the four men were sitting around the table playing cards. As I grew drowsier, I seemed to hear their voices as through a wall. "Hit me," one would say, then another, "goddam, what a hell of 'uh hand." There was the sound of something heavy being set down on the table after an explosive "hah."

The next morning there was a jug sitting on the table, and its corn-cob stopper was on the floor. The young man called Heck was asleep with his head on his arms, his upper body supported by the table.

I would leave a note since I could hear snoring, but there was no paper or pencil. My little black diary was in a saddle pocket. I slipped away from the house, saddled Bally, and we made our way back up Dry Prong.

Spot was so excited that he danced around Bally, barking, and she would lower her head and snort, pretending annoyance.

I had stopped at the heronry in the tremendous sycamore tree many times, and now we stopped again. The great blue herons were coming in from their foraging to alight on their brush-pile nests.

I had at times attempted to climb to them, since I needed a great blue heron egg for my egg collection, but fortunately I had never succeeded. They with their rapier beaks could have attacked so effectively that I might either have been made to fall from the tree, or had a serious stab in the face, perhaps had an eye put out.

So on this day I only sat Bally and watched them yearningly.

While deer hunting last autumn, I passed the old stone walls of the house; the roof had fallen in, and since that night long ago when I slept there, an acorn had fallen close to the south wall, and last autumn there was a great red oak leaning away from the wall. The ax-split shingles of the barn had fallen but were resisting decay.

There were corrugated-soled boot prints in the moist earth of the trails. There were empty beer cans where some deer hunter had still-hunted, and gum wrappings along the trail, and a cast-away paper cup.

A sort of sacrilege. But not so the deteriorating old vats and brass worms that, according to the cowboys, [are] just visible under the cliffs where they were once in use. The vats and tanks, they say, are crumpled and twisted, and there are ragweeds growing up through the rust holes.

~

The Mitschers had now moved back to Oklahoma City after Oscar A. Mitscher's term had ended, and Frank Frantz, a Captain in Teddy Roosevelt's Rough Riders, became agent.[53]

After Tucker's I had a year at a parochial school under the Sisters of Lorreto.[54] I don't remember having an eighth-grade year, but entered High School and the usual activities, mostly athletic, and this cut deeply into my knight errantry, but I still had the summer months, and now older and with my Chester A. Reed's bird guide and my certificate from the Northwestern School of Taxidermy of Omaha, Nebraska, through correspondence, I began to stay out for weeks instead of days, and rode farther, and lived off the country with the aid of Spot and my rifle.

And there was progressively more purpose in John-Without-Purpose's errantry. He now carried in his saddle pockets not only the side of bacon, with flour, meal, salt and crackers, but the just mentioned field guide for identifying birds, as well as a vial of arsenic and one of alum. These latter were for the preservation of skins, and they were well marked. P.J. Monk of the drug store had pasted the classical skull and crossed bones on the arsenic vial.

Now this new interest: the skinning of birds for mounting. Bally and Spot were never impatient with me when I sat for hours by some stream preparing skins. Bally grazed or dozed standing under a tree, and Spot was glad to be able to doze and dream. Especially was he glad to rest during the hot summer months when his tongue almost touched the ground, and there were gurgles in his throat. He would lie for minutes in the water, or on the cool sand, and when he became tired of this he would nose about the area seeking excitement or amusement, or both.

It was about this time that I was given a commission. Mr. Puryear of the Owen & Puryear Drug store had bought a golden eagle from a mixed-blood cowboy, and they asked me to mount it spread-winged, agreeing to pay me five dollars.

He stood high on the prescription partition and mused on the people who came into the store. He had lost some of his native imperiousness in transition from wild, sentient freedom to mummification.

But that is not all my eagle lost.

Naturally when ritualistic-minded Osages came into the drug store, they stood and admired him, and Mr. Owen of Owen & Puryear, being sharp and perhaps not sure that a great bird perched on his partition looking regally down on customers, inspired them to purchase more drugs or carbonated drinks at the soda fountain, felt he ought at least make the bird "pay for himself." In order to compensate for the five dollars he had paid me to mount the great eagle, he suggested to the admiring Osages that he might sell a few tail feathers. The tail was not really visible anyway.

He must have had a difficult time pulling the feathers from alum-tightened and arsenic-preserved flesh. There is evidence of his struggles in the strange, awry, remaining tail feathers, now visible.

From the great bird's perch now in 1966, he muses on the visitors to the Osage County Historical Society's museum.[55]

Now in the autumn-touched air, when we came back from after-school questing, we often came down the agency village's dusty main street, and Bally would catch a glimpse of her reflection in the new plate glass of the bank, and she would begin lifting her feet high and begin to prance sidewise. She seemed to want to lope all the way up the hill.

Of course she was nervous, not excitable, but certainly an exhibitionist. I don't remember of ever having mounted her when she was standing still; I had to hold the left rein short as I put my foot into the stirrup, and she would inevitably start off in a lope while my right leg was still in the air over her back.

Neither my father nor Q. believed that her plate glass reflection inspired her to prance. Q. said: "She's jist high-strung, like that Steel-dust daddy a'her'n" and my father said, "It's funny, but a good hoss can feel its rider, know almost what he's thinkin'—especially a hoss and a kid that's been brought up together like you two. It's the other boys and people who might be watching you ride into the agency, and your mare can feel the "show off" in you, and your pride and vanity, so she shows off. Her reflection in the plate glass of the bank, wouldn't have anything to do with it."

87

I have told of my flaxen-maned, flaxen-tailed beauty's being excited over her reflection, and her sidewise prancing with mane and tail flowing; her short jumps all the way up the hill to our barn, for so long and so often that now I intend to believe it.

And it is just as easy to believe now, looking back over my shoulder to those days long ago.

After my freshmen year in High School, there were only the summers for errantry. In the autumn from September to Thanksgiving day we had football practice every afternoon after school, and every Saturday played some neighboring High School team.

There was the hiatus between football and basketball, but this hiatus endured only for a few weeks, when the days were the shortest. During this time I hunted quail and prairie chicken and ducks, and rode Bally to the wolfhounds. Strangely enough, filled though she was with the joy of living, she never cared fervently for coyote hunting, and became annoyed if a hunter tried to tie a kill behind my saddle.

From the beginning of my sophomore year in September to April of the next year, Bally and Spot and I had to contain our activities searching for that-which-might-happen.

During the autumn, the hunter's moon, there was scarcely time for quail hunting with my new double-barreled L.C. Smith 12 gauge, which I received as a gift on my sixteenth birthday.

By this time the old Osage Reservation was no longer a "Nation" within a Nation, but a county in the new State of Oklahoma, the forty-sixth. On my thirteenth birthday, the sixteenth of November 1907, the bell of the old Osage Council House rang with such vigor and so dramatically that it became stuck upside-down. This was the very first time it had been rung by the excitable French-Osage mixed-bloods and the euphoric Amer-Europeans, and this proved too much for the old bell that for years had called with dignity to the dignified chieftains to convene in council.

The dreams of the common man had for centuries, through the necessities of the patricians, been contained within himself, and it might seem that the pressure had built up to the point that his dreams like steam escaped through safety valves in the trans-

Mississippi River area of the United States exploding into emotion, came whistling and screaming out the valve when he contemplated the glorious future of the new communities and the new importance of himself. When a railroad was to be built through their community, or even just rumored, the people shot off firearms, had fireworks displays, applauded marching bands, waved flags, made speeches, and had picnics.

Thus, down the dusty ways of the agency village, a band marched, children marched, the bell of the old Council House rang dramatically, until like a terrapin turned over on his back on cement, it couldn't make it back to its feet.

People of the agency stepped out onto their porches and fired their guns into the air. There was the sense of impending glory in the atmosphere, and there were no restrictions on dreams. The agency village now called Pawhuska, would become a great metropolis. St. Louis and Chicago had done it.

Now town lots would be sold in the agency village, at the trading post of the Upland Forest People and at the village of the Big Hills, and town lots would be sold on the high prairie and at the settlement of a chieftain of the Heart Stays People. Now people could come into the old reservation as they willed, and needed no permission from the agent and the Osage Council.[56]

The mixed-bloods walked about, or stood and talked in groups, filled with the impending glory, while the fullbloods danced and feasted as they had always done, and after the feasting they sat under the shade of the oaks and the elms and talked of their war honors and their war movements against the Pawnees, the Cheyennes and the Arapahos, of the last century.

I think my father had a sense of impending glory, as immaterial as a dream, but he said nothing to me about it. We went quail hunting on this day which promised county seat importance for the agency village.

~

Entering High School one entered the thick atmosphere of sex-consciousness and the euphoria that suffused the 'teen-aged youngsters, and generated a false pride, and the self-reproductive potential inspired a sense of superiority, and one ceased having sympathy for the ignorance of one's parents and other elders; the adult world in general as a matter of fact, became tediously commonplace, and one felt a sort of sneering tolerance for their drab stodginess.

Wisdom, of course had suddenly made its appearance with the euphoria inspired by the reproductive potential, a wisdom that appeared mysteriously and employed as its embodied instrument, glorious youth.

The High School students knew quite definitely that a gleam of light had finally appeared in the benighted world, so long dark and prosaic under the control of the cautious adults.

But along with this euphoria of sex-consciousness and potential came hypocrisy and pride and arrogance and empirical as well as moral restraint. The Victorians taught that there was actually sin in just thinking of sex, and rather serious sin in the sex urge and desire. This induced the moral restraints. On the empirical side there was the Scarlet Letter sort of tragic disgrace as a result of female venturing.

Then there was the earth law very much in effect at that time which applied to all animals. This was the absolutely necessitous training and control of the universal "sophomore," whether he be colt, cub, kitten or fledgling, by his parents and his elders of the herd, the pack, or the flock. This was necessary for success in the earth-struggle to survive, and the man was no exception.

However, the Victorians would believe that this was not an earth law, but heaven's own, and this belief in its source sharpened their responsibility toward its enforcement, and it became a matter of sins of the children reflecting on the fathers rather than the matter of the sins of the fathers reflecting on the children.

Definitely Romanesque. The Victorians were also in a way, ancestor worshipers, and dynastic.

Certainly the romantic theories of John Dewey and others, concerning the uniqueness and special category of the child acquiring freedom of expression in education were unthought of in the southwest. The child was still no more a special creation than were his parents and teachers, and still attached as were all other mammals to the earth, and he had to conform to Victorian fogyism which was religiously and socially ornamental, but still retained its placental attachment to earth.

Peer conformity among the 'teen-agers would remain through the years just as unfractured in the 1960's as it was in the first decades of the century, but their conformity now is to a new, starry-eyed, earth-detached chimera, that hasn't the virtue of animal self-knowledge.

In the 1960's astronauts are carrying Medieval and Victorian fetishes into space with them.

There was a well-known picture of a tragically distraught girl with a shawl over her head, and falling over her infant, standing at the door of her father's house, as the snow falls. The father's arm is straightened over her head with the index finger pointing into the distant blackness of the night, as he says with grievously wounded pride: "Do not darken my door again," or words to that effect.

This struck deep with the High School girls of my youth, even though they often joined us boys in ridicule. We would say to each other with mock severity, "Do not darken my door again."

I don't remember being especially excited about girls. It could have been that I was almost completely absorbed by my knight errantry, my quail and prairie chicken hunting, and my taxidermy, and my discouragements in the science of ornithology. Also some time before entering High School I had sent away for pit game eggs, and the success of my cocks in defeating the community's dung-hill cocks, inspired other little barbarians, and these others were raising their pit games and we staged cockfights first in one chicken pen and then in another, often to the dismay of our mothers, but protected by the indulgence of our fathers.

My pit games fascinated me with their red saddles and hackles and their eyes that were embers from a fire. Even after some of my cockfighting companions had dropped the pit game hobby for High School dancing and hay rides, I carried on with mine.

There were of course football and basketball, and hunting during the hiatus between football and basketball, represented by the two months between Thanksgiving and the end of the Christmas holiday.

During this period of suddenly descended wisdom and sex arrogance, girls ought to have had special attraction for me, and I suppose I did attribute graces, and beauty and etherealness to them, which they didn't have, and perhaps placed them along with my sisters in the "in with Heaven" category. However, since I was brought up with four sisters, I am sure I never went full out with my attributions.

Of course I had no way of knowing at that time that my sister Josephine was epitomizing the universal female in her jealousy, intensified by the fact that she was seven years older than I was, and by the fact that during those seven years, she was the darling; the spoiled child of parents harassed by fear and superstition, through losing three babies between Josephine and me. Then I had come along and lived, and was a male and spoiled it all.

She had been a beautiful, imaginative, histrionic, willful little girl, and even after the rest of us had come along she continued to "get her way" with our parents.

My princeling arrogance and bright but taciturn enthusiasms, and my parents' pride in their one male, must have disturbed her deeply, and generated resentments that might in a less rational mentality have been lethal.

I had no way of knowing that my sister Lillian was epitomizing the American female in her compulsion to be the first with the latest despite inaccuracies. She seemed to enjoy threatening me with "I'll tell papa on you." However, if one of her "I'll tell papas" had resulted in punishment, she would have wept inconsolably.

Later, we called her "Je Sais Tout."

However, I didn't think for a moment that my sisters' inadequacies were shared by the lovelies of High School with their sweet graciousness, amiability, their readiness to please, their conscious good manner, and their soft concern and dramatic appreciation of one's athletic ability, but I certainly, being fundamentally sister-wise, if not girl-wise, stopped short of associating them with the heavenly mysteries; stopped quite short of natural urge-blind apotheosis.

I suspect also that I must have expected some homage as an inherent right. My life thus far certainly had been full of indulgent females; full of an adoring mother, sisters, female cousins, at least two adoring aunties and a grandmother who laughed indulgently at my little boy's independence and called me "mon petit sauvage du ciel."[57]

. . . [58]

The cinema had come to the prairie and the blackjack hills, as an expression of civilization from the outside, and the theatres where the films were projected were called nickelodeons, and Professor Downing with typical Victorian male know-all assurance, sneered at the "moom pitchers" during assembly and elsewhere, calling such houses of tom-foolery, "nickle-dood-lums."

Of course there was some argument in the "nickle-dood-lum's" favor; their films were atrocious, but there were no suggestions for sex-disturbed youth in them, only vicarious romance. No long, long, embarrassingly long open-mouthed kisses, or young women lying seductively on tiger skins or suggestive attitudes in the love scenes. It might be supposed that most of the lush young women were frantically hanging from cliffs, or straining at the ropes that some dastardly villain speaking beautiful English, had used to bind them to the rails.

The "moom pitchers" harmfulness lay not in suggestions to sex-burdened youngsters, but in the fact that the dastards were made to speak almost flawless and beautifully unhesitant English, while the hero was made to speak unvarnished, down-to-earth, plain good ole "American," full of solecisms and dripping clichés.

This sort of thing was comforting to the vindictive ex-common man refugee from centuries of suppression, in Europe and England, but imitation of this virtuous American hero-talk, would bottle-neck and tarnish many a bright idea in future adulthood.

We were actually propagandized, unconsciously of course, by the racial-memory vindictiveness of the immigrant Europeans and Englishmen, etc., who became basically the free men trying to convince themselves of their social importance in which they didn't really believe. We were inspired to associate beautiful English and suavity and polished manners with those not worthy of trust.

Professor Downing taught physics, and didn't believe in "highfalu-tin'" talk, and I believe he hated the "nickle-dood-lums," not as per-verters of youth's morals, but as nonsense. He had very likely never thought about the seeming paradox of his own part in the civiliza-tion of the youth of our area, through education and culture induce-ment, and the vindictive ridiculing of fine manners and speech, not only at the "nickle-dood-lums" but in the common-man culture of which the cinema was a reflection.

His Victorian male arrogance was not intrusive since he had little of Victorian pomposity. He was virile and large and deliberate, and smoked a corncob pipe on the front steps of his front porch, having apparently long, long thoughts; some of them perhaps Rabelaisian.

In his thinking of his responsibility to young America, and of wasted time at the cinema, he didn't seem to consider the pleasure the "nickle-dood-lums" brought to the entertainment-starved people of the blackjacks and prairie.

The importance of the medicine man, with his treacly cajoleries under the light of a kerosene torch was fading; people had begun to sneer at him and at the sweating Fourth-of-July speakers; local law-yers who grew frenetic with patriotism both on the Fourth of July, and on the 30th of May from a platform in the cemetery.[59]

So the cinema filled a vacuum, with its flickering figures running about with the movements of solitary wasps; its heroes talking good ole common sense "American" and its heroines, who never, never, despite their wild running about, their hanging from cliffs, and their struggles to free themselves from dastardly villains, appeared disheveled.

Someday the cinema heroes and heroines would fill another vac-uum in the American life of the common man, the royalty vacuum created by the Revolutionary War.

Since the heroines were never sweat-stained or disheveled, there were racial memories among the women in the audiences of the rare appearances and the immaculate, royal dignity of queens, especially did this occur much later in the 1920's, the lack of dignity unnoticed.

But, after the development of radio and the television, the medicine man would have a rebirth.

As I write this story of my life I am periodically aware, dimly, of the long ago forgotten Victorian taboos that were handed down to us from our parents and teachers; believing that there can't be a vestige of them left, one is suddenly almost startled by one appearing out of limbo: a deposit lying unnoticed, from the atmosphere of one's youth.

This slightly disturbing taboo of the past, and the present generation's concern with both heterosexual and homosexual proclamations in print and over the air, makes it almost necessary for me to make my position clear.[60] My reticences are not fogyism and my philosophy is from, and of the earth, and when the word symbols necessary to express my thoughts are needed I shall call upon them as I have always done, and not in the least inspired by the atmosphere created by the vociferous rediscovery of sex, and the refurbishing of vulgarity.

One who has lived close to the earth, and has not lost touch with his fellow men and their urges and struggles and ornamentations, realizes that there are three primary laws that govern all life: self-preservation, reproduction and the Force, and if this is an oversimplification, it is not meant to be pedantic or scientifically biological; it is simply what I have believed and do believe, and this is *my* story.

 . . .[61]

In High School I made no dates for the dances. I wasn't timid or indifferent, but I feel now that I ever wanted to be free from responsibility, even the most trivial responsibility. I was, as a result, the perennial stag in my High School days and of course stags had their role.

I don't remember walking hand in hand or kissing in the corners or in the shadows, and since I was quite normal and filled with *joie de vivre*, I have often wondered about this attitude, and have come to the conclusion that from the beginning of my memory I have had to be self-protective from female aggressions, which in themselves were a hint that man's assumptions of the female's demure indifference was in conflict with the laws of the earth.

I had been brought up under the protective dominance of an energetic mother and bossy sisters. Often, I have heard my mother laugh reminiscently at my babyhood insurgency. Her favorite story was about angry revolt. She would hold me between her knees and comb my hair, then as soon as I was released, I would muss my hair and try to comb it myself.

But in High School I got along quite well, even as a loner, since I was not really a loner, but very much a part of the life of the school; I was a loner only in spirit. There is some ethereal chemical in each one of us that is often felt by others, and to which these others react in accordance with their natures, a sort of spiritual exudation that intrigues or repels, or by some is not felt at all.

There are people who are cold or passive, or non-obtrusively ego-centric, to whom others defer because of these ethereal waves, and their selfishness and passivity and indifference are excused, and they receive respect. These self-contained non-aggressive people often become leaders through promotion by their empathic peers who are under the spell of their aura waves.

Innately male passive, I was in perfect harmony with the earth's laws, and having never during my High School days, been forced to defend against female possessiveness, even though my passivity did seem to be at times a feeble challenge to them, but I can't now remember clearly if it was, since there is naturally nothing in the shabby diary to indicate this, and certainly it wasn't spelled out there, since I couldn't possibly have had any understanding of such matters at that time.

. . . [62]

~

As the village of Pawhuska grew into a town and became the County Seat of Osage County in the new State of Oklahoma, doctors, lawyers, cattlemen, merchants, realtors, bankers, insurance, title & abstract men came to swell the population and the pride of the mixed-bloods and the traders.

The Osage Mercantile Company built a new building, but it still retained the mélange of odors of the old building, since they [sic] still sold everything from chocolates to Indian wagons.

P.J. Monk was an Englishman, and had come over in the employ-ment of an English cattle company, but left them to become a pharmacist of the agency. His pharmacy was one of the magic places of my childhood.

You had to climb steps to the creaking, splintery pine-floored porch. On each side of the door was a window. In one window, there were three amphorae-like vessels of glass, each filled with a different colored liquid: one with red, another with blue, and the third with green. In the other window were a mortar and pestle.

When you opened the door you were met by an odor which was indescribable: a mélange of freshly peeled cherry bark, crushed black walnut hull, and wounded cinchona tree. The odor never varied; the components were the same and of the same value.

P.J. [being] far away from his pelagic England had a model sailing ship mounted on the high structure that separated the front of the store from the prescription room. This model was the embodiment of his nostalgia.

He frightened and fascinated me at the same time, and when I went into the store with either parent, and later alone, his eyes looking out from under his heavy eyebrows seemed to pierce my soul. His actions were deliberate and hesitant as he started back to the prescription room to fill a prescription, leading one to wonder if he really intended to fill the prescription or changing his mind accuse one of some misdemeanor, and might even be considering whether he ought to put poison in the prescription.

His speech was of the Midlands and slightly tinted with Cockney, one might believe, perhaps erroneously. There was the very slight hint of neglected H's.

He had no soda fountain in the early days, but later when he had moved into a new building, after statehood and after the agency had become a town, he installed a soda fountain that became the Mecca of the High School students.

The summer following my freshman year was one of special gregariousness and social gatherings among the 'teen-agers, and there were dances, hayrides, and swimming parties at the swimming holes on Bird and Clear Creeks, where we male exhibitionists climbed high into the sycamores and dove when we had managed to focus attention.

While John-Without-Purpose had not abandoned his horse and dog and his summer prairies, something new and subtle was happening to him, and my father felt it. He apparently couldn't think of anything for me to do on the Ridge Ranch, so he asked P.J. if he would take me on as a "soda jerk" for the summer. This would give me a sense of responsibility and I could open a savings account.

This was a bit naïve on the part of my parents who had a sixth sense about girls and me. Here to the soda fountain came the sex-restive, gregarious 'teen-agers: mostly girls since the Victorian Age father always found something for their sons to occupy their time. The girls came to banter and chaff with the boys who stole away for a few minutes from their jobs as delivery boys, or as merchant's helpers, etc. They sipped drinks interminably, loitered, sang snatches from ragtime, then finally left reluctantly, as if leaving unfinished business.

My father would come from the bank, usually in the mid-afternoon, pretending I believe now that he needed some cure-all. He was not a hypochondriac at all, but a sort of drug fetishist. He took little pills with some ceremony before going to bed, and his face after taking [them] had just a hint of the expression mother's face carried when she came home from mass.

However, he had a medicine cabinet full of drug fetishes, and certainly didn't need more, so his carefully casual visits to Monk's drug store, I found later, were for the purpose of spying on the Newcomer girl, who came almost every afternoon, bathed and crisp and bright-eyed, to sit long over her drink, dawdling, pretending high merriment, when the boys arrived stealing time from their jobs, or when a bevy of High School girls came to dally over their drinks.

Skirts in those days reached almost to the ankle, but A. Newcomer seemed always to be pulling at hers with a sort of exaggerated sense of decorum. She laughed readily when there was nothing to laugh at, as though in this manner she was releasing some pent-up, expanding, uncontrollable emotion, and one day when the little M. boy came in with his older brother, and lost his pants as he tried to climb onto a high stool at the fountain, she quickly bit her lower lip and feigned shock, but there was a hint of roguery behind it, and this lit up her face.

On or near the first of August each summer, the upland plover from the northern prairies came over on their way south, and my father was pleased when I asked if I might ask for a day off from the soda fountain to hunt plover. He said: "You've worked anough for the summer. Give P.J. notice so's he can get someone else to take your place. Your hoss ought to be in good shape now, and the weather's not so hot; better go out and get her."

When I told P.J. Monk that I wanted to leave, he looked up at me from under his heavy eyebrows, and didn't answer when I asked solicitously if he could get someone to take my place. He studied me a moment, then said: "How much Osage blood do you have, by the way?"[63]

Osages didn't have that virtue known as "git up and go."

I smiled with appreciation. I wasn't afraid of him now. I had reproductive euphoria and wisdom that came with it, and he was just a beetle-browed transplanted Englishman, whose vocabulary was ever so slightly short of H's.

From the warm heart hidden by the crust of his austerity, he said: "This is the first—the flight don't last too long, does it? Go ahead today; we can make out."

The upland plovers came to the Osage prairies in the thousands to join those that were indigenous and had nested there. They ran across the prairie catching grasshoppers; they flew up in typical shorebird flocks, and had shorebird habits though they were not shorebirds, even though they had shorebird beaks and long, wading legs and shorebird conformation. When alighting they held their wings high above their backs a few seconds as if there might be a momentary malfunctioning of the wing sockets.

We shot them of course, only on the wing, and this was as sporting as shooting woodcock, although their flight was not so erratic as that of the woodcock.

They were often so fat from eating grasshoppers, that they burst when they hit the ground, and greased their breast feathers.

When I told my father that I had ceased being a "soda jerk," that very day, we hitched the black Morgans to the C-spring buggy, and drove out onto the prairie to shoot.

On our way home, I learned the reasons for my father's unusual visits to the drug store. He said, laconically, after a long silence: "We'll fetch your hoss tomorrow," then after another silence, "that Newcomer girl'll get a fella into trouble."

~

[1911]

Both Floyd Soderstrom and I made the football team; he became an outstanding defensive end, and could easily have made all-state. I played fullback, despite the fact that about this time I was built like a sandhill crane. Our coach Jake Duran once said: "Whenever I see one of them big tackles get into the secondary and blast yu, I shut my eyes and pray; the good Lord musta put your joints together special, with some kind of extry wir'in'."

The sandhill crane had the advantage of wings, and I had to remain on the ground.

When I came home late from after school practice, Bally would watch me with her head over the yard fence and Spot would leave off his day-dreaming, and come to me wagging his tail expectantly. And there were the Canada goose and duck swarms down the Plains Flyway, and the quail and prairie chickens were sharp-scented, and frost came and the sumac dropped its leaf-like blobs of blood.

There were girls with pennants and there were bonfires on Friday nights, and dances at strange High Schools on Saturday nights, and strange girls, brightly excited. These were days of bubbling importance and simple existence-thrill, but I note that my diary of that time deplores my neglect of Bally and Spot and hunting.

It was a wonderful thing, however, to glance at the sidelines (we had no grandstand when I played High School football) and see the glow of pride on your game-mad father's face, vicariously playing fullback, vicariously kicking a field goal from a difficult angle.

Once when I kicked one such field goal in the last minute of the game, winning it like a true Dick Merriwell, my father walked back home with me, jabbing the earth with his cane trying to keep pace

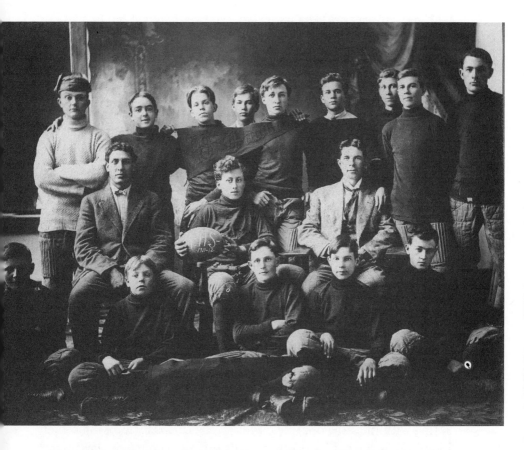

The Pawhuska football team, with Mathews at center holding ball (Courtesy of the Osage Tribal Museum, Pawhuska, Oklahoma)

with me. He was suffused with élan. His eyes laughed but he was not smiling. This was characteristic of an elated and prideful Mathews. I noted that his hands trembled uncontrollably, the free one; the other gripped the cane tightly.

Since our games were sometimes played on the Osage Boarding School field, only a short distance from our house, I came home to bathe after a game, leaving the crowded school showers to the others. He sat and watched me bathe, his eyes still smiling and the glow of élan in his face undiminished. He said pridefully, "You're getting a little flesh on you."

Once, even when his stomach was experiencing little electric shocks waiting for the kick-off whistle, the fullback of the Pawhuska High School football team, standing almost under his own goal posts, heard a flock of Canada geese passing over the field like a pack of trail hounds. He was watching them when the ball hit the ground near him and bounced, fortunately, over the goal line.

He became captain the next season, however.

. . . [64]

The sandhill crane type was useful in basketball, especially at center. We played from just after Christmas until the first of March, and this year we had an especially talented team.

My father came to every game and to many of the practice sessions, sitting with the glow of pride on his face, vicariously jumping center. I have no idea what he really thought the night we were playing our most important rival. I fell, then rose and made a basket for the rival team. He said nothing, nor lost the prideful glow of his face, nor the faint, tight, vindictively smug little smile of victory. He came back to where I was showering; leaning on his cane he ran his eyes over me, then said as if trying to reassure himself: "Son, you'll fill out, time you get older; you won't look so tall then." I was perhaps six feet, and sixteen, but had barely passed puberty.

The next season I was elected captain of the basketball team.

∽

By this time, with full reproductive potential, the mysterious, ethereal chemistry working within me, had by now created a definite aura, under which I walked and from which flowed the impulses which more and more influenced people to promote my leadership, my passivity notwithstanding. I had no need to be vociferously eager, and embryo ringmasters inspired disgust in me.

But ideas yeasted, and even though they were expressed calmly to others, they received their glow in the minds of others.

When my sophomore year ended in June, three of us were acting on a rather gossamer plan to go by boat to New Orleans, by way of the Arkansas and the Mississippi Rivers.

Raymond Seeley was a talented mechanic, but Floyd Soderstrom and I knew nothing whatsoever about motors. Raymond found a cast-off hull, and with the aid of a carpenter refurbished it, and somewhere he had found an old motor, [and] worked it over almost ecstatically.

My father was happy to aid us and furnish money. He had the box taken off the Indian wagon, so that the boat could be loaded on the running gears. Then when it was loaded and ready, he decided to take us the 25 miles to the mouth of Salt Creek where it ran into the Arkansas River. My sister Josephine, sensing a lark, decided to go along, and drive back with our father on the running gear. A unique experience to be talked about when the chaffing dish group convened again the next winter.

In those days the roads were little more than two wriggling ruts connecting two towns, meandering over the prairie and over the blackjack ridges, flowing down into valleys and across streams.

A good team of horses could travel at the speed of perhaps seven miles an hour, and often ten, but the latter only if they could trot most of the way. The road between Pawhuska and the town that grew out of the Grey Horse village, the village of the Big Hill division of the Osages, was rough and dusty.

The trip both ways would consume about eight hours, so my father and sister had to leave immediately after the launching.

We put up our tent and established a camp on the sandy banks of Salt Creek, happy and insouciant and thrilled with our sophomoric dreams. A bevy of High School girls had come to see us off at the agency, and had broken a bottle of something or other on the bow, and my cousin Eleanor Wheeler had christened the boat "Samaris," and the name had been duly painted on the bow before we left.

I doubt if anyone expected us to arrive at New Orleans, and when the motor became temperamental, there were probably doubts in our minds as well, but one had the impression that Raymond the born mechanic was actually happy about it.

Floyd and I became impatient, and even became disinterested in shooting squirrels for the skillet, although Floyd fished constantly, and I wandered about studying the birds. Raymond worked inside the hull, then pulled off his clothing and worked on the motor, his body slimy with mud.

Finally, when the motor was running well again, we got as far down the river as Ralston on the Pawnee side, where we went for supplies, and were just barely able to make it back to the mouth of Salt Creek against the current.

We ventured into the current of the river no more.

One night a storm broke over us, and our tent ballooned and we each sat on a corner to keep it from taking off. The roar was deafening, if only momentary, and when it ceased, there was the roar of the flood. With 'teen-age indifference we went back to sleep without even getting up to have a look. Raymond had assured us that the "Samaris" was tied securely, the painter being tied to the limb of an elm which would allow it to ride the flood.

The next morning we realized that we had weathered a tornado. Great trees were uprooted and were criss-crossed over each other, leaving triangular spaces, and in one of these spaces was our tent, untouched through some miracle.

It was difficult to climb over the boles of the fallen trees. The Samaris was straining at her painter, and the chocolate-colored water was curling about her bow.

This ended the 'teen-age dream of three week's duration. I walked into the little town of Fairfax and contracted with a man to come on his wagon's running gears and pick us up, and he and his helper had to chop their way to the boat.

We became thrillingly newsworthy, and the *Muskogee Phoenix* asked me to write a feature story about our experience. This was important, since Muskogee was one of the large towns of the new state, and I made the most of my opportunity. I built the situation up dramatically, and of course never mentioning the fact that we hadn't known we were in a tornado until the next morning. On the thin ice of our insouciance, under which we didn't even untie the flap of the tent to have a look, I wrote as one might write who walked on thin ice, depending entirely on the reader's assumptions. As I remember the story, even dull unimaginative readers could watch with us the toppling of the trees.

But on the solid ground of reality, I left no doubt in the reader's mind concerning the dramatic tenseness of the fraction of a minute that seemed an hour. I dramatized the necessity for sitting on the corners of the tent, especially.

It was dramatic and very interesting when you appreciate the mechanics and the incredible freakishness of tornadoes. The air of the normal atmospheric pressure and weight was trying to escape from the interior of the tent and fill the vacuum created by the tornado on the exterior: the vacuum which each of us had been assured by Professor Downing, is abhorred by nature.

I don't know how the air escaped from the interior of the tent in its urgency to fill the vacuum, possibly through the little circular holes around the poles that held the tent erect, or through the door flap; but we were fortunate that it did escape, since our tent which became a perfect balloon in shape might well have taken off as a balloon. The whims of the tornadic winds were indulgent that night; they could have carried our tent off flapping like a rag, and us with it. But the miracle of course, was the manner in which the whimsical winds had arranged the boles of the fallen hackberrys, elms and red oaks, leaving the triangular space where our tent remained intact.

The over-dramatized story about the three brave, plucky high school boys in a devastating tornado, was illustrated with snapshots taken by Josephine during the time of the launching.

The new author's first published story, except for editorials in the *Trumpeter*, the High School publication, was illustrated, no less. The

Call Of The Wild, White Fang, Wild Animals I Have Known, Kindred Of The Wild, had all been illustrated, as well.

There were a few men in town who were interested in other things than their businesses or professions, baseball and horse racing, and one of these few was Judge Musseller.[65] He was an amateur ornithologist. His daughter Crete was one of my High School teachers, and she had mentioned that her father knew something about birds and had many reference books on ornithology.

As I wandered through the Salt Creek bottoms around our camp, I remembered this when I saw a grotesquely colored bird of the finch family: a bird that had as a habitat the brushy river bottom, and which I had never seen during my questing over the prairie or the high sandstone ridges. I made notes on its coloration, which reminded one of an artist's palette, its manner of flying, its length, the shape of its beak, its feeding mannerisms, its voice, and entered these notations in my diary, which I carried at all times in my hip pocket. I made a sketch of him and marked off the areas of his cardinal colors.

Then one night by the light of a lantern, I wrote a letter to Judge Musseller transcribing the descriptions from my diary, and mailed the letter when I walked into Fairfax for groceries. Walking in the hot sun, along the dusty trails into Fairfax for groceries was an adjustment to the original plan to buy our supplies as we floated on the currents of the Arkansas and the Mississippi Rivers, stopping at quaint little villages along the river's banks.

When we arrived back home, Judge Musseller sent for me to come to his home. I saddled Bally and rode the short distance—perhaps a mile and a half—to his house.

Later, after the automobile came into general use, one might say, "I jumped in the car and drove over," but in those days, of sporadic cars, we said, "I threw the saddle on and loped over," or "I hooked up the team, etc."

Judge Musseller was a sedate Victorian with a face like Bismarck's, and I worried about where I could tie Bally, since he had no hitching pole.[66] I had never seen horses nibble hollyhocks, and I wondered if Bally might have a whim to nibble at the tall, dusty ones that nodded to her over the picket fence. In my worry, I stupidly admonished her, and she looked at me in such a manner that I became aware of how inane my admonition was.

I was nervous, but I didn't know why. I hadn't a thought in my head: only the Bismarckian image.

As a Victorian judge and head of a family, he had his study, in the otherwise modest house, and I was ushered to it by Crete. As we approached the door, she smiled at me and said, "Father's excited about you."

I remember a vague uneasiness surging. Perhaps he might bring up the piece in the *Muskogee Phoenix*, misled by one of my exaggerations, and wishing to discuss it. There were several things in the piece I couldn't defend. I was afraid that Bismarck would stare at me, deep into my fiction-spawning soul, then later dismiss me with a polite sneer, since there is no one who demands natural science facts so stubbornly as a natural science hobbyist. And one had heard of judges taking people back to their chambers for the purpose of talking things over, but there was no misdemeanor, just an over-dramatized distortion of a certain natural science fact that perhaps Judge Musseller wanted very much to believe.

Crete knocked at the door lightly but with assurance, and a gruff voice said "come." Crete took me by the arm and led me forward into the room, saying, "This is Jo Mathews."

The stern Judge rose from his chair, came forward and grasped my upper arms and said, "good, good—come sit down," ignoring his daughter completely.

I can't of course, remember much of the conversation, and I didn't put much of it down in the little hip pocket diary, but it must have endured for two hours, and with relief, I found that the Judge's interest had been inspired by the letter from the Salt Creek camp about the extravagantly colored finch.

The bird I had so accurately described was a painted bunting, and he showed me several pictures, from his several books on ornithology, already open and lying on the table.

I became inspired; here was someone who was actually interested in birds and knew much more about them than I did. The stern old

Judge's face began to glow and soften, as he thumbed through his precious books, and he listened intently when I talked of the vultures, the red-tailed hawks, the prairie falcons, I had watched while lying on my back on the prairie, envying them their powers of flight. I would never have told anyone in all the world about this: about my secret yearnings and my frustrations and my dreams—not even my father, nor my mother, to whom I was very close.

And, the Judge told me of the medical men who accompanied the armies to the Plains and the Southwest during the Indian wars, who were ordered by the U.S. government to observe birds and make notes about them, as a matter of fact observe all flora and fauna. These men who came after Audubon and Michaux had birds and trees and animals named for them.[67]

He went to the door with me with his hand on my shoulder, and at the door, he said: "My boy, go home and tell your father you're a born natural scientist."

I didn't tell my father.

I can't remember now if I felt prideful, or rather that the princeling might have taken such things for granted. I suspect the latter, since one of my lifetime characteristics is my tendency to place little confidence in other people's opinions of me, and I must have had the same characteristic then. Perhaps I thought in harmony with my nature, that if I really were a born natural scientist, why shouldn't I be? This distinction might be one that you might expect a princeling to have, a sort of an appanage, but the very fact of the birds themselves was of much more importance.[68]

The image of the helmeted Bismarck had faded, and there was now in its place the kindly old Judge, wetting his thumb to turn the pages of his several books, placing slips of paper here and there between pages as bookmarks: hurried at moments, as if the bird he searched for might quickly vanish as birds often did in the field.

Judge Musseller had inspired me profoundly, had given me his adult, dignified very important understanding, then had praised me; but still there was something which prevented me from becoming starry-eyed with ambition and dreams. I can only guess at what it was; it must have been formality, the scientific necessity; the birds imprisoned both as to image and character on glossy pages. I wanted them to be called by their proper names and I even made it a point to learn the genus and species names, but I suppose I didn't want them in a manner of speaking, card-indexed.

But this is not clear, even to myself now. I suppose I shall be compelled to use the phrase, I wanted to play it by ear; I wanted to play natural science, where it dealt with sentient beings, by ear. I later became a student of geology, and here there was no conflict between scientific card-indexing and my rather romantic devotion to the study of the earth, except that I stubbornly refused to measure the duration of geological periods by calendar years.

~

[1912]

During my second year as fullback on the High School football team, I had a desire to become proficient as a passer, since I seemed to be doing so well as a dropkicker and a placekicker, so that when Leo Bellieu rode with me to the Ridge Ranch, he riding Queen and I on Bally, we took a football with us and threw it to each other as we rode along. I seemed to have a definite objective when rarely I rode out with someone else.

We tossed the ball back and forth to each other, then kept tossing as we went from a walk to a trot, and ultimately a lope, fumbling often.

Leo was a natural end and played with a private preparatory school in Kansas. He was a mixed-blood Osage, and his uncle had a ranch just north of "Aunt Sue's," and his uncle Sylvester Lawrence and my uncle Jim shared a breezing track.

We had known each other since we were quite small.

When we walked along together, he would suddenly run and jump a wall, or over a fallen tree, or across a ditch. He was tall, amiable, and attractive, an inherent athlete, and he loved hunting as much as I did, and we read aloud to each other from Charles G.D. Roberts, Ernest Thompson Seton and Jack London.

So, it was quite natural that my idea for adventure during one summer would include Leo. As soon as the idea came to me, which had to do with a pack trip and camp in the Rockies, Leo and Floyd began burnishing it in their own minds and soon we were lying on our bellies on the floor of my room studying the map of Colorado. This idea was far superior to the New Orleans one, and what's more, quite probable.

As I have written, we all three were devotees of London, Seton, [and] Roberts and had read about Kit Carson and Jim Bridger and my own great-grandfather "Ole" Bill Williams, who before becoming a mountain man had been known at Harmony Mission on the Osage River in Missouri as Reverend Williams.[69] One supposes he got "the call" much as Buddha and Mohammed got it, but didn't have their luck, and instead of waiting like Mohammed, he went to the mountain and lost his followers along with his own Christian soul.

We searched the map of Colorado for the wildest spot we could find in the Rockies; an area farthest away from the conventional symbols indicating towns and other concentrations of people, and finally found one such area in the northwestern part of the state.

Our choice was partially influenced by the mountain lake called Trapper's and the name of the mountains which formed the northern border of the basin in which the lake lay. The mountains, Williams Fork Mountains, had been named for my great-grandfather.

This was real romance.

And, Romance guided our fingers as we ran them over the map and up the Yampa River, over the divide and down to the lake, and found our fingers in the White River National Forest.

Again, my father was delighted.

Out of Denver, we took the famed Moffatt Road, the railway to Yampa. The wooden coaches creaked as though in pain all the way up the Continental Divide, and then on the western slope, the wheels screamed as they were forced against the rails on the curves.[70]

Taking "The Moffatt Road" over the Rockies was an adventure, and tourists held tightly to the arms of their seats, and often became white-faced, and women would venture a glance at the white waters of a mountain stream far down in the bottom of a gash canyon, then stop the conductor and ask: "How long before we get down out of the mountains?"

The officials of the railroad were aware of this tenseness in their passengers and especially their tourists, so they had a news-butch-spieler for comic relief. He would walk through the train calling attention to the interesting view, or point out a peak, or canyon, or a band of deer, very seriously, then quite suddenly he became important; he was no longer a news-butch, but an entertainer, with faces and ears turned to him, becoming the important focal point for the perhaps important tourist from the East.

His spiels were supposed to relax taut nerves of the ladies especially. I entered one verbatim in my diary, but I seemed to be more interested in the manner of the spieler than in what he was actually saying. As I remember the different ones, this one may be typical; at least it seems to be the one that has remained in my memory all this time, but it was not entered verbatim.

He would shout through a megaphone: "Lay-dees and gentlemen, if you'll be kind enough to look out the windas to your right, you'll see a place there where they was a strike whin the Moffatt was bein' built. The workers got scairt and cold and tar'd, and they up and quit. They had their camp right there on that there spot your'a lookin' at right now. Well, they wasn't nothin' for the road to do, if they didn't want to be ruint financialee, so they sent East and har'd 'em some of them eastern dudes at high wages, ah rekon.

"Well sir, them dudes come out a-wearin' fancy clothes and cellaloid collars, figurin' on kindy a'lordin' it over the natives, ah guess. They brought 'em out here and unloaded 'em at that place you're a-lookin' at right now.

"Now, these dudes from the East wasn't used to these mountains and this mountain railroadin', so they got shed of them fancy duds, tuk off them cellaloid collars and flung 'em away. Course, when they pulled stakes to move to another camp on down the mountain, there was them white cellaloid collars, a-layin' there.

"Well sir, I'll tell yu what happened; they's a herd of elk come a-mosey'n up the mountain, seen them white collars, thought they was snow and froze to death."

His face was aglow with smugness as he left the car to enter the next one where he would repeat his spiel.

As he passed our seat, he winked at me, afflated.

There was a little station on the very crest of the Continental Divide, and there was a bar there. The train made a long stop here, and the "double header"—the two locomotives necessary to pull the train up the steep grade—seemed to pant from exhaustion.

The three of us got out and went into the bar. A woman right out of Robert W. Service came toward us expectantly, her golden incisor gleaming.[71]

Immediately, she became serious and hardened by suspicion.

"Say," she said, "how old are you kids? Beer's all I kin sell yu." She held up her hand as if to guard against protestations, "they hain't a-one of yu that's dry behind the y'ears yet."

Floyd was eighteen, I was seventeen, and Leo was sixteen.

The Hotel at Yampa was of pine and was weathered to a dove-grey. The Yampa River flowed quickly through the village, as if it had very important business elsewhere.

We stayed a few days in Yampa negotiating with the local livery stable man for horses: a string of pack horses and three saddle horses, and a saddle horse for our guide Frank Wright. We must have seven horses and a guide for two days: a day for traveling from Yampa to Trapper's Lake and a day for the return of the string.

Our duffle was ready to be packed on the horses early the next morning. We were sitting on the splintery porch of the hotel, 'teen-age-bored, when we heard a hoarse voice shouting, "Fire—fire." The groceryman came out of his store running, the livery stable man left his stables, the bartender came running out of his bar, with fingers fumbling at the strings of his white apron. The hotel clerk left his desk, and as he passed us on the porch, he shouted to us, "Come on boys and hep us."

This was the business—excitement! The three of us, even though altitude-winded we were fleet, and reached the firehouse in time to pick up the tongue of a hose cart, and followed the cart in front of us.

Until they got the steam pump going, we formed a bucket brigade from the river to the fire, but athletic Leo, finding this too prosaic, left the line, and climbed a ladder to the roof of the house and started tearing off shingles for the insertion of the hose nozzle. People began to shout to him to come down before the smoke obscured his escape. He liked this sort of thing.

The fire dead, we walked back with bursting lungs in the high altitude, with the groceryman, the stableman, the hardware man, the hotel clerk and the bartender. The latter said grandly, waving his hand toward his place of business, "Come on in, boys, it's on the house." We followed him into the bar. Even the hotel clerk, with an anxious glance toward the hotel, decided to have a quick one.

We stood with our feet on the brass rail, and took our Bourbon straight with the others. The bartender looked at us: "I sure as hell won't ever know how old you boys is, if you don't tell me." He wiped the bar, contemplatively, "En even iffen you did tell me, doubt iffen I could hear; now en agin at certain times I'm deef as a board."

This little incident got full treatment in my little diary.

We strung out up the Yampa River, laboring up the trail to the pass in Williams Fork Mountains. The snow gleamed in cambered patches in the late June sun and at times the trail was blocked by a patch and we had to break trail with the saddle horses, so that the going would be easier for the pack horses.

This was Jack London'ish in a way, only Smoke Bellew would have had to break trail for the dog team.

My horse was smoky-brown, and had been ridden by Teddy Roosevelt, when he hunted cougars out of Meeker some years previously. This could have been a fiction but even if I had had my doubts about the authenticity of the story, I would have insisted on believing it.

Teddy Roosevelt missed by a slight margin being one of my tin gods. Despite his life in South Dakota, he still had almost invisible shreds of dude'ism clinging to him. Perhaps his brashness also kept him from joining Thomas Jefferson, Sir Ernest Shackleton, Marcus Aurelius, and Charles Darwin.[72]

But riding his old cougar hunting horse added to the thrill of the snow, the savage peaks, the very fact of the pack string, and in seeing my first Rocky Mountain ptarmigan who stood and looked at us stupidly. They were now mottled grey-brown and white: in the transition stage between the protective white of winter and the protective grey-brown of summer, with only a hint of the winter's white remaining, now in June.

These birds high among the snow patches didn't know about men, so stood watching us.

Trapper's Lake was primordial, and rimmed by the savage White River Plateau. Its wavelets murmured against the granitic pebbles of the shoreline, like lazy, subdued conversation.

On the west side of the lake, the White River rushed out of it down the mountain. It roared at times, it laughed, it murmured, it gurgled in eddies and it foamed in madness when constricted by the sabre-gash canyons. Unlike William Cullen Bryant's Oregon, it heard more than its own dashings; it heard the challenge of the bull wapiti under a September moon, the winter song of the wolf and the scream-growl of the cougar.

We heard none of these that summer, I suspect because it was summer, but one night when we heard a strange yeowling from the rim-rock, we looked at each other significantly, hoping that one of us or the other would not didactically prove that it was really not a cougar. So, we said nothing, but went outside the tent and listened, with the contented fall of the river, the theme song under the savage stars.

We put up our tent a few yards from where the river left the lake with urgency, under conifers which I seem to remember as being blue spruce. Or is it that I would have them be?

Close to the little creek that flowed into the lake from the north stood a ranger's log cabin, and between our camp and the ranger's cabin was a dilapidated cabin which had been built by a trapper, perhaps. Its logs were losing their chinking, and the sod roof was nourishing columbine and some sort of aster.

One afternoon of watery light after the daily shower, we saw smoke rising from the ranger's cabin, and looked at each other with expressions of disappointment. Another person or persons on "our" lake would do things to the romance of our venture; both to our dreams and the wonderful reality of our primitive, thrilling solitude.

The talk in the tent that night was desultory. Who could the trespasser be? It was more likely than not that there might be several of them: perhaps a party of brash, vociferous, poker playing, cigar chewing fishermen, who characteristically would treat us condescendingly.

If they were a party we wondered how they got to the lake, since we had seen no horses, and that would mean that they didn't come up the river trail or over the pass from the Yampa; they could only have come up the Glenwood Springs trail which was much longer. One had to come to the lake by pack train or afoot; there was no other way.

The next morning as we were preparing breakfast we kept glancing toward the ranger's cabin; then at mid-morning we saw a man riding toward our camp accompanied by an Airedale terrier.

The man was large, not quite the horseman type, one thought, and his disinterested horse looked as if he might have been selected from a pack string. As the large man dismounted, the horse had to change the position of his feet to keep his balance. The saddle tilted and squeaked.

The man looked about the camp. There was a 30-30 Winchester leaning against a tree, and the skinned carcasses of two snowshoe rabbits hanging from a limb.

The man said: "I guess you boys have got licenses?"

Licenses? We hadn't thought about licenses. We said that we didn't know we had to have them, since-since, we weren't really hunting.

He pointed to the rifle: "Wouldn't call that a bow and arrow or a fishing rod, would you? Besides you got to have a fishing license to fish, too."

We said we hadn't either fishing or hunting licenses.

"Well," he said, "if you're all over sixteen, you've got to have licenses to hunt and fish. It'll be three and half apiece, if you're residents of the state; course for non-residents, it'll come some higher."

His saddle almost turned as he mounted. He turned and said: "I'll be back tomorrow afternoon with my book of licenses."

We talked about our money supply, and wondered how we could possibly buy non-resident licenses, and after worrying about the thing for several hours very seriously, we finally decided that we would be "residents" of the state of Colorado. My mother and sisters would be in Colorado Springs for the summer, and I could give their address in Stratton Park as mine. Manitou would serve Leo, since his family were summering there, and it so happened that Floyd had an aunt living in Grand Junction. Why not, we asked of our consciences; my family and Leo's family were actually residents of the state for the summer, and Floyd's aunt better still, was a bona fide resident?

The wisdom and trickery of the presumptuous, arrogant 'teen-ager is like the wisdom of the "sophomore" coyote who furnishes a much easier run for the hounds than his elders. Our wisdom was really hidden from our elders to avoid difficulties but it was real, if not blatant. It had to be secretive since our Victorian parents and overlords were in rather severe control, and therefore more exasperatingly ignorant of their own stodgy frailties. Our wisdom had to be continent, when face-to-face with their much flaunted "wisdom of experience."

When Frank Hays, the game warden, appeared the next afternoon, we coolly gave our names and faked Colorado addresses, and paid the resident fee for our licenses—combination hunting and fishing licenses.

Floyd fished most of the time, while Leo and I climbed to the plateau above the rimrock, or seriously hunted snowshoe rabbits.

We knew that Frank Hays came up from headquarters in Glenwood Springs periodically, accompanied by his dog, and when he appeared at our camp a few days later, we in our sophomoric security attached no significance to the visit.

He was quite pleasant.

He pushed his hat to the back of his head, and as he sat with his back against a tree, he picked up a pine twig and cut it methodically into sections with his knife, meditating.

He said: "I ought to take you kids back to Glenwood with me. Guess you get practice lying to your teachers, but you sure need more practice. Your names are on the register at the hotel in Yampa—your addresses and all, and you bragged about bein' from Oklahoma in the saloon, and they say in Yampa that you bellied up to the bar like miners and took it neat."

There was a very awkward silence: a very long and very uncomfortable silence.

He closed his knife, heaved himself up and went to his saddle pockets, pulled out his license book, and turning pointed to the 30-30 Winchester.

"I guess one hunting license will do, if that is the only rifle you got with you. Haven't got a shotgun, have you? No? Well, I'll tell you what I'll do. I'll let you off—this is purty serious business; your lying that way. The law says I could-a taken you into Glenwood, when I first found you with no licenses, let alone your lying. Les see now; tell you what I'll do, if you fellas'll buy one non-resident hunting license and one non-resident fishing license, I'll let you off. That'll come to $30.00 since the fishing license part of it can be what they call [a] short time tourist license, but a hunting license is a hunting license, makes no difference whether you're hunting elk or snowshoes."

My diary, in which I entered the incident in detail, does not indicate that Frank Hays was careless about verb endings, which one might expect him to be. I had a sophomoric meticulousness about faithfulness in recording speech, I have noted. And it was a matter of faithfulness since I was no purist. It was a matter of faithfulness and my delight in words which seemed to fit the background of the speaker. The manner in which one spoke quite often was part of a personality sketch. Frank Hays's word endings were a surprise and didn't fit his role, I felt.

We accepted Warden Hays's indulgent offer with deep relief, and invited him to have dinner of trout with us.

Since we were all football players, we had some idea that the 10,000-foot altitude would condition us for the 1,000 contour of home on the Osage prairie, so we rose each morning and trotted along the edge of the lake for a mile and then back to camp, pulled off our clothes and had a swim in the icy waters.

Sometimes Leo, full of the joy of his athletic prowess, would trot on out of sight among the pines, looking back over his shoulder, challenging us. But Floyd was anxious to push away from shore on our homemade raft, and whip the lake for hungry trout.

I once saw him cast three leaders to which were tied three flies: a coachman, a silver king and a gnat, and take three trout.

While Floyd fished, Leo and I explored the Flat Tops, the plateau that rose above the lake, he carrying the 30-30 rifle and I with my revolver hung from my belt. We flushed bands of does and fawns, and one day among the snow patches I shot a ptarmigan with my revolver.

Leo waited patiently while I skinned him for future mounting. We had had experience of Frank Hays's cleverness, and I didn't want a scrap of evidence about camp. The ptarmigan would have been a relief from bacon, snowshoe rabbit and trout, and we left the body with regret. When I got back to camp, I sprinkled the skin with arsenic, and shoved it into a boot sock and locked it up in my handbag.

Having to expend the money for the non-resident hunting and fishing license, we had to make some adjustments, and alter our plans. Instead of one of us walking to Yampa (some twenty-five miles, I seem to remember) and having Frank Wright bring our provisions as we needed them, by pack horse, I had to make several trips afoot that summer, and pack the provisions back on my back.

Leo had a football injury, and was afraid of aggravating it, if he tried to carry a fifty pound pack over the pass. The walk into Yampa—we had to climb from the lake to the pass and back up to the pass from Yampa—consumed a whole day to Yampa and consumed the hours from dawn to twilight from Yampa to the lake especially if the pack was very heavy with provisions.

If provisions were extremely low, Floyd felt that he ought to stay and fish, so it was up to me to walk to Yampa, stay the night, spend a day buying provisions, then return to the lake the following day with the full pack.

Secretly, I was happy about this arrangement, but for some strange reason I pretended it was a hardship, and that I might just be making a slight sacrifice. To have expressed pleasure in this arduous hike, would have exposed too much of my soul, and even though my companions knew me quite well, there was the possibility that they might discover something I didn't want anybody to know about my loner dreams. I pretended practicality for every impractical thing I did.

I would start up the trail just at dawn, after making sandwiches of whatever we had left, chiefly fat bacon and possibly the last slices of crystallized bread, or a leg of snowshoe rabbit. I couldn't make a sandwich of trout, of course.

The climb to the pass was a stiff one, but I loved every minute of it.

When I reached the altitude where the snow patches still gleamed, now bordered by the mud from their melting, I looked diligently for the tracks of Ole Three Toe. Ole Three Toe was an old tom cougar, who claimed the Flat Tops and the White River Plateau, Williams Fork Mountains and Coyote Flats as his domain. He would wander over this domain in a wide circle of perhaps fifty miles radius, and according to Frank Hays, he would complete the "beating of his bounds," making his well-known "scrapes" and leaving his urine messages all around the periphery of his domain, arriving back at the Flat Tops about this time of the year.

I failed to find his tracks the several trips I made over the pass on the way to Yampa, but there were tracks of mule deer bucks, and ptarmigan tracks that were like some kind of early American stitching on the mud and the snow patches.

I trailed a black bear for perhaps a quarter of a mile, following his tracks in the mud; they were like the barefoot tracks of a flat-footed man.

I dawdled often, during an hour or more on the trip to Yampa, always above timber line, where I searched for tracks, ever hoping that I might come on the imprint of Ole Three Toe, who got his name from the fact that he had left one of the toes of the left front foot in a trap.

I was a little unhappy to see the village of Yampa far down in the river valley.

I dawdled little on the way back to the lake with the pack on my back.

On the way back with my pack, I had to swing it off periodically and rest but I tried to find as beautiful a spot as possible along the trail; I mean of course a particularly beautiful spot, since the untouched-by-man country was all beautiful. I would find a spot where a mountain brook gurgled and tinkled and laughed, or throw my pack down in a grove of petulant aspen.

I would sit thoughtless and motionless, trying to be as much a part of the life about me as I could possibly be. There was of course no pipe or cigarette to warn wildlife of danger. Smoking, we football players believed, "cut the wind."

One day when I had been immobile for some time and was completely lost in the primitive atmosphere, my man spirit camouflaged much more effectively than my physical self, a band of mule deer, does and fawns crept closer and closer to me, wondering what that strange lump under the aspens could possibly be. I was unaware of their cautious, noiseless approach and may not even have seen them if a slightly angry, much worried old doe hadn't decided to stamp her front foot and whistle (bark) challenging me to declare myself.

The band stood there with every ridiculously large ear forward. They felt no need to move their ears, one back and one forward constantly like radar reflectors (archetypal radar reflectors, certainly) since they could actually see the object of their curiosity.

On these return trips, when I could look down upon the lake silvery in the twilight, there was again, the ever so delicate sense of unhappiness. Momentary, and only of the spirit, since I was usually fatigued and hungry.

After a few weeks we moved into the dilapidated old trapper's cabin, and then later we were allowed to move into the ranger's cabin. Here we had bunks attached to the sides of the cabin and a real stove. Close by the cabin a complaining feeder creek ran into the lake and was silenced.

Here one day some rangers came from the state fish hatchery to strip trout. They trapped them in this little stream, then "milked" them into tubs which they loaded on pack horses and carried back down the mountain.

We watched them with deep interest. The bead-like eggs of the females squirting out when pressure was applied between thumb and forefinger on each side of the belly and pressed to the rear and into the tubs containing water. The sperm of the males which was like "glacial milk" responding to pressure exerted by the thumb and forefinger would be squirted over the eggs.

The slab-sided fish would then be thrown back into the stream.

I had no contemplative, neutral thoughts about the business as one might have watching the interesting process. I remember feeling uncomfortable, and apparently didn't try to analyze my discomfort in my diary. I think it might have had something to do with the fact that man was interfering with the natural processes; taking over, sort of thing, in his usual arrogance and assumption of having been specially created, therefore superior. There must have been a feeling that there just might be a throwing out of the natural rhythm of man's relationship with fish, in some strange, inexplicable manner, detracting from the very idea of sportsmanship, and thus mechanizing and commercializing it.

My thoughts were something of this nature as I stood watching the strippers, and I had no logical reasons for my feelings then, and certainly haven't now, but the attitude remains the same, certainly.[73]

Floyd fished from the raft most of the time, but we fished downriver as well, whipping the gyrating holes of water below the rapids and the rapids themselves. This peripatetic fishing appealed especially to Leo and me, and Floyd would have been a dedicated fisherman under any circumstances. Whipping a trout stream is as exciting as hunting.

We even went downriver far enough to catch an occasional whitefish; the extremely unpalatable-looking carp-like fish, but the nine- and ten-inch rainbows were a delight.

The air was sometimes very cool after the afternoon rain or even sleet showers, and we wore our football sweaters. They were the old-fashioned kind: the gooseneck type with the big letter covering much of the front of them. The great orange P's on the black sweaters Floyd and I wore were conspicuous, but Leo's emblem was on the left side of the chest, and was stylized and discreet and modest.

One cool day we had fished almost down to the dude ranch called Buford's, perhaps five miles from our cabin on the lake, and as we fished, two dude fishermen from the ranch came by, but we merely recognized each other with a courteous salute despite the fact that human beings were rare on the White River at that time. However, fishermen passing each other with un-filled creels have little time for chatting.

Within a few days one of the cowboy-guides of Buford's came to invite us to lunch at the headquarters on a certain day.

We started early and fished down to the ranch, and as we approached, we saw two young women got up nattily in western style riding clothes who seemed to be unusually interested in us. As a matter of fact one of them was flushed with expectancy, and it was in the face of this particularly pretty one that I saw the expectancy displaced by disappointment as we were introduced.

There was the tremendous orange "P" on our black sweaters which ought to have identified us as Princeton football letter men, and suggested romantic possibilities. Instead here were two unsophisticated, slightly unsure 'teen-agers from some unheard-of high school in outlandish "Äklahomer."

I have always felt a little distressed about this unconscious, unfathered hoax of many summers ago, as if I could really have been carelessly responsible for the disenchantment of these obviously hopeful Vassar girls. I felt this even later that afternoon after lunch, when courtesy demanded that we remain for a few hours, and the young women's attitude during that time seemed slightly vindictive and almost rude, due to their frustration.

Their courtesy was not only listless, it was not even mannered, but labored.

The pretty Vasserite, despite all this, did intrude on my dreams several days later as I wandered alone above the rimrock, with the eternal hope of seeing Ole Three Toe's tracks.[74] Once, when sitting with my back against a wind- and snow-distorted and dwarfed spruce, dreaming of actually seeing Ole Three Toe, I suddenly saw myself as a Princeton football hero, again at Buford's sitting with the lovely college girl from Vassar, playing a guitar in the savage moonlight of the White River.

It was near the end of our stay, and we had been comfortably situated in the ranger's cabin for some weeks, and I was preparing breakfast when Frank Hays came in with his Airedale, leaving his sleepy horse to stand unhitched.

He had come often that summer in making his rounds, and I am sure we amused him. We seemed to act as a safety valve for the emotion built up in him by the river and the tall pines and the mountains. He was obviously full of love for the lake, the river and the mountains: a love and deep appreciation that welled and frustrated him because he had no means of expressing himself.

He was large, rough-hewn and inarticulate, but he could recite "Thanatopsis" verbatim, and one felt that he only recited it aloud when he was with us, just sitting, feeling the empathy of the ungrooved ones. He recited "Thanatopsis" several times that summer, and we the untried, romantic youths listened and believed.[75]

He would recite the poem dreamily, then would rise suddenly, step out of the cabin, pat his dog, and mount his horse and leave without looking back.

Frank Hays was definitely not histrionic.

This particular morning when Frank Hays came as I was preparing breakfast was the last time we saw him. I had just come from Yampa the night before, and we had some special food, and were happy to invite him to eat with us, but he declined.

I had made this last trip to Yampa afoot because we were out of money and had to have money in order to pay Frank Wright to bring us out by pack train. I had telegraphed my father as soon as I arrived in Yampa, and I had to wait for two days for the money order.

I walked back to the lake with a full pack: a pack full of canned luxury food.

That morning Frank Hays sat for some time in a silence that seemed an unhappy one, or at least a not too pleasant one. Then when he spoke he spoke to my back as I attended a skillet: "You gonna take that porcypine skin all the way home with you?"

"I want to if I can," I answered.

"Be kinda hard to mount, won't it?"

"I'll try."

"Never remember seeing one mounted," he said. "You've got a Rocky Mountain jay and a Clark nutcracker skins, I guess."

"Yes," I said, but I thought it better to refrain from talking further about my trophies, and purposely kept my back to him.

Then it came: "Say, I tell you what'ud make a purty mount—a ptarmigan that hasn't made up its mind to be all white or all brown, this time of the year up among the snow patches."

I felt his shrewd grey eyes on the back of my neck. I was afraid to turn my readable face to him.

He continued: "Wouldn't have one, would yu?"

I didn't want to answer, but I knew I would be damned if I didn't, but before I could answer, he said, "Of course you haven't."

He rose, picked up his wide-brimmed ranger's hat, and said, "Well, good luck, boys." When he got to the door, he turned to me: "Say, when yu get back home, get someone to carve yu a piece of wood that looks like a rock, then stain it kinda dirty white for snow, and mount 'im on that. Slant his back some, so's he's natural. They like to sit on little patches of snow or on a rock kinda slanty-backed."

I walked to the door and watched him disappear among the pines, the Airedale bounding ahead.

As we ate our fancy end-of-the-adventure breakfast of lamb chops and eggs, Leo said, "We coulda eaten the ptarmigan, if we'd known."

He had a greed that was unusual, and at times transformed his whole personality which was normally amiable and adjustable. In the presence of food he became serious and humorless and over-eager in protection of his rights. This manifested itself in the fact that he was a scrupulous divider, employing fairness as a protection against incident that might jeopardize his own share. When his turn came to cook, he became stiffly defensive, especially if anyone manifested the ordinary interest in what was being cooked, even though refraining from making suggestions or giving advice.

His selfishness and his Don Juan confidence (even at sixteen) were submerged by his shy, natural amiability. The presence of the female sex even exaggerated his queer shyness, but food brought his selfishness and greed to the surface in a sort of sneering defensiveness, which at times was almost startling.

Even this outstanding morning over lamb chops and eggs, his memory of the abandoned ptarmigan from which I took the skin, inspired a defensive stiffness, as if I had done an injury to him.

Our adventure was a very pleasant one, however, and Floyd and I had soon grown accustomed to Leo's incredible greed-born defensiveness, and since his time to cook came only every third day, Floyd soon learned not to ask for gravy, and I ate my snow shoe rabbit leg down to the pink without comment.

~

After we left the lake—I left reluctantly—Floyd went to the Sand Hills of Nebraska to spend the remainder of the summer with his sister and her family. Her husband, John Renfrew, had filed on a section of land among the Sand Hills, fenced the acreage, built a small house, a shed and outhouse, drilled a well and put up a windmill, then planted a patch of small grain.

After staying with my family at Stratton Park, Colorado Springs, for a week or ten days, I joined Floyd in the Sand Hills to shoot sharptail grouse.

This was the latter part of August and the young sharptails were excellent food. The "sophomores" of course were a bit too stupid to afford the sport which the old ones gave. The old ones flushed forty and fifty yards ahead of the dogs, then flew fast and far.

The little Renfrew house was like an excrescence in a trough between two sand ridges, and the outhouse and the shed that served as a stable were flakes from the excrescence.

The house seemed submissive and tired of fighting the sand-laden winds, and the Renfrew family should have been submissive as well, but on the contrary they were happy and confident about something that was certainly invisible the two weeks I stayed with them. Whatever that Something was, it surely could not have been waiting in the sandy expanse, where there was no shade except from the fence posts and the house in the mornings and the late afternoons.

John gave the impression that he was waiting for something and was as a consequence perennially ebullient like a seventeenth-century voyageur, while Hannah's attitude was one of belief in John and the good intentions of Fate.

Floyd and I were hunting grouse for the table most of the time, and the three of us—John, Floyd and I—drove in the wagon to Mother's

Lake to stay for several days fishing and shooting young mallards.

I spent many hot afternoons in the shade of the house, preparing my grouse and harrier (marsh hawk from Mother's Lake) skins, then late in the afternoon we hid ourselves in the grain patch, and awaited the foraging flight of the grouse.

There were trips with the irrepressible John to the little town of Bingham for groceries, and Floyd and I hunted grouse on the way. Later, just before we left, the Kincaiders decided to build their own village and called it Ashby, and we had to make frequent trips from the little house to the location.[76]

John had only a team and wagon, and we crawled over the sand hills like a philosophic terrapin, sometimes having trouble and stalling in the sand that had blown across the trail since our last passage. As we crawled over ocean swells of sand, John in his ebullience would chaff Floyd, then giggle with appreciation at his own humor, tap the dreaming horses on their rumps, with the reins and say "giddap-giddap," as an involuntary expression of bubbling self-appreciation.

He claimed his 640 acres of sand and sky under the Kincaid Act, whereunder a dirt farmer could come into this cattle country and try to "prove up" on his claim within the period of five years. Naturally, the cattlemen hated him and the other Kincaiders, but the war was never as important as in other areas of the west where cattle and sheep and plow met.[77]

When I came up from Colorado for my visit, after the lake, I rode in the caboose of a long freight train from Alliance to Bingham that must have looked like a segmented insect crawling among the Sand Hills. I was fascinated and my diary is full of my wonder, but I had no idea when we reached Bingham. I looked out of my high observation window in the caboose, and saw that we had stopped at a spot where there were a few buildings, and a flagstaff and a flag plopping in the wind.

Across from me a cowboy had been asleep with his hat over his face from the time we left Alliance. When the train stopped, he awoke, looked about him, stuck his head out the window, picked up his bag and climbed down.

I said, "Is this Bingham?"

"Hell yes, cain't yu smell the goddam place?"

I had only my rucksack as luggage, so I decided to walk the five miles to the Renfrew claim, but I had to get directions, so I asked several loafers and a cowboy. Only the storekeeper knew, apparently. The cowboy looked at me and asked: "Is that goddam Kincaider a friend-a your'n?"

"No, I've never met him," I said, "but my friend his brother-in-law is staying with him and I have come up to visit for a week or ten days." Then I added, "What's wrong?"

A loafer sitting on a barrel, answered: "Rekon, he's alright, fur's anybody knows—the on'y trouble is, he's a Kincaider." This was one of the men who had at first said he didn't know him. Then he repeated, "On'y trouble he's a Kincaider."

I had begun to wonder what I had got into. Kincaider might be the name of an outlaw gang, but it sounded more like a religious refugee sect from Russia.

"What's wrong with Kincaiders?" I asked.

The loafers looked at each other significantly, and I was beginning to feel quite uncomfortable. The storekeeper must have noted this, and after all he had to sell groceries, so he tried to explain: "Why, young fella, they ain't nothin' scairy 'bout it—him bein' a Kincaider. It's a fella whose aimin' to prove up on guv'mint land. John Renfrew's alright."

I had just got to the door, when one of the men in the store said: "They's rattlesnakes and it's a good five mile; maybe more. I kin take yu out fer two and a half."

I accepted.

Now the visit was almost over, and the Kincaiders were building Ashby, and in their plans a dance hall–restaurant loomed with importance, but for music they must depend on a piano and fiddlers from among the settlers.

Hannah had insisted on bringing her piano out into the Sand Hills, and it looked incongruous in the faded little space-subdued house. John had persuaded her to allow him and his partners to move it to the restaurant–dance hall to use it until they could buy one.

She stood in the sun and wind, with arms folded over her bosom and watched the three of us loading her piano into the wagon. This piano was her solace when the winds whipped the sand out of the "blowouts" on the points of the sand ridges, and in the winter when it screamed about the little house, and she could not escape from it when the blizzards came, except through the piano.

On the way to Ashby, Floyd and I stood in the back of the wagon and held the precious piano which swayed with the movements of the wagon. I looked back and Hannah was shading her eyes from the sun, watching us.

~

[1914]

The summer following my graduation by the High School was the last of errantry for John-Without-Purpose. The long purposeless, romantic days of Boy, Horse, and Dog were coming to a close. In this wonderful first decade and a half of the twentieth century, besides the development and proliferation of the automobile, wireless across the Atlantic, Vickers and Maxim machine guns, Einstein, Freud, Bleriot flying the Channel, electric power development and the many other inventions, which would try to cut man's placental connection with the earth, there were two incidents that were to affect my life almost startlingly and dramatically: one immediately and the other within a few years.[78]

I was mildly interested in the story of the Wright Brothers making the first controlled flight in a powered flying machine in the history of the world, at Kittyhawk, December 17th 1903. I think I might have been much more interested if I had been old enough and could have read about it and understood it at the time of the flight. The mechanical alienation of man from the earth was not yet developing at that time and young people, like their elders, were influenced by an atmosphere of distrust for ornamental mechanical intrusions, which automobiles and airplanes were supposed to be.

But even so, some years later, I was interested enough in mechanical power flying to go with mother to Wichita, Kansas, to watch an exhibition of flying, and was sufficiently inspired to read every scrap of information I could come by, concerning flight and its development.

As a matter of fact I became enthusiastic.

I read a book by Gustav Chanute, and was fascinated by the story of the Brazilian Santos Dumont circling the Eiffel Tower in a balloon. The balloon had already enjoyed a vogue in the nineteenth century.

At the flying exhibition in Wichita, I remember we stood in a large crowd and watched the flying machines; there might have been three of them, and I seem to have a vague memory that one of the pilots was named Ward, another Ely, and another perhaps, Beachy, but I am not sure about this.

I do remember that a man stood on a raised platform with a megaphone, explaining to us the pilots' maneuvers.

"And now lay-dees and gentlemen, Mr. Ely will make a left bank, then fly straight on and if you'll watch carefully, he'll make a right bank. The next attraction lay-dees and gentlemen will be Mr. Ely and Mr. Ward up in the air a thousand feet at the same time."

While this man-flight excited me I got no encouragement from it. It seemed flimsy and precarious and even boastful but without arrogance. When I came home I watched again the soaring of the vultures over the prairie and the circling of the red-tail hawk, and had a definite feeling of hopelessness.[79]

I now watched them more closely, noting through the binoculars how the wing tips of both the vulture and the red-tail became flexible, and the shafts of the latter's primaries seemed to twist automatically as he banked. The planes at Wichita seemed to have the dihedral of the vulture's wings but not the camber of the hawk's wings.

I hadn't been especially aware of these things before Wichita. I was like a person who has looked upon trees and landscapes all his life, and then suddenly when he learns to paint in oils, he becomes aware of highlights and color nuance which he had not been aware of before.

Watching the vulture play about on his thermals for an hour or more without flapping, without power, became a new obsession.

There could have been some sort of ontogeny here, since primitive man must have felt deep frustrations, watching the birds. Reason came to him, and he cooked his food and used articulate speech, took the skins of animals to protect himself from the elements, but he was still earth-bound, and could only dream of flying as the birds could do. And flight being beyond him, in his dreams he would attribute such power to supernatural beings, such as angels, which his Force-inspired urge might lead him to create.

The Greeks gave wings to Victory and to the lion and called him sphinx, and the Assyrians and the Persians gave wings to bulls. Wings were given to dragons, bulls, lions, etc., and the very fact of the wings was sufficient evidence of their otherworldliness, their superiority, their powers both benevolent and malevolent. And why create gods and devils and beings of mystery if you don't attribute to them the greatest powers you can possibly conceive of, and certainly flight took them out of the province of earth-plodding man. Not only had man chosen the most powerful of beasts that walked the earth with him as mystic power symbols, but he was compelled to give them wings, the ultimate of his power in creations.

And not contented to attach wings to the powerful of the earth which he inherently feared and respected, he created dragons and other beings, and attached wings to them.

Later the Christians gave wings to angels, figments, and in order to make the devil more powerful and sinister, they gave him the bat wings of the mysterious dusk.

But the civilized, poetic Greeks could create Pegasus, and playfully have him discover a spring on Mount Helicon.

So my absorption by bird flight and the mild frustration since I had seen men in the air borne by mechanical wings was not really a matter of ontogeny after all; I tend to stress too much the frustrations of primitive men as born of the same urge as my own. In my case my frustrations had passed with my pre-'teen-age boyhood, and I didn't even have any tendency to heroize Beachy, Ward or Ely. With an incredible modesty, I seemed to assume that people who flew might well have had some special qualification: born with some special attitude as well as a very special aptitude.

Fascinated by, and now academically interested in the flight of hawks, vultures and eagles, I was contented to remain earth-bound with Bally and Spot.

The other incident which was to affect my life, and eventually end the chapter of it titled Boy, Horse, and Dog, occurred June 28, 1914, in Sarajevo, Serbia. However, after a few days, and scarcely noticing the assassination of Franz Ferdinand of Austro-Hungary in the first place, I forgot it when the newspapers dropped it from the headlines.

Naturally, I could have no premonition that this was the last summer of errantry for John-Without-Purpose, and I seemed to have ridden farther and stayed out longer, as though there had been some biological urge to crowd the hours.

I remember sitting on Bally as she stood on an escarpment of a limestone and flint ridge in the Big Green Pasture, which was part of the old Stonebreaker Ranch, and from this wind-whispering emptiness, looking down into Kansas across the border. I remember the smug feeling as I noted the little farmsteads of 160 acres. I had seen no house, not even a wandering cowboy for three days as I rode over the Osage prairie.

We must have looked like statues there against the skyline; even Spot was standing panting with head raised as though he too was interested in the nesting seabird clusters of the farms of Kansas. We were a statuesque group, and the only movement was the wind playing with Bally's long mane.

I believe I must have thought then that there was something wholly satisfying and perhaps slightly romantic about those few moments when we were like statues looking down into Kansas, but now as I write this, there is rather a sense of bittersweet nostalgia in retrospect, since one in retrospect must feel the symbolism in the group, during these last days of Boy, Horse, and Dog.

In July of this summer, Josephine and I were packing for England, and she was more excited and didactic than usual, and she had put so much pressure on mother that mother came to me in the latter part of July to urge me to finish my packing. As a matter of fact she had already done most of it for me.

She said: "Put in the things you'll need besides clothing; that's already packed." Then an afterthought: "Your father says you'd better take your horse to pasture tomorrow. He says you are to take Queen and Brownie along; we'll drive out and pick you up."

Things were becoming a bit prosaic; packing a trunk and leaving Bally at the Ridge Ranch. Was going abroad with P.J. Monk and party worth it all?

We had our passage booked on the *Mauritania* (I seem to remember) for the first of August—or it might have been for a later date.[80] Then during the last days of July, I learned about the importance of the assassination of the bad-tempered Franz Ferdinand who hated the world because he had been attacked by tuberculosis for part of his life, and had contracted a morganatic marriage, and in his vindictive anger had not heeded advice and had gone on a state visit to Serbia at the worst possible time.

I was not very concerned about the cancellation of our passage, but when war was announced in headlines, I felt a deep shock. I remember it distinctly. I entertained inescapable treadmill thoughts about the possibility of a bitter, haughty, disagreeable Archduke in faraway Sarajevo being able to affect my very pleasant life in the Osage hills. I had no idea that my country would ever be drawn into the war, and gave that probability no thought; my thoughts were on my own personal dejection, and were unbelievably strange as I try to remember them and analyze them.

As I recall, or attempt to recall my shock and dejection of that August long ago, my thoughts are even more difficult to understand. I think I might have been unhappy because in my own mind I had decided that men were too civilized to go to war with each other in the bright, sane, logical twentieth century.[81] To use a Victorian phrase, it wasn't done.

My mother's uncle Eugene Regnier had served in the Civil War on the side of the North, and had told me of blood and disease and rats and filthy prisons and men more vicious than any other species of the animal world.

And there was the shooting down of my grandfather John Mathews who had tried to make Kansas a slave state.

I heard both stories over and over and I had been impressed by the incidents of the Civil War since the time I was quite young but these things had happened in the dark nineteenth century.

I had no idea of that which had really happened at the beginning of and during the first years of my span, and if I had known I shouldn't have been especially interested; I shouldn't have been especially interested in the fact that the twentieth century had arrived seething with the common man's bitter defiance of the overlords, not necessarily the landed and the royal overlords, but the comparatively new industrial ones. The workers were fighting for shorter hours and higher wages in Europe and in the United States.

"The Man With The Hoe" was not with them marching and vociferating, nor was the vengeful peasant, prototype of the man carrying the banners with the hammer and sickle emblazonment.[82] It seemed to be an industrial matter at that time, led chiefly by soft-handed histrionic intellectuals as often as not; and these intellectuals seemed to have been divided among themselves as to the nature of their objectives, and on the fringes of their divisions were the usual mad anarchists.

There was no one to tug my sleeve or clutch my horse by the bridle and point out these things to me, and if they had, I repeat, I shouldn't have been interested.

I, in my sophomoric assumptions, had decided along with others of my age, no matter how inquisitive or disinterested we may have been, that "our" age was quite the brightest, and there was certainly behind these assumptions, the faintest hint that we the "sophomores" had made it so. Therefore I couldn't understand that there could possibly be a recurrence of the wars and the social conflicts of the dark ages of the nineteenth century: the century of our parents and other adults. Of course during the first years of my formal training, I had been induced to swallow only the slick worms of Chauvinism, and had memorized statistics concerning wars and Kings and Presidents, and there were no woolly caterpillars of Why.

I knew nothing whatever of wage slaves, as the industrial workers were dramatically called by the frenetic intellectuals: a term that seemed highly dramatic at that time, which in retrospect is transformed into realism.

It wasn't until perhaps a quarter of the new century had passed that

I became aware of the important historical incidents and their significance.

The Spanish-American War was no more to me than a chauvinistic shout about Dewey and Manila Bay, and a brash hero with tombstone teeth and spectacles, with sabre arm raised dramatically. I don't believe I associated this latter image with either Manila Bay or "Remember the Maine," unless I took time to think about the matter. I remember Roosevelt above the others because he had hunted and ranched in South Dakota. Eventually, he almost became a member of the select company of my "Tin Gods."[83]

The Boer War meant chiefly the Jameson Raid, and a granitic old man named Smuts. The Boxer War in China wherein the Chinese attacked foreign missionaries and diplomatists with "Righteous Fists" (which also covered sticks and stones and knives and guns) I remember because of an Osage Indian who was the first man of the foreign allied army over the wall, and had missed fame because the fourth man over reached down for the flag, and planted it on the wall.[84] This incident of the turn of the century was still being talked about and commented on in my town and county in 1914.

Later, when my curiosity had been nourished by collegiate learning, I asked Bonnicastle, the Osage, about the flag incident. That which he told me might epitomize the difference between the Quixoticism of civilized European influence and the protective-coloration consciousness of the Neolithic man.

Bonnicastle said: "Them fellas shootin' at us could see me better with that flag."

There were such incidents as the assassination of President McKinley, which thirteen years later I became more interested in as a highlight in American history, but the United States army playing hide-and-seek with Aquinaldo, through my full appreciation of it, later, was much less thrilling than when my father talked about it when it was a living part of our history.

But the historical disturbances which came in with the new century; the Spanish-American War and its Aquinaldo aftermath, the Boer War, the Chinese "Righteous Fists" skirmish, the Russo-Japanese War, and Teddy Roosevelt's association with the Panamanian

Revolution, and even the mad men anarchists who seemed to murder from personal resentment rather than as really altruistic champions of the "wage slaves," seemed to me to be merely the tidying up for the proper entrance of the twentieth century. The sweeping out from the dark corners of the litter from the nineteenth century and all the dark centuries that preceded it.

Despite the glory that was Rome, the Golden Ages of Greece, the Renaissance, the great Peace of Genghis Khan, Confucian China, the Pax Britannica, the long awaited Glory had really come with the twentieth century, and I the egocentric "sophomore" full of wisdom had arrived with it.

I went back to the Ridge to get Bally. She saw me when I was still a quarter of a mile away, and with tail streaming and mane like a pennant, she trotted toward Spot and me, then stopped and with ears forward studied us as if she were suspicious. We walked up to her and she lowered her head and she and Spot touched noses.

I saddled her happily; there was before us the whole month of August, and the unpleasant thoughts about war in the new century would be lost in the prairie winds.

$\sim$

It was a yellow August that year of 1914. This was the time of the year which the Osages called The Yellow Flower Moon, and the August-September period they called The Peacemaker.

There were violet-blue asters, purple gayfeather and bull thistles, but the predominant color as usual was yellow. The Peacemaker was pastel, as it should have been: yellow with goldenrod, broomweed, compass plant, four species of sunflower, partridge pea, coreopsis; and when you looked to the far horizons, the bluestem had a golden cast, which in certain lights of a bright overcast, was almost terra cotta, but in other lighting appeared gold-washed.

The "sophomore" quail talked excitedly and ran down the trails in line before lifting, and the "sophomore" prairie chickens squatted, then raised their heads to see what was going on, in violation of cryptic freezing.[85]

The "sophomore" coyotes, lanky and full of wisdom, ran to the top of a ridge then stood against the horizon and watched us as we passed. Spot paid no attention to any of them, unless I became interested.

One day he flushed a flock of wild turkeys in the creek bottom and the old ones melted into the landscape, but several of the young ones flew up into tall bottom trees, and this, to Spot, was such a novelty that he began to circle a tall sycamore and bark and slaver.

Up among the branches sat a young gobbler, with his head stretched earthward watching us and saying "quit-quit." I had my shotgun along, since I carried no meat except the side of bacon, depending on the kill for my meat.

I couldn't possibly do anything about preparing and eating the turkey, but Spot was so excited that I had to do something about the business, so I fired and the turkey left the limb far up and slanted forward to earth wounded, but despite this set off running, and Spot gave chase. This was the way Spot hoped it might be.

I came upon them within a quarter of a mile: the turkey dying, as Spot kept him down with one foot, and panted happily.

I had to cut short my questing for that day and bring the bird home. The young know-all and Spot's enthusiasm had forced this return home upon me. The silly young bird had flown to a white branch of a sycamore where he was most conspicuous; otherwise we may not have seen him.

Never was there such a Peacemaker. The yellow-tinted world of prairie waved and bowed gaily in the breezes. But it was too hot in the creek bottoms for comfortable sleeping; there the breezes were cut off and the cicadas made so much noise that one couldn't tolerate them; they were crowding the hours to complete their cycle, and this was their love song—both a love and Swan Song, since they would mate and die.

I threw my "soogin" down each night on the prairie, preferring a swell, where the night breezes could play over me, without obstruction.

The lazy prairie winds of the Peacemaker did blow my strange poetic depression over civilized man and war away, and by early

September, I again took Bally to the Ridge pastures, and Spot and I watched her walk away without even looking back.

~

My father was not quite happy about my going to the University of Oklahoma. He preferred the Naval Academy, and specifically the Naval Academy for the oddest reasons which he could never have expressed, and didn't really know the source of his preference, therefore couldn't reveal it. But later I was able to deduce from his repetition of one sentence the reasons for his choice. His reasons, I deduced much later, were inherent in the one sentence unconsciously repeated during the later years of his planning for me.

"Well, son," he would say, "if you are a naval officer aboard a battle ship you've got your bed with you at all times, and your food is served at the proper times and there will be plenty of it."

Most men who had suffered such deprivations as boys as he had suffered, fleeing the Union Bush-Wackers with his brother Ed, might have dedicated their lives to seeing that their sons "might have it better than I did," and this meant money, but my father was not vindictive for me and sought no vicarious victory over the bitterness and impoverishment of his 'teenhood and perhaps the economically powerful people who must have been associated in his mind with the ugliness of that phase of his life.

His scar was not of the spirit, but deep in the animal, definitely the scar recalling animal discomfort, the deep, still painful wound in retrospect.

But still he wanted me to be a "hossman," an athlete, and a "stem-winder" orator. These accomplishments he valued above all others, but obviously he was ready to sacrifice horsemanship and fame as an orator, for the sake of having my bed with me at all times and my food always available and plentiful.

Besides his game-madness, he loved fine horses, as I have mentioned, and I have memories of him giving William Jennings Bryan's "Crown of Gold" speech, and Shakespeare's Richard The Third's "a hoss, a hoss, my kingdom for a hoss."[86]

~

The University of Oklahoma is built on the Permian Redbed Plains. When I arrived, there were only a few buildings of bastard Gothic, in red brick; the law "barn" in white limestone, and the Fine Arts building in bastard Gothic in red brick. The Science Hall and the Library facing each other across the Oval were small and modest and tinted by the winds that blew across the Redbeds. Besides these there was an engineering building and it seems that there were some shacks, for overflow from the classrooms in the Administration building and the Science Hall.

The students were deadly serious; that is, most of them certainly were, especially those who came from the prairie-plains. Their parents had made "The Run" onto the Unassigned Lands in 1889, and onto the Cherokee Outlet in 1893, and they had fought against drought and grasshoppers and blizzards and watched the horizon for tornadoes. At times they had to pick up the weathered bones of buffalo and send them to market for the making of fertilizer, and they had often to depend on the indulgence of small trading posts in the nascent villages for credit.

These settlers who had run onto the Plains to stake homesteads, experienced the "buddy" spirit of soldiers, since like soldiers they faced a common enemy, and since they were all in the ranks, no one was superior to another, and if one family went under, this inspired in the others much more than simple sympathy, but vicarious fear and empathy. The acrid, smouldering ugliness left by prairie fires, the sun-tortured gardens and fields, the de-feathered chickens and the dead cattle, and the barns and lean-to's that had been swirled to the northeast by a tornado (the settlers were quite often safe in dugouts) made them much more than their brother's keeper, but their brother's comrade in the presence of the ever-present, relentless enemy.

And they were not only attacked by the elements but by disease, and in their hopes for their children's survival they must take into consideration percentages.

The children of these settlers who were sent to the University, were eager and serious and staunchly believed in Christian brotherhood, but there was no test facing them at the University, since no Negro was allowed to stay in the town of Norman overnight.[87]

The parents and grandparents of the students from the eastern part of the state, which before statehood had been called Indian Territory, had come into the Territory, and had resided in the territory which had later become the state, since the early part of the nineteenth century. These were members of the Five Civilized Tribes, mixed-blood members of these tribes, and other settlers. Their part of the state was wooded and mountainous, and musical with mountain streams. They too had had their hardships; many of the Cherokees had come to the state over the Trail Of Tears, and when they arrived in their new homes, they found the Osages: "buffalo Indians" from the Woodland-Plains, dedicated to hunting and war; and they themselves had brought along with them the dreaded disease cholera.

They had to consider percentages in the matter of their children's survival as well, and the prairie chickens devoured their grain and the panthers took their hogs. The prairie chickens had known only acorns, ants, grasshoppers, buds, leaves, berries and wild grains, and the panther had known only deer, wapiti, colts of range mares and wild turkeys. The domestic grains were concentrated, conspicuous and plentiful and there was no necessity to hunt for them. The swine of the settlers knew nothing of protective immobility in order to take advantage of protective background; they could only squeal and couldn't run away.

Here was manna, and these two eagerly made the most of it.

Some of these mixed-bloods and a few of the others who had been forced to leave their plantations in Tennessee, North Carolina, and Mississippi by the United States government, and settle in the area which became western Arkansas and eastern Oklahoma, carried across the Mississippi much of the Southern culture with them into the wilderness, and tried to nourish the plantation culture there, despite cholera, smallpox, typhoid fever, malaria, prairie chickens, panthers and Osage Indians.[88]

Some of them had brought their slaves with them, and this meant they also brought their caste. This might have died out in their struggle with the wilderness, where Christians might be expected to stand shoulder to shoulder in their struggle with the earth, Osages, drought, disease, panthers, and prairie chickens, if there had not been an infiltration during the nineteenth century into the hills and woods of the Indian Territory, low-livers, and criminal refugees from the laws east of the Mississippi; driven out of the states east of the river through the progress of culture and law development. Their presence and savage depredations, and way of life, alone, would have been sufficient incentive for the settlers to yield to the ancient, inherent necessity in man to create caste, even though the imported caste from the South might have grown feeble under the new conditions.

However there was no evidence of this among the students of the University from that part of the state. There was only a certain nonchalance which might not have been noticeable if it had not come face-to-face with Plains earth-struggle seriousness.

I made the freshman football team, but when we scrimmaged against the varsity, it was revealed to me that I was not a college football player. I was put into the line as a tackle (of all places for a sandhill crane) by the freshman coach, and the varsity tackle opposing me was one of the Hott brothers, and he must have been the deciding factor in my football career. The Hotts were both linemen and built like tanks, ham-handed and dedicated.

I don't believe Benny Owen and his assistants were concerned about my inadequacy at tackle, since they had a line with the Hotts, Red Phillips and others, and the backfield was full of real football players, and the next year the varsity was all-victorious without me.

But I stayed on the freshman team, and the next year I made the "Yanigans," the name for the un-lettered football pariahs.

But during my freshman year, when the game with an outstanding rival was played someone got the idea of reproducing The Run of 1889 at halftime. There were covered wagons driven around the cinder path that circled the playing field, and of course two students on horses circling in opposite directions, carrying staking flags.

Members of the freshman team were given this duty, and I borrowed a horse from Neil Johnson, who played half back on the varsity and was a member of a prominent ranch family who had their home in Norman.

When all was ready Tom Hill and I rode in a dead run, he down one side of the cinder path and I the other, and at the end of the run we reined in our horses, causing them to hook brake with their hind feet, then jumped off and planted our symbolical claim flags.

It all seemed rather silly to me, even at that age, but my father was present at this all-important game, still with burnished hope, realizing that his future All-American couldn't play with the varsity as a freshman. He didn't know anything about the Hotts and about the coaches trying a sandhill crane out at tackle, a fact which might indicate that Benny Owen, head coach, hadn't been reading the *Osage Journal*.

I saw my father in the stands with a striped tie and his Stetson hat, and there was the old look of approbation lighting his face. Even though the princeling was only a freshman yet, and not suited up on this thrilling day, his attitude, when he came to the fraternity house after the game, seemed to say that anyway there was a hoss in the affair, and son had ridden him well: in a dead run standing in the stirrups with his staking flag waving. His attitude indicated that he would have liked to discuss this particular phase of the game, but none of the young men seemed to think the incident worthy of mention.

His face was lighted during the few hours he remained at the house; people naturally deferred to him.

. . . [89]

Looking back on that tranquil period, one experiences an indefinite nostalgia, and despite the conscious maleness among the young men and the careful propriety of the young women, there was freshness and hope and a fascinating naïveté that puerile pride tried to dissemble.

Conscious maleness covered the practice of greeting each other on the walks of the campus, with "hi, men" and shaking hands with a vise-like, sometimes painful grip. Wristwatches were considered effeminate; not even transfers from Rutgers or Princeton or

Yale wore wristwatches. As far as I know, before the war of 1914–1918, no "he-man" dared to wear one. Even the girls might have felt uncomfortable with wristwatch-wearers, as they might have been with a "queer" or a Lesbian.

These were the prewar days of tranquility and naïveté.

~

[1915]

I went out for freshman basketball, but one March night my sister Josephine called over the telephone to tell me that our father was dying.

There were no cars on the campus, only a few Fords called "jitneys" running on shuttle from the campus to the center of the town and back. There were a few horse-drawn hacks for hire; as a matter of fact I had arrived in one from the inter-urban station, when I came to the University.

My fraternity brothers felt the drama of the situation, and they got McIntyre, the livery stable man to come out and pick me up to take me to the inter-urban. They had got him out of bed, and he was unhappy, drowsy and surly.

As we clop-clopped in the hack to the inter-urban, he seemed suddenly to realize that after all this call must be very important, since we were in the midnight hours, and the surliness had left his face as I paid him. He was especially helpful about the luggage, a thing he was not noted for.

He said: "I hope it ain't nothin' too bad."

"My father," I said. He became clumsily apologetic in manner only; he said nothing.

The family had sent a team to meet me at Nelagony, the junction of the casual Midland Valley Railroad, whose roadbed was so new and wavy that the locomotive's bell tinkled periodically on its own, in mild, hesitant protest, and the important Missouri, Kansas & Texas road.

It was about four in the morning when I arrived at the house, and my sister Josephine was alone, the nurse having gone to sleep. She came to me without tears and with no sign of her accustomed dramatics, and said: "He is afraid of coma, and he wanted to—to—to, I guess, say goodbye."

We stood and looked at each other for some time, and then for the first time the beauty of soul that neither one of us had ever been aware of in the jealousy-dominated spoiled child, for the moment was ascendant in the young woman.

I had a short talk with my father, about the things we usually talked about, then the nurse came in to tell me it was time to go. My father frowned and said, "Why does it hafta be this way?" He plucked at his sheet, then said, "Why can't a man die like a man, and not like a baby?" He shook his fist at the nurse: a gesture that was mock anger and at the same time evidence of dissipating control.

We waited. As we waited I recalled incidents of my boyhood and my father's association with them, and suddenly I was shocked to realize that he was almost fifty when I was born, and he was in his sixties when we camped and slept under the Indian wagon, deer and turkey hunting. He was in his sixties when we hunted behind the bird dogs, and shot plover on the wing, and when he, himself hauled the Samaris to Salt Creek and drove back on the running gear of the wagon. We were both impossible as fishermen, but we tried, usually going fishing during the time some game bird was in season, even when we took mother and my younger sisters to camp with us.

Before the final coma, he said, "I've had the horses taken to pasture, Son."

I didn't think of the pride I felt as we followed the hearse that March day; the pride I felt in noting the black crepe on the closed doors of the stores and the people along the way with their hats off; this pride I didn't think of as a sin. This couldn't possibly be a species of sin living on from the imbuement of my childhood, since sin no more existed for me. The pride I felt—a sort of weepy pride—could not possibly be a taboo remnant with me, but the consciousness of it haunted me for many days thereafter, and I seemed unable to keep back the thought, that I had somehow been disrespectful to the memory of my father.

These kaleidoscopical thoughts came during my stay at home with mother, and became even more uncomfortable when they were joined by the unpleasant thoughts created through the suggestion by our lawyer E.E. Grinstead, that I stay home to aid mother with the business affairs. I hated anything that had to do with business.[90]

Mother, the Frenchwoman, secretly believed in the superiority of the male; it was more than just a Victorian pose. She believed this especially since her special male had been eighteen years older than herself.

She hadn't the least interest in whence came her material comforts, or what circumstance allowed her libertine charging at wholesale prices at the Osage Mercantile Company. She had known no restrictions: only those represented by the limited luxury stock of an Indian trading post. Fortunately the towns in "the States" during the early days were out of her province of action. Not only did these little towns present for sale wonders in merchandise, but you could order things all the way from the East to be sent there for you.

However, she could only get to these emporia by team and buggy, and this had been impossible without my father or another driver. My sisters and I had heard our father say many times, after taking off his glasses and pointing them at a pile of bills: "We'll end up by all goin' to hell in a hand basket."

But, he did nothing to stop her, and made no attempt to teach her the value of a dollar.

So, since this insouciant Frenchwoman had been appointed administratrix, and since I was the only son, it was decided that I should stay home and work with mother and the lawyers and the business adviser, Clyde Lake.

Though I was unhappy, my mother and I were very close, and there was compensation when I could read her face and see there the confidence and comfort my presence inspired, especially since she might have been left alone, my younger sisters being in boarding school.

It mattered not at all to either of us that I was as inadequate as she was, and hated the whole thing as much as she did; what did matter to her, was the fact that there was a male as a prop for her, even if that male was only her son, whom she had nursed and prayed over from birth. The fact of his being her son only added glory to the ordinarily prosaic protectiveness of maledom, and having this glorious son in the role of the protective male, filled as he was with male wisdom, what possibly could go wrong?

Nothing did.

I worked with the cautious, honest, serious lawyer E.E. Grinstead of the firm of Grinstead and Scott. I watched his chalky hands turning pages of documents, his finger going to his lips and tongue between page-turning.

I watched the ebullient Clyde Lake who was now cashier of the Citizens National Bank, which had evolved from the old Citizens State Bank. He smoked light brown cigars, and was quick and self-assured. He exuded bright efficiency, which precluded any urge to be casual. This efficiency even extended to his long light brown cigars, which he smoked with delicacy; never tonguing a chewed one from one side of his mouth to the other. He stuck a toothpick into the end of it, lit the other end, and held the cigar in his mouth with the toothpick between the teeth.

Like many completely absorbed business men, he laughed often—at nothing. His laughing was like that of certain other business men, protective; you couldn't see his thoughts beyond it: a veritable smoke screen, or even a species of distraction display, as practiced by the brooding killdeer or the upland plover.

He had been a favorite of my father's, and he kept faith. My mother and I were fortunate in our advisers.

One day when mother, Judge Grinstead, Clyde Lake and I were not meeting to place our documents and other legal papers in neat little piles, to await probate, a day off from studying, thumbing, discussing documents, since we were almost finished with the Amer-European formalities, and on this day when there was no worrisome posthumous business for mother and me, the Big Hills came riding up our dusty hill. There were perhaps five or six of them from the Buffalo and the Buffalo Face gentes.

They had ridden from their village called Greyhorse in the southwestern part of the old reservation, some twenty-five miles away. They tied their horses to the fence at the place where mother's lilacs had overflowed the yard, and were spilling over into the "alley" (the road that led between our barn and the government barn, and separated our house from the agent's house), and mother watched them anxiously from a window.

I have forgotten whether there were five or six of them, but they were led by a member of the Tallchief family of the Buffalo Face gens, but I have never been able to identify him (he might have been Eaves Tallchief).

I went to the door and held it open for them, and they came in one after the other as if they were on the trail, seeming, as they actually did on the trail, to step into the exact footprints of the one in front.

They walked to the back of the room without making a sound, not even uttering the usual greeting "haugh." They gathered in a group in front of a portrait of my father, and there with faces uplifted to the portrait, they chanted the Song of Death, wherein The Great Mysteries were asked why they had taken away the remaining days of my father.[91]

There was in this chant no assurance, or satisfying rote or a feeling of liturgical completeness as in the prayers of the Christians or in Judaism, nor was there the mechanical exactitude and weary completeness of Allah's Muezzin from his tower, or the endless unit by unit completeness of the bead-counting of the Buddhist.

As in the morning chant to the morning star, the Song of Death ended in a sob of frustration; like the snapping of a violin string during an emotional crescendo.

The tall men then walked out in line as if on trail, in the same manner in which they had entered, saying nothing, not noticing me.

They were already untying their horses when mother came from her bedroom to which she had fled when they had begun their death chant to The Great Mysteries. She was carrying a pair of scissors and she made no effort to stop her tears. She said as she passed me on her way to the door, "I'll cut them some lilacs."

When she got out into the yard the visitors had started down the hill, so she stood, scissors in hand and watched them go. She smiled, when she suddenly realized how ridiculous such a gesture would have been. The gesture would have been both ridiculous and disturbingly

Eugenia Girard Mathews, John Joseph Mathews's
mother (Courtesy of the Osage Tribal Museum,
Pawhuska, Oklahoma)

poignant, but as it was, her laughter at herself banished her tears and obliterated her grief for the moment.

I have never known anyone who could laugh so wholeheartedly, and without histrionics at her self, as my mother, profoundly amused by her own frailties. She often used a term from her Missouri backwoods childhood, "greenhorn." I have not the least idea of its derivation; it might have had its source in French back in Normandy. "Oh," she would say of herself, "what a greenhorn."

Our yard was a jungle of lilacs, wisteria, honeysuckle, trumpet vine: a province where roses must be satisfied with understory mediocrity.

When people stopped to admire the lilacs in April, mother would study them, weigh their words for them, search for worthiness in their faces and attitudes, then if she approved of them she would invite them into the yard, and cut for them an armful of lilacs.

My sisters and I used to greet each other with "guess who's in?" and the questioner would end by mentioning old Mr. So & So, or a new government nurse or a teacher, to whom mother had given lilacs.

It was decided eventually that I might be able to go back to the University to finish the term, if I came back on weekends, and after I left, mother reported that the Big Hills had come several times more to sing their Song of Death, weeping before my father's portrait, and she was becoming terribly upset. But soon, they came no more.

My instructors of the University were especially considerate, and for the month or more I had been absent they set special papers to be turned in. In English 1, a humorous essay; in Geology 1, a paper on the stratigraphy of the Redbeds on which we stood; and for Greek 1, a long, long, dreary drilling in phonetics, in which my very bright friend Charles Rider coached me. In History, a paper, or almost a thesis, on the Age of Jackson, with whom, even by now, I was almost fed up.

~

Although the unconscious philosophy of some of the instructors of the University might have favored the "inducere" method of acquiring learning above the "educere" method, they were indulgent with me. I fell flat on the humorous essay in English 1, since I had apparently said it all in the title *Wild Animals I Have Et*, a travesty on Ernest Thompson Seton's *Wild Animals I Have Known*. My English instructor had been enthusiastic about the title and had read it with amusement to the class, and was visibly disappointed in the fizzled development of the amusing idea. The essay on the Redbeds brought an A, and in Greek I received a B, which indicated the generosity of Dr. Paxton.

The essay on Andrew Jackson was unacceptable since I had whimsically, and with small knowledge, postulating instead of presenting the results of reasoned research, suggested that Jackson knew the war of 1812–15 had ended before his post-bellum histrionics at New Orleans, which were artificially blown up out of all proportions to the facts.[92]

"Inducere" methods had little influence on me during the course, since I had an ingrained contempt for Jackson's encouragement of the tobacco juice–spitting mobs who despoiled the sacred rooms of the sacred White House, during his inauguration. I could never understand why some people in the history department could, especially after chauvinistic speeches, not only condone this wild, barbaric emotionalism, but actually champion Jackson as the epitome of the American traditions and spirit. Since I had by now begun to think for myself, I incorporated my own conviction in my unimportant little essay, ignoring completely that which had been offered me by my instructors in the classroom.

Since I had left the well-trodden road of didacticism, and found myself in a sort of cul-de-sac, I had to find my own way out, and I found my way out through the close, but perhaps specious study of one of the people of the history department.

This man pretended to sneer at intellectualism, economic wealth, community social standing and at European royalty; his pretended contempt, I would believe later, was a matter of racial-memory vindictiveness.

But he also had a smug attitude toward the uncultured and uneducated, and his sneering at them seemed more sincere, while his sneering at royalty, wealth, social position, certainly more stressed, seemed less sincere, and somewhat of a protective pretense.

He seemed to be constantly aware that his self-attributed intellectualism made him superior to the uneducated, and, he hoped, superior to many of the wealthy, and to royalty suffering from hemophilia.

So he and others seemed to find in Andrew Jackson the embodiment for their vindictiveness, and championed him as against the intellectual Thomas Jefferson and the Adamses; the thinkers and tranquil rationalists like Morris, Madison, Marshall, Lee and Carroll.

The Dastards of the old High School "nickle-dood-lums" again, this time represented by Thomas Jefferson and others as opposed to the good old American Tommy Playfair represented by Andrew Jackson.

This racial-memory under-dogism vindictiveness given expression by a few of the University instructors might later come into its own through Fascist and Communistic leaders, but certainly had no place in the institutions of Democracy.

According to my diary, I had at this early age—at least for one who had been brought up on wild prairies and blackjack ridges—begun to wonder about Truth. The instructor who sent me off the highroad of "inducere" education, because of his own common-man pride, contributed unconsciously to "educere" education. I don't believe my possible intelligence had much to do with it, since the arrogance of self-designated and vindictive "intellectuals," was almost offensively obvious.

～

[THE RHYTHM BROKEN]

My father's affairs were in excellent order, and there was no trouble in the probating, but my poor mother found herself restricted in her wholesale buying at the Osage Mercantile Company. There was more than a hint of injured innocence.

I was free from affairs that summer because of the efficiency of

Judge Grinstead and Clyde Lake, but one had a disturbing feeling that just overleaf was the end of the chapter.

The Lusitania had been sunk by unrestricted German submarine warfare and our cultured President was making speeches in which I believed, but that early June the prairie breezes failed to sweep away my intangible perturbation.

Bally was grass-fat and shone in the sun as if she had been lacquered, and Spot was joyous. He was keen and whimsical and there was so little of interesting scent in the June breeding season, and having little to amuse himself with, he played with a female upland plover, who was trying to lead him away from the spot on which her brood had frozen at her warning, through distraction display. She would fly up and then on quavering wings just scrape the grass tops, then suddenly fall to the ground, and flutter onto her side, with one wing held up quivering.

Solely for the sport of the thing, Spot, would pretend that she was actually deceiving him by her mimicking of a wounded bird, and he would rush her, and she would elude him to fly again above the grass tops farther away from her well-hidden brood.

He would never have paid any attention to the mother plover at any other time, but on this non-hunting, feebly scented day in June, he was having sport even if it were pallid. He knew he couldn't catch her if he had wanted to, and I feel sure that if he had wanted to molest the young ones he would have gone back to the spot from which he first flushed her.

My little soiled diary of this period also tells me that I was suddenly quite happy one day as I sat on a prairie swell watching a group of turkey vultures, sailing, dipping, banking, wheeling, zooming (the term "zooming" had, I believe, not yet been coined) over a carcass lying in a ravine that cut the swell, downwind from us.

The two coyotes that were tugging at the carcass paid no attention to the hesitant vultures. Two of them had already landed and were keeping their distance. A crow was more bold, and was walking about the carcass like an Indian woman, trying to decide just where to attack with her knife.

But the prairies had lost their rhythm for me this summer, and instead of a smoothly flowing stream of thrilling contentment, my periodic happiness was in its flow checked by exotic weed growths; the legato of *joie de vivre* interrupted.

According to my little diary, one day I received a slight shock. I was suddenly awakened from my day-dreaming when I heard Bally blow through her nose at something in the grass roots where she was grazing with reins dragging.

It was only a terrapin.

But, before going back to my day-dreaming, I watched Bally grazing for a moment and as she grazed close to me, I noted that just above her eyes there were nascent hollows. I went over to her and examined her teeth, much to her annoyance. She was becoming a "smooth mouth."[93]

My beautiful horse was growing old, and I was just starting the wonderful adventure that was life beyond the prairies. I looked at Spot sound asleep in the grass, like an old man taking his siesta.

The thoughts of that particular June day filled two pages of my diary, and at the bottom of the second page, was written: "But, I have heard of horses living to be twenty."[94]

~

[1916]

I saddled Bally only a few times during the summer of 1916, since I wanted to give her every chance to foal, feeling that at her age, she must be given every consideration. I had asked Tony to breed her to a Steeldust, and I planned to have a colt from my old playmate for sentimental reasons, if for no other.

The Morgans were too old now for driving, and they had been retired to the Ridge pasture, along with Brownie and Queen.

The chickens had been sold and the chicken house torn down, along with the old smokehouse, and the bumble bees came no more to the cedar roosting poles, where Tom Mitscher and I used to bat them down with shingles, as they flew into the door. In that part of the barn where we had kept the carriages and the wagon, was mother's new Sterns-Knight.

My father had considered well, the new-fangled thing, the internal combustion engine as motive power for the "horseless carriage," and after some months of deep thinking, had come to the "horse sense" conclusion that the connotation of combustion—internal "explosion," couldn't mean anything else except destruction. Explosion and combustion were really the same thing, and if they weren't, why weren't they, he'd like to know? How, then could one expect to get motive power out of destruction?

Steam, he believed, was quite another thing. Here you had dormant, potential power, not created, but waked up from sleeping to become active, simply through the heating of water, which resulted in steam, and all you had to do was release it and channel it into useful work. What about the great locomotives clanking and screaming across the Continent?

Automobiles were raising hell with traditions built on "hosses," and if the "hoss" was to be replaced let the replacement at least be "horse sensible," like something powered by steam. This, despite the fact that he had once said, "You take your life in your hands every time you board a train."

When he died there already had been much war news concerning the airplane, and aviation was just entering the realm of Romance, just a dozen years after Kittyhawk. Bleriot had flown across the Channel in 1909, and already in 1911, the year of George the Fifth's coronation, the gentry of England were landing their private planes on each other's parks or lawns.

My father, however, seemed to think that motive power through explosion in the air was perhaps too ridiculous to discuss, and one might assume that he with millions of others over the earth, must have still believed the airplane to be a vogue and a plaything.

As a matter of fact the Nations meeting at the Hague in 1907 prohibited the launching of projectiles from balloons, "for another five years." Even militarized Germany saw this ban as no deterrent to her progress toward military ascendancy, and the self-interest-watching of the Nations at the Hague seemed to think that airplanes were not worthy of discussion as possible military weapons.

So the very spring he died my father was preparing to enter the age of the "horseless carriage" but he would drive into it in a Stanley Steamer.[95]

"You see, son," he said, "you can go to the barn and start the fire in the fire box, and by the time you're ready you've got a head of steam, and you've got natural power and silence, and not all that popping you have in an automobile, like a shootin' match."

The first motor car that came to the agency, the harbinger of automation and technology, was driven up to the stepping stone and hitching rack in front of the agent's residence. The driver wore goggles, gauntlets, and a long duster and a cap. The passengers, except for gauntlets, were dressed in the same manner except that the women wore veils tied tightly behind their necks, and no goggles.

The car and its passengers might have been from Washington, D.C., and in recalling the wriggling, sandy roads of the Osage country, I am at this moment of writing, wondering how they ever got to the agent's residence at all. Could they have brought the car on the train, and had managed to drive it over the sandstone and dust, the six miles from the junction, Nelagony?

I can't remember who occupied the agent's residence at that time; it could have been Frank Frantz, and I was possibly called from playing with young Frank, to go on this great adventure all the way to the village of the Thorny-Valley People, perhaps two miles away.

I remember some of the conversation among the ladies of the party. They seemed to visualize a stampede of Indian horses, and women, wild-eyed, herding their children to the bushes, or into their lodges. They thought this sort of thing, the frightening of horses and people might be improper. Their worry was tinged with fear, I thought, but the men of the party reassured them.

The Indian women looked out from the flap-hole doorways of their lodges, and the children with their little owl-faces peeped from behind their mother's wrap-around skirts, but there was no panic.

The horses raised their heads, and several of them trotted off with heads high and manes streaming, and there were snortings and whistlings through their noses. They all stopped after a short run and looked at the strange, crawling thing, with a plume of dust behind it.

The vicious dogs came from their day beds snarling and trail-barking, and some of them ran alongside of the car, with raised hackles, yelping.

The tall, dignified men pretended that they had not seen the miracle.

If the Frank Frantz family did occupy the residence at this time the incident of the first car occurred before statehood, since Teddy Roosevelt had appointed his Rough Rider, Frantz as the last Territorial governor.

But by the summer of 1916, two of the streets of the village were paved, and the agency village had been the County Seat of Osage County for some nine years. And now there were several cars in town: a Haynes, an Oakland, a Keeton, an Imperial and a Ford or two.

Dr. Richards had a temperamental contraption which one might visualize, when someone mentioned "horseless carriage." The bug-like thing would stop, apparently without cause, in the thick dust of the center of the village, before pavement, and in trying to start it with the crank one hot day, the doctor fainted and fell into the dust. The last upthrust of the crank as the doctor fell, started the motor, and the car ran over him and snaked its way on down the dusty street.

My father had seen this from the bank window, and he came home that happy day with proof of his doubts concerning "internal explosions" as successful motive power.

When mother asked him if Dr. Richards had been hurt, he gave the impression that if he had been driving a steamer, and not an internal combustion outfit, he might have inquired about him.

The impact of the motor car on the life of the prairie and blackjacks, this superimposition of technology, even a toddling technology, demanded adjustments that were both humorous and tragic.

I have never known a more limited-minded and more dedicated follower of the teachings of the Church, or one who wore a closer fitting blind bridle of liturgy, than the local priest of my boyhood. His celluloid front-to-back collar was seldom cleaned, and his black clothing had every crease and fold filled with the dust of the village.

When some cowboy or rancher or farmer came riding into the agency on a sweat-dripping horse, or driving a foam-dripping team to ask him to come to the bedside of a dying member of the family or a neighbor, he backed his disinterested horse into the shafts, and became immediately oblivious of everything except getting to the communicant in time to give Extreme Unction.

While his thoughts wandered about in the other world, his neglected horse died one day from exhaustion; the Spirit was concerned only with the driver, not the lower form. My mother and other ladies of the Altar Society bought a Model-T Ford for him. On his way to save souls and comfort the dying in his "auto'mobul," nothing mundane could frustrate him.

People of the village knew him and got out of his way, when he came bouncing down the dusty streets tense and whispering to God.

But one day a trustful drummer (traveling salesman) was crossing the street from the Pawhuska House with a toothpick in his mouth, contented and dreamy, when Father Edwards came popping along the street on his way to a bedside west of the village.

The drummer's after-lunch reactions were inadequate, and the T-Model hit him and knocked him down and ran over him, and the shocked Father Edwards suddenly became earth-conscious, and braked.

The man was not hurt since the T-Model had a high clearance, and he was up behind the car brushing the dust from his clothing. However, Father Edwards thought he was still on him, and excited and distraught by the people running to aid the unfortunate stranger, backed up and ran over the drummer the second time. This time the motor decided to stop while the car was still over the man, and people had to push it off, but still the man was unhurt and unvexed, when he saw the priest's collar and noted his deep, saintly concern.

It seemed during this period men boasted of their cars and their own performances as drivers, more than they had ever boasted of their fast, beautifully matched buggy teams. There seemed to creep into men a scarcely tangible arrogance, which had never been noticed before, as if this mechanical power, an almost miraculous power under control by them, had inspired hauteur, giving them caste, as horses had once done, in transmuting trudging men into chevalier and caballeros, and creating the Age of Chivalry.[96]

But the mechanization of the civilized world already had a good start before the turn of the century, and the few car-owners, despite their arrogance, had not time in which to create caste, in the incredible development of mechanisms nourishing a much broader based prosperity. These few men able to own cars in the beginning when there were only a few, lost their distinction in the flood of car owners almost immediately, about the time Henry Ford spawned the T-model, and this made the creation of a Technoarchy impossible.

But they could boast of their cars as if they had made them themselves and spoke at every gathering of their virtues. They challenged each other to races on the natural roads by "honking" as they passed and boasted of making someone "eat my dust."

Soon the cars were rolling over the prairies, running over prairie chicken nests, and during August and September loaded with gunners, who shot from the cars. There were very few, of course, but one car could cover many a section in a day.

Before the doves learned to fly up from their gravel picking along the primitive roads thousands of them were killed, and the vultures soon learned about the smashed bodies of rabbits and opossums and skunks along the natural roads that twisted over the prairies.

The clever coyotes kept their distance, watching the strange animal, man-animated and stinking. They watched the car out of sight, and eventually learned to come back at twilight, advancing cautiously to the roadway to find the food the strange beast might have provided for them. Not even the "sophomores" were hit by the monsters, except at times when they might be confused by the headlights.

When we began hauling the running hounds—gaze-hounds—out onto the prairie, coyote hunting in cars, we could not really be accused of unsportsmanlike behaviour, since the danger to the hunter over hunting from horseback was much greater in the high center of gravity cars of those days. However, hunting in cars was never to be compared with hunting on horseback; the latter was the very highest form of sport.

So now the barn was empty except for the smug Sterns-Knight in the old carriage compartment. The hens sang no more or pridefully cackled over their just-laid eggs, and there was silence at dawn; no roosters crowing and no more Osage prayer-songs from the hills across the creek. Periodically during the day, motors would labor up the dusty hill which now became Grandview Avenue.

The old manure pile had disappeared from under the window on the west side of the barn; mother having given it wheelbarrow by wheelbarrow full to gardening neighbors.

Technology had arrived among the blackjack hills and prairie.[97]

~

[THE WAR OF 1914–1918]

[1917]

I wasn't particularly worried about the war, and apparently I was finally reconciled to the fact that civilized man could have wars since he was certainly having one at the moment: a very bloody and lousy one in France. There was something imminent, and I am sure we all felt it and felt that our country would finally be brought into the conflict on the side of the Allies, despite the fact that Woodrow Wilson, who ran for the Presidency on the slogan "He Kept Us Out Of War," managed to defeat Charles Evan Hughes in November.

Most of us lost interest in our studies, I seem to remember. My own attitude was not the "What's the use?" type, like the attitude of almost a half century later inspired by the atomic bluffing, and certainly must have been similar to the animal restiveness which affects horses and other animals during a barometric low.

If I did feel sure we would be going to war, I couldn't possibly have felt that I had a rendezvous with death, since one of the classical Fates who seemed to have been especially interested in me and my existence up to the moment, certainly wouldn't want to end the whole thing she had been so interested in developing. I certainly, in my self-confidence, could have felt that I had some understanding with at least one of the three Fates; even though I couldn't have named them at that time, the feeling was the same. This Fate who might have had a special interest in me I now would assume to be Lachesis, who determined the length of human lives, and who would have no intention of destroying her special work, which I could have easily thought myself to be.

I probably felt that my rendezvous might well be with Life instead of Death: an expanded, romantically revealing life.

I was reading more than the sports page of the newspapers now; romance of the war in the air was gripping me. My heroes were Guynemer and Richtoffen and Lufberry, and even though Guynemer had been a frail physical misfit and a probable introvert, which facts might have given me a warm glow of confidence in myself as a possible flyer, I was still of the opinion that I was not one of those special people born to fly.[98]

There was not only the thrilling fact of flying, but the war in the air was quite primitive, as yet a species of chivalric aerial jousting, while down on earth war had become cold, mass mechanized killing, in which the individual was like the tooth of a ratchet.

Coming with the spring of 1917, there was something exciting in the air. The samara of the elms, which Dr. Boyd had so lovingly planted at the turn of the century to make some shade on the Redbed Plains, were twisting down to the campus walks, and as usual there was the thudding of the tennis balls, and the frogs and the peepers and the bevies of sorority girls strolling and singing toward the Varsity Shop.

But this new thing that had come to the campus with the spring of 1917, was intangible and "buzzy." It wasn't a thing we talked about, but felt deeply and transmitted to others unconsciously.

It was completely an unreasonable euphoria.

When the articulate President gave his declaration of war message to Congress, his self-righteousness borne on the wings of his immaculate English, was also our self-righteousness, the bright self-righteousness of a virtuous unit of society innocent of European sins.

The Kaiser's men had already claimed the assistance of God in the motto on their belt buckles, "Gott Mitt Uns," but we asked of Him to not only consider our righteousness but definitely approve of us, and favor us above the Germans.

We of the University were formed into provisional companies and drilled under a few undergraduates who had attended military schools. We were lectured concerning war and military training and the duties of the soldier, in the Science building auditorium.

However, that which was much more important, now that war exhilaration had suffused us, was the Pan-Hellenic "military ball," and we all came in some kind of military uniform and the girls came in nurse's or Red Cross uniforms.

We had to search diligently for uniforms and I borrowed a most elaborate one from Professor Jacobson, School of Fine Arts Director. I think he must have been an officer in some royal guard of one of the Scandinavian countries, and he must have been slightly softened by patriotism to have lent his precious uniform to a barbarian from the Osage country.

Most of the girls were charming in their Red Cross and nurse's uniforms, and I seem to remember that we were all elevated on thermal currents of self-appreciation and imminent romance, which had only a conscious touch of patriotism. There must have been something akin here to the romantic unreason and the dramatics of protective maleness, when the South took up arms for the beginning of the Civil War. Like the gentlemen of the South we were transported spiritually with the compulsion to ride off in all directions, shouting slogans and waving flags, and kissing our clinging, brave, keeping-back-the-tears sweethearts, but we had to be contented with our daily classes and lectures, waiting impatiently for the call to arms from Washington.

Ours was not just a sophomoric emotionalism; the Nation was emotionalized. The sedate, academically cultured President of the United States walked down Pennsylvania Avenue heading a "Preparedness Parade" carrying a flag.

Those impatient for glory joined the National Guard, who had just come back from chasing Pancho Villa home to Mexico under Pershing.[99]

We knew of the Plattsburg idea for the training of citizen officers, and when the states of Oklahoma, Arkansas and Louisiana were given an officers' training camp, I joined the 1st Cavalry of the 12th Provisional Troop.

But while waiting to be transported to Little Rock, Arkansas, for training, I made a search for an epaulette from Professor Jacobson's elegant guards uniform.

I failed to find it but as in [the] case of Mr. Herbert of the School of Journalism and the editorial I failed to write, I experienced a degradingly apologetic feeling. I still have this feeling when I periodically see Professor Jacobson, whom I also admired. Professor Jacobson had all the virility and ruggedness of one of his own landscapes, and to me as an undergraduate he personified the classic gentleman, in direct descent from Chivalry, Scandinavia conditioned. Even today I associate him in my thoughts with fiords and mountains.

At home preparing to leave for Little Rock, I went to my uncle Nick Girard's house to visit with Jeanne Girard, my grandmother. We sat in her room and talked of war, and she was excited about my going, and this might seem a strange attitude for one whose father had left France to escape being drafted by Napoleon 3rd.

She had a map of the war area pinned to her room's wall, and she had it stuck with colored pins to indicate the position of the armies, and she moved them daily or weekly after reading her *Kansas City Star*.

Her pretty pins indicated a bow into sacred France, but what matter, the *sal Bosche* would soon be pushed back across the Rhine, and her interest in America's entrance into the war indicated that she approved of it, especially since she criticized only Great Britain. However, she wouldn't say definitely that the entrance of the United States into the war would save France, only intimating that the war would be made easier for France, and that "it was about time," remembering, one supposes, Lafayette.

Of course she was never disloyal to her adopted country, only jealous because France had become second rate. Chauvinism dies hard in the hearts and bloodstreams of Frenchmen.

As a matter of fact, I could see as I kissed her goodbye, that she was deeply proud of the United States, her Gallic vindictiveness melting.

On the train to Little Rock, I wondered if I could ride an army saddle, a McCleland saddle, as they were known. I wondered why the army didn't make use of the strong, rugged, bronc-busting, steer-roping stock saddle, like my Frazier.

I also pictured my horse. I had seen pictures of the white horse or the black horse troops, and naïvely wondered if our 1st troop of the 12th Provisional would have horses all of one color.

But my dreams which were titillating, due to the imminence of exciting action associated with horses, were often broken even on the train to Little Rock to admit Guynemer, Richthofen and Lufberry, diving out of the sun like a falcon or a golden eagle.

I remember being startled out of my dreams about black or white cavalry horses and aerial Chivalry over France, when the thought came to me that neither my French mother nor my French grandmother had evinced emotion when I kissed them goodbye. I know that my mother had kept her Latin emotions deep at that moment but my grandmother showed only a slight excitement and pride, like perhaps the Spartan mother who reminded her warrior son to come back with his shield or on it.

Our Citizens Training Camp was on a mountain top on the site of the old Fort Logan H. Roots, and one could walk out from the camp some distance and look down upon the writhings of the Arkansas River.

I had my own nostalgic-soldier spot there on the rim rock, where I spent many hours.

The companies and troops of cavalry were in new barracks, one company or troop to a barracks, and one was soon able to re-create in his own mind the atmosphere of seasoned obedience, the band concerts and the social amenities among the officers and their wives of the old forts of the last century. And here at Fort Logan H. Roots, the Boots & Saddles atmosphere still clung; not only emanating from the old mess hall, the officers quarters and the administration building, but during the band concerts on the parade ground some late afternoons and early evenings, it had a striking revival. As I watched and listened, I often thought of Bret Harte.

There was a species of dignified boredom among the regular officers and their ladies, but among most of us citizen-soldier pariahs in
our bob-tailed tunics and satchel-seated britches there was the boredom of limbo.

United States military prowess had become recently recognized by
the panoplied Europeans, but didn't quite speak the language. In the
United States there had been no theatrical military traditions as there
had been in England, France and especially Germany and Russia.
Our Revolutionary soldiers often wore mop-like scratches and backwoods homespun or leathern britches and woolen stockings and rib-
bons to distinguish rank, and both the Blue and the Grey must have
had their uniforms thrown at them by the commissaries.

At Fort Logan this obtained; we were given hats that originated in
the Indian wars—campaign hats. They were like the modern Shikari,
Forest Ranger, hats adopted by Baden-Powell for his boy scouts. So
as not to confuse us with soldiers the army had our hat cords made
in replica of the officers' hat cords, except that instead of being black
and gold interwoven, they were red, white and blue, with familiar
"acorns" in front, where the cords ends were joined, and hung free.

I was permitted after protest to go bareheaded until I could be fur-
nished with a seven and five-eighths size hat. The incident that made
flexible the inflexible regulations, happened on the parade ground
when my too-small issue hat had blown off and under the feet of
Captain Hays's horse, causing him to snort and sidestep.

There seemed to be two regular officer's attitudes toward us citizen
soldiers. One, that we must be accepted into the sacred military category (but not into the caste) because of the present emergency, and
as a military gesture of obedience, and the second one had to do with
the fact that we could never quite become gentlemen, no matter what
rank we might receive at the end of the summer's training. The regularly enlisted men were already calling us "90 day wonders."

We of Troop 1, drilled in the manner of cavalry, but there was only
one horse in the whole troop and he belonged to Captain Hays, the
troop commander, and "latrine news" had it that there would be no
horses; and there weren't, ever.

I trained with the Troop in cavalry drill, swinging into troop front like an obedient cavalry horse, and all summer I saw only two horses: the one ridden by Captain Hays, and one exercised every late afternoon by Captain Kuznic of the 8th Company.

Captain Kuznic would stand with a long rope in his hand, the other end attached to the horse's halter, and he would make this strikingly beautiful horse alternately trot and lope the periphery, cracking his whip like a true ringmaster.

I often went there to watch.

One day in from the drill ground where we had been drilling like the horseless cavalry, which of course, we were, we wiped the sweat-muddied dust from our faces, and some of us were lying on our cots, looking at the ceiling with perplexed expressions, thinking nothing like good soldiers. Some of us with shoes and socks off were rubbing our feet solicitously.

Woody stood at the entrance to the barracks, hot, sweat-muddied like the rest of us, and as he looked down the long rows of cots, he seemed to be the only one who saw any humor in the situation.

Woody was below average height, perhaps, and his weight was perfect for a cavalryman; he even had bowed legs as if Nature had been planning a career in the cavalry for him. But this was only Nature's dream, and busy shaping his legs and watching his weight, she forgot horse orientation for him.

He was one of those delightful people who have a tremendous respect for the seriousness of life, the rights and opinions of other people, the social and religious hierarchies, and realizes that he ought to recognize the Proprieties and practice seriousness, but breaks over like a compulsive sinner.

He could look up into your eyes and in his naïveté, become very serious about the war or horses or citizens training, then in the middle of a sentence, break into an impish smile as if he suddenly realized that he was being a querulous hypocrite.

He said to me one day, as if to assure me that he meant no discourtesy to me in his attitude toward horses (I never did learn why he was a member of Troop #1—mixed-up papers or something, and perhaps his fear he might be summarily sent to the ranks if he stood against even confused orders).

"I've only seen beer wagon horses; never even touched 'em. Glad we won't get 'em. Take me and a horse, now; neither one of us would know what'ell to do. A horse seein' me for the first time might figure that his turn had finely come."

On this hot day he stood a moment, sweaty and apparently sad. Then he broke into silent laughter at the rows of dejected troopers, the kind of smile that had it been anyone's except Woody's might have invited a barrage of army shoes from the nearby cots.

Suddenly, impulsively, he came nikkering down the aisle between cots, kicking a cot on one side then on the other, making explosive, farty sounds with his lips as he loped along.

Dejection, sore feet, muddy sweat were forgotten and, men even sat up on their cots to laugh.

Suddenly someone shouted "Ah-Ten-*Shun*."

At the opposite end of the barracks, Woody came face to face with Lieutenant Recalled. They stood and looked at each other. The Lieutenant trying to decide what his new dignity demanded since he had been recalled from retirement as a sergeant and commissioned, and his silver bars were placing a tremendous responsibility on him—a responsibility to the Nation and to the Army.

Unaccustomed, he felt around for superiority and formality. This sort of thing was not in the much-read Officers Manual.

While the Lieutenant hesitated, Woody rounded up his wits, which never wandered far, clicked his heels together, stiffened and saluted, staring with military immobility at something near or on the Lieutenant's right shoulder, possibly a fly, and said: "With your permission sir, may I go ahead with my lessons to the boys on seat and reining, and, and movement?"

Recalled nodded; he was happy to get out of this one. Woody turned sharply on his heels and as he came between the rows of troopers now stiffly standing at the foot of their cots, at attention, he said: "We'll continue after the Lieutenant's inspection." Since he was preceding Recalled, he was wearing his usual impish smile, and we standing at attention had a difficult time controlling our faces.[100]

~

Guynemer with his feminine features and his onetime rejection for military service had given me mild encouragement, which was not nearly strong enough to banish my misgivings, and I was no nearer being convinced that flyers were not specially endowed.

But, now, Phil, a pale, sedentary fellow from one of the infantry companies, came to tell me one day in adenoidal tones that he had applied for entrance to Ground School, which were formally called Schools of Military Aeronautics, pre-training for the Aviation Section of the United States Signal Corps.

He was a chain smoker and his fingers were stained with nicotine, and he was no athlete, but apparently despite all this he had been accepted by the Signal Corps, and was now waiting for an opening in a Ground School, and would eventually fly.

I talked with him for several hours at different times, each time wondering anew at his paleness and slightly annoyed with his smugness.

Suddenly I felt "buzzy" about something but didn't know exactly the nature of its source. I awakened at night to feel a slight thrill, and there was the "buzzy" feeling as I played horse with my fellow troopers on the drill ground.

Finally, I found the source of this nascent emotion in Phil and Guynemer, in Phil's cigarette-stained ineffectiveness and in Guynemer's frail, feminine beauty.

I can't quite understand in retrospect why I was so modest about flying. As I remember my outlook on life in general created by my family, and my non-competed for and careless successes, unbroken from the beginning of my consciousness, I am still more uncomprehending. Having always been fascinated by bird flight; their easy mastery of the air, especially the red-tailed hawk, the harriers, the golden eagle, the vultures and the swifts and swallows, I suppose I had felt so meek and earth-bound and inadequate and humble, as I spent hours lying on my back on the prairies as Bally grazed and Spot dog-napped. I can remember my emotions, and once, when I was quite young actual tears of frustration.[101]

As early man in the creation of his gods, had given them wings, and as the Christian concept gave wings to super-humans they called angels, which placed them unquestionably above man's earth grubbiness, so had I invented a certain type of man, born to fly, as naturally as one might be born to become obese, or tall, or ugly-faced, or short, or aggressive, or meek.

Now after talking with Phil, and after spending one night where anticipations replaced dreams, and one day on the drill ground, daydreaming as I played horse with my troop, I went to Captain Hays and asked permission to take the examinations for Ground School, and if successful to transfer from the Cavalry to the Aviation Section of the Signal Corps.

He looked at me critically, and I saw for the first time that he didn't think much of me as a possible cavalryman, *his* service. This was due chiefly, I learned later, to the fact that I failed to come up with the right answer to a grain supply problem, given us one day after a practice scouting maneuver in which the Captain himself had complimented me on the handling of my squad. Then as I learned later, Lieutenant Recalled had come to him with my messed up arithmetic, the valuating of which had taken several days. The problem had to do with the amount of grain necessary for a troop, covering a certain number of miles over a certain type of terrain (they always mentioned terrain; army people loved that term) during a certain season.

The Captain's orderly, "dog robber" in the vernacular, told me later after the war, when I met him in Yellowstone National Park where he was working, that Captain Hays had frowned when Recalled had brought the papers to him, and with his stubby finger on my sloppy arithmetic had observed: "He's a college man too."

I think I made Captain Hays happy that day I asked permission to transfer, since I have a feeling that he could not have conscientiously recommended me for a commission in the Cavalry, after my not being able to work out the amount of grain on a certain terrain for a certain number of miles, during a certain season.

It seems to me also that the hypothetical enemy territory might have been a factor in the problem—the territory of the Plains Indians or Villa's Mexico.

Anyway, he not only gave me permission but recommended me as having the proper conformation (cavalrymen love this word "conformation," applied to men and horses) for flying which he didn't know anything about, but it was a double-edged statement, which intimated that I didn't have the proper conformation for a cavalryman.

He had never seen me within touching distance of a horse.

But he was a kindly, humane, conscientious person, and I do believe that if I had got the grain problem worked out correctly, he might have wanted to keep me, but since I had flunked it, he must have believed that I might as well consign myself to the la-dee-da Aviation Section of the Signal Corps; I had asked for it.

Very few self-respecting army men over the world took aviation seriously, and perhaps thought that it was the perfect service for the unmanly and the misfits. An English officer in France was irate, and appealed to the War Office about war planes, complaining that "the bloody things frighten the horses." General Pershing was careful not to get any of it on him, and Foch encouraged publicity about the successes of Guynemer seeing to it that they were blown up to the size of miracles for the purpose of *esprit* in the trenches and in the streets of Paris. France could be vicariously triumphant in the person and the heroics of Guynemer and other pilots without attaching great importance to war in the air.

Only Lord Kitchener, apparently—or at least he was one of the few of the army men—appreciated the importance of the aviator, saying that he supported effective leadership on the ground.

Captain Hays was certainly not alone in his attitude, and this kindly man avoided the very unpleasant duty of withholding my commission in the Cavalry. A dedicated Army man would have wanted to save good cavalry material from error.

In my memory I consider Captain Hays one of my most important benefactors.

I was accepted for ground school and now changed my status from citizen in officer training to cadet in training for a commission in the Signal Corps, but I stayed at Fort Roots until the training terminated, then went home to await my orders.[102]

～

My orders were for the Ground School at Austin, Texas, and in harmony with the suddenness and the magnitude of war on our great unprepared democracy, we were housed in the buildings of the Institution for the Blind.

We were now cadets and wore white hat bands around the same old Shikari, Boy Scout Leader, Forest Ranger hats of the Indian Wars and the Rough Riders.

Our curriculum was straight from England, based on her war in the air experience, while our physical training and general regimentation was from West Point. We studied motors, alignment, wireless, meteorology, map reading, and machine guns, the latter which we had to learn to take apart and reassemble blindfolded. When your gun jammed in combat, you had to be able to do something about the un-ejected shell fast.

We drilled each afternoon except Saturdays and Sundays.

On Saturday afternoons we boarded the trolley which shrieked and rasped down the hill into the center of Austin which we explored: our thoughts, of course, on girls.

Austin being the seat of the University of Texas, we were of interest to the co-eds. We were like a migration of robins from the north, taking the places of the indigenous robins, the men of the campus having migrated to every branch of the services, and some had gone to France and England.

We were a new experience and perhaps a thrilling one for the co-eds, with our clipped words, suffixed "ers" from New England, and stressed verb endings; the plateau-like inflexionless speech of the mid-west, the tell-tale speech from the Plains and the prairie, and the beautiful, soft, viscous speech of the South, which had come from the South east of Texas' natural drawl.

There were theatrical entrepreneurs from New York, All-America football heroes from the mighty Big Ten Conference, Harvard classical scholars, Yale Sheffield scholars, clear-eyed and duty-bent collegiates from Kansas, Nebraska, Iowa, who dreamed of going back to the land or industry after we put things tidy again at war's end.

I believe a college degree or three years of college were the basic academic qualifications for acceptance by Ground Schools; or it may have been two years of college, and I had the impression, and the feeling still clings, that some of the academically able and physically acceptable ones were refugees from the fix bayonets and thrust-for-the-belly, squads right, squads left routines of the Citizens Training Camps of the land. Guynemer's exploits, as great as they certainly were, but blown up for Allied *esprit* and universally publicized, may have made of physical unfitness and feminine delicacy convenient criteria for Citizen Training Camp commandants, thus giving them a catch-all in the Aviation Section of the Signal Corps for their few "la-dee-da" over-sensitive ones.

I believe, if I am right in the first assumption, that the percentage of these "refugees" who made it through flying school was small.

The four years of West Point regimentation were crowded into the few weeks at the Institution for the Blind, which had become our Ground School, and at the end of that time you were qualified to enter Flying School. But before you were a worthy candidate for Flying School, you must have completed the course without a failure in any subject. If you failed in one subject during any one of the weeks you were dropped, unless your other qualifications overbalanced this single failure, then you would be given another chance, and were dropped back one week.

It was a terrific test, both physical and mental, and by this time England would be telling us that in early 1916, the German Fokkers had forced on England formation flying over the lines and the enemy had bombers bombing ammunition dumps and troop concentrations, and bombers being slow and cumbersome had to be protected by fighters, and in trying to cope with these fighters, they England, were learning something new every day, what with the Germans taking the initiative in speedier and speedier planes, much, much more efficient than anti-aircraft. England had to do more than simply defend against these improvements, but themselves produce faster planes, climb to higher altitudes, bomb across the lines.

These improvements were her defense.

So as she learned through experience, England passed the knowledge on to us with a silent plea, "I say, *can* you shove it along a bit— it's becoming sticky here."

We were up at reveille, lined up for morning roll call, ran back to barracks to make our bunks, ran to the mess hall to get into line again and march to our seats at table; out of the mess halls to lectures which we didn't dare miss, and then classes and lectures until noon, with no interim. We had the mid-day meal, then out to drill and back later to practice wireless, etc., etc., etc., into the night.

I have seen men fall asleep over their writing pads as they sat on their bunks writing on their knees to their girls back home.

England was urging us to "shove it along a bit."

I had no girl back home, but I got letters from my family and a roast turkey at Thanksgiving time from mother, which having no priority, took a circuitous route, was held up, and arrived spoiled. I had a letter from my youngest sister, Florence, addressed: Cadet J.J. Mathews, United States School of Military Aromatics."

Every Saturday just after the mid-day meal, we crowded to the bulletin board where the weekly grades were posted, to see how we were doing. The tension was sharp from mental and physical fatigue.

One day I saw an All-America football star from the Middle West weep when the bulletin board told him that he had flunked motors for the second week.

I went each Saturday afternoon to the bulletin board and over the shoulders of others read my grading. It was something like Sewanee's bulletin at the entrance to the chapel. Satisfied, and with a light heart, I went downtown in the complaining trolley, drove out to the University in a taxi, picked up Mary Wilkins at the Kappa Kappa Gamma House, and we went to dance all afternoon, where the dust from the floor danced in the beams of light coming through the windows. The room was above a store I believe, somewhere on some street somewhere in Austin.

Mary was a beautiful girl, and we were very happy playmates. She seemed to understand my idiosyncrasies so readily, especially my *joie de vivre* insouciance which dominated my sense of humor. Serious people seemed to find this attitude toward life too light, intimating in their reactions to it that there must be something more than just the joy of living behind it. People often, by their manner, seemed to accuse me of over-stepping, even to the extent of *lèse majesté* and sacrilege, despite the fact that my manner was not the least obtrusive.

I now suspect that this characteristic of mine could possibly have been put on the scales by Captain Hays with the grain supply problem, and aided in overbalancing my qualifications as a cavalry officer. Anyway, a natural sense of the ridiculous wouldn't have suffered from malnutrition during the training of horseless cavalry for the Military Manual's "success in battle."

Mary didn't resent my attitude through interpreting it as arrogance, and appreciated my tranquil humor, and we became self-appreciated dancing playmates on Saturday afternoons.

Then on New Year's Eve, I remember vividly an attack of jealousy. I had been assigned to guard duty as a necessary part of our military training. The brilliant lights of the State Capitol shone down upon me, since there was a light in every room it seemed. I could hear the music faintly, or at least I imagined I could hear it.

I walked my post in my long top coat: too long and not regulation, yet there seemed to be no definite regulations in the Aviation Section of the Signal Corps, except the white hat bands and the general-issue tunics that flared up into a sort of ballet skirt behind, and the britches with their nineteenth-century Turkish bagginess. For top coats we pleased our individual whims, and our vanities often chose leather leggings, instead of the canvas ones or the ugly wrap-arounds.

Why bother about regulations for such a la-dee-da ephemeral service?

As I walked my post in my long surcoat, I felt like a Cossack. I wore a knitted helmet under my hat (had to use a chin strap to keep my hat on) and a pair of especially knitted wristlets sent to me by a very concerned friend of the Oklahoma University days. The helmet I needed on this cold night, but the wearing of the wristlets was a courtesy, since I hadn't had time to answer her letters or thank her for the fruit cake.

My conscience urged the wearing of the wristlets.

Up and down, up and down and the lights of merriment gave out into the night. Suddenly, I realized that Mary would be there where the lights were so cheerful, and I was out in the cold. Mary would be dancing with someone else; some other cadet, since I seem to remember that this was the Governor's party, and some members of our squadron certainly had been invited, or someone from Camp Travis even. If she were dancing with a cadet, it could be the soft-voiced, very handsome man from Atlanta, who was as unconsciously arrogant as I was. Obviously Mary liked my arrogance, then why not his, and he would be one up with his beautiful Southern voice—they could be soft-voiced together as they danced.

It could be the Yale man, or the Harvard man who gave the impression that he was making mental notes on the amusing folkways of Texas. Mary's beauty would mess up his thoughts and his condescending amusement.

I was relieved at 2 a.m., sometime after 1918 had arrived among the merrymakers, and Mary would still be dancing with an infatuated unknown.

This jealousy, I remember as being rather strange, since I can remember being jealous only once before. Sue Lessert was not at her sorority house when I called, and later I met her walking with John Carey.

I had supposed that there would be no need for a display of jealousy where there is no competitive spirit and where passivity is the dominating characteristic and where there had ever been the assurance of being favored. This assurance did absorb all nasty little innuendos and satirical vindictiveness, and all urges to vengeance in others. The spirit of vengeance being ill-nourished and ephemeral in my being, I had very little understanding of it.

I mention this incident of jealousy, since without basis it was unique, and seems to have been born of my discomfort and what I believed to be a very silly occupation on that cold New Year's Eve.

So we were rushed through our telescoped, concentrated training, in order to sooner aid the Allies in countering German ingenuity in the air: Classes, drill, lectures, wireless, meteorology, motors, alignment, from dawn until darkness fell.

There was no survival training, since in those days we didn't survive our ships.[103]

The atmosphere was charged; the results of the un-natural pressure were fatigue, tension, fear of failure and constipation.

I wrote to my mother telling her of the frenetic program, and intimating that there was scarcely time for healthful functioning. She sent me a tin of brownish little tablets, but I didn't dare take them. Later, after the war, my sisters told me that our mother in recommending these same little tablets to a friend, assured the friend with her usual linguistic entanglements, that her son had taken them and had "passed every thing in the army."

Mother considered a second Lieutenancy an achievement.

But even at the end of the course, as I stood at the bulletin board which assured me that Mathews J.J. had passed all his examinations satisfactorily, I was not assured by this that Mathews J.J. might qualify in another category, since the graduation from Ground School didn't necessarily mean that I would be accepted at Flying School since there were matters of co-ordination, temperament, attitude, and our instructors had kept notes on us.

I had not graduated brilliantly by any means (what had happened to the "Ancient Greek"?). Motors had been my nemesis, and I finally had to commit to memory the lectures on motors, and transfer the memorized lectures to paper, and even then barely passed. I hadn't known a camshaft from a crankshaft when I entered Ground School, and was still a little hazy about the matter when I graduated.

Then the day came when we stood in squadron front and waited for our names to be called since those whose names were called would be recommended for flight training.

As I stood at attention waiting, I had never realized that there was such a great distance between A and M, as there was at that moment in history. I also hadn't realized that there were so many L's in the 24th Squadron, and it seemed that my name might never be called out.

When it was finally called out, I remember having a deep feeling of responsibility; so much depended on me now, and I seemed to know at last that men need not be Fate-pampered in order to fly.

I remember, in my deep self-satisfaction, that I looked up at the flagpole where our 24th Aerial Squadron's pennon hung limply as if it too had felt the tenseness of the weeks just passed. It bore the circle emblem of the Allies, the emblem which Allied planes carried under their wings; and there on the pennon was the Allied plane dropping a vaned bomb plumb on the tower of Potsdam.

I was assigned to Kelly Field, just south of San Antonio, Texas.

~

[BOY BECOME A PEER
OF THE RED-TAILED HAWK]

The now teeming, roaring airfield called Kelly was built west of south of San Antonio, Texas, about 5 miles. The necessary acreage had been scraped and shaved, but around the edges still grew the original mesquite, huajillo and huisache like the fringe of hair of a cleric's tonsure: a flat-headed cleric. There was a long line of hangars and a straight ribbon of blacktop running along back of the hangars and dividing them from the barracks and the officer's quarters.

In front of the hangars was the "line" and the field.

The United States Army had established the flying field here in April 1917 with only a few planes and a very few flyers, most of them civilians. They took advice from England concerning the necessities of war in the air. Eight months after its establishment when I arrived from Ground School, the field was of great military importance. The U.S. Army Signal Corps had the J.N.-4 trainer, and only these as trainers. England had warned them against having several of a variety of models, with which they couldn't fly proper formation, and formation flying had become a necessity over the lines when Germany had begun aerial attacks on their artillery spotters and their reconnaissance planes and later their bombers. To attain uniform and successful formation flying, you had to have uniform planes.[104]

England had been offered the Wright Brothers' cooperation within seven years after their successful power flight in 1903, when they suggested to England that they buy their invention, but the War Office had turned the proposition down.

175

England had become the most powerful unit of society in the world through her insular position and her sea power, and she didn't want anything to disturb this advantage, and this new flying Thing wasn't to be nurtured, since her power might be diminished, or even through military development of the airplane be placed in jeopardy. England wanted to "keep in touch with the movement" of aerial navigation toward a military weapon "rather (than) to hasten its development."

The attitude of 1911 had to change quickly in 1914 in order to keep from being beaten by the Germans in the air. England found herself depending on France for her motors.

So after the Fokkers in diamond formation began to attack, the reconnaissance and spotting planes, the English had to send their planes over the lines protected by planes in formation, and they were learning many more things which they passed on to the flyers of Kelly Field.

The success of the Fokkers caused the English to make their reconnaissance from higher and higher altitudes, and the camera became a necessity and very effective in revealing trenches, gun emplacements, troops and ammunition dumps, that the naked eye couldn't hope to discover. Thus began the feverish development of aerial photography, and their findings were passed on to us. They assured us of the great importance of weather forecasting, and that wireless was imperative.

The Fokkers forced the development of aerial photography, the necessity for high altitude flying, wild goose and diamond formations, and the beginning of the attacks by the Fokkers on the English observation planes inspired the quick development of aerial gunnery. Long before this the English pilots had left their revolvers and carbines and rifles on the airdrome and began to mount Lewis and Vickers machine guns.

In 1914 they dropped small bombs over the sides of their planes, and hurled flechettes, and had some difficulty in hitting the Continent.[105] Later they had bombs attached to the undersides of the lower wings which were released over the target directed by a bomb sight located on the edge of the cock pit on the pilot's arm rest. They had to work fast in the development of adequate defense in the air, and the enemy of course were their inspiration.

Had the Fokker not appeared in February 1916, the English pilots might have carried on with their aerial jousting, with their top section machine gun, and flying about in their vulnerable, low-altitude artillery-spotting planes, and their low-flying reconnaissance, not even dreaming of flock protection at high altitudes which made aerial photography absolutely necessary, and they might not at this date, spring of 1916, have developed a plane called the De Havilland #2 and through its frailties inspired the maxim "stunt or die" which was so dramatically appealing to us Americans at Kelly Field.[106]

The D.H. #2 built for speed and altitude was fitted with a motor too heavy for the body, and its controls were so sensitive that it could go into a spin with startling suddenness. This sort of thing got the pilots' "wind up" especially since the D.H. had a tendency to burn as it spun to earth.

There were no parachutes for the pilots of 1916.

The pilots called the plane that seemed otherwise to be a match for the Fokker "The Spinning Incinerator," and after several pilots had the experience of falling into a spin when they were attacked by the German pilots, they realized that while actually spinning they became a difficult target for the German aerial guns. Soon, they learned how to come out of a spin, and began to practice this maneuver as defense acrobatics along with other "stunts."

At the battle of the Somme the English had the mastery, but soon after this the Germans recovered it, and the English had to come up with more advanced planes and acrobatic maneuvers, as well as trying for higher and higher altitudes.

They had learned to loop, spin, sideslip, stall, roll, fly with the erratic flight of the woodcock, and imitate Max Immelmann's turn. The Immelmann was a half loop: nosing up as if to go into a loop, but at the top of the loop, slipping off on a wing, then pulling the plane out so that it was then flying in the opposite direction from the one in which it was flying before the maneuver began.[107]

However, many of these stunts might have remained chiefly

defensive, if Rolland Garros, Frenchman, and Anthony Fokker, Dutchman, the latter detained by the Kaiser and his advisers, had not solved the problem of synchronizing the whirling propellers with the firing of a machine gun attached to the cowling just in front of the pilot, which made of the aircraft a firearm itself. Now one had only to aim the plane, as one might aim a gun.

Rolland Garros was another military "misfit." He was a concert pianist and an exhibition flyer. He was flying his Morane in Germany when the war came, where he would descend from his flights and then amuse his crowds by playing the piano.

When the war came he was shocked to find himself a prisoner, and was informed that he would be held for the duration, and perhaps used by the Germans in their experimentations in the air.

But one night when his guards were guzzling and singing in the post's bierstube, he crept out to his Morane, started it and launched himself into the night to become one of the first night flyers. Aware of his dwindled gasoline supply, he made for the nearest border, which was Switzerland's.

From here he went home to France and joined his country's Air Service.

He worked with another French flyer, one Eugene Gilbert, on the idea that the aircraft could be made an arm itself if they could discover a way to fire a gun through the revolving propellers.

They mounted a Hotchkiss gun back of the propeller, then fastened V-shaped armor plate to the butts of the propellers, and when trying it out aiming at sandbags on the ground, some of the bullets ricocheted and killed two of the observing officers, and after this Gilbert gave up.

Garros kept trying.

He found that firing 300 rounds a minute from his machine gun at varying speeds of his propeller revolution, that less than 7 percent of his bullets hit his armor plate deflectors.

Then he went hunting Germans, with his Hotchkiss machine gun mounted just in front of him and with a cable reaching from his stick to the trigger of the gun, and in this way he could fire the gun with the same hand that held the stick.

He downed an Albatross in April of 1915, and he had, after this five victories in sixteen days, and received the title "Ace" from the dramatic American journalists, and was cited by the Legion of Honor from his own country, and one might presume that he not only became one of the first night flyers during his escape from Germany, but according to a French pilot who came to advise us at Langley (or was it Ellington?) he was the very first Ace of the war. If these things be true one might wonder why the French government didn't heroize him through publicity in order to imbue the soldiers and the hero-hungry populace with *esprit*? Perhaps if the American journalists had been less flamboyant in attaching to all flyers who downed five planes the term "ace" they might have presented him to the world as a hero, delivering him from an undeserved obscurity. Before the war the French had referred to Grand Prix winners and other winners as "aces," and here the dramatic journalists found their term.

Although Anthony Fokker had to perfect the synchronization, the idea seems to have been Gilbert's and Garros'. The later Vickers machine gun firing through the propeller did for aerial chivalry what Edward 3rd's "bombard" (canon) did to the "flower" of French chivalry in 1346 at Crécy.

According to the story, Garros was bombing a railroad siding at Courtrai, and in order to come in over target, he cut his motor, but when he gave it the gun after dropping his bombs, it failed and he had a forced landing in German-controlled territory. He tried desperately to burn his plane, but the high humidity and a wet plane made this difficult, and soon a squad of German soldiers came and took over, called the air people, and they flew the plane to Berlin to Anthony Fokker, and the secret was out.

Fokker devised a mechanical interrupter gear, bolted a cam gear to the back of the propeller boss that through a series of metal rods actuated the trigger of the gun. Thus when the blade was opposite the muzzle, the trigger release was taken out of action and there was interrupted firing.

Fokker's perfected devise was taken into action as early as June 30, 1915, and the German flyers became ascendant again, but were under orders to remain over conquered territory, to avoid being downed over the lines. However, one German flyer got lost in a fog and was forced to land in French-controlled territory, and Fokker's improvement on Garros' idea was revealed.

I believed aerial chivalry didn't die for some years yet, but the "flowers" of French, British and German aerial chivalry fell in greater numbers.

The British Royal Air Corps fed our instructors and they fed us this defense knowledge as the former learned it from experience. These defensive and offensive acrobatics which they and the French flyers learned over the lines in battle with the ingenious Germans, they learned chiefly to imitate, often not quite understanding the technicalities, and therefore they were able to pass on to us little more than the mechanics of the maneuvers, and our American instructors parroted to us that which had been parroted to them from England and France very much as I parroted my instructors in motors at Ground School. The British didn't seem to know why in a steep bank the elevators became the rudder, or why the compass "went crazy" in a fog. They learned defensive acrobatics from necessity, just as their ancestors had learned to put on chain mail.[108]

But we Americans loved mottos and slogans, and even if the British were not able to pass on to us the technological reasons for their acrobatics and other aerial phenomena, it seems we would have been more inspired by the motto "stunt or die" than by the academic knowledge, and with this motto we could, with the usual American verve, and the practical experiences gained by the British through life-and-death circumstances, build a powerful Aviation Section of United States Signal Corps.

And now since the British planes had been forced to become fighters and bombers instead of just artillery spotters and reconnaissance which had once been the role of the cavalry, it was time to identify them as an independent unit of military service, but their name wasn't changed from Royal Air Corps to Royal Air Force until almost the end of the war, and we were eventually to have an independent title as well.

Thus the American spirit and emotionalism inspired both by patriotism and excitement, had made Kelly Field within eight months of its founding, a busy primary training center.

There weren't a sufficient number of American commissioned pilots to act as our instructors, so some of us cadets had our first flying lessons from civilian exhibition flyers, and despite the fact that their salaries were higher than the salaries of the commissioned officers (I didn't see a flyer at the time with a higher rank than first lieutenant) they seemed to have little enthusiasm for either teaching cadets or for war, being completely absorbed as they must have been, by just the fact of flying.

They were taciturn men, and I admired them; as a matter of fact I even found the commissioned flyers much less cocky than the "90 day wonders" of the other services. In those days there was something about flying that wouldn't allow one to forget for a minute one's vulnerability, and besides the "wing and a prayer" imbuement, strangely enough there was evidence of fetishism, and charms and amulets and good luck pieces were carried—in case prayer didn't work, a logical mind might conclude.[109]

I had begun to wonder if Mathews J.J. would ever be assigned to an instructor. But one morning wearing a leather flying coat, a soft leather helmet and raised goggles, stepping forth in my shiny, new non-regulation polished cavalry boots, (why bother about clothing regulations for Ephemera?) I reported to my civilian instructor at the line.

I have never been a hero worshiper, only a respecter of men who accomplished success in those provinces where my own interests lay, and I facetiously referred to such men as "tin gods." I had already at my age then, collected several: There were Thomas Jefferson, Audubon, Carl Akeley, Sir Ernest Shackleton, Charles Darwin, Guynemer, Lufberry and Richtoffen. Eddie Stinson was among the second order of "tin gods," and I had hoped that I might be assigned to him for my first instructions in flying.[110]

England had a flyer quite as great as Guynemer, of the French, Richtoffen of the Germans and Lufberry of the American Escadrille. This was Captain Ball, and I hadn't even heard of him because of British Patrician conservatism and sportsmanship.[111]

The French and the Germans and later the Americans blew up the images and deeds of the three really great flyers, in order to aid *esprit* among the civilians and the military, making of them the emblems of the power and the glory of their respective nations to inspire patriotism and Chauvinism. Another "Hun" dropped by Guynemer was a victory for the *amour propre* of the French people, and the same with the Germans when Richtoffen, "The Red Knight," downed another allied plane. These were images which were caused to be blown up by the respective governments and military hierarchies, but very likely Lufberry and others of the Lafayette Escadrille became journalistic super-heroes.

The British believed it to be not too sporting to throw the bright beam of universal publicity onto Captain Ball as the symbol of British glory, while the British Tommy and his officers fought and sweated and bled for Old England in the filth and mud of the trenches.

Even though Captain Ball was as great and as courageous and dedicated as the publicized ones, I had not up to this time heard of him, and as a matter of fact didn't know he had existed until after the war.

My instructor and I taxied to the end of the run, turned into the wind, then he raised his goggles and looked back at me in the rear seat and said: "This is dual control; you see your stick? Don't touch it. I'll handle 'er, and I want you to watch ever'thing I do; might look at your rudder bar and look out at the aileron flaps. We'll make three turns of the field then land, and you'd better watch what I do when I'm fixin' to land: how I cut the motor and ease 'er down with the 'gun' if I need to."

Something came up from deep inside and lodged in my throat, as I said "alright" but I couldn't hear that I had said it.

Before I was aware we were off the field and there underneath me were the hangars, and then under us suddenly was the earth's pelage, the mesquite, the cactus and huajillo, and then to the left far down was the tonsure of the flat-headed cleric—Kelly Field with its row of tiny hangars with the row of doll houses behind them.

I forgot to watch the slight movements of the rudder bar, the adjusting movements of the aileron flaps. I forgot everything except the fact that I was at last brother to the golden eagle, who circled so arrogantly above the Osage prairies, taunting me for my earth-anchored stodginess.

Between flights my instructor quizzed me, and seemed to be pleased with my answers—or was he just bored?

The next flight, he allowed me to hold the stick, after he had taken off, and I was actually flying the plane around and around the field, he taking the stick for landing and taking off again. He referred to the take-off as "getaway."

We got along beautifully together. He was silent and seemed bored and I was silent and drowning in my own emotion.

He was tall and thin and I admired the manner in which he rolled a cigarette in the wind. I don't remember his name but he wasn't Stinson.

After several flights I was getting the feel of the ship: beginning to fly by the "seat of my pants," I believed, but yet not trusted with the stick for taking off and landing.

I came to the line one morning to find in the place of my civilian instructor a commissioned one, with very new silver bars. He was of the first crop of flying school graduates, who in the army's necessity were awarded first lieutenant's commissions. They, I believe, at least in some cases were less than "90 day wonders."

He exuded hauteur, I thought. He was short and I got the impression that he was bent on doing something about it.

He made no greeting; he looked at a notebook, then up at me and asked: "Mathews?" and I answered "Mathews, J.J."

"Sir," he warned sharply.

"Sir," I said.

He looked at me for some time as if he didn't believe that I was Mathews; that I had stupidly made a mistake in *wartime*, no less. He acted as if the U.S. Army had imposed on him. He spoke no word of instructions or encouragement, as we buckled our belts.

As we flew around the circle, monotonously without the slightest agitation of the stick from the front cockpit that would signal me to take over, I fixed my gaze on the back of his head and hated him.

Later, when I had learned to take off and land, he would turn in his

183

seat after the landing and with a sneer, say: "You're gettin' your tail down okeh now, but you're pancakin'."

When he wanted control returned to him in the air, he would shake the stick violently, as if he were thoroughly disgusted with my stupidity, and as if I couldn't possibly understand anything less obvious.

Even after a perfect three-point landing there was no praise, only silence as we taxied back to the line, and he walked away without saying anything, except once or twice he looked back at me and said, "Tomorrow, we'll try it again" intimating that the business of teaching me to fly was hopeless.

One day he said sneeringly, "Do yu think yu'll ever solo?"

I said, "Yes sir."

"What'yu base your optimism on?"

I thought for a moment, then a wonderful thought appeared, and I said with all the private-first-class humility I could fake, "Your ability, sir." He was caught off guard, and I hastened to say, "But of course I don't want to strain it too much, sir." I should have said that I didn't want to put strain on it.

He leaned against the trailing edge of the wing, and looked at the horizon as if he were pondering some weighty matter of great importance, expecting a sign there which might point to a way out of a dilemma. Then suddenly he said, "Alright, take it."

I said in disbelief, "You mean?"

"Course I do; get in. Rear seat, of course, on account of balance, as you ought to know by this time."

He looked into the cockpit to see if my belt was properly buckled, then as he backed away said, "Now take it up and break your neck."

When I got into the air and had made the first turn, I was astounded by the number of planes in the air; it seemed impossible that there had been just that many every day.

I felt like a schooling fish.

When I had made my last turn and had cut the motor as I nosed down, I could see my short instructor far down on the field like an erect beetle. He had warned me to land as close to him as possible, and seeing him there far below, I thought, "Maybe I can hit the bastard"!

I made a decent enough landing if not quite a three-pointer. He had only to walk a short distance, but I knew he would have no favorable comment, and he said just about what I had expected him to say: "If yu can't do any better than that, I'll havta get back in and nurse yu along some more."

During the third and fourth circlings of the field there seemed to be fewer planes in the air, and my fourth landing was a perfect three-pointer. I wouldn't have known that I had touched the earth if I had not heard the tail skid, rasping.

He climbed into the front cockpit and we taxied to the line, then we both got out and raised our goggles, and unbuckled our helmets, and stood awkwardly, before he took out his pencil and wrote something on a pad, handed it to me and then said, "Take this to Lieutenant _____ when you report to him tomorrow morning."

"I've soloed in eight hours?" I asked.[112]

"Yep," he said, "and I am goin' back to the quarters and offer up a prayer of thanksgivin'," and he walked off without extending his hand, or saying goodbye. I looked at his supercilious back and hated him again, but only momentarily. I was now a flyer; the hell with overweening assembly line pilots.

Now came the monotonous taking off and landing, taking off and landing, and a little later the flying of figures of eight over two very important looking tombstones in a nearby cemetery, and over the stupa-like, or kiosk-like bat roosts.

After a period of solo flying I went to the cross-country stage, and this was joyous. There was cross-country flying and formation flying, and now I was doing exactly what I had always longed to do: fly above the woods and look down upon the rivers—the pelage and the arterial system of earth—alone. There was only one drawback; one had to report at the objective landing field within a given time, then fill up with gasoline and fly back to the parent Kelly Field. One was at least alone and free between the parent field and the auxiliary fields.

But I feel that the British, seasoned by aerial battles, might have been less restrictive of their cadets than were the academically knowledgeable non-flying, dismounted cavalry officers who were in command of the flying fields. These horse-detached, unhappy and disinterested men must have felt disgraced to be in command of military pariahs.

In cross-country flying we flew directly to our objective by aerial map, and our orders called only for landing and refueling. We had time to smoke a cigarette and perhaps talk with the citizens from the little towns near the primitive little auxiliary fields scratched out of pear cactus and mesquite, and perhaps parade a little before the 1918 version of the "khaki-wacky" girls, who might well have been called "wings-wacks," but there was no time to do anything about their wackiness in case they might have wished to venture.

However, you could make a great ado about examining dramatically your flying and ground wires and their turnbuckles, striking the wires sharply with the edge of the hand. You could be importantly deliberate in arranging yourself in your cockpit, and saying "contact" with grave authority to the mechanic who whirled your propeller blades to start the motor; you were the focus of all eyes.

Then you would lift majestically over the little weathered shed with its gasoline drums, and over the up-turned faces of the impressed villagers, waggle your wings as a gesture of farewell (poetic this) and disappear into the great Blue Yonder.

After many of these joy-flights alone over the earth, a strange thing happened; my plane began to be a sentient thing like Bally. I sensed the slightest nosing up or down, the air on either side of my face when skidding ever so slightly, and I was very sensitive to the slightest of motor coughs and plane vibrations, and was mechanically ready for the thermal updrafts over ploughed fields or over chained-out areas of the Brush Country and was always aware of the faint disturbance from "electric winds" from distant cumulonimbus clouds.

So this lifting himself from the earth was what man was dreaming about during the long centuries of his plodding, and his attempts to differentiate himself from his brother animals. He had attributed flight to angels, and had coined words like "ascend," "above," high," "heavenly," "rise," "empyrean," and now he could look down, in his euphoria, and say to himself that since God had always been able to see things hidden from men, that now perhaps God and man may come closer together in understanding. However, the Irish linen of the wings, the ash of the struts, and the flying wires and the ground wires that held man's ship together were frail contrivances of aspiring man, not having the solidity of the Tower of Babel, and yet far more comforting than Icarus's wax wings.

I often became so absorbed by my thoughts and dreams while flying that I could land at the field and sit for some time with my motor idling, brought to awareness by the sudden appearance of the line sergeant. I was quite aware of other planes in the air and landing, even though my landing was mechanical and my thoughts far away, and I didn't jeopardize other flyers since my instincts were alert and on sentinel duty as my mind wandered—perhaps to Allenby and Palestine, since the war there was highest romance to me.[113]

I had now a sentimental attachment to the old oil-spattered "Jenny" to which I was assigned most of the time. I don't remember her number but I became as attached to her as I did later to the Curtiss-H 38075. I was flying now by the "seat of my pants" and she seemed to respond as had Bally, when I made the lightest movement forward in the saddle or stood in the stirrups. This was imaginary, but my plane did seem to be sentient.

One day flying in formation at 6,000 feet, I felt the faint quiver of my plane, even before I heard the sparkplug misfire. Her coughing and trembling increased and I had to fall out of formation like a wing-shot goose: the one shot in the wing breaking it when the flying pressure was greatest.

I swept in wide circles down and down more like a golden eagle now, trying to determine if the object far below is rock or fawn, searching for an area on which I might be able to land; everywhere under my wings was low brush, and I began to worry, but I was chiefly worrying about my undercarriage. I didn't want anything to happen to my Jenny, nor did the United States Government.

This seems rather silly now in retrospect. Of course I didn't have much to worry about as far as my own safety was concerned, since I could have pancaked my plane onto the brush, even with a dead stick, but the wings would have been pierced and the undercarriage

The Curtiss JN-4 airplane, as flown by Mathews during
World War I (Courtesy of the Canadian Department
of National Defence, Library and Archives Canada,
C-024435)

smashed, and I would have another plane assigned to me with quite
different idiosyncrasies, and it would be something like mounting a
strange horse.

As I circled lower and lower, I saw a spot that had been "chained-
out," and the ground was rough and the vegetation had begun its second growth to climax, but I managed a dead stick landing, examined
my plane and found it intact, then sat in the shade of the wings and
smoked a cigarette, awaiting the trouble shooter from the field.

Even with our heads full of theory about airplane motors, we were
not allowed to even examine a sparkplug in such circumstances, and
this was a great boon to both myself and the Aviation Section of the
Signal Corps.

The people of the scattered little ranches and farmsteads, had seen
the sick plane circle down out of the sky, and since practically none

of them had seen a plane except in the air, and that rarely, they came to stand about. The dozen or more of them who came had never seen a plane on the ground close up, they informed me. They stood about and wondered; they asked permission to touch the fabric, examine the cockpits.

Some of them invited me to come spend the night at their homes, but I told them I had to stay with my plane: military orders. They were visibly impressed and I felt terribly important. Soon they melted into the expectant twilight of the Brush Country.

Last to go was a veritable "Uncle Tom" with his kinky hair rimming a bald spot like a soiled cotton halo. He had stood apart and at a distance. After the others had left, I motioned to him, and asked, "Would you like to come closer." He came up smiling and said, "Ah rekon you duh fust aeroventilatah, Ah done evah seed."

He touched the wings, looked into the cockpits, then backed away holding his hands clasped behind him. I said, "What do you think about it?"

"Yas'suh, hit's the fust one Ah evah seed, and you de fust aeroventilatah Ah evah seed."

"If you want to ask questions, go ahead."

"Yas'suh, Ah cain't haw'dly fenacitate, what yu'all do when yu'all gotta do a job up dere."

Pride had urged the others to refrain from asking questions that might in some manner have indicated that they were not men preeminent themselves, and which might have fractured the illusion that we were all knowledgeable males together. They smiled smugly when their women asked questions and they were noticeably, vaguely embarrassed: questions which they might have liked to ask, themselves.

Being practical people who watched the clouds, and were interested in every whim and manifestation of Nature and every important natural functioning, "Uncle Tom" had probably asked the question which had come first to the women's minds, and which they naturally didn't dare ask.

Later, when I was alone in the darkness, the yellow light of a lantern flashed jerkily on the brush, as it approached the plane. A settler appeared with some blankets over his arm and a tin of coffee and a sack with fried chicken. As he handed the sack and coffee and blankets to me, he said patronizingly, "The woman sent this stuff; yu know how women are."

He stayed for some time with me and talked about the goddam Kaiser.

Periodically during the night, when I slept under the wings, I was awakened by the chorusing of the coyotes. As I listened, there was a hint of homesickness; not really home sickness, but nostalgia—a prairie-sickness perhaps, since there was not the faintest suggestion of self-pity.

～

Entering into the acrobatic stage of primary flying, I was taken for my first loop. Sometimes in the J.N. 4's, the "Jennys," when you reached the top of the loop, gasoline dripped from the rocker arms, and during each loop there was the odor of raw gasoline, and the motor sometimes coughed and sputtered.

There was ever present the danger of fire, but we seemed to have paid little attention to this hazard, lost as we were in the joy of looping.

I can't think of anything that comes closer to the complete expression of the urge to express *joie de vivre* through physical action than a series of loops, pulling out of them only when you have lost so much altitude that you must do, and we learned to pull out of the last loop of the series close enough to earth to be able to land.

This last was chiefly a stunt, without being essentially a military defense.

The defensive virtues of the stall, the loop, the sideslip, the vertical bank, the Immelmann turn, the roll and the spin, were obvious defensive maneuvers, but they were also offensive. Looping to get rid of the enemy on your tail, you would be using defensive tactics, but as soon as you pulled out of it you might be on your enemy's tail, unless he looped following you, and the maneuver immediately became offensive action.

But still man was imitative of those things which he had seen in Nature; I had seen harriers (marsh hawks) and falcons do Immelmann turns.[114] Once when Bally and I were going through a patch of horseweeds as high as her back, a harrier flying low, was so intent on field mice trails on the ground, that he didn't notice the projection above Bally's back until he was within a few yards of us, and face to face with dangerous boy, he did an Immelmann.

Birds can also stall, loop, sideslip, zoom, dive, make a vertical bank, and when shot, hawks go into a tail spin, having lost power like a plane that spins.

Falcons do Immelmanns when the prairie chicken they are attacking suddenly dodges, and turns back. It was the quickest possible change in direction.

Spinning was deceptive. I was surprised to learn that in spinning through 1,000 feet, the plane made only three or four revolutions. One might have guessed at least thirty.[115]

When we had finished acrobatics we were finished with primary training, and we were, as I remember, free to practice our cross-country and acrobatic flying.

A cadet was grounded for stunting over Brackenridge Park.

I was fascinated by the sinuous, lazy San Antonio River, lying far below my wings like a great, listless snake, and the human beetles, erect and complaisant, living with it. I flew over San Antonio often, and by now the citizens had become accustomed and there were no groups of people standing on the streets gazing upward, as happened when one flew low over towns and cities that had no airfields near them.

But still I liked cross-country flying best. I could circle over Eagle Lake, one of the auxiliary fields like a vulture or an eagle, and between fields I could see the earth as the wild goose or the sandhill crane sees it. I was a young man training for war in the air over France, but I was actually imagining myself as a bird, joining the birds in their *joie de vivre,* and had become a peer at least through my ability, of the earth-inspecting, messenger angels.[116]

I have no hesitancy admitting this illusory transmutation, since I had passed a rather rigorous mental as well as physical examination by the United States Medical Corps.

But flying in 1917–18 was rather a dangerous business. We had no parachutes and when the ship was disabled, we came down to earth with it. Naturally, the instructors flying from the front cockpit were highly vulnerable, but during my training at Kelly, I remember only cadets being killed; almost one a day I believe I have heard, but even as an average this must have been a dramatic exaggeration; perhaps having its origin with some cadet "Mezzanine Flying" on Saturday afternoon at the Menger or the St. Anthony Hotel, in the presence of one or more girls. A one-a-day casualty would not have dimmed his glory one bit as a survivor.

This strutted misinformation eventually became "Latrine News."

I have never been interested in checking this; Washington would know. I only know that the young man of the bunk to my left failed to come back from cross-country flight, and another whose bunk was the fourth down from mine, tried to climb too steeply on take-off, and that one cadet near the end of the barracks failed to come out of a spin, and one in the middle of the barracks failed to come out of a loop.[117]

When we saw the "Meat Wagon" roll across the Field with the white-coated medical corps people clinging to it, standing on the running board, we considered the crash in the light of an object lesson, and we assured ourselves that we wouldn't have made the same mistake which the mangled flyer had undoubtedly made.

I have always believed that rather unusual courage was necessary for an instructor: a cold courage if one had a vivid imagination. This sort of courage was certainly necessary when one was an instructor in the primary stage of training. There was always the danger that a cadet might "freeze" the controls in panic, and the instructor wouldn't be able to shake the "stick" loose.

There was one story, and I always suspected it of being of "Mezzanine" or the "tea dansant" origin. It concerned the primary training instructor, who unable to shake the cadet's panic grip on the stick, had managed to knock the cadet out with a wrench, but tragically the cadet fell onto the stick in his cockpit and they both died in the crash.

Excellent "Mezzanine."

But this one happened. Instructors not only had to have courage, but they seemed to have pride in the success of their cadets since their adequacy might reflect on them, the instructors. They watched with pride when their cadets first soloed. They stood on the field and watched like a mother watching her child cross the street.

I was standing by an instructor whose cadet was soloing, and we were following him as he circled the field. That day there was a wind from the Gulf, and the Flyers had to come in over the hangars to land into the wind.

As the cadet soloist came in over the hangars, it was evident that he had cut his motor too soon. He floated with a wobble over the hangars, and even I, the just graduated Primary trainee, along with the agonized instructor made a mechanical movement toward an imaginary throttle, as if we would "give it the gun."

Flying speed was synonymous with control.

The cadet pancaked on the field and bounced and the instructor waited for him to taxi to the line, filled with inexpressible anger, which had displaced agony. The cadet brightly lifted his goggles, and his face glowed with his accomplishment.

The instructor walked up to the ship, but he only sputtered; his anger bottlenecked by Army Regulations concerning swearing at non-commissioned men. He could only sputter, "What in the name of common sense were yu doin' up there over the hangars? What'dy tell yu 'bout a steep enough glide so's your wires sing? Don't tell me yu heard your wires singin'—damn it to hell."

The cadet said, shame-faced, "I thought I did."

"THOUGHT yu did? THOUGHT yu heard your wires singin'— well, if yu DID hear 'em singin', what in hell were they singin', s'what I'd like to know."

The cadet was silent again; growing rather serious after a flash of amusement had appeared on his face when the instructor asked what the wires were singing.

"Well," continued the instructor, "I'll tell yu what'thu hell they were singin'— they were singin', 'near oh my God to thee,' that's what they were singin'."

One day during my training in acrobatics, as I walked from my ship to the line, I saw my old Primary stage instructor waiting for me. I gave some greeting weakly, but as usual he didn't respond, but handed me a Fort Worth paper.

There were banner headlines informing the United States that their dance idol had been killed. Vernon Castle and his wife Irene were the embodiment of Romance. They not only danced divinely, but by being able to do so had elevated themselves above human-swarm grubbiness, and along with the cinema actresses and actors, were helping to fill the royalty-vacuum that had existed deep in the souls of Amer-European masses since 1787. Ward McAlester's Four Hundred were a bit more mass-alienated. The masses could feel possessive in the case of cinema actors and the Castles.[118]

Captain (now promoted from his 1st lieutenancy) Sutton watched me closely as I read, then as I handed the paper back to him, he said sarcastically, "Killed on one of those steep climbing turns, you always liked—in a hurry to leave the earth." He was silent a moment, then lifted the paper slightly, and said, "Now, he'll hafta wait for Gabriel."

I looked down into his serious, virile face, and I was aware of something which he couldn't hide, and he became aware that I saw it. Most citizen-officers when ill at ease shoved their civilian hands into their formal military pockets, and thus made of status a farce, becoming ridiculously slouchy, but Captain Sutton only put out his hand, barely touched mine, and said, "Remember: keep your nose down on a take-off climb." He walked off then turned and said back over his shoulder, "Good luck."

A warm wave of appreciation came over me and I said to his back, "Good luck to YOU." Suddenly I was very fond of old Primary instructor; I now knew instinctively that the feeling was mutual.

It took years for me to learn about my princeling self-assurance, that was not quite arrogance, but might have offended the *amour propre* of others. It was not, as I have intimated, in the least aggressive, and there was inherently in it a faculty for attracting people to me, almost a paradox.

How well Captain Sutton had understood me, and how wrong was my first impression of him. Tom Mitscher had made me fight with him, and Captain Sutton had made a flyer of me by bringing out a natural ability and the competitive spirit of pride. Tom Mitscher had called me "curley" and Captain Sutton had pretended despair over my lack of intelligence and co-ordination, hating my placid, genial self-assurance, which disturbed the self-esteem of others, and besides Captain Sutton seemed to realize that one couldn't be carelessly successful in flying.

We never saw each other again.

Sometime during the cross-country training, we were confined for a period to the post: perhaps the vanguard of the terrible epidemic of influenza had made its appearance. Anyway we were confined to the post at Kelly, but whatever the reason, my mother got wind of it and came down to San Antonio with my youngest sister Florence, to see for herself what might be happening to her son. Possibly she had visions, inspired by the Civil War stories of her uncle Eugene Regnier, of her son lying ill in a tent hospital, where there were too few nurses and there were blood-letting doctors and rats and a dearth of antiseptics. She must have had images of her father Joseph Girard's death through neglected pneumonia in a Union Army hospital.

We had just "washed out" flying for the day and I, oil-smeared, walked up the road with several other cadets. I had just landed from a cross-country flight.

One of the group noticed the taxi in front of the headquarters building: a most unusual sight during the strict quarantine. We conjectured as to the meaning of this strange thing and then one of the group said, "There's a woman in it" and another said, "Only a woman could get past the guard; they certainly'ud hold their fire."

I said facetiously, "I know one woman who might do that very thing—no, I know two women who couldn't be stopped by either guns or regulations: my mother and my grandmother."

When we came near the taxi, mother got out and came toward me and my kid sister Florence with hair flapping on her back, ran ahead to greet me.

Apparently they called the field from their hotel in San Antonio, and they were warned that the field was under strict quarantine, and that they would not be admitted under any circumstances. They hired a taxi and came anyway.

There are two versions of what happened at the gate to the field. My sister Florence, who now lives in Washington, D.C., has just written in a letter the following:

"I called Kelly Field and was told that it was under quarantine. Mother insisted on going there anyway—we took a taxi. Upon arriving at the gate we were told we could not enter. Mother leaned forward to the taxi driver and even though a guard was standing in front of the taxi, commanded him to drive on, which he did. The guard jumped aside, and the driver took us to the commandant (Of course he was waiting for us)."

The corporal of the guard told me later that the lady was very nice but firm, and that when she told the driver to drive on, he had answered as he pointed to the armed guard in the middle of the road, "But mam, he won't let us."

According to the guard's story, my mother then said, "Well, then run over him."

In any case the commandant handed me a pass, which gave me the weekend free to spend with my mother and sister.

Later, he seemed to want to excuse his indulgence by dressing it up in semi-military accoutrements. When I appeared before him later as ordered, he immediately ordered me to be "at ease," and then seemed to want to impress me with something which he didn't believe himself—that he had preserved his cavalry officer dignity before my insistent mother. He seemed to be trying to convince me, the private first class, that he the strict army officer had relented and fractured his own regulations pertaining to quarantine, under the influence of special circumstances, which under the old Boots and Saddles cavalry regulations could not have been relaxed for a moment, but could now be made adjustable to a unique situation wherein this la-dee-da civilian experiment, aviation, was concerned: a situation created by this strange experiment.

He seemed reluctant to end the—the, whatever it was—and as I saluted stiffly on being dismissed, I felt that he hadn't justified himself to his Boots and Saddles self, nor to a la-dee-da aviation cadet either, which left him even more annoyed with himself than he had been before.

The story and image of Pontius Pilate both became quite clear to me, suddenly.

~

[1918–1919]

We all knew through "latrine news" that the fighter pilots would very likely be sent over to France or England to receive further training before being sent over the lines, and naturally, almost all of us training at Kelly, when we finished our primary training had made fighter pilot training our choice.

However, there were pilots needed for bombing and reconnaissance and for the training of cadets, and our instructors themselves had studied their cadets; their attitudes, their abilities, their dedication and their mannerisms in general. This was rather surprising since our instructors were only a few months and a few flying hours ahead of us, and had been themselves, only a few months before college graduates or undergraduates, and themselves eager to get to France.

They must have had to fill out a chart from Washington, in addition to studying each cadet's individual Pilot's Book.

Anyway, my dreamy dedication to cross-country flying, a dedication and obvious interest in such flying, must have led my superiors to believe that I was interested in making acute observations of terrain and of objects on the earth and that this serious interest might have future military importance, and the "90 day wonders" presented their recommendations to the fed-up cavalry officers who were in command, and got their nonchalant affirmation.

I was recommended for training in bomb raiding, so after a short interim at the flyer's clearinghouse at Dallas, Texas' Love Field, I was sent for advanced training in Night Bomb Raiding to Ellington Field, Texas, between Houston and Galveston.

Having nothing to do at Love Field, as a young second Lieutenant, except shine my new RMA wings (Reserve Military Aviator) have my English hunting boots shined and have uniforms made to order whose tunics and britches were more companionable than the satchel-seated britches and the ballet skirt tunics of the general issue. And I of course went dancing and had dinner at the Adophus with the Burtons.

The Burtons had turned their home over to something or other patriotic and had taken a suite at the Adolphus Hotel, and here I spent many very pleasant, very satisfying hours. They seemed to have adopted Jap French who came up with me from Kelly and Ben Allan Ames whom I had known at the University of Oklahoma. The latter had come from Camp Travis, I seem to remember.

The Burton apartment became a civilian home for the three of us, and we had dinner with the family often, and once I was invited to be present at a review of troops at Fort Worth. The Burtons thought this might be interesting and I am sure the whole thing was arranged by Amon Carter, who apparently could accomplish almost anything in Fort Worth.

The Canadians had a flying school there, and there was an army training camp there as well, and one had the impression that even Canada's and the local U.S. commandant might defer to Amon Carter in Fort Worth, Texas. This was my impression only, the impression of a not very much concerned young man.

I seem to remember that the troops on review were leaving for France, and the air was filled with patriotic fervor. I, a second Lieutenant, found myself standing by the reviewing Colonel as the troops marched by. My new RMA wings shining in the Texas sun.

Between marching and saluting companies, the crystallized old foot soldier would have a quick look at me, and it seemed to me that he was about to growl, then he would face the oncoming company and stiffly take the salute. I must have embarrassed him, since no one would be silly enough to mistake me with boots and wings, for a member of this old infantryman's staff.

Later, the Burtons thought it was amusing.

The short, whirly adoption by the Burtons was made quite exciting by the fact that they had three very attractive daughters, one of them engaged to the remarkable Amon Carter.

I was loath to leave Love Field solely because of the Burtons: dinners, dancing, gaiety and beauty. Otherwise I might have tried to get the bit in my teeth, since there was no flying, just waiting until the army had places for us in the advanced training schools over the country. But with the Burtons, waiting had been an exciting interlude.

Ellington Field had been scraped out of a savanna, nourished by soil that had only recently been the bottom of the Gulf of Mexico (geologically recent, of course), and was a large field for that time, and when I arrived there they were still building buildings. There was no barracks for me, and I was quartered in an army tent with three other flyers from primary flying school over the country.

Of course we were military peers: second Lieutenants.

I was rather disappointed in being assigned to Night Bomb Raiding; the romance was on the side of the fighter pilot, but as I have mentioned I had shown too much interest in cross-country flying at Kelly, by actually gloating over being a brother to the eagle rather than training for success in battle. My dreams as I flew over the beautiful Guadalupe and the Hondo Rivers, and looked down upon the mesquite and sycamores and as I flew over the savage Brush Country, there could have been no thought of military glory or of rivers in France and Germany that led to Troops concentrations or ammunitions dumps.

I had longed for aerial knight-errantry, but in flying cross-country from Kelly, I took few liberties, since there was much to absorb my interest under my wings as I followed the charted course between parent and auxiliary fields, but I varied my course, once at least I remember, to fly over a bewildered coyote that my shadow had disturbed as he lay in his day bed among the mesquite, and when he decided to flee from this roaring, materialized chimera, I followed him. When my shadow caught up with him, he turned sharply, using his bushy tail as a rudder, then swung it in a circle as the hunted ones did when a running hound was about to take hold of one: a trick which baffled the hound and he always sped past the turning of the coyote, and this enabled the quarry to gain time and distance. Turning as my shadow came over him and swinging his tail in a circle were associative defense actions. However the flying monster kept him in its shadow; overflying him and having to turn and come back to the game. This particular coyote of the roadless, harsh area had been frighteningly introduced to the machine age, having missed the motor car stage in the development, as were the wolves, bears, bighorn of Alaska when the bush pilots arrived after the war.

I wanted to tell someone about this, but there were so few who might understand; most assuredly it was not in my report to my superiors.

I also tried to clock a flock of Canadian geese. I made them break formation, but we had no Pitot tubes yet by which to measure ground speed. As a matter of fact all we had in the "Jennys" were a tachometer, an altimeter, a compass and a fuel gauge. We knew our r.p.m, our altitude, direction of flight and the amount of gasoline left in the tank.

At Ellington I was soon fascinated by night flying, and I soloed rather quickly, because I was fascinated by it and began to learn all I could about it; again not for success over German ammunition dumps and troop concentrations, but for the thrill of being up high above the earth in the darkness, and knowing that on certain nights, that I was the only human being flying high above the Earth and its prisoners in all America.[119]

My enthusiasm for night flying was mistaken also for military dedication by my superiors.

Of course, not all of us on the field were night flyers; as a matter of fact the three officers with whom I shared the tent were in training for day light bombing and we were "washing out" night flying at 3 a.m., so that I arrived at the tent a few hours before they started their day, and I saw little of them except when we "socked in" on account of the weather. Two of them, one from Massachusetts and one from New York City, were convinced that I lived on a desert: therefore my contentment with Texas.

The British had been compelled to take up night flying when they discovered that German cavalry were shooting down and capturing their day bombers, even after they had learned about formation flying and the necessity for fighter protection. So they got the "wind up," and asked the War Office to send them planes whose wings could be folded so that they could be rescued and hauled along the French roads to the Allied lines by tractors or trucks faster than the German cavalry in pursuit of them.

This was during the period of the greatest naïveté, and the idea was never developed, never seriously considered by the War Office, and night bomb raiding became a necessity.

They began to send formations of night bombers over the lines with bombs now attached to racks under the wings and which could be released from the cockpit. Also they had invented a bomber sight that fitted on the edge of the bomber-observer's cockpit, and there was no more of tossing the bombs overboard, as at the beginning of the war.

We had all this knowledge at Ellington Field. We attached dummy bombs under our wings, and used a Wimpers Sight that was quite accurate for those days. On our return from practice bombing with dummies, we landed by the lights of the field, but when we were practicing forced landings at night we had flares attached to the underside of the lower wings and we set the flare off at the right moment from the pilot's cockpit for the landing.

We also practiced accuracy in bombing over a camera obscura; flying over the camera emplacement in a special building, and our course over the camera was charted and it also registered the moment the trigger was released which would in turn release a hypothetical bomb.

The observer-bomber assigned to me when I was practicing flare landings was an Alabamian and I had some trouble understanding his viscous accent. His laissez faire tranquility impressed me, since he must depend completely on me and the plane, and had no power whatsoever to save his own life if either I or the plane faltered.

I wondered if his complete trust and his placidity might have to do with his girl's silk stocking. Each day when he came out to fly with me, he pulled the stocking out of a special little bag which he carried in his breast pocket, and carefully tied it to a strut, without the least embarrassment, seemingly unconscious of my presence.

My keen sense of the ridiculous of course inspired a facetious observation. If he had not had the very interesting accent from some Alabaman hinterland, and had not been so short and humorless, I might have refrained from my facetious observation, having no intention whatever of being discourteous.

After my remark, he stiffened with dignity, and stood looking up at me in a sort of hand-on-sword-hilt attitude. I knew better than to smile, but I wanted to and barely managed to control my face.

I said simply, "I'm sorry."

He said nothing; there was not even any sign of relief in his tense face, and his facial expression said quite clearly, "You'd better be."

The incident was completely forgotten, and he tied his stocking to a strut of the Curtiss-H we were flying, each night, as if I were not present. We became good companions and I was impressed eventually not only by his trustful tranquility but by his courage.

There wasn't anything unusual about the carrying into the air with one "luck charms." It was a common practice among flyers both at Kelly and at Ellington and probably there were more exotic fetishes at Ellington than there were at Kelly.

After I became an instructor in Night Bomb Raiding I attempted to make a list of them. Some amulets remained hidden in the pockets, and the flyer, whether pilot or bomber merely fondled them before buckling the seat belt, or they were brought out and tied to a strut.

My list is not now available, although through the years I have kept practically everything of the least importance, but I seem to remember that there were rabbit's feet, lucky coins, stockings, and one horseshoe at least. The night flyers often gave the silk of the parachute flares to their girls who had panties or step-ins made of them, then they gave them back to the donors as fetishes after being consecrated through being worn. D's girl had sent him her step-ins from New York City.[120]

The fetishism of flyers seemed more noticeable than in the case of other fetish worshipers, I suspect, because the airman's fetishes were more in evidence than the usual "luck pieces" or amulets. They were often tied to the struts of the planes, almost ceremoniously before the pilot of the bomber climbed into his cockpit, but more often they only fondled them in their pockets, or wore them on the person. But for some reason or unreason some of them—a small percentage per-haps—had to be seen to be effective, and since they were in many cases associated with female apparel or attributes, such as locks of hair, etc., they were really true fetishes rather than just amulets; pant-ies and stockings were in preponderance, but a neat little hank of hair possessed by one flyer was unique because it was pubic hair.

This last was the fetish protector of a Rabelaisian cynic, and although he carried it in the breast pocket of his shirt, one know-ing him found it difficult to believe that he could possibly be a seri-ous fetishist, but he was. One evening he came out to the line, felt of his breast pocket, then ran back to the barracks to get his fetish from the shirt of yesterday. If he had been ridiculing the other wear-ers of amulets, etc., he wouldn't have run all the way back to his bar-racks, leaving his plane idling and ready, and anyway he would have needed more than the line sergeant and me for an audience if he had intended to be derisive.

He was one of my students in Night Bomb Raiding: a Cajun from the muskrat country of the Mississippi River Delta, and he wore a St. Christopher medal pendant from a chain about his neck.

The paradox of the Man-From-The-Muskrat Country puzzled the young Philistine from the Osage prairies whose background and criteria for analysis and thought was the natural world, even in 1918 when life was so absorbed by flying. Even though this particular night flying student who had been sent to me for instruction inspired me to spend much time wondering about this paradox, my thoughts were of necessity drusy, and they are not much clearer now in 1965.[121]

One can't help wondering about the reversion of modern civilized man (by his own estimate) to the primitive stage in his development, when face to face with man-contrived mechanical dangers, and who seems to have an urge to propitiate this man-made power manifes-tation, just as his primordial ancestors tried to propitiate the natu-ral manifestations after attributing to them super-natural power and designs.

Stockings and panties tied to the plane's struts and amulets at fin-ger tips in the pockets were to propitiate what or whom? Not the Christian God with sex symbols?

What was it? Was it probable that deep down in the soul of civilized man, somewhere in his racial memory is the necessity to revert to the worship of primordial symbols of the protective female progenitor—the symbols of generation and perhaps pre-natal protection? Did the panties, the hanks of hair from the head and the pubic regions satisfy to some degree the atavism of the night flyer, as did originally the carved statuettes exaggerating the female conformation, stressing vulva and the breasts, satisfy the fearful primordial man?

Man had got himself into the air—toward heaven—by mechanical means and this was a new experience, and there was nothing in his earth-dwelling, racial experience (since his concepts and creations were based on earthy things like floods and fires and lightning,) out of which he could create the omnipotence and mysticism which had given him security on earth, but not above the earth in flying mechanisms. He couldn't very well displace these earth-anchored symbols of his earlier creations with his above-earth fetishes, so like the Man-From-The-Muskrat country, he considered both the Christian medal and the fetish protective, potent spirits.

But why visible; why not secret amulets? Perhaps the idea here is also primordial, since primitive man took no chances, and wanted them to be seen, but by whom? Not his brother flyers, not the command staff; in the latter case the result might have been new regulations or revived old ones.

Logically, the primordial urge was to have some non-entity, some not-yet-conceived Mystery to notice them.[122]

By the time I had been instructing in Night Bomb Raiding for several weeks, I became even more interested in flyer's fetishes, since I had to report in detail on each student and I had to watch them carefully and to know them, and my academic interest in fetishes grew.

Perhaps the racial memories from primitive man's nights, when he huddled in his cave listening to the scratchings and sniffings of the saber-tooth or the bear, were deeper in the soul of man and nourished the racial memory giving greater impetus to fetishism, especially among night flyers.

Civilized man has not quite rid himself of the incubi of the primitive man. He still feels and fears the evils of darkness. The primordial man's attitude toward night and day still influences his thinking and his life and his language similes. One is enlightened or one is benighted.

I felt vicariously this racial-memory reaction to darkness in my students, when they came out to their assigned planes at twilight, and I noted too that the students most disturbed by darkness in this strange element, for man's venturing, the sky, were the more unimaginative ones, while in almost every other confrontation of man with hazardous undertakings, or even certain death, the lack of imagination is often mistaken for cold courage, while on the contrary the imaginative ones must have the real courage.

The flying was much more pleasant at night, since the air was almost always calm, and there were no thermals to contend with, and we "socked in" on the Night Bomb Raiding stage when there was just the slightest hint of turbulence or even a thin ground fog, but even when the moon shone or when there were stars, there remained the incubi of primordial man.

After I became an officer of the post, and lived in a comfortable barracks, and especially as an instructor in Night Bomb Raiding, I had more freedom, but the unhappy thought that I might never be sent out to fly for Allenby in Palestine, came to bother me often. He had called for flyers, and the romance of his campaign had begun to call to me.

But Jo-Without-Purpose, the loner, was in his element, and this time not riding over the Osage prairies, but high in the starlit sky over Texas, and happy even though as an officer of the post I was obviously anchored to my pleasant freedom, and Allenby might be compelled to advance to Damascus without me.[123] However, I was free and playful, and I could take a plane off the line any time I chose.

The cumulous in the afternoons were cones of whipped cream, and the cloud floor beneath one with its little monadnocks, and the windows through which one could look down upon the green, grey and the brown of the earth, gave one the feeling of being in a strange, new world.

Then there was moonlight making lustrous the cloud floor, and this produced in me a disturbance, since there could never be a satisfying expression of my emotions; thoughts went in circles. Instead of tranquil happiness and/or even ecstasy, there was rather the sort of frustration which I think Spot often felt when he was filled with *joie de vivre* or intense emotion and could only slaver in his bafflement. One night I remember I said aloud, "Oh!"

A sudden jerk, a quiver in the plane when flying in the moonlight over the unpeopled earth, because of a fouled sparkplug, made a return to the field imperative. I have always thought of these sudden jerks and quivers while flying in the moonlight as symbolical of life: a quiver or a jerk as one is filled with physical well-being and spiritual happiness, then down, down to earth, not knowing the character of the area on which he must land.[124]

Once I had to come out of the moonlit sky and use my landing flares. An oil line had been ruptured but the terrain was kind to the plane and me, and I sat the remainder of the night watching the moon slide from the zenith to the horizon, listening periodically to a great horned owl, a coyote, a frog and a distant hound barking at moon shadows.

One night there was lightning against a cumulonimbus that was purple-smoky in the moonlight, and since the zenith was bright and clear and the cloud was like a curtain on only one horizon, I flew toward it.

The lightning played along the cloud curtain like the momentary fire that plays over a flat surface upon which a few drops of gasoline have been poured and lighted. When I came near, I almost did an unintentional wing-over, then the whole ship shook. I turned away immediately. There had been dramatic tales about the effects of "electric winds" from storm clouds, on planes. True or not I was ready to believe them, and hadn't the courage to experiment further.

I liked flying over the lights of Houston, where the motor cars being sporadic in those days, were like beetles; their headlight shafts were their antennae, feeling their way over the city. They crawled in radial lines from the heart of the city, and occasionally there would be a lone determined beetle hurrying along the road from Houston to Galveston. In those days there was little traffic outside of the military, and not much of that either.

The lights of far away Galveston danced and blinked, detached from the earth.

One night when I was giving dual control instruction to a student we ceased the monotonous circling of the field when I felt the student had got the assurance he needed to leave the comforting lights of the field, and flew toward Galveston and I shook the stick as a signal for the student to take over. I felt quite a bit of confidence in my advanced flying students, and after releasing the stick, I sat looking down at the earth: a thrill that never palled.

Then suddenly the plane was zooming, and turned sharply to the right. I immediately signaled that I would take over, deeply comforted to realize that my student had not frozen the controls, always the first thought that comes into an instructor's head in such cases.

I came into the traffic lane and landed.

I turned to my student, "What was wrong?"

"A plane coming right at us," he said.

"So you zoomed over it," I suggested, "but you didn't see it pass under us, or pass on either side of us."

He realized that there was something amiss now, and hesitated, then said, "I could see the wing tip lights, and—"

I interrupted him: "But they were both uncolored lights not green and red, and not only that, they were in Galveston; I've noticed them before—they are level with each other and just about a wing span apart."

This young officer was an excellent daytime pilot. For some flyers judging distance at night was like judging distance on the sea or on the plains.

As an officer of the post and especially as an instructor, my playfulness was curbed. No more flying over towns unaccustomed to airplanes, to enjoy groups of people with up-turned faces causing traffic tie-ups, or playing with other pilots as we did at Kelly during primary training, playing follow-the-leader. This latter boys-will-be-boys adventure had to do with following the leader under the span of a river bridge. Some of the cadets playfully used to throw fire extinguishers at deer and coyotes in the Brush Country.

Here at Ellington, before I became an officer of the post, I flew one afternoon to Rice Institute (later a great university) and "buzzed" the campus during the period when the students were passing from one lecture to another. I waved idiotically at the knotted, gazing students, and waggled my wings as I left.

I didn't know even one girl there, and this was my last aerial playfulness, except for permitted looping at twilight pretending to test the ships before my students appeared at the line.

This may seem odd to people now who jet all over the world in all kinds of weather, during the night or the day, but one must remember that we were flying just fifteen years after the first powered flight in the history of the world, and naturally planes were new, exotic and exciting, suspect and highly romantic.

Romance was thrillingly ascendant on the nights when you were the only human being high above the darkened earth in all America. After night flying had been "washed out" at approximately 3 a.m., and the field darkened, I would connive with Sergeant Maynard, and take a ship up to fly alone for perhaps an hour, then land and wake up the sergeant who had fallen asleep in the hangar.

My dreams of being sent to Allenby in Palestine were sharper now, and I made application to be sent in citizen-soldier naïveté, however pleasant my anchorage to Ellington was and however free I was.

I could take a plane up just at sunset or before and fly away from the field, climb to perhaps 9,000 feet, then go through a series of loops out of *joie de vivre* and there were no other planes up: the interim between day and night flying. This was the best time of all: the time when [the] daylight of man's self-assurance and self-importance faded into the mystical darkness. The air was usually still.

I could leave the field as I have mentioned and fly away into the darkness of the moonless early mornings, after night flying was over, and become Jo-Without-Purpose: Jean-Sans-Effet again, questing in the mysterious starlit space over Texas. The very few earth lights, like the eyes of jack-lighted deer, would be incredible to flyers now, who may now see earthly galaxies splashed over Texas. My scattered earth-eyes were chiefly red kerosene eyes of 1918.

I had forced landings, but fortunately only one with flares, and once I had to land in a rain storm on what I supposed must have been a rice field since I bounced over earth corrugations. The storm had come suddenly and the rain slanted into my face (we had only open cockpits) and it was like the pricking of a thousand needles. I had a difficult time getting back into the air after the rain ceased, bouncing into the air from the man-made ridges of the field.

How arrogant we were with wings. We called the non-flying officers of the post kiwis, for the New Zealand bird that through the centuries had lost the power of flight, and they knew about the epithet and hated us. Many of the higher ranking cavalry officers of the field had never even been up in a plane and in our winged, sophomoric wisdom, we patronized them. Only of course on the Mezzanine floors of the hotels, during the tea dances and during dinner on the Rice Hotel roof and on the ball room floor of the Galvez Hotel in Galveston. Added to these officers' original contempt for the silly experiment of the Signal Corps, called the Aviation Section, was the flyers' intolerable assumption that they belonged to a higher order of human beings, notwithstanding the difference of rank. Contempt turned into hate.

Our wings were passports to dances, teas, drawing rooms, hearts, not to mention the excited "wings-wacks," who still-hunted in pairs.[125]

Two more of my students in Night Bomb Raiding dodged the two lights in Galveston, and had to go back to day flying, where at least one of them was sent on to advanced training for fighter pilots and stood out as a daring and tricky fighter.

Besides the queer revival through racial memory of the incubi of primitive men, there was the inability to measure distance in the darkness; the nemesis of several excellent daylight flyers.

But the test that sent most of the aspiring night flyers back to daylight flying as well as to their deaths or to the hospital was the searchlight stage of night flying.

The students were supposed to fly back and forth over the searchlight emplacements, and the lights would find them and follow them as far as they could reach them, then they returned and the lights played on them again, like several fire hoses from different spots and angles. This simulated of course the light beams that found Allied flyers over their targets, enabling the enemy anti-aircraft guns to shoot them down. When the searchlight beam both in reality and in practice found a plane, the operator tried to keep the plane in its beam, and the pilot had to get out of the beam anyway he could, so he might try any acrobatic maneuver in order to do so.

This was tricky business in this glare which blinded the pilot, and he lost his horizon which always gave him a sense of stability and he had to depend on the air against his cheek, the pressure of his life belt, the laboring or the racing of his motor, and if he failed to straighten himself out, even after escaping the light beams, he might crash, despite the fact that at the field the student was given plenty of altitude in which to maneuver.

Some of the students expecting to go into the searchlight test within a few days were often white-faced and seemed absentminded.

There was one ridiculous incident which might have had tragic consequences. This was an incident of the Night Bomb Raiding Stage.

A big extrovert, having finished his primary flying at some ground school in Illinois, was sent to me for Night Bomb Raiding instruction after he had finished his primary night flying. He had polished up his brass bars, and advanced to me with an exaggerated, stiff salute with a manner that said, "I'm your equal in rank but I salute you only as an officer of the post and my instructor, all of which means that I have learned all there was to know at military preparatory school, and I conform to military customs as a correct officer of the United States Army."

I had on first thought, on recalling the incident and reviving rather clearly his image, the tendency to refer to him as The Tackle, but on second thought I realize that I have never known a college football player who had not been more or less humbled by sweat, competition, opposing position superiority, bruises, sprains and fractures and ego-submerging teamwork, so in recalling him, I think he was more the Lord Jim type of Joseph Conrad's novel of that name: "His voice was deep, loud, and his manner displayed a kind of dogged self assertion—It seemed a necessity, and it was directed apparently as much at himself as at anybody else."

He glanced cursorily at the map I smoothed out on the wing for him, and his attitude said that he couldn't afford to lose time going over it in detail. This was a map of the area, and the points where we had placed targets were indicated, along with the number of minutes from the field and the direction. These targets were a series of concentric circles on a cleared area on the ground, like a rifle range target; the concentric lines of whitewash and the bull's-eye an electric light. Some distance from the target were the observation houses, where the observers could mark the hits by triangulation.

The extrovert landed back at the field and I asked him if he thought he might have scored well. He looked at me as if he would make sure that I wasn't joking, and said, "Good enough, I guess," his military correctness forgotten.

At nine the next morning an orderly came to my bedside and said that the commandant wanted to see me immediately. He would accompany me to headquarters.

I knew the orderly didn't know why I was summoned and I immediately thought "Allenby needs specialized bombers."

The commandant was thin-lipped and severe, and he searched my face in silence as if he would find signs there of un-military thinking.

He ordered me at ease, then told me a story that was supposed to be a reprimand of me and one of my students of Night Bomb Raiding. Apparently a student from Night Bomb Raiding had flown over a ranch house during the time the rancher's little daughter was having a party under the trees of the yard, and the trees were hung with Chinese lanterns, and damned if a 50-pound bomb hadn't fallen near the yard and another in the corral. Of course these were dummy bombs.

I wasn't in command of the Night Bomb Raiding Stage; I was only an instructor, so the commandant dismissed me after the object lesson, and I was so relieved to be allowed to go back to my interrupted sleep that I had not learned just what had happened, whether the incident of the bombing of the Chinese lanterns of the rancher's daughter's party was a current one of the night before, and my extrovert had been involved, or rather the incident had occurred sometime before. My extroverted, self-protective bluffer didn't report back for further training to my stage.

We flew to Beaumont, Texas, and other cities, in large formations, and our duty was to drop little red cards with the following printed on them: "This card was dropped by an aviator from Ellington Field; It could have been a German bomb: BUY WAR BONDS."[126]

After we had dropped all our cards, we watched them volplane, twist, tumble to the city streets, you with the others landed by turn on the improvised field where the mayor and the band met us, and where there were speeches under the flag. Later in some building in town, a tremendous luncheon was served, and we were surrounded by fluttering women, and we were introduced to "Miss United States War Bond" and her entourage, and I seem to remember there was a "Queen" of something or other and a "Princess This or That," who not only helped fill the racial-memory royalty vacuum, but indicated the dawning national nympholepsy which would develop in the 1920's to rather ridiculous importance.

We danced for several hours, looked at our wrist watches, and were driven back to our planes, and took off by the number, circling the community waiting for the last plane to take off, then like migration-inspired Canadian geese we formed our V and flew back to the field at Ellington.

By this time the most rugged and hairy of males wore wrist watches; for in the trenches, the soldiers had found them necessary, and we in the air couldn't possibly have fumbled under our flying coats, under our safety belts to get at our pocket watches.[127]

⌒

Spanish influenza came to Ellington that summer, and we were confined to the post. Ellington was a very large field, and many soldiers and some flyers and perhaps some staff officers died.

I realized the seriousness of it when I over-heard talk of it at Officers' Mess. The medical men, most of them commissioned as majors out of civilian life, were visibly perturbed. When I casually asked several of them what I should do as a preventive, they in 1918 could only advise: "Soon as you get up in the morning, stand out in front of your barracks and inhale as deeply as possible, hold it for as long as possible, then exhale."

I did this with little conviction.

In order not to destroy *esprit*, the staff had the ambulances come to the field to take away the bodies at about the time we of the night flying stages washed out at 3 a.m. Every morning at this time, as we came to our barracks I saw the ambulances in line, waiting at the back doors of the hospital, their drivers and assistants in groups smoking and whispering. This caused me almost every morning to think of Shakespeare's mysterious figures in a dark street of Genoa of the sixteenth and seventeenth centuries, plotting murder. The very atmosphere was macabre.

With my sophomoric assurance, I was above death, and these things affected only my tragi-poetic sense. I was above making the mistakes the lost flyers had made which plunged them to their deaths, and influenza would attack someone else.

D's death was not from influenza; he fell out of a climbing turn just after take-off, and since he was an officer of the post, this placed his death in another category, and four of us were told off to accompany his casket to New York City. We, for some reason—perhaps a special request—were ordered to take planes from Mitchell Field and fly over the cortège, but something intervened; perhaps weather.

We, the four of us who had accompanied D's body and had been grounded, were compelled to crawl along with the cortège, and that night we shamelessly went to a smoky, speak-easy sort of place, blithely threw rings at little posts and won dolls and teddybears and other gewgaws for the titillated "wings-wacks." I refrained from pairing off with one as the others did, since D's girl, she of the fetish step-ins, had wanted me to come to her.

She seemed to find solace in a rather eager, weepy nymphomania, and after every tumble, she would weep, her sniffling jerky.

Once she said through her sniffling, "Oh! what do you suppose reely happens to people—you know, after—," then after several slightly explosive sniffles, she said, "Is there a heaven? He wouldn't be watching us, would he?"

I had an image of D's face; the face of a cocky egocentric who consciously limited his obtrusions because he wanted more than anything else to be voluntarily noticed and appreciated. He would undoubtedly have been quite busy up there ingratiating himself, with no urge to spy.

I kept my facetious thoughts to myself, but strangely enough, I did feel just a little like a passive, un-scheming Richard The Third.

The next time the orderly came to summon me to appear at head-quarters, he came at the night flyer's rising time at noon. When I entered the commandant's office, Anderson the "blind flyer" (one who flew with instruments covered; they were also called "cloud fly-ers") was there before me. We were soon informed that we were to report to Langley Field immediately. Langley Field was situated at Hampton, Virginia, which in turn was almost an extension of New-port News, a well-known embarkation port.

This time I knew it must be Cairo, Egypt, and to Allenby's advanc-ing lines of camels and sheiks in white burnouses and swarms of turbans, and above the romantic swarm Mathews, J.J., Second Lieu-tenant of the Air Service might soon be flying a British D-H-9.

Anderson didn't seem to care where he might be sent. He was a midwestern farm boy whose chief object in life was to get the busi-ness over as soon as possible so that he could get back to his long rows of glacial soil. He was honest and efficient, candid and modest: the epitome of the American ideal.

John Joseph Mathews in World War I pilot's
uniform (Courtesy of the Osage Tribal Museum,
Pawhuska, Oklahoma)

We were allowed four days in which to report to Langley, so we each stopped over for a few hours with our families.

I could visualize Anderson at the farmstead in Iowa (perhaps), talking seriously with his father, not about the war but about the corn crop and the number of feeder-cattle they might be able to take from the Southwest and from the Plains. I could see them walking down the corn rows, here and there pulling the shucks back to reveal the beautiful grains. They, as they walked down the rows, and examined the ears, would also talk of beef and hog prices in Omaha and Chicago, and as the family stood on the station platform talking with Anderson through the coach window, he might say, "I COULD be back by plantin' time."

For me there was the matter of barn repairs since the last flood, but as I drove across the prairie, the thirty miles to the ranch house on Beaver Creek, there was no thought for flood-slanted barns, and washed out drift fences; there was no room for such thoughts along with the visions of swarming retreating Turks, and white burnoused Arabs on camels, and long strings of lorries flowing down into the *wadis*, and out onto the volcanic emptiness again, like segmented, interminable serpents crawling toward Damascus.

This, I daydreamed, is what I shall soon be seeing under my wings.

Les Claypoole was alone at the ranch house, and upset.[128] His wife had left him. Her son, his stepson, had been stationed at an army camp in the southern part of the state, and while she was visiting her son, Les had hired a housekeeper and cook.

As we sat on our heels with the flood-bullied barn slanted over us, he talked as he whittled: "Whin we's a-settin' in the evenins, a-waitin' fer bed time, 'course they wasn't nothin' to do; the chores all done. So after I hep'ed her with the dinner dishes, we jist set. Well, one evenin she gotta snappin' her garters a-settin there en kindy smilin' at me."

After a silence, he said: "Well, yu know how t'is."

Back across the prairie to the Ridge Ranch, and still there was no room in my thoughts for slanting barns and down fences.

At the Ridge, I rode out into the pasture to have a visit with Bally. She stood like a statue, ears forward, and looked at me as if she had never seen me before, then trotted off with her flaxen-tailed colt, now a yearling.[129] Her mane flowed in the old manner, and her long flaxen tail was raised and looped gracefully and even fancifully as in a later Kiowa Indian stylized painting.

When she stopped, I dismounted and walked toward her, and just then a whimsical eddy carried my scent to her, and she came toward me. She sniffed my hand as I held it out to her. I could now see the grey hairs on her muzzle, and the hollow above each eye.

A smooth-mouth now, but she was fat. I pulled the cockleburs from her forelock and her mane, and allowed her to go to join her suspicious, staring, sorrel son.

I arrived at the offices of the commandant of Langley Field just under the deadline, which was par for Jo-Without-Purpose, and naturally Anderson had been in Hampton since the day before, and he was now waiting to be called before the commandant.[130]

The commandant was surprised and obviously confused. He evidently had no orders concerning us. He advised us to find lodgings in the town of Hampton since there were no quarters for us on the field. We would report every day, until orders came: every day at 2 p.m.

We found lodgings with a very pleasant family and reported dutifully, and soon it was quite obvious that the commandant might never receive orders for us, and we sat in our room and concluded we were lost, and we became very unhappy; Anderson wanted to get on with the unpleasant business, giving the war his best as he did everything, and I was convinced that my orders for Palestine were hung up somewhere in the War Department, but I hadn't quite the courage to ignore regulations and appeal to a Senator from Oklahoma.

Finally, the commandant looking up at us and shaking his head in a tired, un-military manner, every day at 2 p.m., came down from his regular army dignity and commiserated with the bewildered citizen-soldiers. Eventually, he made arrangements for us to become officers of the post, and we were given duty.

My dreams of Palestine were fading.

Langley Field had been named for Samuel Pierpont Langley of the Smithsonian Institution, who along with the French-American Octave Chanute, railroad engineer and bridge builder, had given the Wright Brothers advice, and had guided them to reading in aeronautics at the turn of the century and thereafter.

The field was just out of Hampton, Virginia, the little town at the mouth of the James River, and influenced by the whims of the sea. The town smelled of brine and fish, but the field had only the odors of the wide Atlantic Ocean.

Where Ellington had trained both day and night bomb raiders

Langley trained reconnaissance pilots and observers, and here was located the Science and Research department of the Aviation Section, and it seemed rather in character, I should think, that a lost "blind" (instrument) flyer and a lost night bomb raider should become aerial chauffeurs for scientists fumbling in the strange new province of aerodynamics.

I became nocturnal again periodically, but only periodically, and my immediate superior was Captain Webster who had been called from his Stanford University physics laboratories and given a Captain's twin silver bars, then shook hands all around. Then he was shown where to attach his bars, and ordered to Langley. He had to leave his lead-insulated workshop, where he had dreamed of the split atom. He walked in a dream and was not of the earth's struggle but was searching for something behind it.[131]

But he was tall and rugged, and at times could have the presence of an efficient colonel, until he returned your salute, then his hand stopped halfway to his cap, and he immediately began explaining the next experiment on bomb trajectory. Although he had momentarily left the mysterious frustrating world of the atom, to attend to military things at hand, he was surprisingly earth-coordinated and adept in his new province of research.

We worked beautifully together since he understood perfectly the nature of my aerial problems with weather, and never in his apparently all-absorbing dedication, and in his scientist's impatience to get on with an experiment, forgot the realities of man's mechanical flying.

He stood out in his earth coordination through comparison with the other scientists from the great Universities. One lost his captain's bars from his left shoulder and failed to notice the bars' absence, and another opened his penny box of matches upside-down, consistently. Another couldn't seem to avoid stepping in mud puddles.

Anderson and I were officers of the post with all the privileges of position, but we remained as strangers among the other officers of that category, and I knew very few of the reconnaissance pilots.

We knew well only the militarized scientists.

I had the same freedom that I had at Ellington, and took a ship from the line when I chose, usually on some pretended military or scientific business, and flew over the Tidewater. The Tidewater of Virginia was in contrast with the Brush Country of southwestern Texas and the savannas of the Gulf Coast.

Here one flew over tranquil inlets and peninsulas covered by great trees which surrounded sleepy villages. In the forest openings there were mansions with their rows of slave cabins. I flew over these villages and mansions circling lazily like an eagle.

The war workers who had been concentrated at Newport News were like ants during the shifts, and ships moved in and out of Hampton Roads, their wakes focusing your attention. The wake of a ship as seen from the air is more conspicuous than single objects on land, due perhaps to the many patterns of earth's vegetation, with which single objects blend as in protective coloration. Of course this applies to the natural state; anything that man has touched usually looms like the clearings in the forests, and the mansions and the village and the roads were brusquely conspicuous.

Now, in 1966, men in orbit often stress the conspicuousness of the ship's wakes.

Of the many scientists and others who were sent down from Washington to give their inventions a try, one was a representative of the American Optical Company, whose people had perfected a new goggle for pilots, which I believe in some way diminished the sea glare, or was not affected by oil spray. I have forgotten which, perhaps both. Oil spray on the goggles was a nuisance in the earlier days of flying; both the J.N.-4 and the Curtiss-H speckled the pilot with oil periodically.

The personable representative (he could have been an executive) of the company gave me a pair of the improved goggles, and climbed into the observer's seat behind me. He watched the line sergeant adjust his seat belt with concentration. The percentage of people who at that time had been up in a plane must have been a fraction of one percent.

We flew out over the sea, then to the mouth of the James River, and over the war-busy shift-changing swarms of workers far down in Newport News. We may have been flying a bit low, since the workers stopped and massed in the streets and along the docks, turning their faces up to us and waving enthusiastically.

I had turned my head to look at my passenger once when we were testing the goggles over the sea, and he didn't seem to be thinking about goggles, but was holding tightly to each side of the cockpit, and now when I looked back he was looking down on Newport News fearfully.

To relax his tenseness, I said through the speaking tube: "You know, about 50 percent of those people down there are wondering if we are going to fall, heh, heh."

His voice in my ear was tense; there was no ring of levity in it. He said: "You know something, Lieutenant, exactly 50 percent of us up here are too."

Then there was the little man with a long beard and Thackeray spectacles. He talked constantly to himself in a murmur, in German perhaps—I suppose it was some other Teutonic or Slavic language however, since anything German was suspect in the United States at this time.

The little scientist had his assistants, the line sergeant and several mechanics of the field haul a tank-like container to the plane, lift it to the cockpit and arrange it there; then he squeezed in behind it.

He had waited for a particular type of weather condition which characterized this day, a day of large conical, bubble-edged cumulous, and eagerly pointed to the one he wanted me to fly through. I held up my index finger to him as one might do in warning a child; he had a tendency to be bossy, but the pilot as always is in command in the air, like a captain of a boat on the high seas. I made sure that the tank-like thing was securely bolted to the fuselage, and that the scientist himself was safely belted.

In a cloud, without the horizon visible, a flyer can easily lose his sense of stability, and may know when he is side slipping by the rush of air on either side of his face, or when his nose is down or up when his motor is racing or laboring. Also he must depend on the pressure of his safety belt.

Twice in a cloud I felt the pressure of the belt on my abdomen and righted the plane, but apparently my passenger noticed nothing. (I can't remember why Anderson, the true cloud flyer didn't have this assignment in the first place.) Clear of the clouds I turned for more directions to my scientist in the rear cockpit. We had just cleared the last of five or six clouds, and I wanted to say that we might not have gas enough for one more cloud.

He was talking to himself, and had his eyes fixed on another cumulous ahead; his long beard waved back over his shoulder like a banner; like the tail of Halley's comet.

I pointed to the earth and he assumed a frightened expression and pointed to the cloud at which he had been gazing. The duration of our flights of course were limited by the capacity of our tanks, unless there was an auxiliary tank above the pilot's head on the center section.

My gasoline gauge was giving me a warning, and I turned toward the field. I felt a poke in my back, and when I turned back, my scientist was pointing to a tremendous cumulous that had somehow eluded him, and was now just at the edge of Chesapeake Bay and running for the sea. I pointed to my gauge and made pantomime of great concern and fear, edging on the tragic, but he kept pointing to the magnificent cloud, and his attitude and manner seemed to say, "We can't bother with gasoline now—that's the best cloud yet."

When we landed, instead of the usual courtesies and sometimes effusive expressions of appreciation, he went immediately to headquarters, like one of my sisters of my childhood going to "tell papa."

That night at the officers' mess, I described my passenger standing in his cockpit, anchored by a specially devised safety belt for the experiment, pointing excitedly at the cloud, with his beard streaming out behind in the propeller's wash like a pennant.

Captain _____, formerly Dr. _____ (meteorology), said: "You know what you two were trying to do up there playing among those cumuli?"

"It wasn't play," I said. "I had helmet sweat in one cloud. But what were we doing?"

"Trying to make it rain; when we get to France, and become tired of fighting, we'll call you war birds and seed a cloud, and it'll rain on the Huns, then we can all go back to our badger holes and finish the card game."

Captain Webster had a problem with bomb trajectory: something about the variation from the true perpendicular when it was falling to earth on a target. I went up several nights a week, and flew over a designated spot and released bombs from 6,000 feet. As soon as a bomb left the rack under the wing, a bulb in the tail fin lighted up and the Captain and his assistants were ready with the cameras.

The trajectory of a bomb from plane to earth target, was a slightly bent one I understood, and I never knew whether it bowed in the direction of the plane's movement or in the opposite direction, but the knowledge gained would aid in bombing accuracy. I didn't know enough about the matter to even discuss it speciously with Captain Webster.

I was the aerial chauffer for [the] cloud seeding experiment, for the photographing of the bomb trajectory, for the non-glare goggles, and several other inventions brought down from Washington by competing and cock-sure enthusiasts, but there was no disaster: only a near one.

We were experimenting with plane to ground station telephony, and one afternoon I flew out over the Bay at differing low altitudes, then circled and came back facing a ground station. The technician was in the rear cockpit working silently over his gadgets. We flew this figure of eight for several hours. (We had to land and fill the gasoline tank perhaps twice.) I felt a poke in the back, and when I picked up the speaking tube, the technician's voice came over it as calmly as if he were talking about the favorable weather.

He said: "Lieutenant, I'm afraid we're on fire."

We had been drilled in defense against just such emergencies, quite as effectively as we had been drilled in tactical defense and attack. Our planes were highly vulnerable. The fabric was Irish linen painted with "dope" which in itself was highly flammable, not to mention the gasoline from the rocker arms, during an Immelmann or a loop or a roll.

When fear came suddenly, we sweated under the helmet, or at least I did, and I talked of it lightly with others, and we referred to it as "helmet sweat." It came when one went into a funk, and at times even dripped down the face.

I remember I had a bad case of helmet sweat as I threw the plane into a side slip. This would cause the flames or the suffocating smoke to fly upwards, instead of back into the faces of the occupants of the plane. Over land you would have to come out of the side slip and land normally, and in this few moments the flame and smoke would stream back into the pilot's and observer's faces again, but we were over the Bay when the fire started, and we needn't come out of the side slip, but plunge into the Bay.

I shouted back to the technician, "Unbuckle your belt," and he shouted back, "It's out."

I just barely came out of the side slip to avoid hitting the water, and later the technician said that our wheels actually touched the water ever so slightly.

I suppose jet pilots, and even their blasé passengers, might smile with indulgence at the naïve appreciation of earth's wonders that flowed under our primitive wings, and be amused by our delight in looking down upon the trees, the mountains, the deserts, the rivers and the villages that looked as if they might have been dropped to earth from the air as a solid, then fractured on impact. We felt at all times our relationship with earth, and knew we were not weaned from her. Sentient earth was our most dependable map and the smoke from sporadic fires gave us wind direction, and the stars were our most dependable compass, and the dash instruments were almost useless without the horizon.

The sensations, the emotions, the euphoria, the cockiness, and the sense of thrilling adventure we experienced, might seem puerile to jet pilots and their passengers escaping boredom through watching a cinema screen, but I must repeat, we were flying just fifteen years after the very first powered flight in history.

We flew by the seat of our pants.

Allenby with his Tommies and his Arabs had done it without me; they had swarmed into Damascus.

The day we got the news of the Turkish defeat and the occupation of Damascus, I was serving as Officer-Of-The-Day, and as I made my rounds of the post that night, I had ample time to think about the unaccountable slip up in Fortune's plans for me, but maybe my guardian Fate, Lachesis—she who controls one's stay on earth—had taken a hand in the matter, since it was also well known that she also guided destinies, and had influenced the War Department to "lose" me at Langley.

For several days I was dejected.

But as always, wings were a source of comfort, and I was ordered to accompany several Reconnaissance pilots by train to Little Silver, New Jersey in order to ferry some Curtiss-H's back to Langley.

I didn't know the military category of Little Silver. There were barracks there and officers' quarters and pheasant shooting, and that is about all I ever knew about it.

One might suppose that the planes were sent there from the factories, then air-ferried to the several fields where needed. This is an assumption, which of course, in no way excuses my lack of interest in such things at that time.

The pheasants were important.

I couldn't resist circling the Statue of Liberty, and flying up Fifth Avenue, before turning southwesterly over New Jersey to begin my flight over early American history.

Princeton was a doily set in a cleared space in the woods, and after flying over monotonous freeholds (so marked on the map) and barns and houses too close together, and smoke and factories and man-soiled meadows, it was a delight.

I landed at Bolling Field just at sunset, and of course stayed the night in Washington, D.C., since we had orders against flying at night while ferrying planes. I had asked permission to fly back at night, with my wings efficiently loaded with flares, but the commandant at Langley didn't think it advisable to risk flare landings in case of a "conked" motor or other trouble. Also there were no landing lights at most of the fields in those days.

This was disappointing since the romance of romances was flying at night, and especially did I want to fly at night over Colonial America.

After taking off from Bolling Field and circling for direction, I volplaned and circled the Washington Monument three times, entirely too close and too low; but at that stage in flying, by the time watchers and officials got over their excitement induced by my playful circling, the regulations came to their minds too late, and they couldn't have remembered the plane's number anyway.

The officers at Bolling had asked me to take along with me to Langley a technical sergeant, who had been assigned to our field. He had never been in a plane before.

I could feel his nervousness all the way to the field.

The Rappahannock called to me and I turned from my flight line to fly down the peninsula, between the Rappahannock and the York Rivers, to the Bay, and there played over Mathews County and Mathews village like a euphoristic, September red-tailed hawk. I circled low over the town many times, and people stood in the streets too interested to wave. They came out of the County Court House to look up, judges, clerks and stenographers.

I spent too much time flying down the peninsula and lazily circling over Mathews, and when I looked at my gauge, I was startled and immediately began to climb to a safer altitude and set off for the field at Hampton.

However, before I arrived there, while flying at 6[,000] or 7,000 feet, there came the familiar jerk of the ship and the cough of the motor. I had to unbuckle my belt, stand up and turn on the auxiliary tank, then the engine caught with confidence, and there far below and ahead was Langley Field.

I looked back over my shoulder to say something encouraging to my passenger, but he was so tense that I turned back without saying anything.

There were dances at the Chamberlin Hotel at Old Point Comfort and at the Richmond and the Jefferson Hotels in Richmond, and somehow one met here in the Tidewater more conservative, mannered girls than the Wings-Wacks, although there were a few of the young ladies who were wing-wacky, albeit mincingly.

It was sometimes hot during the early autumn when we danced at the old Hotel Chamberlin at the Point, and the rigid collars of our tunics almost choked us as we sweated, and while English riding boots (the cavalry used to do the spotting for the artillery, and do the reconnaissance work, and being a mounted service their officers wore boots; planes had by now taken the place of the cavalry in spotting and reconnaissance, and the mounted traditions were transferred with the duties; hence commissioned flyers wore boots) could compete with the naval officers' white shoes with some assurance, our sweat-tightened military tunic collars, and our sweat-spotted tunics made us self-conscious in the presence of the white duck uniforms and the golden wings of the Navy.

I thought Richmond was delightful, with an atmosphere as definite as that of San Francisco or New Orleans, which fascinated me later. Among the people of Richmond there were assurance and tranquility and an aura of self-assurance that was almost a boast. Prideful ladies from the old families made sure you were aware of their social ascendancy, and their sometimes garrulity about it in their lovely voices was more attractive than boring.

I am sure that Ethel Ann Sutton had much to do concerning my pleasant associations with Richmond. I went there often to visit her and dance at the Richmond and the Jefferson Hotels. We spent many hours driving about the Tidewater during the weekends; then on Sundays I would take [a] boat down the James River to Norfolk and ferry over Hampton Roads to Hampton.

I reported at the field at my convenience unless called for aerial chauffeur duty, but when there was no duty, I took a plane from the line at the magic twilight hours and flew ad libitum over the Bay, ending my aerial junket with acrobatics.

The life of the cat.

I was no longer agitated by my dreams of flying over the Arab swarms in a D.H.-9, and I was becoming contented in just keeping my flying edge, knowing now that if I ever got away from Science and Research, I would fly over the lines in France at night to blow up German ammunition dumps and bomb troops.

France had of course been the objective, and all our training as all military training should do, was to enable us to be successful over the German flyers, so that we could bomb their troops and dumps and bring down their reconnaissance planes. But Allenby's entry into Damascus had in some intangible manner eliminated the romance of war in the air for me and I actually began to think of that which I had not theretofore thought of: that in France, as the field people serviced my bomber at twilight, and I stood about puffing my cigarette, I would suddenly appreciate the fact at last that I would be no more than an aerial lorry driver, delivering my cargo, like an efficient truck or lorry driver, then turn and fly back along a previously laid-out route, lucky if I didn't have a German fighter on my tail and a dead or wounded bombardier, or a tail gun out of commission—a laboring, slow, almost defenseless aerial truck trying to get back to the Allied lines.

The fighters attending me would experience the romance of combat.

So, I adjusted to the cat's life, and became more and more attracted to auburn-haired, lovely voiced Ethel Ann, anticipating the weekends in Richmond, where we would spend the hours together.

I was losing my enthusiasm for my future role as an aerial trucker over muddy, bloody, sordid trenches and barbed wire in France. And anyway Romance had died there about the time of the tanks in 1916 and later the dirigibles over England had killed it there, and if there was a scrap of Romance it was lingering among the fighter pilots of both sides; there was a remnant of chivalry left when a downed pilot on either side of the lines might often be taken prisoner and then wined and treated as a noble enemy, worthy of all the chivalric courtesies.

Now, I know that in my country, the year 1918 saw the end of war euphoria and belligerent Chauvinism. One saw the spirit of the fifes and drums of 1776 muted in the summer of 1918, when the casualty lists were printed each day.

The chivalric jousters of the air would have their long bow men and their Crécy later.

My war days like my life from infancy were pleasant under the aegis of Lachesis, but when the Armistice came there was a feeling of incompleteness and regret and just a faint touch of uneasiness which one might experience if one had been a slacker.

The cavalry officers in command of the fields and the "90 day wonders" with RMA wings had misinterpreted John-Without-Purpose's dedication to cross-country at Kelly, and had recommended him for bombing; then at Ellington his dedication to night flying was misinterpreted as dedication to bomb raiding, then he was "lost" at Langley.

I shall never know if I was really lost along with Anderson by the War Department at Langley, or whether Science and Research had called for a night flyer in order to carry on with night time experiments, such as Captain Webster's bomb trajectory photography and others. It is not unlikely that my gleeful interest in night questing might have been mistaken for scientific interest, and I was chosen for Langley above other available night flyers of the field.

I had no reason really, to believe that I might be sent to Palestine; it was a matter of my having wanted it so intensely that I made myself believe that I might be ordered there. I had asked to be sent there when I was at Love Field, but there is no reason to believe that this request might have had any effect on the War Department.

Lachesis probably had a hand in it after all.

But now it was over. Every available ship on the field was in the air over the Tidewater, in wild goose formations divided into groups. We were led by a hospital ship painted white with a large red cross under the wings and on the fuselage.

We flew over Hampton Roads and you could see the steam from the ecstatic whistling of every boat in the Roads; you could see the flags waving in Newport News and Hampton, and there were far below the happy people in the streets like shoaling fish.

I was flying number three in one group, and the hospital ship was at the point of the V as the leader. It kept losing altitude and sank slowly, and we could only watch her sink. The white paint, or whatever it was, was too heavy; much heavier than "dope."

I felt flattered when the War Department asked me to remain in the service—the Air Force now and retain my rank. I had to think about it for some time. I really wanted to carry on with flying, but even at that time, even noticed by an insouciant young man, were many signs that the Air Force might become the War Department's stepchild. I had no way of knowing that bitter, nostalgic, horseless cavalry officers would not continue to be my immediate superiors. From what I had experienced, I could easily believe that the infantry and cavalry generals, even now, after France, might believe us to be a damned extraneous non-military growth—a malignant one, no less. There seemed to me to be little chance for Air Force pilots under these circumstances.

General Billy Mitchell's experience with the generals of the War Department confirmed my sophomoric guessing later.[132]

I don't remember that I had prescience concerning the very important future of aviation both in peace and in war, either, but I am sure that I would have been quite contented to stay in the Air Service had it not been for the brittle attitude of the earth-anchored old-line generals, who were the War Department. To indicate that they were brittle, is not to say that they were not very able and flexible as ground tacticians; they just didn't believe in a mechanical device composed of Irish linen, wires and ash, powered by a gasoline motor, as being of military importance, then or in the future.

There were definite reasons for England's disinterest in the development of the new factor in earth struggle. As mentioned previously, she wanted nothing new whose development might jeopardize the importance of her ships and other instruments of her world power, as well as nullify her insularity. She had stubbornly and fearfully tried to ignore this new factor of air power, retard its progress, but she met Reality in the form of Fokkers, and later dirigibles, and frenetically sent to France for motors and more motors for her planes that were waiting while she kept "in touch with the movement."

The United States War and Navy Departments had not really been conditioned to the new idea in earth-struggle, since they had not experienced that which the French, the English and the Germans had experienced; they had not faced the Realities long enough and intimately enough, to adjust completely, an adjustment which might mean giving up their Boots & Saddles and John Paul Jones traditions; and they couldn't possibly understand how this new-fangled idea of aviation could effect the tactic of amassing a great number of troops at a point of defense, or how bombs from a plane could possibly sink a battleship.

England had been forced through four years of war, and war in the air development, through intimacy and through the necessity for self-protection, to adjust to the idea, no matter how it might affect her traditions of ships and insularity.

The Ancient Greek Ideal of brain and body could be developed as I flew, but Oxford University and world travel came into sharper focus on the screen of my many drusy, kaleidoscopic ideas, and I finally decided to become only a reserve officer in the Air Force. There would be periodical flying to keep an edge, and there would be freedom from the post-war airfield doldrums, which I felt would be inevitable due to War Department apathy.

The old line general's frown was the frown of Jupiter.

Back home during the summer of 1919, Bally seemed not to have changed much; there was more grey on her nose, and the hollows above her eyes were slightly more conspicuous. She had not been shod for some time, naturally, since she had not been ridden for some time, and her front hooves were chipped slightly, but not in the least splintered. Her wild, suspicious, sorrel colt trotted away as I rode nearer, and she seemed to think she ought to follow, prancing away like the horse of a Kiowa painting again, her mane in the wind like flame.

When she stopped and looked back at me and my strange mount, I dismounted allowing my horse his freedom, and as he grazed, I lay down in the grass, knowing that with pronghorn curiosity she would be compelled to investigate this strange behaviour. After a few minutes she was blowing through her nose at my inert body, and the familiar scent of me was strong, and when I sat up she didn't shy away.

Her facsimile sorrel son with flaxen mane and tail, the future outlaw, kept his distance.[133]

⌒

230

I was in my junior year at the University when I went into the military service. It was too late to apply for matriculation at Oxford University, so I matriculated at the University of Oklahoma in the autumn.

The war heroes were back now with deep seriousness. A poker player pre-war who had spent his weekends in the whorehouses on California Street in Oklahoma City began preparing for the ministry. A perfect preparation for the ministry, he would know what he was talking about when he preached, and be convincing.

Charles Rider, my friend, [who] with starry-eyed honesty had intended someday to be the Chief Justice of the United States Supreme Court now took up the study of geology and dreamed of oil riches. Most of the girls I had known before the war were gone, having been war-panicked into marriage, rupturing their own designs on their chosen ones.

There were too many of us heroes and near-heroes, and we strained the University's capacity to take care of us, coming in a postwar, eager flood, as we did, to augment the normal matriculations.

I personally had one and a half years left of my planned four years, but my remaining academic hours devoted to the attainment of a B.A. degree were put on the scales and then balanced by Ground School aerodynamics. The faculty of Arts & Science seemed to be more interested in the perfect balancing that would achieve my B.A. in one semester, than in the academic value of my aerodynamics. As a matter of fact they couldn't have evaluated them since they belonged to other provinces as well as Arts & Science.

I seemed more interested in girls now, but I think it wasn't wholly a matter of more interest, since I had always been interested in them, but it would seem that since my war experiences, I saw them as they were, and this gave me more confidence. The Southern Womanhood inculcation of my father was still strong, but the wings had vanished and the nimbus was grown dim.[134]

I danced more often now, and I had several playmates, but my special playmate was Dorothy Prouty. She had rather taken the place of my last pre-war playmate, Georgia Shutt, who sang *Macusla* beautifully and belonged to an honorary society. Dorothy was also a member of a women's honorary society, the Owl & Triangle.[135]

She walked across the campus with long Junoesque strides to her 8 o'clock class eating an apple, her large full moon earclasps bright in the morning light.

We walked to the river, we danced, and during the spring field meet when the High School seniors from over the state were rushed by the fraternities and sororities, I brought the family car down to help her impress Theta rushees; again, the "Theta pimp."

I was still Jo-Without-Purpose, not having been seasoned by battle over France, but Oxford University became an objective rather definitely now, and I had the odd feeling of just marking time.

I was on the staff of the collegiate daily paper, and had been on the staff of the University's annual, and I rather listlessly was a candidate for editor of the annual called *The Sooner*, and lost, even with the able and knowledgeable Herbert Fuque as a "campaign manager."

Athletics of some nature might have absorbed my interest adequately, but I had what I referred to as my "airplane ankle." During the time I was an instructor in Night Bomb Raiding at Ellington, one of my flare-landing students at the stick was met head on by a student from another stage. The student from the other stage was soloing in night flying, and became confused, got out of his traffic lane. We fell as a unit, the two planes meshed.

I got an injured ankle and a severe burn on my right forearm from the exhaust pipe.

I couldn't even go out for polo, which was post-war-new at the University.

It was pleasant marking time, and waiting for graduation before making application to enter Oxford, and somehow it never occurred to me that I might not be accepted. However, the idea was only an ember, really, which I know now could have been quenched by some greater enthusiasm, if Walter Stanley Campbell had not come to the fraternity house with bright enthusiasm to talk with me about a Rhodes Scholarship.[136]

He had been one of the first Rhodes Scholars from the new State of Oklahoma and at this time was on the staff of the Department of English Literature. We had only just met, and of course I had not said anything to him about my idea. It must have been my strange aura again; sending out its little waves.

His enthusiasm blew the ember into a blaze. "You don't have any idea of it, of course, but you are the perfect type for a Rhodes; you are archetypical—the type Cecil Rhodes himself might have had in mind, and I know you're the type that Oxford visualizes as American and Colonial scholars. You *must* have a try."[137]

He was on the Rhodes Scholarship board for the state, and he sent me an application blank, and since I had to have a sponsor, he suggested my fraternity. This was easy. I was at the time Number One (President) of the chapter, and I had to sign my own application along with the secretary and the treasurer and other officers, after the unanimous vote. I have smiled about this many times.

My grades for my three years at the University, if charted would look like a sharply serrated mountain range; Sewanee would look like an Alpine plateau.

The more I thought about them the less interested I became in appearing before the Rhodes board, and especially I felt I might embarrass my sponsor, W.S. Campbell.

I went to him and suggested that I apply and if accepted, go independently. "Wonderful," he said and with a most hurried and unusual enthusiasm got me accepted at his old college, Merton.

He must have blown up my athletic ability, practically dormant since high school, and my scholastic ability, which like a hibernating insect came out only when sun-warmed by whimsical enthusiasm.

I was notified by Merton College that my rooms would be ready for me at the beginning of Michaelmas Term, in October.

After graduation by Oklahoma University, I had intended to go to E.W. Marland of the Marland Oil Company and ask to be sent on geological reconnaissance to some foreign field; now I would wait until after Oxford. Also, now I could escape the bank and the Osage Mercantile Company. Being the only boy in the family, and manifesting little interest, the Tucker brothers of my father's old partners became disinterested in carrying the estate along as drones, and made a buy or sell proposition to my family, and we had no choice and sold our interest in the merchandise, but retained our interest in the real estate.

I was free.[138]

~

[1920]

After arriving home and after the flurry of my sisters getting off to college and boarding school, I became restive, I could have filled the hours and the days between this period in September and the beginning of Michaelmas Term at Oxford by hunting coyotes and quail, but I had not bothered to get another bird dog since Spot's death. He had died while I was at Ellington Field. He died of old age, but in so doing he had upset mother, since he died immediately after a long drawn-out howl of unutterable poignancy, which her Gallic mystique took to be an omen. She nodded her head knowingly when it was discovered that the night Spot had howled so piteously, and died, was the night I had crashed at Ellington.

My restiveness increased after all preparations for sailing in October had been perfected. Then the idea flashed; I could go out to Wyoming and be in camp by the time of the full moon, when the bull wapiti would be challenging, and before the black and the grizzly bears began their hibernation, then arrive back in time for my sailing date in October.

My big-game hunting fever had attacked on Mt. Washburn in the Yellowstone when I had ridden into a band of Rocky Mountain bighorn. I remember distinctly when it struck, and I had descended the peak in a sort of trance. Also one could see cow wapiti here and there in the park; cows and calves since the bulls had not come down from their summering higher up in the mountains.

A mule deer buck had stood, the "velvet" on his antlers like a fungoid growth, and watched me rowing two of my sisters on the lake.

Black bears of course were everywhere; they came to the garbage cans in the late afternoons, but left reluctantly and sometimes

Mathews, in nature, with pipe (Courtesy of the Osage Tribal
Museum, Pawhuska, Oklahoma)

growling when a deliberate grizzly made his appearance, bluffing them like some 'teen-age bully among grade school children. The black bears begged along the edges of the Park roads much as they do today.

Naturally when the fever had struck, I talked with hunting guides in Cody but had made no arrangements, but now the fever at its most disturbing state, I telegraphed Bill Barron asking him to meet me at the train at a certain time on a certain date.

During the time I was making my preparations, my brother-in-law Henry asked if he might go along. He was not a hunter, but my preparations excited him.

We picked up our saddle horses and pack string at Holmes Lodge on the Shoshone River, on the trail to the east gate of the Park. Besides the five saddle horses, one for Bill the guide, one for Jim the cook and one for Wuff, the wrangler and one each for Henry and me, we had a string of perhaps fourteen or fifteen pack horses.[139]

We crossed Two Ocean Pass and came into the drainage of the Snake River, and finally camped on Pilgrim Creek, a feeder of the Buffalo Fork of the Snake.

This was the country Bill loved above all others. He was sixty then, born in 1860. Fed up with the aftermath of the Civil War, and people in general, he came West, the Wild West, and settled in Cody, but he spent his winters in the mountains looking for gold, and in order to finance his search for gold, he guided hunters in the autumn and fishermen during the summers.

In camp the first night still on the Shoshone drainage, he said, as he roasted his meat on a stick over the coals: "I was sure glad to get your telegram 'bout huntin'. I sure got a belly full of herdin' ewes and lambs this summer—girl scouts and their herders. While I'se settin' up their camp for 'em the old hens'ud be cluckin' 'round with ridin' britches stretched across their fat bottoms, like shoats tryin' to git out from under a blanket. There's sure better ways a-makin' a livin'."

Bill was like twisted rawhide and coyote-clever. He wore a walrus moustache that hung over the corners of his mouth like drapes. He neither smoked nor chewed tobacco, I believe—at least I never saw him do either, but his nemesis seemed to be whiskey. He admitted it.

"One time," he said, "I had me a fine grub stake and was ready for the hills when a friend of mine asked me to have just one drenk with 'im." He stopped talking and gazed into the fire for a moment, as if he might see there something there that might tend to make the memory less graphic. He continued: "Well, they ain't much more than that to tell; when I finely come to, I had used up my grub stake, and they told me I'd given a dance at the Irma."

He told no stories of the "old days." He told no stories of his hard-ships when he camped along the feeder streams of the Yellowstone and the Snake, searching, searching, searching for gold. He told no stories around our camp fires, but sat and conjectured aloud where the big bulls might be, and wondered about the grizzly tracks he had seen as we came down the Fork.

He appreciated deeply his own frailties, and therefore was generous with the frailties of others. How well he knew his own: having ample time to know them in the months of his solitary gold-seeking, and in his secret thoughts during his outward subservience as guide to "ewes and lambs," and to arrogant and ignorant "creampuff dudes," who didn't know fat cow from poor bull.

Whatever went wrong or whatever he might have to suffer would be his fault, he felt. Those characteristics which he found in himself which were not worthy, despite what his vanity might urge, he did not try to project to others. So he lived with them and accepted them and smiled over them, but his modesty had not the slightest taint of inferiority.

We would ride up the shoulders of mountains, tie the horses, then hunt afoot, walking, or better, climbing and descending for perhaps five or six hours a day.

Henry had been fortunate enough to get his bull the second day, so thereafter, being a non-hunter, he stayed in camp, eating, making sorties for wood and indolently flipping pebbles at chipmunks.

Bill and I hunted from dawn until twilight each day for a week, but had not yet had a good shot at an outstanding trophy.

Bill could see that I was enjoying the search for a trophy just as he had enjoyed the search for gold, and realizing this he was a bit disappointed: not disappointed in not being able to show his hunter a desirable bull, but in the evident fact that I had lost myself in the

hunting rather than in the quick kill, and not for a moment considering the taking of a day's rest in camp.

One midafternoon we were sitting on a fallen lodgepole pine, trying to locate a deep-voiced bull, so that we could stalk him. But as we
listened we heard a challenge to him reverberate among the mountains far to the west, and our deep-voiced bull's acceptance reverberated from the mountain sides and faded as he trotted toward his
challenger.

We looked at each other. Bill said: "Better call it a day." He sounded
weary.

"I think I know the country fairly well," I suggested. "I believe I'll
try it alone tomorrow."

"I bet you're wrong 'bout what you think I'm gonna say," he said.
"I'm gonna give you my blessin'—no use puttin' on; I'm tar'd, and
there ain't no call to lie to you, cause you'd know I'd be lie'in.'"

I smiled with pleasure. I had been looking forward to a day absolutely alone, and the canny old man saw my pleasure. I said: "After all
you're only human, and we've been going all day every day for a week."

"Yeah," he said as we walked toward the horses, "they ain't no
doubt 'bout me being human, but a man'ud hafta look twice at you
and the Honourable _____. He came from England and he actually lowered on a whoppin' big bull sayin' he wasn't ready to take a
head yet. I felt plumb whipped. Like this now, it was the sixth day,
and I wanted a day in camp to kinda rest up.

"Well, that night in camp, I said, 'I see you got'cha a pair of fancy
chaps, and you'll need 'em tomorrow.'

"'Really,' he said.

"'Yep, sure will,' I said. I'd just stepped out a minute before and I
could feel the big wet snowflakes. He'd just had them chaps special
made: angora hair and fancy—heavy leather.

"Well, he put 'em on next mornin', and by then it had snowed a
couple-three inches and was still snowin'; them big wet, September
flakes. When we left the horses higher up it was snowin' good, and
it wasn't long 'course 'til that angora hair was soakin' wet, and that
leather had sopped up melted snow too, but by the time to call it a
day he was still goin'.

"Back in camp, I pulled off my wet boots and socks, changed pants, and fell back on my bunk and didn't wake up 'til the next day. 'Course, when I woke up he was gone, a-wearin' his chaps; he never did get the point."

His eyes twinkled: "Fellas like you and him don't come along but once in a blue moon. That bull yesterday was in range." He looked at me sharply.[140]

As we approached, the horses were dancing around the trees to which they were tied. As we rode down the mountain single file, he turned back and said: "It's time for a big snow, and if one sets in we'll hafta get back over the pass pronto, so you'd better let one down tomorrow."

I rode next day high up under the rimrock, and sat most of the afternoon just listening to the primordial, soul-disturbing challenges of the bulls. I was fascinated and disturbed and even frustrated, in trying to, man-like, pigeonhole my emotions. To me the bull wapiti's challenge is the most primordial and disturbing voice in Nature. I have tried to describe it many times, and now I have it taped.

I still can't describe it except to say that it vibrates a deep Paleolithic racial-memory chord in the soul. Chiefly I must depend on images; it brings images of prognathous, slant-browed men with hairy arms over their heads squatting around a fire, or a circle of these hairy men squatting around a deer carcass with their bloody hands and blood-smeared faces.

The challenge in the moonlight is beyond even images and word symbols.

The next day after a day in camp Bill was with me again, and after noting his concern with the "buttermilk sky" of that particular day, I decided to shoot the first bull I could get a shot at, no matter the size of his antlers.

We trailed a wary bull in the snow, and I had to lie flat on my back and shoot between my feet. He ran downhill for fifty or sixty yards, then fell dead with a crash.

Bill was so happy he trembled. Getting their "dude" a shot is a matter of honor with guides, and seeing their "dudes" kill when the game is shown makes them vicariously triumphant.

After Bill had gutted my mediocre bull, I said, "Help me with the head, I want to have it mounted with 'cape.'" This was an unusual request, and a difficult business with only our knives; the wrangler and the guide do this when they come up to quarter the carcass so that they can pack it on pack horses; the head is usually severed at that time.

We had some difficulty in severing the head properly for mounting "with cape" with only our hunting knives. Bill carried my rifle and I carried my precious head down the mountain to the horses, not able to count the times I slipped on the snow and the head tumbled down in front of me.

John-Without-Purpose and his all-absorbing obsession with the primitive atmosphere, the trees, the echoing challenges, passing up takeable bulls, and his dreaming, delaying, had thrown Bill's plans out, so the morning I had set out alone and Bill hadn't even gotten out of his bedding roll, Wuff the wrangler left on his horse, leading one pack horse, to buy some provisions from Ole Beavertooth who had a little store on the edge of Jackson Hole.

He had been excited; it had been like a trip to another world for him, and we had talked about it—just the two of us, the night before.

Wuff was a derivative of the mountains, rugged, natural, granitic and illiterate, with a soul overflowing with poetry he couldn't express. Such esthetic urges imprisoned by the lava crust of complete ignorance, oafish peer conformity, and male pride, created frustrations which were poignant at times.

There was something about the "dude"—perhaps my youth drew him, and when he squatted on his heels by me away from the others, I instinctively described to him the country he would see from the pass: the Teton Mountains, Jackson Hole, the Lake, etc.

Like many illiterate and uncultured men, trying heroically to understand, he held his mouth half open as he listened, as though he would have every gateway open in order that the magic that my words carried could enter into his consciousness, and be classified.

"When you leaving?" I asked.

"At the crack of dawn, I guess."

"Well, you can take it easy and you'll be getting to the pass j-u-st about sundown. On the pass you'll be looking down on the Lake and the Tetons will be reflected in the Lake, and then behind the Tetons the sun'll be setting. You may hear a wolf about sundown, back up in the mountains on the Park side; I once did, just after the sun had gone down."

Just visible there was a fleck of saliva at each corner of his mouth, then he closed his mouth and swallowed. He rose abruptly without saying a word and went to his pup-tent.

He had been left on a settler's doorstep, and had never been given a name; a proper sort of name, so he knew no name, and had been called "Wolf" which had eventually become "Wuff."

He was back from his journey into strange lands, by the time we got my bull's carcass down on two pack horses, and as I sat and watched Bill and Jim hang the meat, Wuff came over and squatted by me. I knew he was brim full of emotion, but I said nothing—I waited.

He began cleaning his fingernails with his knife, frowning down at them. There was a long silence. A beaver slapped the water of Pilgrim Creek with his tail, and that seemed to break the silence.

"Well," I said, "did you make it to the pass at the right time?"

"Yeah, I shore did." A silence, then, "But I didn't hear no goddam wolf."

This time there was a much longer silence. He folded his knife and put it into his pocket, set his hat on the back of his head, and he seemed to be worried about something.

Another lead: "I hope it wasn't cloudy so you could see the sunset."

"It shore wasn't," he said, "it SHORE wasn't." He seemed to be searching the ground for something, then he raised his voice slightly: "Just like you said, them Tetons was a-shinin' in that watter, en-uh— en-uh, that sun was a-wallerin' en-a-raisin' hell behind them Tetons, a-bloody-'n them white peaks."

Here his thoughts finally jammed, and his unaccustomed words broke down under their heavy load of emotion; finally he managed in a voice gravelly with emotion, "It was the purtiest son of a bitchin' thing I ever seen," and his rough fingers worked ridiculously, as if he were actually trying to get hold of his emotions, as he might subdue a wild ranch calf.

241

I felt I had to make some comment, so I said, "I know."

The beaver slapped the water again, and this seemed to bring him back to horse wrangling. He jumped quickly to his feet and went toward the improvised corral. He stopped, and looking back at me asked, "You got your riggin' ready for packin' in the mornin'?"

We got over Two Ocean Pass before the snow became a barrier; our horses waded belly-deep in it.

We made camp in the deep snow on the Atlantic side of the Pass, and I was awakened during the night by the wolves. They were not running or hunting; they seemed to be standing each on his own lookout howling at the hard, empty white night in exasperation.

Arrived at Holmes Lodge, Henry left the hunt, when I decided to try for bighorn in the Sunlight country, and since this would cause me to miss the Michaelmas Term at Oxford, I went into Cody with my wapiti head, and after taking it to the taxidermist, I telegraphed the Cunard Lines in New York to have my passage canceled on the Aquitania, then telegraphed my family. With a fresh supply of provisions I made preparations for bighorn hunting.

My cabin at Holmes Lodge was at the edge of a mountain stream that gurgled and laughed all night.

The interim between the Buffalo Fork hunting wapiti and the Sweetwater to hunt bighorn was very pleasant. The food was excellent and my cabin comfortable with the mountain stream laughing and talking just under my window.

We got off up Sweetwater Creek, but this time the pack string was smaller, and I insisted that one horse be packed with fresh eggs. The culinary art of Jim had limitations not only in technique but in creativity, and fresh wapiti meat has a subtle, sweet taste that one doesn't appreciate in game. It always ought to hang several days.

I had the same white horse, whose name I have forgotten. I remember with pleasure his pelage that blended so perfectly with the snow, and that he was sure-footed without being agonizingly cautious. Since rams have telescopic eyesight, and we hunted in the snow, my white horse was a boon.

Just over the pass we came into Yellowstone River drainage from the drainage of the Shoshone, and strung out down Sunlight Creek.

This Sunlight country had a special association; as a matter of fact it was sheer romance. Leo Bellieu, Floyd Soderstrom and I had read a story about a ram of Sunlight—the *Sunlight Ram* whose author's name I am sorry, I have forgotten.[141] We read this thrilling story when we were still small boys, and we had said to ourselves that someday we would go to the Sunlight country. Now, I was there, and I would be hunting a Sunlight ram myself.

We camped in a steep V-shaped canyon, carved by Sunlight Creek, and from here we hunted the shoulders and the rimrock of Dead Indian Peak.

It was hard going, and we were unable to take the horses very far up the flanks of the canyons, and had to leave them below the rimrock, and as we climbed, we often slipped, fell and slid down the canyon wall. I had to sling my rifle—my rifle, Bill carried no rifle—onto my back, and we had to use the dwarf furs as a cordelle in order to rim out. Once on the plateaux above the rimrock, where the winds had swept the surface clean, we lay on our bellies side by side, and played the 12x binoculars over the trails that wound up the face of the canyons.

When the grey granitic and the smudgy basaltic ledges seemed suddenly to move in blobs, we watched with intensity. The blobs would move along the trails, their smoky-grey blending beautifully with the canyon walls. These animated blobs would stop for some time, suddenly start to move again deliberately, disappearing one by one around a shoulder. We saw no rams with these ewes and yearlings.

We spent hours playing the binoculars over the sides of the canyons, but we saw no rams.

After several days of this very difficult climbing, slipping, falling in the snow, cordelling, Bill became fatigued and stayed in camp for the remainder of the stay on Sunlight.

Each day I urged my horse up as far as I could kick him toward the rimrock, so that I wouldn't have so much climbing to do; urged him up through the snow until he started groaning, then tied him and hunted the Alpine meadows above the rim.

One perfect morning of no wind over the Alpine meadows, I

scrambled up over the rimrock. The brightness of the sun on the snow was blinding, and I found the snow difficult; this was a snowshoe day, really. But the sun was a boon; it brought into dark relief a trail a quarter of a mile away.

The hoof prints were elongated like those of bighorn, and the bellies of the two trail makers had scraped the deep snow, and this was characteristic of bighorn—mule deer bellies would clear the snow.

The trail led me down under the rimrock and across the timber line. I was so close behind my quarry that I could note the scarcely noticeable fragments of snow falling back into the tracks.

I would stop and stand perfectly immobile as long as I could do so, trying to sweep the area with my naked eyes, without noticeably moving my head. I believed I was trailing bighorns, and they would be watching me. This would be something if I could approach within range of bighorns without being seen by them.

I moved slowly, penetrating every shadow, my heart beating a little faster than usual. Then suddenly the identity of my quarry was there written in the snow in the form of still-steaming deer droppings. Obviously I had been trailing two old bachelor mule deer who had spent the summer on the meadows above the rim, and foraging among the lenses of snow-melt and moss, and without the necessity to move about much, their hooves had grown elongated like those of bighorn sheep. The bighorn-like belly scrapes indicated that the snow was much deeper than it appeared to be.

These bachelor friends now feeling the urge of rut, were moving down below the timberline where they would find a band of does. Then the bachelor friendship of the summer would end—could end, as a matter of fact, in locked antlers and death for both.

I could shoot a buck deer much closer to camp, where he would be accessible to pack horses, but a ram would have been worth the trouble of dragging him down to the pack horses.

One or both of the bucks might have been trophy heads, but disappointed, I left off trailing and sat with my back to the bole of a Douglas fir, and studied the mountain side across the canyon. The world was white and silent and the bright, high-altitude sun made mauve shadows beneath the trees.

There was only the movement of snow falling from the branches of the conifers; the limb relieved of its burden regained its original position like a spring board. The muffled thudding of the snow fallen from the branches was the only sound.

As I played the binoculars over the snow and the shadows, the writhing tail of a cougar came into the field of the binoculars. He was across the canyon. He was playing with a saddle blanket dropped by some hunting outfit earlier in the season. He had dug it up out of the snow because it was still heavy with the scent of horse; the scent of meat he loved the incentive, and he played with it through an urge to keep bright his powers to remain in the struggle of earth's life. ("The object of military training is for success in battle.")

It took some moments of inspection through the 12x glasses to finally identify the piece of oblong weaving, as a saddle blanket. I at first had entertained the dramatic thought that it might be wearing apparel.

I watched this play, this training for success in struggle, suddenly inspired by the scent from the saddle blanket, until the cougar left it and melted into the shadows, tired of his plaything.

I plodded back through the snow to my restive horse, happier than I would have been if I had shot a trophy head. With endurance, and persistence, and keen desire, I could eventually shoot a bighorn, but during the rest of my life, I would never again see a cougar in the snow playing with a saddle blanket.

Jim Milstead was not a professional camp cook; as a matter of fact he was not a cook at all. Bill Barron had asked him to accompany our outfit as a cook, at a time when he had a slack period in his work or his profession; I never knew just what he did for a living.

He was genial and enjoyed his duties as well as the long hours on his bedding roll reading paperback Westerns. Some of the stories which he devoured would in some strange manner effect his self-esteem as a true westerner especially, and as a westerner who believed himself to be knowledgeable on the subject of arms, hunting, bears, deer, wapiti, and bighorn, as well as western manners and mores.

I, the young "dude" must have inspired didacticism in certain older natives of the mountains, who might have felt the need to bolster their self-esteem, but Jim was never didactic. Bill's profound knowledge and experience, and his almost constant presence might have had their effect.

Once he came rushing out of the cook's tent, and threw one of his magazines into the fire, swearing. When he saw me he pointed accusingly to the fire and said: "Why that goddam 'dude' that wrote that story don't know turds from wild honey 'bout pack-in huntin'— er nothin' else. Why hell's fa'r, he—" Here he choked on his injured vanity, and disappeared into the tent still searching for words strong enough to express his vindictive contempt.

I remember being intrigued by this incident, and kept thinking about it, and wondered why Jim had been so upset, even if the story or the article was fiction. Why should that affect him? I finally came to the conclusion that Jim was really upset and contemptuous because the "dude's" story had been published, and Jim's practical knowledge as a true westerner, must remain forever obscured.

Bill had not only become fatigued but he became ill, and I reproached myself with having fired his guide's vanity, causing him to overreach himself. He was reluctant to break camp, thereby ending the hunt for bighorn, since he had been unable to show his "dude" a ram.

He could barely sit his horse on the long trail back to Holmes Lodge, and he and Jim were driven into Cody immediately.

After Bill and Jim left (I believe I have forgotten to mention that Wuff did not accompany us to the Sunlight) I hunted with the Cougar Hunter of Holmes Lodge, shot a passable mule deer buck, and surprised a black bear who had delayed his hibernation.

The Cougar Hunter owned Holmes Lodge I seem to remember; however, I am not sure; and he had hired a Mrs. Shauber to run it for him. Perhaps he only had a lease on it.

He had come from the East. One found men in the mountains; chiefly those areas that had been romanticized through novels or songs or by Ned Buntline and Buffalo Bill. Many of these men were graduates of Yale, Harvard or Princeton, and I seem now to find a parallel between them and the English Remittance Men, but these American men were usually financially independent, and possibly bored by life in the East and Europe. You found them in unlikely places doing unlikely things.[142]

Some of them affected moccasins and fringed buckskin leggings and buckskin shirts with fringes. I don't believe any of them went so far as affecting Buffalo Bill's gauntlets, or carrying a beaded quirt.

They were obscure exhibitionists, sufficient unto themselves as one might strut before a mirror.

One, a Princeton graduate, had bought a sheep ranch, dressed himself in fringed buckskins, and had been whiskey tiddly ever since the false armistice of October 1918. One wondered why sheep? Cattle would have been much more romantic.

Even though they were older men—in their forties or late fifties, one supposes—it was pleasant knowing these men of culture and education, if only for a very short time, but I think it was the fact that I had known them which placed Teddy Roosevelt in the second-order category of my "tin gods." Had I never known these men, he would have been among these of the first order. He was of their genre, but differed from them in the fact that he found strutting before a mirror insufficient, as did Buffalo Bill.[143]

But still, these men were not really strutters-before-a-mirror, nor yet real exhibitionists in their moccasins and buckskins; their obsession may have been closer to Narcissism, and just simple Romanticism; quiescent Buffalo Bills.

I knew nothing about the Cougar Hunter; I can't even recall his name by which he was introduced (melted snow now joined the sweat and the blood to blur the pages of my diary, here). The "Cougar Hunter" is the name I gave him for my own convenience; my epithet.

I have no idea whence he came in the East, but his accent gave him away, as well as his profitless, sportive, almost wild-eyed dedication to cougar trapping. He certainly was of the genre.

He set his traps then ran them three times a week, riding out on his stout mountain horse. When the trails became snow covered he would dismount, catch his horse by the tail, like an Osage Indian crossing a river in spate, and the horse digging his toe plates into the slippery trail pulled him along to the next trap.

Despite this empirical, year around trapping (cougars no less) he had much in common with the scientists of Langley Field who opened penny match boxes upside down. He forgot to cinch his saddle one morning but managed to mount without turning it, but slid off over the rump of the horse still in the saddle, when his horse started up a steep mountain trail.

I believe he broke his leg once while running his traps, but in general and in other incidents, his dedication seemed to serve him as a sort of insulation, and he survived where a seasoned self-protective native hunter might have been killed.

His eyes shone with a sort of wild ecstasy one night, when he was telling me of the cougar that got away with one of his traps. The trail was easy to follow, and he knew the remarkably clever cat was just ahead of him the whole afternoon, but of course he was never able to see him.

Finally he stopped to catch his breath, and at that moment he was attracted by a pine squirrel scurrying along a fallen tree trunk. Just as the squirrel was passing along the trunk a great paw was lifted and fell on it, and momentarily the Cougar Hunter could see the head and shoulders of the cougar before his almost instantaneous cryptic freezing again, with just the top of his head visible above the log and his protective blending in his immobility would never have been penetrated if he had not lost his temper, from pain caused by the trap and through being pressed by the erect animal he was afraid to attack.[144]

The Cougar Hunter knew that the head of his cougar had never disappeared behind the tree bole when his shoulder and paw did, but he couldn't actually see since now it was perfectly blended with the shadows, the high lights, the bark of the trees, the snow-melt, the soiled snow, the stones and the bits of visible earth.[145] There were not even conformation lines of the round head suggested to the hunter.

So the Cougar Hunter kept his eyes on the spot where the head seemed to have disappeared behind the fallen tree, took careful aim and fired, and then excitement. The cougar being head-shot, jumped into the air, fell, kicked himself in a circle in the snow, growled, and then with his tail straight in the air he died and the tail then writhed and fell limply to the earth.

The cougar along with grizzlys and black bears and jaguars, leopards, rhinoceri, cape buffalo, tigers and arid land rattle snakes have the shortest tempers of any animals I know about. Many animals and birds and reptiles will break cryptic freezing out of nerve failure or funk, but the cougars among the others mentioned have short tempers that are more often than not self-destructive.

The Cougar Hunter told me of his incident in detail, because it was his best story, the most dramatic incident of his life. He finished his detailed story with his almost fanatical eyes boring into me, and his smug smile of triumph a long time in fading. All this without really boasting.

He was with me the day I shot my mule deer buck (gunless; not as a guide but just for the hell of it) and we were late arriving at the Lodge. We had gone afoot into the higher elevations, and the snow was difficult. Afraid of being over taken by darkness he taught me a trick he had possibly learned in Switzerland, since later my Swiss guide to the chamois habitat re-taught me to do "le glissade." He showed me how to place my gun between my calves and my thighs as I squatted, then holding the rifle in place glide down the mountain side on my heels.

It was strange to me to meet such a sense of well-being and self-satisfaction in a man who was not anticipating monetary profits.

Back in Cody, Bill Barron had revived and walked about in a mild state of excitement: walking, strangely enough, in the reflected glory of his friendship with Caroline Lockhart the novelist, who among other novels wrote *The Fighting Shepherdess*, wherein a sheep rancherette out-virtued, out-witted, out-fought and out-lasted a group of unethical, nasty old enterprisers (all male). His glory reflected from Miss Lockhart would come in introducing his "dude" to her, to impress the "dude."[146]

She like the male refugees from the factories and the brittle mores of the East had come out to Cody and its environs for atmosphere and illusions. The reflection of figures of Romance, in which Ned Buntline walked, and which he had helped create through his sensational journalism just after the Civil War, was still bright enough for the American counterpart of the English Remittance Men and Caroline Lockhart, with this difference: in the case of the interesting men I met, they needed no remittances, and I assume Miss Lockhart was pulling her own weight through her novels. They seemed to be the kind [that] young girls of the East of that time might read lying on their beds face down eating chocolates.

Bill took me to meet her with a pride that caused a dim glow on his face.

She wore cowboy boots, a buckskin skirt, if I remember correctly (my diary is useless here—I might not have gone to meet Miss Lockhart, but remember that which Bill said about her) and had a bar in her house with saw dust on the floor in order to create the Old West atmosphere.

I have no memory of her face or voice or personality, but she must have been a young woman of culture who found rugged, honorable, kindly, sincere old Bill interesting.

Bill's subdued excitement remained, and he persuaded me not to leave Cody until after the weekend, since he wanted to give a dance in his "dude's" honor in the Irma Hotel's prohibitionized bar room.

A dance in this sparsely settled area was like a County Fair at the County Seat in Iowa or Missouri; everyone from miles about came, and I feel sure the invitation to it was an announcement in the local paper. Anyway many people from the ranches and the town came, and I suspect some of the ranch people brought their lunches.

There were no drinks sold at the bar, naturally; its honorable old whiskey and beer stains seemed to continue to exude the old odors and it was too cold this November evening for open windows.

Everyone had his own bottle.

I was asked to rooms by people I had never seen before. There were groups of men and women drinking; they handed me drinks and patted me on the back, and praised me effusively without knowing why.

In one of the several rooms I visited, the host was one of the Old West's nostalgic re-creators, the refugee from the East genre. He had been graduated by Harvard bright-eyed, jilted by his girl while he was in the trenches in France, and had chucked it all. But apparently he was not quite satisfied with the creation of atmosphere wherein he could walk in a state of euphoria; he must be transported spiritually into his make-believe world through alcohol.

As his guests talked he was suddenly transmuted into an Old West cowboy, or a bad man. He pulled his pearl-handled revolver and emptied the cylinder into the ceiling.

Several of his visitors left, not precipitately, but with controlled eagerness.

I stayed from curiosity, since he didn't re-load and remained sitting on the edge of his bed, still the genial host.

Nothing happened. There was no apologetic manager tapping on the door, to ask what was wrong as if he didn't know.

In the old barroom, there were wapiti (always called elk), pronghorn (always called antelope) grizzly and black bear heads and buffalo heads hanging all around the room, and on the floor close to the wall was a complete buffalo cow and calf, and apart from them a buffalo yearling calf, that seemed continually to trip up the free style dancers, after their repeated visits to the rooms upstairs.

The fiddlers were indefatigable; they were being handed drinks in coffee cups, and as the night wore on they were pounding their specially constructed dais with their heels instead of simply tapping out the rhythm, and one in his ecstasy fell out of his chair and off the platform.

I saw my original host, Bill, only once, early in the evening, with the glow of triumph on his face.

I danced with tall girls and women, with short girls and women, with plump girls and women, with eager girls and women, some graceful and some just determined, but I can remember no names and no faces. I remember only "Widow" Kelly, a hard, handsome,

sun-browned woman who smelled of home made soap. I think I
remember her chiefly because she was a friend of Bill's and wrote [a]
letter for him to me later in England.

Her ranch was high up the drainage of the Shoshone River.

I had sent my heads and bear skin into Cody to have them mounted
by Richardson, and I now went around to visit with him and watch
him at work.

Richardson was a most meticulous artist. He was not only an artist
and a naturalist which Taxidermists ought to be, but he went about
the business with a scientist's fervor. He went hunting in the mountains during the height of the bull wapiti's rut, and skinning his animal in the field immediately he got to it, he made a plaster cast of the
swollen neck of both deer and wapiti. There were the impressions of
arteries and muscles and when he cast the model in this matrix, it
became the perfect model from which he worked.

I was fascinated by his dexterity and his Alchemists' dedication.

Bill and Jim came to the station to see me off, and Bill handed me a
letter which Widow Kelly had written for him. It was a letter of introduction to the other "dude" whom he had honored with a farewell
dance: the Honorable _____ of England.

~

At home waiting for me was a letter from Merton College, Oxford,
written in cold-fingered angular script, folded into a cramped, quite
ordinary-looking envelope. The letter hinted that perhaps I hadn't
really appreciated the rare privilege of having been accepted by Merton College as an undergraduate, and certainly I must be aware of
the fact that there were many on a waiting list who might be more
appreciative of the privileges granted by Merton and the University.
The letter ended with an assumption that I indeed intended to appear
at the beginning of Trinity Term the next spring, and occupy the
rooms that had been waiting for me since October.

Also there was a letter from my worried sponsor, W.S. Campbell,
informing me that when he had heard that I had gone hunting in
Wyoming, he had written to Merton, and they had answered that

they would be expecting me for Trinity Term, and that my rooms were waiting.

He should have expressed disappointment, one might suppose, but when I went down to Norman to visit with him before leaving, he met me with a happy smile, and said, obviously delighted, "You're getting away with murder."

At the time I thought of this as an exaggeration, and forgot about the whole thing during my stay at Oxford, and really had given no thought to it through the years until I came to this present stage in the writing of my story. Now, quite suddenly, I am sure that I was not "getting away with murder," even when I am now remembering the tense seriousness of the scholarship young men, and the others who desperately wanted to be accepted by the very old and very great University of world prestige.

If one still believed that I was "getting away with murder" based on the above he must be looking at the matter solely from a single point of view. Perhaps from a "granted scholarship" point of view, only.

Had I been elected as a Rhodes Scholar, my privileges would have been passed to my alternate no doubt, and if I had been an English scholarship boy, my scholarship would have been withdrawn. And I further believe that if I had not been Jo-Without-Purpose (and "Purpose" must take on another shade of meaning along with the original one here) and rather an intense non-scholarship American, who had been accepted on the grounds that I was an oarsman, a football or tennis player of national notice; or a hockey player, or an American boy who had attended Eton or Harrow, etc., I believe the reasons for my non-appearance for the designated Term must have been more rational, logical and important than "gone hunting in Wyoming."

But just as Frontier Histrionics of the Old West inspired and nourished by sensational journalism, magazine stories, penny terrible books and novels, was still alive when I made my first big game hunt, but perhaps flickering, so was the old order of Patrician ascendancy atmosphere still bright, but perhaps flickering in England after World War I.

The charming academic anchorites who accepted me as an undergraduate of the University were not only oriented toward

The author, circa 1977, with his first published work, *Wah'Kon-Tah*
(Courtesy of the Osage Tribal Museum, Pawhuska, Oklahoma)

the Patrician Order, but were imbued with it through the generations, and very much a part of it unconsciously. They were under the influence of the centuries.

These delightful, coldly chivalric, highly civilized men, had no criteria for judging the Oxford-worthiness of John-Without-Purpose, except W.S. Campbell's blown-up prep school boy who had captained his athletic teams, and on the "mind" side had been the editor of his school annual. And of course there was the war in the air record.

These things, these images taken out of contiguity, these highly cultured anchorites of Oxford could understand, but they could have no conception of Tucker's or Pawhuska High School in the middle of the wild blackjacks and prairie.

And when W.S. Campbell had written that J.J. Mathews, Esq. had gone hunting, they could understand, and might say among themselves that which a nineteenth century Master of University had said when he allowed the undergraduate Lord Edgmont to be absent from lectures twice a week in order to go hunting: it is "so suitable."[147]

The only criteria the academic gentlemen of that period were aware of made Public School captains and hunting gentlemen with academic interests dutifully and traditionally acceptable, since their University was what it was through the wholesome influence of the ruling classes and their privileges.

They couldn't possibly have conceived of a young barbarian of French, Welsh, and Osage Indian descent, brought up among Neolithic men, cowboys, traders, freighters in a beautifully primitive country of sky, prairie and blackjacks, but still having enjoyed the patrician privileges (minus social) of England.

So J.J. Mathews, Esq., was allowed to postpone his matriculation as an undergraduate of Oxford University from Michaelmas Term in October to Trinity Term the next spring, I assume now, because it was "so suitable."

∽

I found Bally almost fat, and she seemed in good condition even in her winter hair. She came to the bridle and I saddled her and rode her over the Ridge Ranch, but I didn't dare ride her to the stag-greyhounds after coyotes. There was danger that she might fall and break a brittle leg.

She could have lived until I could return, but not likely. When I slipped the bits from her now very definitely "smooth" mouth, she slobbered on my hand. I slapped her on the rump, and she whirled on her hind legs as in the old days, but stumbled slightly, then trotted off a little stiffly.

I watched her disappear into a growth of running oaks behind the barn, then stood for some time after she had vanished—holding her bridle, an empty bridle.

This was the end of the first chapter; more fittingly the end of Liber Primus, and John-Without-Purpose was about to be transported from the animal world of boyhood to the earth-alienated world of man's ornamental creations.

Notes

~

Introduction

1. John Joseph Mathews, *The Osages: Children of the Middle Waters* (Norman: University of Oklahoma Press, 1961), 15, 107. Hereafter *Osages*. Louis Owens notes in "'Disturbed by Something Deeper': The Native Art of John Joseph Mathews" that Mathews's "body of writing . . . has yet to be fully recognized for the contribution it makes to American literature" (*Western American Literature* 35.2 [Summer 2000]: 162).

2. In his Guggenheim application of September 1938 for the fellowship he received for 1939–40, Mathews avows that he has been investigating the relationship between the Osages and Amer-Europeans for twenty years; thus, by the time *The Osages* was published in 1961, his study had spanned forty-three years (John Joseph Mathews Collection, Box 3 Folder 14. Western History Collections, University of Oklahoma Libraries, Norman, Oklahoma. Hereafter, works in this collection will be referred to by initials, box number, and folder number, as in JJM 3.14). His focused work on the volume began as early as January 1952, and he began writing in July 1955, according to his diaries (JJM 2.3, 2.7).

3. Diary, 1961–1971: 30 August 1961 (JJM 3.1–3.10); 7 August 1961 (JJM 2.14); 27 January 1963 (JJM 3.3). Mathews intended to steal from himself the title of his 1943 manuscript, *Without the Sword*. His 1963 concept was for a novel on the predicament of men and nations when they have lost their power, while the original *Without the Sword* had been a nonfiction attempt to discuss the importance of the biological imperatives shaping human behavior to attempts to solve conflicts in international relations. The title derives from Hobbes's *Leviathan* (pt. 1, chap. 17): "And Covenants, without the Sword are but Words, and of no strength to secure a man at all." See Diary, 19 February, 26 July 1943 (JJM 1.46); Lottinville to Mathews, 9 November 1943 (JJM 1.28); Lottinville to Ewing, 10 November 1943; Mathews to Lottinville, 11 November 1943; Ewing to Lottinville, 16 November 1943; Lottinville to Mathews, 19 November 1943; Mathews to "Heimer" (Lottinville), 17 December 1943; Lottinville to Mathews, 21 December 1943. (All letters listed after the first one are in the Oklahoma University Press Collection, Western History Collections, Box 94 Folder 5, University of Oklahoma Libraries. Hereafter, works in this collection will be referred to as OUP 94.5, etc.). See also John Joseph Mathews, *Talking to the Moon: Wildlife Adventures on the Plains and Prairies of Osage Country* (Norman: University of Oklahoma Press, 1945), 214–33; hereafter *TTTM*.

4. Diary, 2 January–6 December 1963 (JJM 3.2, 3.3); 25 January 1962 (JJM 3.1); 27–28 May, 1 June 1965 (JJM Sound Recording [SR] #2274).

5. Diary, 1965–1971, 1978 (JJM 3.4–12, 13, JJM SR #2274–2279).

6. *Wah'Kon-Tah* 359; *Osages* 97–103; Willard H. Rollings, *The Osage: An Ethnohistorical Study of Hegemony on the Prairie-Plains* (Columbia: University of Missouri Press, 1992).

7. *Osages* v–viii, 789–90. Mathews's father joined an Osage delegation to Washington, D.C., sometime between 1900 and 1904, perhaps as a member of the tribal council (Osage Tribal Museum Archives and Library, image #5580); Mathews himself served on the tribal council, thus showing their embeddedness *as* Osages not just their descent from them.

8. *Osages* 772, JJM 3.15, JJM 2.1. Allotment was an assimilationist policy instantiated through both federal and state laws, most famously the Dawes Act of 1887. Collectively held tribal lands were broken up into allotments of private property held by the individual tribal members, variously defined. Rather than dividing the total land acreage by the number of tribal members, the government would often assign a predefined number of acres per capita, and then throw open the remaining "surplus" land to non-Native settlement. The result was sometimes a checkerboard effect that further impeded the political and social cohesiveness of the tribe. Allottees often leased their lands to non-Native farmers or ranchers rather than accepting the attempt to "civilize" them into male-centered farming or the Western-dominated ranch economy. As Mathews observes in *Sundown*, mixed-bloods often advocated in favor of allotment. Mathews explains in *The Osages* that lands in Osage Territory were allotted through an act passed on June 28, 1906. "The Osages . . . by the act would hold their land intact but not communally as they held their hydrocarbons. The land was allotted in severalty to the 2,229 members of the tribe, each member receiving a tract of 160 acres tax free and approximately 498 acres 'surplus,' which would total for each member of the tribe approximately 658 acres. . . . The tribal trust funds would be divided, and the pro rata share of each member of the tribe would be credited to his account in the United States Treasury, and the interest and the royalties from the exploitation of hydrocarbons would be distributed per capita to the members of the tribe quarterly, after the agency operating expenses were set aside." Three large tracts were set aside as communal property for those "who wished to continue the traditional village life," and three smaller reserves were set aside for other community purposes (*Osages* 772–73; see also Thomas Biolsi, *Organizing the Lakota: The Political Economy of the New Deal on Pine Ridge and Rosebud Reservations.* Tucson: University of Arizona Press, 1992).

9. Theodore Rios and Kathleen Mullen Sands, *Telling a Good One: The Process of a Native American Collaborative Biography* (Lincoln: University of Nebraska Press, 2000), 3; Hertha Dawn Wong, *Sending My Heart Back Across the Years* (New York: Oxford University Press, 1992); *Native American Autobiography: An Anthology*, ed. Arnold Krupat (Madison: University of Wisconsin Press, 1994).

10. Diary, 1 June 1965–11 March 1967 (JJM SR #2274-2275, JJM 3.4, 3.5); *Boy, Horse, and Dog* Manuscripts (JJM 4.31–4.35, 3.13, and binder in Box 4 unnumbered as of 8 June 2009. The last is hereafter referred to as *BHD* MS).

11. Diary, 19 February 1968 (JJM 3.6).

12. Diary, 10 February 1968 (JJM 3.7). In his Guggenheim application, Mathews notes that the family Bible recorded his birth as November 16, 1895, whereas the Osage Agency records had it as 1894 (JJM 3.14). He consistently used the agency date with one or two exceptions.

13. Diary, 26 September 1966 (JJM 3.4); 13 March, 10 April, 13 April, 28 October 1967 (JJM 3.5); 9 January, 20 January 1968 (JJM 3.6–3.7); 24 August 1969 (JJM 3.8); 13 August 1962 (JJM 3.1); Richard D. Lyons, "Seymour Lawrence, 67, Publisher for a Variety of Eminent Authors," *New York Times*, obituary, 1 January 1994 (available at www.nytimes.com/1994/01/07/obituaries/seymour-lawrence-67-publisher-for-a-variety-of-eminent-authors.html); "William Morrow," HarperCollinsPublishers, 2010 (available at www.harpercollins.com/imprints/index.aspx?imprintid=518003). It is unclear whether Mathews sent the manuscript to Knopf, his stepson's publisher, as planned in 1968. He later mentions that the University of Oklahoma Press has it, and three years afterward that the press turned it down, but he does not say whether the press peer-reviewed it, rejected it for reasons of genre and fit, or suggested the cuts he suddenly embraced that year. See Diary, 5 May 1968; 24 August 1969; 12 July and 12–13, 23 November 1972 (JJM 3.6–3.7, 3.11).

14. 9 March 1966 (JJM 3.4). Here and elsewhere, I have generally corrected minor typos and spelling errors in Mathews's diary entries rather than interrupt this essay with an unnecessary series of "verbatim" or "sic" disclaimers. For example, Mathews in this quote typed "busines," "dullnes," "verry," and "goddamed." Words like "homosectuality" in the previous quote have been allowed to stand, as ambiguously reflecting Mathews's intentions.

15. Diary, 21 January, 23 January, 14 October 1967; 8 September 1961; 18 January 1962 (JJM 3.5, 2.14, 3.1).

16. Diary, 3 April 1943; 31 January 1945; 4 November 1946; 13 March and 30 June 1948 (JJM 1.46–1.48, 1.50)

17. Diary, 1967–1973, 1978 (JJM 3.5–3.13, JJM SR #2278–2279); Diary, 1 September 1978; 10? August 1967; 10 April 1978 (JJM 3.12, 3.5). There is no mention in the diary regarding the specifics of Mathews's illness that led to surgery. In August 1967, he recorded the first of a series of nosebleeds that increasingly bothered him. He wrote them off to high blood pressure and appears not to have consulted a physician about them, thinking they were nature's safety valve and that they were caused by changes in atmospheric pressure. He complained occasionally of shortness of breath. Mathews appears to have been a lifelong pipe smoker. (Diary, 18 January 1935; 24 February 1969; 1 January 1958 [JJM 1.2, 3.8, 2.12]). One project during this period was painting the blockhouse on his ranch. Carter Revard, Charles Red Corn, and others are currently exploring the feasibility of converting The Blackjacks into a historical site, possibly a writer's colony, as a memorial to Mathews (Revard to Kalter, personal correspondence, 13 March 2009).

18. Diary, 30 January, 27 May, and 6 September 1967; 2 July, 5 July, and 17 September 1970; 3 December 1971; 15 November 1972; 23 January 1943; 27 January 1966; 29 May, 21

June 1965 (JJM 3.5, 3.9–3.11, 1.46, 3.4, SR #2274). A. LaVonne Brown Ruoff, "John Joseph Mathews' *Talking to the Moon*: Literary and Osage Contexts," in *Multicultural Autobiography, American Lives*, ed. James Robert Payne (Knoxville: University of Tennessee Press, 1992), 8.

19. *Osages* 751. Diary, 1 December 1967 (JJM 3.5); 2 July, 5 July, and 17 September 1970; 1 September 1969; 15 June 1965 (JJM 3.9, 3.8, SR #2274)

20. Diary, 10 March 1967; 3 September and 28 November 1966; 17 July and 8 October 1969; 21 March 1970; 15 July and 8 August 1971 (JJM 3.5, 3.4, 3.8–3.10).

21. Robert Allen Warrior, *Tribal Secrets* (Minneapolis: University of Minnesota Press, 1995) xix–xx; Diary, 31 December 1946 and 17 June 1965 (JJM 1.48, JJM SR #2274); *Osages*. Mathews also read the autobiographies of H. G. Wells, Somerset Maugham, Bertrand Russell, and Vladimir Nabokov to get hints from professionals about how to craft his own. He was also reading Ernest K. Gann's *Fate Is the Hunter* during the period of composition, and his comments about that book suggest that he had already read the great piloting narratives by Antoine de Saint-Exupéry, *Night Flight* and *Wind, Sand, and Stars*. He disdained Russell's earth-detached intellectualism and proclaimed himself glad not to have to review Gann's work. Mathews also researched the historical incidents about which he wrote, even worrying about avoiding plagiarism with regard to one of his sources: *The Territorial Imperative* by Robert Ardrey. Mathews's style, like Gerald Vizenor's, was to research diligently and accurately but not often to reveal his sources or to attribute their contributions to particular passages. See Diary, 3 January 1966; 30 January 1967; 6 July 1968; 27 July 1969; 9 March 1966; 1 September 1978 (JJM 3.4–3.6, 3.8, 3.12). Also see Gerald Vizenor, "Socioacupuncture: Mythic Reversals and the Striptease in Four Scenes," in *The American Indian and the Problem of History*, ed. Calvin Martin (New York: Oxford University Press, 1987).

22. Warrior, *Tribal Secrets*, 25; Dr. Phil Carl Weiner to University of Oklahoma Press, 25 February 1933 (OUP 9.1); photograph of *Wah'Kon-Tah* display table (OUP 37.5). In 1951, Lottinville got Mathews's Osage parentage wrong in the opposite direction, thinking that he was "a sixteenth blood Osage" (Lottinville to Mr. Lewis Gannett, *New York Herald Tribune*, 26 December 1951 [OUP 175.6]).

23. Henry Seidel Canby, "*Wah'Kon-Tah* by John Joseph Mathews," *Book-of-the-Month Club News*, October 1932, ed. Harry Scherman, 2 (OUP 4.5); OUP 4.13, 37.5.

24. Diary, 14 October, 23 October 1967; 21 March 1968 (JJM 3.5–3.6)

25. Diary, 1 January 1970 (JJM 3.9); cf. *TTTM* 224.

26. Diary, 23 March 1966 (JJM 3.4); Sara Jane Richter, "The Life and Literature of John Joseph Mathews: Contributions of Two Cultures," diss., Oklahoma State University, 1985, 14; Autobiography MSS (JJM 4.31–4.35); Diary, 3 June 1978 (JJM 3.12), 1967–1972, 1978 (JJM 3.5–3.12, JJM SR #2278–2279).

27. Autobiography MSS (JJM 4.31–4.35); Diary, 29 August 1961, 2 March 1966, 25 October 1967 (JJM 2.14, 3.4–3.5); William Wordsworth, Preface to Lyrical Ballads, *Prefaces and Prologues*, Vol. 39 (Harvard Classics, New York: P.F. Collier & Son, 1909–14); Bartleby.com, 2001, www.bartleby.com/39/36.html.

28. Diary, 1 January 1970 (3.9). Disgusted that the world preferred reading about Joe Namath, Muhammad Ali, and Billy Graham, Mathews wrote: "I shall have the pleasure of writing it, even if it's never published, it will be in the archives, and some future researcher will be compelled to stumble over it."

29. Diary, 5 April 1963 (3.3; on this day, Mathews spoke to Dr. Gibson about creating a collection of his papers at the University of Oklahoma archives). Revard to Kalter, personal correspondence, 24 May 2008), Mathews to E. Hunt, 14 June 1940 (JJM 1.15).

30. Mathews to E. Hunt, 14 June 1940 (JJM 1.15).

31. JJM SR #2274–2279, Diary, 13 June 1921, 1962–1963, 1966–1972, 13 March 1966 (JJM 1.44, 3.1–3.11).

32. D'Arcy McNickle was also reviewing for the University of Oklahoma Press. He was one reviewer for a rejected manuscript by C. J. Milling titled *Red Carolinians*. Though his impression of the book was favorable, he felt it difficult reading (OUP 48.4). It was published in 1940 by the University of North Carolina Press. Mathews had met McNickle by 1940 (JJM 1.39). John Milton Oskison reviewed Rachel Caroline Eaton's "A History of the Cherokee Nation," a manuscript that the University of Oklahoma Press rejected. Elaine Goodale Eastman was a Press reviewer during this era as well, at a time when the Press rejected a manuscript by her husband on Sacajawea based on the critiques of Muriel Wright and Mathews's mentor W. S. Campbell. Her manuscripts and Oskison's were also under review during this same era (OUP 50.18, 9.10).

33. John Joseph Mathews, review of *Blue Star* MS, 10 October 1933 (OUP 50.18); "The Caxton Printers Ltd.: A Brief History" (2007; available at www.caxtonprinters.com/history.htm); Mathews to Lottinville, 18 October 1933 (OUP 9.1); J. S. Clark, "A Selected Reading List," *Chronicles of Oklahoma* 20.3 (September 1942); Oklahoma Historical Society 2001 (http://digital.library.okstate.edu/chronicles/v020/v020p275.html); Lottinville to Hayes, 8 July 1936 (OUP 26.4); Basil A. Hayes, "Leroy Long—Teacher of Medicine," *Chronicles of Oklahoma* 20.2 (June 1942); Oklahoma Historical Society 2001 (http://digital.library.okstate.edu/Chronicles/v020/v020p107.html).

34. Lottinville to Sister Mary Paul, 31 December 1938; Mathews to Lottinville, 4 August 1938; *Osages* 795; Sister Mary Paul to Lottinville, 13 January 1938 (OUP 60.3); Sister Mary Paul to Lottinville, 19 August 1939 (OUP 61.3).

35. Mathews to Lottinville, 9 July 1938 (OUP 48.7); Autobiography MSS (JJM 4.31–4.35).

36. Diary, 7 July 1946, and 7 January and 15 February 1955 (JJM 1.48, 2.6); Lottinville to Mathews, 1 July 1949; Mathews to Lottinville, 20 July 1949; Lottinville to Mathews, 27 July 1949 (OUP 103.3); Mathews to Lottinville, 15 October 1949; Lottinville to Mathews, 19 October 1949 (OUP 128.10); Diary, 4 November 1949 (JJM 2.1) and 27 November 1948 (1.50).

37. Diary, 4 February and 7 February 1953 (JJM 2.5); Orpha B. Russell, "Chief James Bigheart of the Osages," *Chronicles of Oklahoma* 32: 384–94; Oklahoma Historical Society 2001 (http://digital.library.okstate.edu/Chronicles/v032/v032p384.pdf); Diary, 11 October 1961, and 8–9 February and 30 June 1962 (JJM 2.14, 3.1).

38. Diary, 29 November and 1 and 4 December 1967; 22 February 1968 (JJM 3.5–36).

39. Probably the manuscript that became *Spanish War Vessels on the Mississippi, 1792–1796*, not published until fourteen years later (New Haven, Conn.: Yale University Press, 1968), probably because of Nasatir's meticulousness rather than problems with the research.

40. Lottinville to Mathews, 24 March 1954, 3 September 1954, and 22 December 1954 (OUP 211.11).

41. Mathews to Brandt, 12 February 1936 (OUP 4.14); Lottinville to Mathews, 6 March 1936 (OUP 27.5); Mathews to Brandt, 11 April 1936 (OUP 4.14); Lottinville to Mathews, 23 June 1936 (OUP 27.5).

42. I was thrilled to find that someone had finally decided to investigate Mathews's use of the term "queer" in Chal's inner monologue in *Sundown*, particularly given Mathews's brief references to views of homosexuality in the 1920s in his autobiography. Unfortunately, however, Michael Snyder wishfully conflates Mathews's character's sexual concerns with Mathews's own sexuality. While there can be little objection to Snyder's reading of the novel, one must object to the reading of Mathews's life and sexual or romantic proclivities through a novel, in the absence of any other evidence. Evidence strongly suggests that Mathews's antagonism to homosexuality was other than a mask for unacknowledged same-sex attraction. Nor is the fear implied by the term "homophobia" an accurate description of its driving emotion. It is an unfortunate pattern that a writer's fiction cannot be seen for its artistry (however conservative or reactionary), but must be falsely converted into confessional autobiography. See Snyder, "'He Certainly Didn't Want Anyone to Know That He Was Queer': Chal Windzer's Sexuality in John Joseph Mathews's *Sundown*," *SAIL* 20.1 (Spring 2008): 27–54; Diary, 5 December 1924, 18 February 1971 (1.45, 3.10). In one entry about anti–Vietnam War agitation, Mathews talks about "grimy sodomists" and says, "It is a tragic thought that these earth-detached homosexuals can make non-violent protests which might even be named treason while the wholesome young men of the air force and cavalry (mechanized) must die. We protect the degenerate and sacrifice the wholesome young men of the nation. And I am not sure just why we are fighting in Vietnam." His belief that nonviolent protests might be treasonous is puzzlingly contradictory to his fears of a U.S. fascism (Diary, 31 January, 12 February 1966 [JJM 3.4]).

43. Diary, 1 August 1964; 12 June 1963; 30 April 1922, 20 April 1967; 31 July 1968 (JJM SR #2277, JJM 3.2, 1.45, 3.5–3.6). So, like Alexander Posey, whose poetry Mathews knew, Mathews's family background in supporting the Confederacy and the social structure in the Osage Nation and in Osage County during the oil boom shaped his views of African Americans in ways that his acceptance of the timelines of material anthropology reinforced. See Diary, 27 January 1968 (JJM 3.6); and Alexander Posey, *The Fus Fixico Letters: A Creek Humorist in Early Oklahoma*, ed. Daniel Littlefield and Carol A. Petty Hunter (Norman: University of Oklahoma Press, 1993).

44. Diary, 16 August 1970 (JJM 3.9); *TTTM* 75–76.

45. Richter, "Life and Literature of John Joseph Mathews," 3.

46. OUP 37.5; Richter, "Life and Literature of John Joseph Mathews," 156; JJM 1.17 1.23, 1.27, 1.32, 4.30. No diaries are extant and no extensive correspondence is extant for 1905–1921, 1925–1931, 1933, or 1937–1938.

47. *Osages* xiii; Diary, 11 January 1943 and passim. Virginia Mathews was at Goucher College in 1943 (Diary, 6 February 1943). John Mathews, Jr., was attending St. George's School in 1943–44, then went on to Princeton (Diary, 6 December 1943; 19 December 1949). John Hunt, who was his stepsister Virginia's age, entered the Lawrenceville School in autumn 1940 on a scholarship and entered the Marines during World War II, so his college tuition at Harvard was probably covered by the GI Bill. See Mathews to E. Hunt, 27 June 1940; Mathews to E. Hunt, 17 July 1940 (JJM 1.15–1.16); Diary, 28 December 1943 and 21 June 1945 (JJM 1.47). Ann Hunt attended the Burnham School prior to matriculating at Radcliffe in 1948 (Diary, 22 May, 7 September 1948 [JJM 1.50]); Ann Hunt to Lottinville, 5 July 1948; Lottinville to A. Hunt, 6 July 1948 (OUP 103.3).

48. Diary, 31 December 1949; 5, 7–8 June; 5 July 1964 (JJM 2.1, JJM SR #2276–2277); 18 January, 22 July 1946; 3, 30 September 1948 (JJM 1.48); Geoffrey H. Moore. "Recessions," *The Concise Encyclopedia of Economics*, Library of Economics and Liberty, Liberty Fund, Inc., 2002. Recessions are frequently delayed in the Midwest and affect the arts more than they do other sectors of the economy. The three articles were: "Oil and the Osage Indians" for *Service (Cities Service Magazine)*, October 1946 (Diary, 1, 7, 8, and 9 February 1946 [1.48]); "Chief Lookout" for the *Sunday Oklahoman*, April 23, 1939; and "Scholarship Comes to Life" for the *Saturday Review of Literature*, May 16, 1942, according to an author information sheet for University of Oklahoma Press for Marland publicity, October 1951 or earlier (OUP 175.6). He may also have written a fourth: Lottinville said in a letter to Mathews dated 9 January 1939 (OUP 47.13), "*Nation's Business* asked me to recommend someone to do an article on the political and economic status of the Indian, and I have taken the liberty of saying that you could probably do a better job than anybody else."

49. In March 1946, Mathews read and gave suggestions to Elizabeth on her short stories. That August, he posted one story by her and two by her daughter Ann along with one of his own to an unknown publisher or agent. 10 March, 5 August 1946 (JJM 1.48). 19 March, 30 October 1946 (JJM 1.48). On Mother's Day 1948, Mathews's mother was chosen as Osage County mother of that year. Mathews records in his diary his mother's joy and says she exclaimed "my life would make a book." 9 May 1948 (JJM 1.50).

50. Mathews to Henry Allen Moe, 11 September 1940.

51. Diary, 30 January, 19 February, 1 July–26 October, 6 November 1943 (JJM 1.46); Lottinville to Mathews, 9 November 1943; Lottinville to Mathews, 19 November 1943; Mathews to "Heimer" (Lottinville), 17 December 1943; Mathews to Sears, 14 April 1944 (JJM 1.28); Lottinville to Mathews, 12 December 1944; Mathews to Lottinville, 11 January 1945; Lottinville to Mathews, 15 January 1945 (OUP 103.3); Couch to Lottinville, 14 January 1948; Lottinville to Couch, 21 January 1948; Lottinville to Couch, 22 January 1948 (OUP 103.3); Diary, 10, 22 November 1943 (JJM 1.46).

52. Diary, 2–3, 5–9, 12 August 1946; 30 August 1961; 5 September 1970; 31 August

1946; 11 September 1948 (JJM 1.48, 1.50, 2.14, 3.9). He apparently considered the work an "orphan" because of an inadequate marketing job by Longmans, Green. The experience soured his relationship with that press: when he brought Longsmans, Green his next manuscript—the first draft of *Talking to the Moon*—he said privately that it was "worthy of being 'pushed,' and on that I shall insist." Mathews to E. and A. Hunt, 30 January 1943; Mathews to E. Hunt, 4 February 1943 (JJM 1.20).

53. Diary, 1 November 1948, 2, 31 December 1949; 27 August 1953 (JJM 1.50, 2.1); JJM 4.1–4.29; Diary, 19 September 1943 (JJM 1.46); Mathews to E. Hunt, 23 October 1939 (JJM 1.7); Diary, 1 December 1961 (JJM 2.14). Mathews usually attempted to observe a regular Monday-through-Friday workweek, taking Saturdays and Sundays off. With regard to writing anything other than his diaries, he would more likely miss a workday of writing for other business (Museum, Osage Tribal Council, meetings with or correspondence with publishers, etc.) than work on weekends. He generally wrote about three thousand words each writing workday in the 1930s, two thousand to three thousand in the 1940s and 1950s, and one thousand in the 1960s.

54 (Diary, 5 March 1952; 27 August 1953; 12–13 January 1955 [JJM 2.3, 2.5–2.6]).

55. Diary, 3, 20 September 1948; 9 December 1949; 3 April 1943 (JJM 1.50, 2.1); Mathews to E. Hunt, 24 September 1944 (JJM 1.21).

56. In Mathews's letter to Lottinville of 8 November 1950, he writes:

> The Marland book which was on the Fall list of the University of Chicago Press will not appear. I have the MS and my contract with the above mentioned Press is cancelled. At the last minute Couch got some idea that there ought to be more about the first Mrs. Marland. This very unpleasant phase I sidestepped rather gracefully, since I had known Lydie and George from boyhood. . . . I explained that I preferred to avoid this Sunday Supplement story when I first began writing to him about the MS . . . then his letter. I was annoyed. I asked for the cancellation of the contract, saying that I would not do any re-writing. He agreed to cancellation and now I have the MS.

E. W. Marland married his adoptive daughter Lydie about two years after his first wife died. Marland's first wife was Lydie's maternal aunt. In his 14 March 1972 interview with Guy Logsdon, Mathews attributed the break with the University of Chicago Press to the fact that John D. Rockefeller founded the university and implied that its press found him not portrayed kindly through Marland's eyes in the perspectival biography. Perhaps these comments were another astute sidestep designed to keep Marland and his wives' business out of Logsdon's ken (Osage Tribal Museum, Pawhuska, Oklahoma, JJM SR #2281).

57. Diary, 3, 23 February and 24 March 1945, and 9 December 1967 (JJM 1.47, 3.5); Sketches for Marland book (JJM 3.17); Lottinville to Sheppard, 11 July 1951 (OUP 175.6).

58. Diary, 22 November 1948; 4 November 1949; 7–8 April, 27 September, 13, 21 May, 30 September 1948; 31 December 1949 (JJM 1.50, 2.1); *Osages* 689–706, 771–75; Diary, 26 May, 31 August, 1–26 September 1952, 18 April 1953 (JJM 2.3, 2.5).

59. JJM 3.14; Brandt to Mathews, 18 March 1936 (OUP 4.14); Brandt to Mathews, 29 September 1938 (OUP 48.7).

60. Diary, 18 October 1952, 5 March 1953, and 17, 30 January 1955 (JJM 2.3, 2.5–2.6); Lottinville to Mathews, 19 December 1953 (OUP 175.6). Lottinville earlier suggested that "biographical subjects are better treated after their eternal reward than before it" (Lottinville to Mathews, 16 December 1952 [OUP 175.6]); Diary, 27–28 August, 1–27 October 1953; 1 March–1 December 1954; 3–13 January 1955 (JJM 2.5–2.6).

61. Diary, 10 April 1953; 27 January, 30 September, 23 October 1963 (JJM 2.5, 3.2); 14–16, 29 July 1964 (JJM SR #2277; JJM 4.40); Diary, 18–19 April 1967; 25 October 1968; 26 February, 1 June 1969 (JJM 3.5–3.6, 3.8). In 1953, Mathews burned old manuscripts and letters, but clearly *Within Your Dream* was not among the items burned, as he revises it several months later. Possibly he burned merely those manuscripts already published, but his diary does not specify (Diary, 4 May and 27 August 1953 [JJM 2.5]).

62. Logsdon, interview (JJM SR #2281); Diary, 27 July 1921 (JJM 1.44).

63. Logsdon, interview (JJM SR #2281); Diary, 9, 15–16, 18 June 1921 (JJM 1.44).

64. Diary, 19, 23–30 June; 1–13, 15, 17, 20 July 1921 (JJM 1.44).

65. Diary, 23–30 July; 14–20 August, 23–27 September 1921; 6, 9–10, 13 January 1922; 26–27 June 1923 (JJM 1.44). It is important to remember, as Carol Hunter pointed out, that the years 1921 through 1925 saw the murders of at least twelve Big Hills Osages committed in attempts to acquire direct and indirect control over their oil headrights. There is no hint whatsoever in the diaries of these murders or any fear of lethal or financial vulnerability. In fact, later, when his stepson John Hunt wrote a novel *The Grey Horse Legacy* about the events, Mathews privately wrote that he was not especially interested in the story. Of course, such a comment could match any number of underlying emotions. It is consistent with the lacunae in the 1920s, however. Still, Mathews and his four sisters would have been potential targets of black gold diggers and criminals during the Reign of Terror even though they were very bicultural mixed-bloods. See "The Historical Context in John Joseph Mathews' *Sundown*," *MELUS* 9.1 (Spring 1982): 69; and Diary, 7 May 1968 (JJM 3.6). In November 1954, Mathews's older sister Josephine was hospitalized with cancer; he canceled a hunting trip to stay near her. So it appears that she died during this year as only Mathews, his sisters Marie and Lillian, and his wife, Elizabeth, were present when their mother passed away the following year (Diary, 4 November 1954 [JJM 2.5]).

66. Diary, 27–28 April, 1–5 May, 24 June, 2 July, 26 August 1922 (JJM 1.45). This viewing of the Passionspiele in Oberammergau seems quite different from his two depictions of mutilated "Jesus" cards in *Sundown* and in his autobiography. Mathews's scattered but substantial comments in his letters and diaries about his changing religious and spiritual views allow us to trace this development of his thought from 1921 to nearly the end of his life.

67. Diary, 27–28 April, 1–5 May, 24 June, 2, 4, 6–7, 13, 20–21, 24 July, 15–31 August, 1–18 September 1922; 26–27 June 1923 (JJM 1.44).

68. Diary, 1–3 January 1924 (JJM 1.45). Possibly, Mathews was studying for an undergraduate degree, but the timing and details are off. He would have graduated in June

1923, gone to the University of Geneva for the "cours de vacances" in international relations, and then returned to Oxford to study history. In his interview with Logsdon, he hints that he received a master's degree because anyone does who is there long enough. It is a curious statement, especially for Oxford, and implies that that was his aim in 1923–1924 before he entangled himself in a marriage he didn't really want (Logsdon [JJM SR #2281]).

69. Diary, 19, 23 January and 7, 27 March 1924 (JJM 1.45).

70. Diary 24–30 April, 1–31 May, 1–30 June, 1–31 July, 1–26 August, 3, 24, September, 1–2, 9–10, 12–13, November, 26, 28, 31 December 1924; Diary, 9 March 1945 (JJM 1.45, 1.47); Logsdon, interview (JJM SR #2281). In this same segment, he also says that he had a chance after graduating from Oxford to go to Portuguese West Africa as an exploratory petroleum geologist with Sinclair Oil Company. He suggests that the Teapot Dome scandal (which sent Sinclair's founder to prison for contempt of the Senate and jury tampering) put an end to that prospect. Sinclair Oil had had its early beginnings in southeastern Kansas and in Osage Indian territory. "Teapot Dome Scandal." *Encyclopædia Britannica* 2010. Encyclopædia Britannica Online. www.britannica.com/EBchecked/topic/585252/Teapot-Dome-Scandal; Zeck, "The Teapot Dome Scandal Fact Sheet," Montgomery College (available at www.montgomerycollege.edu/Departments/hpolscrv/jzeck.html); "Success Story: Sinclair Founded Career on Brashness and Daring," *Sinclair: A Great Name in Oil.* 1966. Sinclair Oil Corporation. 2008. www.sinclairoil.com/history/history_p2.htm.

71. Mathews to E. Hunt, 1 March 1939 (JJM 1.6); 15 June 1964 (JJM SR #2276). Mathews's article in the *Sooner Magazine: Oklahoma Alumni News* for April 1929 has him still listed as a realtor living with Virginia in Los Angeles. His Osage heritage is not mentioned, but his "ranch in the Osage hills" is. See "Hunting the Red Deer of Scotland: The Thrill of Conquering the Monarch of the Highlands," *Sooner Magazine* 1.7 (April 1929): 213–14, 246 (available at http://digital.libraries.ou.edu/sooner/articles/p213-214,246_1929v1n7_OCR.pdf).

72. Mathews writes that the peak in per capita royalties was $13,000 in 1925 and that they had fallen to $712 by 1932. *Osages* 775; Diary, 24 September, 20 October, 2, 12, 16 November, 28 December 1924 (1.45); Indian Census Rolls, 1925–28, 1930–32, available at Ancestry.com (original data: Indian Census Rolls, 1885–1940 National Archives Microfilm Publication M595, 692 rolls Records of the Bureau of Indian Affairs, Record Group 75, National Archives, Washington, D.C.); Mathews to Moe, 15 November 1939; Diary, 27 March 1945 (JJM 1.47); Mathews to E. Hunt, 1 March 1939; Mathews to "Biddy," redirected to E. Hunt, 1 March 1939 (JJM 1.6). John Mathews, Jr. was apparently twelve years old at this time, and when Mathews opens the door, his son asks, "Is this Mr. Mathews?" Had Mathews's practice of writing every month originated after this meeting, earlier, or later? Mathews also remarks in this letter that he "observed holes in the heels of Sisters [Phyllis's] stockings, and made out another check to the amount of $100.00," the same amount he had just given them for two months' rent.

73. Mathews to Mrs. Henry C. Hunt, 25 October 1932 (JJM 1.1); Diary, 4 April

1945 (JJM 1.47); Mathews to Elizabeth Hunt, 22 March 1935 (JJM 1.2); telegram from Mathews to E. Hunt, 30 March 1935 (JJM 1.25); Mathews to Mrs. Henry C. Hunt, 18 January 1935 (JJM 1.2); JJM 3.14; Mathews to E. Hunt, 13 December 1939 (JJM 1.9); Diary, 6 January and 21 February 1943 (JJM 1.46). Mathews looked into several different kinds of service to the nation during WWII, moreso than has generally been known. In letters to Elizabeth, he mentions the Office of Inter-America Relations, the Office of War Information, the Bureau of Economic Warfare, the Army, a "mysterious" job at the White House that turned out to be a "cloak and dagger" secret mission rather than a job writing the biography of Warren Harding, the Provost Marshall's Office, the Air Force, the United Nations Relief and Rehabilitation Administration, the Allied Military Government for Occupied Territories, and the Foreign Economic Administration. Mathews to E. Hunt, 18 February 1943, Mathews to E. Hunt, 26 February 1943, Mathews to E. and A. Hunt, 16 March 1943, Mathews to E. Hunt, 24 September 1944 (JJM 1.20, 1.21). In August 1944, he received word from the Economic Administration that he would be training for two months in Washington before being sent to Delhi, India. See Mathews to E. and A. Hunt, 5 August 1944 (JJM 1.21).

74. Diary, 3, 6 December 1943; and 25 January, 3 September 1946 (JJM 1.46, 1.48). On 30 January 1945 (JJM 1.47), Mathews wrote in his diary that he insisted on college for his daughter Virginia. Either her mother had suggested that she need not go to college, or Mathews perceived it that way.

75. Diary, 16 November 1969 (JJM 3.8); Richter, "Life and Literature of John Joseph Mathews," 15, 114; JJM 3.15. Mathews and his four sisters apparently each inherited an equal share of their father's headright.

76. Logsdon, interview (JJM SR #2281). The word "heart" is by no means clear on the tape and may be erroneous. He may be saying "out of a man's home" or "out of a man's hearth."

Twenty Thousand Mornings

Mathews did not provide titles or dates in his first several drafts, but he started to title and rearrange his sections in the form of vignettes in the draft in Box 4 Folder 31 (John Joseph Mathews Collection, Box 4 Folder 31. Western History Collections, University of Oklahoma Libraries, Norman, Oklahoma. Hereafter JJM 4.31 and the like. See also Introduction Note 2.). I provide dates and selected section titles from that version as a guide to the reader. One of these section titles is also Boy, Horse, and Dog, the title of this volume of his unfinished autobiography. Born in mid-November 1894, Mathews would have been three years old throughout most of 1898.

1. Mathews was the last of three boys born to the family but the only one to survive to adulthood. The order of siblings in his family was: Sarah Josephine, Susan Frances, George Martin, William Nicholas, John Joseph, Marie Imogene, Lillian Bernadine, and Florence Julia. Susan Frances also died in childhood. (See Sara Jane Richter, "The Life and Literature of John Joseph Mathews: Contributions of Two Cultures," diss., Oklahoma State University, 1985, 14.)

2. From version 4.31, versus "a livery stable, traders' stores" in versions 4.32 and 4.33. Mathews would also add several buildings to the list: the Doctor's House, Council House, Superintendent's Office Building, and hotel. He meant to name the blacksmith and signal that his house, as well as his shop, were in the valley. There is a partly illegible emendation in this 1970s version citing a Delereux, as well as the following note on the importance of the blacksmith: "The Blacksmith was a very important man in the latter part of the nineteenth century—rather a magician to the Osage Indian, since he shod their horses and repaired their wagons, repaired their rifles and war axes. He was called *Mo'n-ce-Gaxe*, 'metal maker.'" *Mo'n-ce* also was the name for the heretofore unknown silver dollar, which later [illegible] became *Mo'n-ce Ska*, white metal" (4.31).

3. ". . . braying laughter. The freighters couldn't obtain whiskey in the Osage Reservation, but in 'The States,' where they must go to get the merchant's supplies they had access to both beer and whiskey and sometimes still under the influence when they arrived at the agency" (4.31).

4. ". . . and the wapiti's challenge. But the lobo's howl was an (earthy) cry of the hunter, and the wapiti's challenge was nuptial. Also the lobo's howl and the wapiti's challenge had endings" (4.31).

5. Mathews changed "god" to "god concept," a potentially significant change (4.31). However, it is unclear how one might communicate with a concept.

6. ". . . the Muezzin calling from his Minaret, or attend the definitive formalities of the Mass" (4.31, 4.33).

7. ". . . "civilized' man" (4.31).

8. ". . . Apostles' Creed; the chant to Allah, the frenzied chant-dancing of Africa" (3.13).

9. Mathews later lists several of these night and early-morning voices: the chuck will's widow, the great horned owl, the screech owl, the restive wild gobbler, the dancing prairie chicken. He also adds: "Later when I said my prayer at my grandmother's knees, I (would) learn about 'Lost Souls.' I assumed with the Osages that the screech owl must be a 'Lost Soul'" (3.13).

10. Mathews's father's name was William Shirley Mathews.

11. This passage may be of particular interest to readers of *Sundown*. In the novel, Mathews converted the religious conflict between superior Protestants looking down on their Catholic relations into both a religious and a racial conflict. Challenge is called a "Little savage" (20). It is important to note that Mathews's cousins were on his father's side rather than his mother's and may have been part Osage or married to Osages. When writing *Sundown*, Mathews also transposed the incident regarding learning how to swear from the freighters from its place in his own experiences to the scene about the prayer cards, and he altered the way the giver of the cards learns that Challenge has treated them in a way contrary to her expectations. The autobiography passage also brings out, apparently, an important dimension of the social aftermath of the Louisiana Purchase and Anglo-French rivalry for North America. Mathews's Anglo-Welsh relatives look down on his mother because she is a French-American woman from the "hills of central Missouri" (Diary, 5 March 1953).

12. Mathews was an aficionado of technologies aeronautic and mnemonic throughout his life. He was filming with an early cine-camera by 1938. Toward the end of his life, he had a large slide collection which he occasionally brought out for entertainment at dinner parties he hosted or attended (Diaries, 1921–1978). His interest in slides possibly corresponds to his narrative interest in the window as a frame that limits both one's perception and one's knowledge. In *Wah'Kon-Tah*, he persistently used the window in association with Major Laban J. Miles to illustrate that character's confinement within his preconceived ideas about events within the Osage nation. To an extent, one can say that by using the memory slide or slide memories in this work, with their resemblance to windows, he figures his own memories in a way that leaves one to imagine what is not seen, noticed, pursued, or understood.

13. "'Q.' was Quopah; a Quapaw tribesman whose honesty and Indian philosophy appealed to my father" (Mathews footnote, 3.13). Mathews includes various spelling for this man's full name in his drafts, including Quapaw and Quopaw in addition to Quopah. He also shifted late in his editing to using Q.'s full name rather than merely his initial, which may have been a nickname. This note leaves some guessing, but is the best explanation for the variations. Later, he adds other footnotes calling him a "handy man of all work" and "my father's stable man and 'chore man.'"

14. ". . . Ee-lon-schka. They danced each afternoon and each night for three days from Thursday afternoon to Sunday afternoon, and on the fourth day..." (4.31). Mathews writes this as I'n-Lon-schka (intertribal dance, Playground-of-the-First-Son) in his book *The Osages*, but Ee-lon-shescah (men's dance) in *Talking to the Moon* (78).

15. Mathews's father was part owner of this store.

16. Excision: section on Josephine's piano lessons.

17. ". . . afraid, frustrated and overcome by a deep sense of futility" (4.31).

18. *Inducere* is Latin for "to lead into, to introduce," especially by persuasion or a motive that acts upon the will. *Educere* is Latin for "to lead out," that is to bring out from a latent or potential existence, to be led forth.

19. ". . . of 'Big Bill's' Barbershop, the week before; demanded by my father to avoid trouble" (4.31).

20. Mathews seems to have been fascinated by the early school fights of young boys. In both *Sundown* and *Life and Death of an Oilman*, such scenes as this one with Gentner Drummond appear in the opening chapters. In *Sundown*, Chal is bullied and called a "white gurl" by a group of Big Hills Osages, then counseled by his father to fight them if they continue because "you got to fight an Indian—just enough to show him you ain't 'fraid" (28, 31). In *Life and Death of an Oilman*, six-year-old Ernest Whitworth Marland is dressed by his mother for a holiday party at a public school in traditional Scottish garb. The crowd of children taunt and shove him until he starts running. They pursue him, tearing from his body the clothes brought back from Scotland by his mother (3–4).

21. I have removed the single-line paragraph prior to this paragraph because it breaks the rhythm of the narrative and is unnecessary: "Back to Tucker's later, but now again with confused chronology, back to my parents."

22. Mathews is probably referring to the yellow fever epidemic that struck New Orleans in 1853, killing more than 8,000 people in a city of about 116,000. Jeanne Girard, Mathews's grandmother, lived until at least 1917 when she would see Mathews off to his service in World War I, so she would have been born in 1828 or later, probably in Normandy where she was educated. If she came to the United States at the age of 16, then, her arrival would have been either in the decade prior to this plague or perhaps in the year it occurred. Given what he says later about her father's escape from service in Napoleon III's draft, the family probably arrived in the United States between 1848 and 1852. Jeanne Girard's daughter, Mathews's mother, was born on April 25, 1866 (Diary, 25 April 1952).

23. It is interesting that as early as 1967, Mathews identifies diabetes as a "European disease," grouping it with three communicable diseases, though it itself is not communicable. Although it seems unlikely that Type I diabetes was absent from the Western Hemisphere prior to the fifteenth century, some suggestions as to its cause beyond simple hereditary predisposition have included a hereditary predisposition induced by chronic poor diet, viral infection, exposure to chemical toxins, early exposure to cow's milk, emotional stress, and other factors that may be associated with post-fifteenth-century conditions in the Americas. See http://chinese-school.netfirms.com/diabetes-causes. html. Type II diabetes has been definitely linked to lifestyle and diet factors associated with those conditions.

24. This vindictiveness probably refers to the precedence of the French in Osage country and to the Louisiana Purchase, which alienated the area from French control. Mathews perhaps felt that his grandmother thought that had the French retained the Territory, these diseases and deaths would not have occurred. Diseases came to the Americas with every colonizer, regardless of nationality; there appears to be no evidence that the French-colonized arenas were less afflicted than others. However, there may be some truth to the idea that the consequences intensified in this area after 1800, given that the U.S. removal policy was made possible by the Louisiana Purchase and that Indians removed from the east to Indian Territory entered the area weakened by these diseases acquired during the journey. Jeanne Girard would have been a child during the worst years of that era.

25. Eugenia Girard Mathews died on March 24, 1955, in her own home in the presence of her son, John Joseph; her daughters Lillian and Marie; and John's wife, Elizabeth. She had spent about seven weeks in the hospital from mid-January to early March, apparently recovering from a broken leg. Mathews wrote of her: "She was one of the most touchingly devoted, delightfully fallible Catholics I have ever known, and her long life was a wonderful example of Christian endeavor. She believed without the least doubt every line of the Credo. . . . She prayed voluminously for me, to counteract [my] straying from religious formality. I suspect she believed me to be a failure in life, since I had renounced both formal religion and money as a standard of happy living" (Diary, 26 March 1955).

26. After the Missouri Compromise of 1820, slavery in the Louisiana Purchase was prohibited north of the 36°30′ parallel with the exception of the new state of Missouri.

When the U.S.-Mexican War ended, the newly admitted territories reopened the question, leading to the Compromise of 1850, which admitted California as a free state and mandated the principle of popular sovereignty in Utah and New Mexico, thus destabilizing the ideological stalemate. In May 1854, passage of the Kansas-Nebraska Act allowed for the admission of these states under the same principle of popular sovereignty, overriding the 1820 prohibition of slavery in Kansas and provoking a race between Free-Soilers and advocates of slavery for control of the territory. The result became known as Bleeding Kansas. In December 1855 an antislavery settler was killed, and in May 1856 a proslavery mob sacked the town of Lawrence. Three days later, John Brown led a small band of antislavery forces in the Pottawatomie Massacre, the killing of five proslavery men living on Pottawatomie Creek in Franklin County, Kansas. Kansas was ultimately admitted as a free state in January 1861.

The killing of Mathews's grandfather occurred at the hands of Union soldiers from Fort Scott in September 1861 (*Osages* 633–34). The southern states had started seceding in December 1860. Mathews had lived in Little Town (present-day Oswego) since 1841 when he had bought a trading post there from August Chouteau, so he was not part of the factions who had moved into the state as a result of the 1854 act (*Osages* 627–28). However, he actively organized Osages, Cherokees, and Creeks against the Free-Staters before and during the first months of the war. Given the complicated land relationships arising from the influx of new settlers onto Osage lands and the complexities of alliances among the federal government, the Confederacy, and the Indian Nations during the war, this passage in Kansas history deserves further scrutiny to unravel Mathews's proslavery sentiments from his pro-Osage and pro-Indian loyalties.

27. "Since being crippled by a horse during his trail herd days as a Civil War orphaned teen ager, he could never . . . " (4.31).

28. William Mathews was neither a lawyer nor a judge, so the term was merely honorific.

29. Chester A. Reed wrote bird and flower guides, and had a pocket guide for birds east of the Rockies.

30. Anthropopathy is the attribution of human emotion to a non-human being, often a god.

31. An uhlan is a special type of cavalryman or lancer in the Slavonic countries and later the German Empire.

32. ". . . born as a citizen of . . ." (4.31).

33. ". . . to be. When a warrior's face after death was not painted with marks of the tribe the gens and division, he could not enter Spiritland, had to wander about at night—a lost soul" (4.31).

34. Excision: passage (and short paragraph below the break) on the urges of boys and "Blank Nameless."

35. Marc Mitscher had been one of the earliest pilots in the U.S. Navy's air fleet during World War I and had gone on to help develop the aviation corps within the Navy. He was a commander at the Battle of Midway and in the Solomon Islands during World War II.

At the command of Task Force 58, a force of aircraft carriers, he led the air strikes toward the capture of Iwo Jima and Okinawa. More details may be found in Theodore Taylor's *The Magnificent Mitscher* (1954), which Mathews may have used to construct these passages (Diary, 29 August 1961). The incident Mathews describes between Mitscher and Mrs. Tucker nicely reframes the image of the stoic Indian, the Indian-in-pain-but-silent, depositing the image into an Amer-European figure and ironically one who was the son of the federal Indian Agent Oscar Mitscher.

36. In their introduction to Zitkala-Sa's *American Indian Stories, Legends, and Other Writings*, Cathy N. Davidson and Ada Norris write of Carlisle Indian Industrial School: "Carlisle, under the leadership of retired army general Richard Henry Pratt, was a Pennsylvania boarding school founded with the express purpose of separating Indians from their reservation and tribal contexts in order to assimilate them into white society. Famously, Pratt's slogan while running the Carlisle school was 'Kill the Indian and save the man!' The methods employed by Pratt and his contemporaries ranged from forced and prolonged separation from family, beatings, and food deprivation to less overtly violent tactics, including a forced work system which farmed out students to area families to be immersed in everyday white culture and 'labor.' To qualify for federal funding, boarding schools were required to practice a strict English-only policy" (xvii). By all accounts, students infrequently graduated and frequently ran away from Carlisle and other Indian boarding schools without graduating as a result of this recipe for personal and tribal annihilation. Between 1879 and 1918, Carlisle enrolled 156 Osage students among its 10,606 students.

37. Barbara Landis, a researcher of the Carlisle Indian Industrial School, was able to provide a list of Osage students with the surname Mathews or Matthews who were students at the school. There is a student with the name Walter Mathews whose parents were both deceased at the time of his enrollment at the age of 20 in 1899 (when John Joseph Mathews would have been five years old). Walter Mathews graduated with the class of 1904 and married a woman named Anna Parker. The records have him living in Osage County in the town of Grainola a decade later. This would fit precisely with Mathews's later mention of him as the brother of Annie Cooper, who lived to the south of his sister near Beaver Creek. There is no record of an Owen Mathews at the school, but it seems unlikely that Mathews's recollection of the twins' enrollment would have been faulty. Continued research into Mathews's extended family might clear up the question in the absence of complete records. The football team mentioned was the one on which Jim Thorpe played, though not until 1907, and was coached by Glenn "Pop" Warner, later to be the coach of Stanford, the team Carlisle beat. Warner was at Carlisle from 1899 through 1903 and from 1907 through 1914. Records of the Stanford-Carlisle game to which Mathews will later refer are not readily available.

38. Mathews had introduced this ironic use of the term "free men" about halfway through his work *The Osages*. At the same time that it distinguished white Americans from slaves, it helped him to remind us that the people who called themselves "free" had never freed themselves of the scarring memories of their history in Europe. Their outra-

geous behaviors in the Americas had to be seen in the context of that escape-without-healing from a repressive social system:

> The Anglo-Saxon invaders had a tribal memory as well as the Little Ones. It was a racial memory of British kings who could have you hanged from a cross-roads gibbet if you killed a deer or a partridge in New Forest or any other royal or ducal preserve; and here in America they were expanding, as though through a safety valve, from the political, social, and economic pressures of the centuries. Not only did they have racial memories of suppression by princes and parliaments and hierarchies, but they might even have fresh memories of the class distinctions in the Thirteen Colonies. These free men were not scholars and gentlemen from the Atlantic Seaboard, but many of them, perhaps most of them, were refugees from the law and were men more savage than those whom they called "Injuns." It was these barbarians who shouted of their freedom from kings and strong governments and princes of both worlds, in the wilderness, and raped and murdered and stole horses and brought the *we-lu-schka*, "the little people," to the Little Ones and took away their "remaining days." (383)

We-lu-schka refers to diseases. The passage and his use of the term thereafter are typical of how Mathews employed empathy in his critiques of the behavior of others, never satisfied merely to criticize but ever looking for a way of pointing out the motivations that led to destructive or inappropriate behavior.

39. ". . . country dance, 'Hoedown' in local parlance" (4.31).

40. This scene can be compared to Mathews's description of the social life in the Osage Nation in *Wah'Kon-Tah*: "There was little social life and no distractions, except the gossip of the Reservation. Sometimes there were dances at Chautauqua or Elgin, and all the young people of the Agency attended. The men pranced and strutted like turkey cocks. . . . When the activities of the drink-excited mixed-bloods were restricted to the Reservation, they burned up their energies in different ways. Some were quiet and pugnacious, some were quiet and jovial, but there were some, who, when they reached a certain stage in their glorious victory over the prosaic dullness of the Agency, began shooting out lights" (155–56).

41. The Oklahoma Archaeological Survey, sponsored by the University of Oklahoma, has identified forty-six sites on Beaver Creek that inform us about the past 2,000 years of human occupation of this area of Osage County, or since about 100 C.E. Overall, they have identified 180 sites in Osage County, some of which reach back to 6,000 B.C.E. and earlier, positing that not all the existing sites have been discovered because they remain buried beneath the prairie sediments.

42. An early draft of the manuscript identifies these "Samaritans" as the Hoods, but does not give their first names (4.34).

43. A song about a father writing to his son to return home on the occasion of the mother's death, hoping to end a separation marked by "angry words."

44. ". . . after forty centuries" (3.13). It was common for Mathews to search widely

through history to touch on the "right" span of centuries for the lag he assumed in the material culture of Western versus Eastern Hemisphere.

45. Mathews misremembered Caligula's horse as "Cincatatus."

46. The Devonian period was the fourth period of the Paleozoic geological era, lasting from 416 million years ago to 359.2 million years ago. Four-legged amphibians (the ancestors of frogs) began to appear at the end of this era. North America and Europe were not yet divided from one another, but formed a continent known as Laurussia or Euramerica. *Homo sapiens* originate much later, within the last hundreds of thousands of years rather than millions.

47. Sir Charles George Douglas Roberts was a Canadian poet, born in 1860, of Mathews's mother's generation. He founded a nationalist school of poetry in Canada. *The Kindred of the Wild* (1902) was one of several collections of his stories about forests and about the behavior, psychology, and realistic predation of animals. Born in England in the same year, Ernest Thompson Seton was also raised in Canada. His childhood in Manitoba led to his authoring and illustrating animal stories, of which *Wild Animals I Have Known* was his most famous collection. Seton was active in the attempt to establish reservations and national parks to protect human and animal populations threatened with extinction, and probably influenced Mathews's views on the connection between these populations greatly. In 1902 he founded an organization for non-Indian youth known as the Woodcraft Indians and helped to found the Boy Scouts.

Later in his life, Mathews met Seton. In August 1935, he attended the "College of Indian Wisdom," in Santa Fe. It was actually a camp established by Seton that brought together for a few weeks a collection of mostly non-Indian intellectuals to discuss how to preserve Indian cultures. Mathews thought the idea good, but useless and doomed to failure (Mathews to E. Hunt, 20, 24, 31 August 1935).

48. This paragraph and the preceding eighteen are a handwritten insert into the 4.31 version of the manuscript, edited as lightly as possible for illegible, omitted, and misplaced words. They have been included because they inform Mathews's later descriptions of flight as well as his boyhood involvement with nature. He described in his diary the circular path of a bird, so the duplication of the word "west" and the omission of the word "east" in his description of the chuck-will's widow beating its bounds has been corrected. An internal title, "Beating Bounds," placed prior to the fourteenth paragraph has been removed.

49. In the 4.31 version, Mathews wrote on the top of the page where this story begins: "We met McCurdy the train robber who later was killed at Okesa and mummified." Two pages later, he inserted into the MS clippings from various sources, including one from the *Pawhuska Daily Journal-Capital* from Wednesday, April 20, 1977, stating that "Elmer McCuardy (McCardy) the outlaw who met his maker near Okesa 66 years ago . . . according to an official autopsy report from California, was found Dec. 7, 1976 at Greer's Amusement Park at Long Beach, Calif., when a film crew with 'The Six Million Dollar Man' TV series discovered he was not, really, a wax dummy, but the mummified remains of a human." The article announces that the outlaw would finally be laid to rest in Okla-

homa, getting the proper burial he deserved, thanks to a state senator and the state medical examiner. The senator served as a pallbearer. Mathews intended to insert information from these clippings and other memories into the manuscript.

50. "Later, when I told Henry Lookout about the incident, he said, 'Was his face painted?' 'I couldn't see it.' I said, 'the body was bent over forward.' 'Hehn,' he said. 'I guess he didn't make it' (4.31).

51. ". . . headwaters of Pa'in Creek (Anglicized as Pond Creek)" (4.31).

52. ". . . better fer bobcat huntin' . . ." (4.31).

53. Theodore Roosevelt appointed Frantz agent in 1903. Mathews would have been about nine or ten years old. He served for three years and became governor of the Oklahoma territory in 1906. Mathews's chronology here is either extremely compressed or slightly misremembered, as Frantz would have left the agency for the governorship before Mathews entered eighth grade or high school.

54. Mathews likely refers here to the Sisters of Loretto, a religious institution of the Catholic Church dedicated to social justice, improving the lives of persons who suffer from injustice and oppression. It was founded in Kentucky in 1812 to educate children on the frontier who could not otherwise afford schooling. It is distinct from the Sisters of Loreto, a religious order founded in 1609 as part of an effort to improve the lives of women within the Church. The order also sponsors schools in North America, but the closest would have been in Illinois.

55. We may compare this story of Mathews's engagement in taxidermy to a scene in Linda Hogan's fictional *Mean Spirit* set in the early 1920s. A narrative about the Osage oil murders, the novel depicts a scene in which the character Belle Graycloud discovers a truck filled with the carcasses of 317 golden eagles. When she tries to protest this massacre, she is thrown in jail, seen by the non-Indian perpetrators as irrational and hysterical simply because the victims are not human (109–10). Considering Mathews's comments elsewhere about the mass murder of coyotes, it is clear that he distinguishes his own taking of individual lives of eagles from their mass slaughter. Hogan cites not only Mathews's writings but his first critic, Carol Hunter, as sources for her story, along with two other writers whom Mathews knew, Angie Debo and Carter Revard.

56. ". . . agent and the Department of Interior" (4.31).

57. French for "my little savage of/from the heavens/sky." In version 4.33, he has crossed out *du ciel*. In version 4.31, he changed it to *un petit sauvage* (a little savage or little savage).

58. Excision: passage on high school dances.

59. Until 1971, Memorial Day was celebrated on May 30, rather than on the last Monday in May.

60. ". . . print and from the stage and the re-discovery of Christ . . ." (3.13).

61. Excision: passage on ontogeny, phylogeny, racial memory, and God.

62. Excisions: passage on Miss Prissy; section on Floyd Soderstrom and his father.

63. Significantly, Mathews emphasizes here Monk's "heavy eyebrows" as he asks the young Mathews a question that marks his Indianness, particularly given that Mathews

elsewhere describes himself as a white man (at least in the perception of, for example, Mexican Indians). In his masterwork, *The Osages*, published about five years earlier, Mathews writes that the Osages referred to the French and later Amer-Europeans from the United States as *I'n-Shta-Heh*, the "Heavy Eyebrows."

64. Excision: passage on hunting coyotes with Tony Fortune.

65. The 1910 U.S. Census for Osage County, Oklahoma, lists a Crete Musseller of the proper age for the judge's daughter. Therefore, I have used this spelling rather than the two variations Mathews used: Mueseller, Muesseller.

66. Otto von Bismarck was the prime minister of Prussia from 1862 through 1890 and the founder and first chancellor of the German Empire (1871–1890). He is remembered for his role in the unification of Germany and the practice of Realpolitik, as well as his archconservatism.

67. André Michaux was a French botanist. In 1785, he was sent to the southeastern and midwestern United States and the Spanish Louisiana territories to collect plants to replenish a depleted forest outside of Paris, but most of the plants were lost in a shipwreck in 1797.

68. An appanage is a provision made for the maintenance of the younger children of monarchs. It might be a province, jurisdiction, or lucrative office, but it could also take the form of money.

69. Mathews wrote about his great-grandfather William Shirley Williams in *The Osages*. Williams is also the subject of other publications, such as *Old Bill Williams, Mountain Man*, by Alpheus Favour; *Bill Williams' Mountain Men*, by Thomas E. Way; *Lone Elk: The Life Story of Bill Williams, Trapper and Guide of the Far West*, by Chauncey Pratt Williams; *The Story of "Old Bill" Williams*, by Frank Evart Wells; and a biography of Williams by Frederic Voelker in *Mountain Men and Fur Traders of the Far West: Eighteen Biographical Sketches*, ed. LeRoy Hafen.

70. David Halliday Moffatt was a banker, merchant, mine owner, real estate man, and investor who succeeded in establishing a railroad across the Rocky Mountains beginning in 1902. Twenty-seven tunnels were blasted through the mountains, and the route was directed over elevated passes and underneath the continental divide. The intent was to connect Denver and Salt Lake City by rail, then build to the Pacific Ocean. It was a spectacular engineering achievement for its day.

71. Robert William Service was a poet born in England in 1874. He emigrated to Canada at the age of twenty and worked eight years in the Yukon. He became a newspaper correspondent during the Balkan Wars of 1912–13 and was a correspondent and ambulance driver during World War I. Mathews probably refers here to images from his poems about the Klondike, such as "The Shooting of Dan McGrew," in which a pioneer woman profits from the murderous mutual jealousy of her current and former lovers.

72. "Perhaps his romantic illusions and his Buffalo Bill–like histrionics also . . ." (*BHD* MS).

73. It is interesting to compare this passage on artificial insemination of fish eggs to the final chapter of David Treuer's *Little* (1995), which takes up a very similar theme.

74. "The prettier Daisy-Chainer, despite . . ." (4.33, *BHD* MS). In October 1967, Mathews referred to the staff of Seymour Lawrence & Associates pejoratively as "Daisy-Chainers" after receiving the manuscript of this autobiography back from them unread and rejected. The less cryptic Vasserite of the earlier draft has been preferred here as more consistent with the collegiate references, the masculine/feminine rhetorical emphasis, and the relative innocence of the incident and associated fantasies.

75. "Thanatopsis" is a poem by the American writer William Cullen Bryant. It was published in *The North American Review* in 1817 when Bryant was twenty-three, six years after he wrote it. The title means "a view of death."

76. "Kincaider" refers to homesteaders who settled on the Sandhills of Nebraska to take advantage of the Kincaid Act of 1904, a congressional amendment to the Homestead Act of 1862. Applicable only to the arid regions of central and western Nebraska, the act allowed for people to claim land for both farming and ranching homesteads of 640 acres, or four times the amount of land allowed under the previous law. Bingham and Ashby were two of several towns that grew up close to the Chicago, Burlington, and Quincy Railroad so that ranchers could ship their livestock for sale. Environmental conditions eventually forced out many farmers, who sold their homesteads to ranchers, for whom the conditions for cattle raising were more suitable.

77. Maria Amparo Ruiz de Burton writes of these "wars" in the context of San Diego County in her 1885 novel, *The Squatter and the Don*. The comparison suggests, perhaps, that the war in California was driven by several factors beyond the mere coexistence of ranchers and farmers: racial and national tensions between immigrants from the more easterly United States to California and former citizens of Mexico who had become U.S. citizens under the Treaty of Guadalupe Hidalgo; the ability of the former to push through state legislation antagonistic to the rancher and favorable to the farmer; and a tendency toward vigilantism and outlawry fueled by racialized self-justification. In Nebraska, both farmers and ranchers would likely have seen themselves as racially united against the Sioux and other Native American groups from whom they had wrested these lands. Mathews's part-Osage background and highly conscious understanding of land wars in general makes these ironies of land displacement even more ironic.

78. The Maxim machine gun was the first fully automatic machine gun. Invented in 1884 by Hiram Stevens Maxim, an American engineer living in London, it was manufactured by the Vickers company of Great Britain. Louis Blériot was a French aviator and aircraft manufacturer born in 1872. He flew across the English Channel from Calais to Dover on July 25, 1909, in a monoplane with a 25-horsepower engine. He became an important airplane manufacturer up to, during, and after World War I, supplying the Allied Powers with much of their air strength.

79. ". . . hopelessness. My exhibitionist man-flyers seemed so inept as I watched the redtail hawk" (4.31).

80. The RMS *Mauritania* was an ocean liner launched in 1906. The ship was the fastest in the world until 1931 and when built was also the largest. Sister ships were the *Lusitania* and the *Aquitania*. In May 1915, the *Lusitania* was targeted by a German U-boat and

sank. The *Mauritania* then began to serve first as a troopship and later as a hospital ship.

81. "... too 'civilized' to ..." (4.31).

82. "The Man with the Hoe" is a poem by U.S. poet Edwin Markham (1852–1940). It was first published in 1899 in the *San Francisco Examiner* and was based on an 1862 painting by Jean-François Millet titled "Man with a Hoe."

83. The war between Spain and the United States took place in 1898 when Mathews was a toddler. It arose out of the Cuban struggle for independence from Spain, which had begun in 1895. The United States entered the war after the USS *Maine* sank in the harbor of Havana. The ship was nominally in Havana to protect U.S. citizens and their property during the rioting in that city against colonial rule, though other "chauvinistic" motives are now commonly accepted by scholars, given the contradictory colonialist/anticolonial sentiment in the United States, the Monroe Doctrine, and U.S. intervention in the Caribbean in general during that era. The war was extremely short-lived. In signing the Treaty of Paris in December 1898, Spain ceded Guam and Puerto Rico to the United States, gave Cuba independence, and sold the Philippines to the United States for $20 million.

Commodore George Dewey was the leader of the naval squadron that entered Manila Bay in the Philippines during the first days of the war. The brash hero with tombstone teeth and spectacles is Theodore Roosevelt, whose Rough Riders, the First Volunteer Cavalry, won a victory on San Juan Hill and helped to capture Santiago, Cuba. He was pictured commercially on a tin tray sitting on a horse with his sabre raised. The tombstone teeth recollection probably comes from later newspaper and magazine caricatures of the politician.

84. The Boer War (October 1899–May 1902) was fought between Great Britain and the Boer republics of the South African Republic or Transvaal and the Orange Free State. (A Boer is a South African of Dutch, German, or Huguenot descent.) It is seen by many as a successful attempt on the part of Great Britain to take over the gold mining region of the Witwatersrand located within the South African Republic. The Jameson Raid was a failed attempt in December 1895 by Cecil Rhodes and Leander Starr Jameson to overthrow the South African Republic, which forced Rhodes to resign his premiership of Cape Colony. General Jan Smuts was a leader of the Boer commandos that almost took Cape Town in 1902. He was prime minister of the united South Africa from 1919 to 1924 and from 1939 to 1948.

The Boxer War of 1900, also known as the Boxer Rebellion, was a peasant uprising in China the intent of which was to drive colonizing foreigners out of the country. The term "boxer" refers to the secret society known as the Righteous and Harmonious Fists, who opposed the increasing encroachment of European nations and Japan into China's economy and the resulting impoverishment of the country and its people. Boxer attacks targeted Christian converts and foreign missionaries. In June 1900, international forces tried to enter Beijing. The empress dowager ordered foreigners to be killed, and several foreign ministers were killed or put under siege. However, leaders in central and southern China worked against these assaults. When the international forces entered Beijing in August, they looted the city and forced out the empress dowager. An agreement stipulating reparations for the foreigners was signed in September 1901.

Arthur Bonnicastle was a former student at the Osage Boarding School, Haskell Institute, and the Carlisle Indian Industrial School. He was a sergeant in the U.S. Infantry during the war who also served in the Philippines, apparently against Emilio Aguinaldo, the leader of the Filipino independence movement against Spain and the United States. According to Garrick Bailey, Bonnicastle was also a peyote roadman (Bailey, ed., *The Osage and the Invisible World: From the Works of Francis La Flesche,* Norman: University of Oklahoma Press, 1995, 26). He served on the Osage Tribal Council from 1908 to 1910 and was principal chief from 1920 to 1922.

85. The preceding 19 paragraphs are significantly rewritten and expanded from the carbon preserved in folder 4.33.

86. Actually called the "Cross of Gold" speech, this memorable piece of oratory was delivered by William Jennings Bryan on July 8, 1896. Bryan delivered it at the Democratic National Convention in Chicago during his first of three bids for president of the United States. Bryan was a liberal who defended the laboring classes and supported the popular election of senators, the imposition of an income tax, suffrage for women, and Prohibition. Mathews confuses the title of the speech because of its most famous final lines. Bryan was attacking the idea that gold was the only legitimate foundation for currency, championing unlimited coinage of silver in a 16:1 ratio with gold. "You shall not press down on the brow of labor this crown of thorns, you shall not crucify mankind on a cross of gold."

In Shakespeare's play, Richard the Third utters this line in the last act during the Battle of Bosworth Field. Richard's title to the crown is challenged by Henry Tudor, the Earl of Richmond. Unhorsed during the battle against Tudor, Richard calls twice for a horse with these words, abusing his ally Sir William Catesby who suggests he withdraw from the battle to receive one and soon thereafter falls to his rival.

This characterization of his father by Mathews helps us to understand the similarities and contrasts between William Shirley Mathews and John Windzer, the father of Challenge in *Sundown.* In the first chapter of the novel, John Windzer quotes from canto 1, verse 13 of Byron's *Childe Harold,* attempting to imitate William Jennings Bryan's voice and tone, during his wife's final moments of labor before Challenge's birth (2–3). "He felt like a great orator standing there in the bright light, and that all the imaginary calumnies that had been heaped upon him were proved false, and he had emerged as a hero; a conqueror, not only by his sword but by ringing words, and this little patch of the world under the oaks, unresisting and tranquil in this savage valley, was symbolic of the world that had ignored him and taken special trouble to persecute him" (3).

87. ". . . night, and a Negro was not allowed to drink from the fountain in front of the Administration Building" (4.31).

88. ". . . mixed-bloods and fullbloods who . . . Carolina, Georgia, and Mississippi . . ." (4.31). See also *The Osages,* in which Mathews details the conflicts between the Cherokees and Osages throughout the first half of the nineteenth century.

89. Excision: passage on dancing and campus grounds and atmosphere.

90. There is an Elmer E. Grinstead in the 1920 Census for Osage County, so this spelling has been preferred to Grindstead.

91. This line originally read ". . . wherein Wah'Kon-Tah was asked why He had . . ." (4.32). Mathews crossed out those inaccuracies, replacing them with a better translation of Wah'Kon-Tah.

92. The Battle of New Orleans, through which Jackson gained fame and honor in the United States, was fought fifteen days after the signing of the Treaty of Ghent, which ended the War of 1812. The defense of New Orleans and the Louisiana Purchase against British capture had immense economic and symbolic weight, given that farmers and merchants in the west relied on the port of New Orleans to ship their goods at low cost and given that Jefferson's plan for the Louisiana Purchase was an egalitarian agrarian democracy through expansion as well as Indian removal. Mathews's "postulating" may have been more reasoned than he implied (though probably less researched than his professor would have liked). It may have arisen from an understanding of Native perspectives on Jackson, which are almost universally negative, and from Jackson's unethical actions during and after the Creek War of 1813–14.

93. A "smooth mouth" horse is at least eleven years old, and therefore past prime. The permanent teeth wear down at various rates related to stabling versus grazing outdoors in sandy areas. Estimating age would have been necessary when a buyer, for example, was unfamiliar with the seller.

94. Excisions: section on term at the University of the South (Sewanee); section on return to University of Oklahoma, dating, and archaeological expedition.

95. The first automobile was steam-powered. Invented in France in 1769, it had three wheels, carried four people, and ran for twenty minutes at 2.25 mph. Steam buses were in European cities by 1800. However, both the perceived and real dangers of steam vehicles led to their being banned. The Stanley Steamer, made by twin inventors Francis Edgar Stanley and Freelan O. Stanley, broke the world speed record in 1906, at nearly 128 mph. It was the first commercially successful automobile in the United States. The cars were made until 1927, when gasoline-powered engines took over.

96. Mathews's early description of this boasting is quite funny: "Men boasted of their car's performance. You might have thought that each owner had made his own car, and with the pride of an artist had often to trespass into the province of fiction to top the boastings of other motorists. A banker boasted that he had driven to Bartlesville and back in neutral in his Imperial; let the A.N. Ruble with his Oakland, W.T. Leahy with his Whatever, A.W. Hurley with his Whatwasit, or even Miss Josephine Mathews with her Stutz Bearcat beat *that*" (4.34).

97. Excisions: section on Floyd and Rozie Soderstrom's claim in South Dakota; passage on fall return to the University, pop quiz, and excursions for his Geology course.

98. Georges-Marie Guynemer was a famous French combat pilot born in Paris the same year as Mathews; he was France's first great fighter ace. Like Mathews, he had not originally joined the air service but attempted to enlist in the infantry and the cavalry to serve in World War I. Unlike Mathews, he began in the service as a mechanic, went

into pilot training in 1915, and had died in combat by September 1917. Prior to his death, he racked up fifty-three victories against enemy aircraft and had been shot down eight times. Manfred Albrecht Freiherr von Richthofen is much better known as the Red Baron, archenemy of the Allied Powers. He was born in Breslau, Germany (now part of Poland), in 1892 and died over France in April 1918. He was a lieutenant in the First Uhlan Cavalry Regiment of the Prussian Army, fighting in Russia, Belgium, and France. He then moved to the infantry and in 1915 to the air service, becoming a combat pilot in September 1916. He downed eighty aircraft before his death, which occurred when he suffered a fatal chest wound as his red Fokker triplane was penetrated by ground fire near Amiens, though rumors attributed his death to a pilot captain in the Canadian Royal Air Force flying a Sopwith Camel aircraft. Hermann Goering, whom Mathews would meet by chance in Switzerland in 1924, succeeded him as commander of the squad (letter against American fascism, JJM 4.40). Gervais Raoul Lufberry is a slightly lesser known French-American pilot who served in the French and U.S. air commands during the war. Born in 1885, he scored between seventeen and sixty victories before his death in 1918. He may have been a victim of the failure of the Allied armed forces to issue parachutes to pilots, which Mathews will mention later.

99. Pancho Villa was a leader of the Mexican revolution. By the end of 1913, he had become the governor of Chihuahua, going on to defeat Huerta in June 1914 and claiming Mexico City. By December of that year, he fled the city with Emiliano Zapata, pursued by another leader of the campaign against Huerta. In January 1916, he executed seventeen U.S. citizens living in Santa Isabel and attacked Columbus, New Mexico, later that winter. Woodrow Wilson sent General John J. Pershing against him, but Pershing failed in his mission. Villa was too popular, the U.S. entry into Mexico too unpopular, and Villa's familiarity with the province too superior to Pershing's. The National Guard to which Mathews refers would likely have been composed of some of the grandsons of the U.S. soldiers of the U.S.-Mexican War, which for some did not end the cross-border animosities as we see commemorated in Cormac McCarthy's *Blood Meridian*.

100. Excision: passage on southern womanhood, Chevalier Blanc, "khaki-wacky" girls, and loss of virginity.

101. "I remember how I experienced a rather childish worship for the Red Tailed Hawk, and felt vicariously his ability to leave the earth, where he seemed to be bound unhappily and launch himself into the sky, alighting only in trees, unless the necessity of prey made imperative alighting heavily on earth.

"I might have chosen the Golden eagle as my symbol of earth detachment or freedom but I was more intimately associated with the Red Tail, since [it] circled high in the air above Bally, Spot and Me, to determine if we might excite some species of game to abandon cryptic freezing through our sudden appearance" (4.31).

102. Excision: passage on coyote hunting after Officer's Training Camp.

103. "When we fell, either in training or in aerial battle we would have no parachutes" (4.31).

104. The JN-4 or "Jenny" was a biplane built by the Curtiss Aeroplane Company start-

ing in 1915. It combined a model J airplane built for the U.S. Army and a model N built for the Navy. It had a 90-horsepower engine and could go up to 75 miles per hour and as high as 6,500–11,000 feet. Because of its weight, it could not climb well. The ailerons were originally controlled by a shoulder yoke, then later by a wheel with a foot bar added to move the rudder. Improvements were made in part because of fatal crashes, and Mathews's JN-4 model would have had the advantages of these improvements. The trainers were not used in combat. More than 6,000 of the JN series were built at up to $8,160 apiece. A well-known stamp—the Inverted Jenny—pictures the aircraft, accidentally printed upside down.

105. A *flechette* (French for "little arrow") is a small, hand-held weapon made of steel—about four inches in length and 60 grams in weight. It was used during World War I to kill troops on the ground from the air by penetrating the helmet and the skull of the targeted soldier. Gravity made it quite deadly, if aimed accurately.

106. ". . . Field. Birds in practice flight formation could have taught them much. Birds feeding on the ground or in trees flush simultaneously when danger comes, warned not by voice warning but by the sudden action of a member of the flock. Birds, also elephants, deer white tail squirrel etc., etc., etc." (4.31). On the bottom of the manuscript page associated with this note, he also wrote: "Flock protection, used by crows, elephants, geese, guineas for time immemorial—man, the arrogant earth walker had to learn from LOWER FORMS" (4.31).

107. "Note the flight of hawk pursuing game—they make Immelmann turn back to catch prey and escape from enemies" (4.31). Mathews also notes that a pileated woodpecker being chased by a hawk will use the Immelmann turn as well.

108. "They learned this chiefly from the birds" (4.31).

109. ". . . one's vulnerability and primitive awe of the sky—'Heaven, the mysterious, and besides . . .'" (4.31).

110. Carl Ethan Akeley (1864–1926) was an American naturalist and explorer in whom Mathews was likely interested because he contributed to taxidermy's use in museums. He also invented a motion-picture camera for naturalists, perhaps one that Mathews later used.

Sir Ernest Shackleton (1874–1922) was a British explorer who tried but ultimately failed to reach the geographic South Pole in 1901–1904, 1907–1909, 1914–1916, and 1922.

Edward Anderson Stinson (1894–1932) was an early aviator whose sister Katherine Stinson was the fourth female pilot in the United States, soloing after only four hours. He instructed pilots at Kelly Field during the war and later founded the Detroit-Stinson aircraft company. He built planes that succeeded in crossing the Atlantic Ocean and circling the globe.

111. Captain Albert Ball (1896–1917) was a British flying ace who died over Annoeullin, France, during World War I. He recorded forty-three victories in the air.

112. It is difficult to determine the average time it normally takes for pilots to solo, as there can be variations due to conditions beyond the pilot's control and present-day norms may not reflect the norms of the 1910s. Pilots queried said that the average

is between fifteen and twenty hours.

113. Edmund Henry Hynman Allenby, the first Viscount Allenby, was the director of the British campaign for Palestine during the war. His initial war experience was acquired in Africa in the 1880s and 1890s. At the start of the war, he was a commander of the cavalry and the army in Europe. He moved into Egypt in June 1917. His first victory there was at Gaza in November 1917 against the Turks, and his forces captured Jerusalem that December. He won the Battle of Megiddo in September 1918, then advanced to Damascus and Aleppo, defeating the Ottoman Empire in the area that became known as Syria. These milestones help to date Mathews's movements in this section of his memoir.

114. ". . . Nature but arrogantly believing he *homo sapiens* had invented them. . . ." (4.31).

115. "Note: Racing toward earth and no horizon" (4.32).

116. ". . . birds in their earth-detached freedom, and . . . least of my boyhood dream bird the redtail hawk through my ability" (4.31).

117. These recollections acquire a deeper meaning when it is known that Mathews lost a nephew during pilot training practice in the spring of 1943 (Diary, 2 June 1943). In the weeks after the death of Henry Benjamin Caudill, the son of Mathews's older sister Josephine, Mathews ruminated over the accident in his mind, at one point remarking to himself that he thought Henry should have bailed out of his aircraft but that he saw in context why he had not (Diary, 16 June 1943).

118. Vernon Castle (1887–1918) and his wife Irene (1893–1969) became a well-known ragtime and ballroom dancing team. They originated the one-step and the turkey trot, and they made famous such dances as the castle polka, the castle walk, and the tango. They were also known for their liberal social views. Vernon Castle died in a training accident over Fort Worth, Texas, in February 1918 toward the end of World War I. He had earlier served in Great Britain's Royal Flying Corps and garnered the Croix de Guerre for his actions. He first began training pilots in Canada before being sent to Texas to help the U.S. effort. Ward McAllister (1827–1895) was a U.S. attorney who dubbed the social leaders of New York City society "the Four Hundred" when in 1892 he told William Astor's wife to shorten her invitation list as there were only about 400 in the high society of the city.

119. The last eight words of this sentence are taken from version 4.31.

120. In the 4.31 version, Mathews consistently changed D's initial to T.

121. ". . . now in ~~1965~~ (~~1974?~~) (1978?) when I refer to my diary of 1917 '18?" (4.31).

122. I have used the 4.31 version of this sentence.

123. Mathews's friends and family referred to him as "Jo" throughout most of his life, and he signed his letters as Jo. His earlier manuscripts retain his self-imposed moniker John-Without-Purpose throughout, but in the 4.31 version, he began to refer intermittently to himself instead as Jo-Without-Purpose. It seems fitting, therefore, to begin here to use that name where he uses it, in a way that honors both his earlier drafts and the intimacy and greater accuracy of the later appellation.

124. ". . . the sleeping earth . . . jerk of some pain or disorder when one . . ." (4.31). One

must wonder, if this emendation was written in July 1978, whether Mathews was thinking of his own pain or the disorder that sent him to the hospital in 1975–76 or the ailment that would end his life within the year (Diary, 3 June, 1 September 1978).

125. Mathews may have meant "still hunted." However, as still-hunting is a common deer hunting practice, he may well have intended the analogy.

126. Between receiving the manuscript back from Seymour Lawrence and sending it out to William Morrow & Company, Mathews corrected these lines by researching his own files for the precise wording on the cards (Diary, 25 October 1967). He mentions that the wording appears on page 324, which matches the 4.31 version. It is unclear whether the lines below are the corrected or the original, but they indicate that the double-spaced version in 4.31 was extant by 1967, though marked as emended in the 1970s:

> OVER THERE—
> The Boys Dig in to keep from getting
> shelled out.

> OVER HERE—
> We must dig in and shell out. Here
> comes the FOURTH LIBERTY LOAN.
> It's Up to Us!

> This was dropped by an aviator from Elling-
> ton Field—THINK—It might have
> been a German Shell.

> BUY BONDS.

127. Excision: passage on Mary Wilkins and wish to fly with Allenby.

128. Osage County censuses show Claypools rather than Claypooles. Mathews writes this name in this manuscript, version 4.32/4.33, as Les Claypoole, as well as in *Talking to the Moon*. He uses Claypool in version 4.31.

129. "... her iron-grey colt ..." (4.31, 4.33). Here and below.

130. "... Jo-Without-Eager-Purpose ..." (4.31).

131. The atom was first split in 1917 by Ernest Rutherford at the University of Manchester. Stanford University's Department of Physics was among its first departments opened in 1891. David Webster began research on X-rays there in the early 1900s. In 1934, he recruited Swiss physicist Felix Bloch, a refugee from the Nazis. Bloch went on to collaborate with Robert Oppenheimer in research and conferences that may have contributed to Oppenheimer's later work at Los Alamos.

132. General William Mitchell (1879–1936) was court-martialed in 1925 for advocating the separation of the air forces from the army and pushing to see the military better prepared in aviation. During World War I, he commanded a joint-forces armada of 1,500 planes and used formation flying to bomb en masse. In 1925, he accused the Departments of War and the Navy of "incompetency, criminal negligence, and almost trea-

sonable administration of the national defense" after the unnecessary loss of a dirigible during a storm, and as a result he was convicted of insubordination. He received a special medal from the U.S. Congress posthumously in 1946.

133. Excisions: section on oil exploration with sister Josephine's husband, Henry Caudill, in Appalachia; passage on trip to Lake Onondaga with Herbert Parker and friends.

134. ". . . nimbus was a bit tarnished" (4.33); ". . . nimbus was slanted" (4.31).

135. Mathews is probably referring to "Macushla," an Irish folksong that begins: "Macushla! Macushla!/Your sweet voice is calling,/Calling me softly,/Again and again."

The Owl and Triangle was a senior honor society for women at the University of Oklahoma begun in 1912. Only the eight highest ranking female juniors at the university were chosen each year for the honor. The male senior honor society was known as Pe-et and chose the ten highest ranking men on campus.

136. Walter Stanley Campbell is better known under his pen name, Stanley Vestal. He was a member of the faculty in the University of Oklahoma's Department of English from 1915 through 1957, and serving during that time in World War I. He had attended Oxford on a Rhodes scholarship between 1908 and 1911, eventually receiving both a bachelor's and master's degree in English language and literature. He also became a Guggenheim Fellow and a Rockefeller Fellow. He is best known for his nonfiction account of Sitting Bull and his positive depictions of the much-maligned (at the time) Plains Indians, among whom he had grown up. He was known inside the field of English for establishing a nationally recognized professional writing program, and it was in this capacity that Campbell appears to have aided Mathews the most, serving as a mentor and voice of encouragement for him because he considered him a talented writer. In version 4.31, Mathews wrote that Campbell was "a historian faculty member whose well known pen name was Stanley Vestal."

137. The Rhodes Scholarship was established in 1902 by Cecil J. Rhodes, a British imperialist, diamond magnate, and prime minister of Cape Colony. The scholarships were then restricted to unmarried men between nineteen and twenty-five. The Rhodes Scholarship is known for promoting an ideal scholar who combines intellectual with athletic attainment, though Rhodes actually established four criteria by which applicants would be judged: literary and scholastic attainments; energy to use one's talents to the full, as exemplified by fondness for and success in sports; truth, courage, devotion to duty, sympathy for and protection of the weak, kindliness, unselfishness, and fellowship; moral force of character and instincts to lead and to take an interest in one's fellow beings.

138. Excision: section on road trip with mother and younger sisters through the Rockies, Plains, and the upper Mississippi River Valley.

139. In an earlier version, Mathews refers to Wuff as "Floyd the wrangler."

140. Mathews's original wording of this passage has been preferred to his edits in 3.13, most of which seem uncharacteristically to overrefine Bill's language.

141. Although the dates do not match Mathews's memory, the description suggests "The Black Ram of Sunlight (Mountain Sheep)," by Hal G. Evarts, published in *The Bald Face and Other Animal Stories* (1921).

142. A "remittance man" is an exile or expatriate who lives on money sent from his former home. Wealthy and noble British families would send their second and third sons away to various locations in their colonies but fund their often vocation-less or profession-less lives.

143. ". . . men—in their forties or late thirties and could have in their own span come under the influence of the enthusiasm of James Gordon Bennett, General Sheridan and General Custer, and American frenetic flutters over the visit of Crown Prince Alexis in 1871, one supposes . . . insufficient. Buffalo Bill had strutted both before the mirror and through Ned Buntline's journalism" (3.13).

144. ". . . attack. He might follow him for miles out of sheer curiosity, but would ordinarily not attack, except in defense" (3.13).

145. ". . . paw did since he must keep an eye on his trailer, but the Cougar Hunter couldn't actually see the head since . . ." (3.13).

146. Caroline Cameron Lockhart was born in Illinois in 1871 and initially aspired to be an actress. She worked as a reporter and short story writer in Boston and Philadelphia until 1904, when she was assigned to a story on the Blackfoot Indians. She moved to Cody, Wyoming, and began to write the westerns that make her nationally known, including *The Lady Doc*, *The Man From Bitter Roots*, and *The Fighting Shepherdess*. The latter two were made into Hollywood movies; *The Lady Doc* depicted the residents of Cody in what they considered an unfavorable light. Lockhart actively opposed Prohibition. She tried unsuccessfully to preserve the Old West, which was already a subject of nostalgia by the time Mathews visited Cody in the very early 1920s. Lockhart also became a newspaper owner and ranch owner and thus represented the new economic freedom for women that could be found in the West.

147. Possibly George James Perceval, the sixth Earl of Egmont (1794–1874), or a relative. Perceval would have captured Mathews's imagination, given that he served in the Royal Navy, fought at the Battle of Trafalgar and the Battle of Algiers, and captured a town on the Penobscot River in Maine during the War of 1812. Whether he attended "University" is unclear. His contemporary Henry Frederick John James Perceval, the fifth Earl of Egmont, had attended Cambridge.

Index

~

287